EXPORT IMPORT MANAGEMENT

JUSTIN PAUL

Associate Professor
Nagoya University of Commerce and Business
Japan

RAJIV ASERKAR

Professor
S P Jain Centre of Management
Dubai

OXFORD

UNIVERSITY PRESS

OXFORD

UNIVERSITY PRESS

YMCA Library Building, Jai Singh Road, New Delhi 110001

Oxford University Press is a department of the University of Oxford.
It furthers the University's objective of excellence in research, scholarship,
and education by publishing worldwide in

Oxford   New York

Auckland   Cape Town   Dar es Salaam   Hong Kong   Karachi
Kuala Lumpur   Madrid   Melbourne   Mexico City   Nairobi
New Delhi   Shanghai   Taipei   Toronto

With offices in

Argentina   Austria   Brazil   Chile   Czech Republic   France   Greece
Guatemala   Hungary   Italy   Japan   Poland   Portugal   Singapore
South Korea   Switzerland   Thailand   Turkey   Ukraine   Vietnam

Oxford is a registered trade mark of Oxford University Press
in the UK and in certain other countries.

Published in India
by Oxford University Press

ISBN-13: 978-0-19-569458-1
ISBN-10: 0-19-569458-9

Typeset in Baskerville
by The Composers, New Delhi 110063
Printed in India by Ram Book Binding House, New Delhi 110020
and published by Oxford University Press
YMCA Library Building, Jai Singh Road, New Delhi 110001

Preface

During the last decade world trade has grown phenomenally in terms of volume as well as value. The reasons for this growth include liberalization of economies across the world, formation of the World Trade Organization (WTO), the ever expanding reach of the World Wide Web, digitization of trade documents, and increasing the cargo-carrying capacities of ocean and air carriers.

This spurt in world trade has evoked interest among academic institutions as also the corporate world and has prompted them to learn more about the different dimensions of international trade. Slogans like "export or perish" are heard more frequently than ever before. This has been a path breaking phenomenon in the corporate history, because in the pre-liberalization days, the focus of the domestic industry was primarily on the home market. This was due to the large gap between the demand of close to a billion consumers at home and the inability of the domestic companies to meet it with adequate supplies. Then it was mainly a seller's market and the only time exports were considered was when the companies had to meet the export obligations, which were imposed as a pre-condition to import of raw material and capital goods.

After economic liberalization in the early 1980s, companies in countries India and China began to feel the pinch of international competition and in order to retain their share in domestic market, they started investing in quality improvement programmes, supply chain management initiatives, etc. The resultant superior products and competitive prices opened the doors of the world market for goods and services. Large retail chains, big automobile manufacturers, multinational pharmaceutical giants and information technology companies are increasingly looking towards the market as a reliable source of a variety of goods and services. The government at the same time has started according importance to infrastructure development which has resulted in the building of better roads, privatization of ports, increasing the number of international airports to support the export-import trade.

In addition, there is a growing interest among investors to invest in manufacturing and services sectors. China still remains a preferred destination for foreign direct investment, but the Indian market of one billion plus consumers is also attracting a large number of foreign investors. India, which was earlier considered an agrarian economy, is now home to foreign automobile manufacturers and other high technology manufacturing companies who have made it their production hub for international markets. This is also a recognition of the skills of workers as well as technical competence of large pool of engineers, technocrats and knowledge workers.

All this has led to a rapid growth in export and import of products and services. Thus, there is a greater need today to understand export-import management in a globally competitive market.

About the Book

This book recognizes the growing significance of export-import trade and the need of the corporate world to understand the nuances of this business in order to compete successfully in the international market on equal terms with foreign competitors. In the universities, International Trade, which is also termed as Foreign Trade is an important part of the curriculum. In fact, a number of universities are offering post-graduation courses in Foreign Trade and International Business to students who wish to specialize in this area. This book, besides catering to the needs of the students of such specialized courses, is a valuable resource for practitioners.

The book is divided into sequentially defined chapters. Each chapter begins with a statement of learning objectives and introduction of the subject matter in a concise manner. This is followed by a lucid explanation of each topic with the help of flow diagrams, illustrations, data tables, etc. covering the conceptual framework. Each chapter concludes with a summary of key issues and includes case studies and a set of questions to test one's understanding of the topic.

Pedagogical Features

The pedagogical features of the text are:
- Learning objectives before each chapter highlighting major learning insights.
- End-chapter exercises such as review questions to enable the students reflect on various issues.

- Examples provided in the chapters with an Indian context to make the subject matter interesting and relevant.
- Copies of export documents provided at appropriate places to exemplify documentation.
- Large number of tables providing export and import data
- Specific chapters on regional/country markets that provide an insight into the business, political, economic, and legal environment of the host region/country.

Coverage and Structure

The book begins by introducing the institutional framework and basics of foreign trade. As regulatory norms are the first hurdle for companies operating in the arena of foreign trade, the regulatory framework and the documentation related to it are discussed in Chapter 1. A good understanding of rules and regulation, and accurate documentation facilitates faster clearances from the regulatory authorities. Chapter 2 discusses the related documentation and step-by-step procedures. Commercial and transport documents are also elucidated.

Chapter 3 discusses types of letters of credit, their importance, limitations and the precautions one needs to take while dealing with them. Chapter 4 discusses export-import strategies and practices. Chapter 5 explores the nature and scope of export marketing activities, strategies of companies engaged in International marketing, and understanding how free trade blocks, like WTO etc., facilitate export marketing activities. Chapter 6 discusses pre and post-shipment finance. Chapter 7 explicates various types of business risks in the international market. These risks include physical risks to the goods as well as commercial risks to the traders. Awareness of such risks and the ways of covering such risks helps to minimize the losses. The cargo has to travel long distances and encounter numerous risks. Mitigation of such risks is an important aspect of this business.

Logistics is an integral part of export-import trade, as the cargo in right quantity has to reach the right place at the right time. Chapters 8, 9 and 10 discuss everything from customs clearance to Electronic Data Interchange (EDI) in customs that are related to the logistics of movement of goods from the point of origin to the point of destination. New developments in customs clearance procedures are also explained.

It is important for a company dealing with overseas customers or suppliers to know about various modes of transportation, their advantages and disadvantages. This helps them to choose the right mode of transportation for their cargo. Another important development in maritime trade is containerization of cargo. Ports across the world are expanding their container handling capacities; also bigger ships are being built which can carry a larger number of containers. Shippers have adopted containerization in a big way to maximize their benefits from multi-modal transport. Shipment of cargo, freight structure and rates are explained in these chapters. Chapters 11 and 12 are devoted to discussion on ports, types of ships and the various aspects of containerization. Shipment of cargo, freight structure and rates are also discussed in these chapters.

Chapter 13 deals with the procedures and documentation pertaining to export marketing. The entire exercise beginning from the search of an overseas client, to making offers and quotations and negotiating on export documents are covered in this lesson. Chapter 14 brings to the forefront the importance of information technology in international business, elaborating the concepts of e-procurement, e-marketing and e-logistics. Chapter 15 on export incentives discusses various incentive schemes offered by the Indian Government which an exporter can avail of to remain competitive in the global market. A good understanding of the procedures to benefit from the incentives enables the exporters to maintain a healthy rotation of their working capital.

Every region/country across the world poses new challenges to exporters. The book has four chapters, 16 to 19, exclusively dedicated to analyses of markets in the Middle East, Association of South East Asian Nations (ASEAN), Australia and New Zealand, and China and Japan. Along with the challenges, each market also offers ample opportunities. An exporter, who has limited resources, has to weigh the pros and cons of entering a new market. An insight into the business, political, economic, and legal environment of the importing country enables a potential exporter to decide whether or not to enter that market. A thorough understanding of the business practices in the target market helps the exporter finetune his market entry strategies.

The book thus attempts to cover a very broad spectrum of issues related to export-import trade in order to facilitate better understanding of the intricacies of this business. There are ample real life examples to highlight relevant issues. At the end of each chapter there are questions to test the reader's understanding, and interesting exercises to put some of the learning into practice. The book concludes with a Test Your Knowledge section. It has a large number of objective type questions that would be useful to the faculty as well as students.

There are a number of unexplored areas in international trade, which we could not focus upon due to the limitation of the scope of this book. We are, however, confident that this book will stimulate the readers to look beyond the domestic market and explore the international market. It will prepare the readers to foresee the challenges ahead; at the same time it will prepare them to exploit the opportunities.

JUSTIN PAUL
RAJIV ASERKAR

Acknowledgements

We are indebted to all the individuals who helped us gain knowledge and insight into various aspects of international trade, including export-import procedures, documentation, marketing, logistics operations and application of technology in the field of Ex-Im management. The sources of learning have been one too many and a complete list of individual references would become encyclopedic.

Dr Justin Paul appreciates the support of colleagues in academic institutions, bureaucrats, industry professionals who influenced his work and "last but not the least" executive participants of his various training programmes in India, Japan, Mauritiius, and Oman.

He makes a special mention of Mr.K.T.Chacko, Director, Indian Institute of Foreign Trade (IIFT), New Delhi and Dr. Rakesh Mohan Joshy (Chairperson – IIFT), Dr. Hiroshi Kurimato, President- Nagoya University of Commerce and Business (NUCB), Japan, and Kyoko Hayakawa, Managing Director, NUCB Graduate School, for their contribution and encouragement in producing this book.

Dr Paul is grateful for the support of family members Mr P.V.Paulose, Ms. Annie Paulose, and Dr Festi. He has also thanked the editorial team of OUP for its co-operation in bringing out the book.

Dr Rajiv Aserkar, appreciates the valuable support of industry professionals like Mr. Shashi Kiran, Divisional Manager, Logistics, Jawad Group, Dubai, for providing valuable information on warehousing management tools as also the management of Dee Tee Industries Limited, Indore.

The support and encouragement of his colleagues at SP Jain Centre of Management Dubai, Singapore, and Mumbai, including its President Mr Nitish Jain are acknowledged with due respect. Professors Sanjay Dalvi, Balakrishna Grandhi, Christopher Abraham, Vijay Sethi, Shilpa Dalvi, and Arindam Banerjee find special mention in this regard.

Dr Aserkar also owes a special thanks to his wife Meghana for standing by him and to his children Sarang and Shivani.

Both the authors have expressed their gratitude towards their students, interacting with whom, they say, was a step towards greater awareness.

JUSTIN PAUL
RAJIV ASERKAR

Contents

1 Foreign Trade— Institutional Framework and Basics

Learning Objectives

After studying this chapter, you will be able to understand
- the implications of WTO on foreign trade
- how to export strategically as an entrepreneur
- the role of government and semi-government organizations

Understanding the context (WTO), steps, process and procedures of export and import has become all the more important due to the ever increasing momentum of globalization. The basics of international trade, role of organizations and the processes involved are covered in brief in this chapter.

WTO AND TRADE LIBERALIZATION

The World Trade Organization (WTO) is the only global international organization dealing with the rules of trade between nations. It was formed in 1995 with the General Agreement on Trade and Tariffs (GATT) as its basis. Table 1.1 provides an overview of the road from GATT to WTO.

Table 1.1 The road from GATT to WTO

Year	Place	No. of Participating Countries
1947	Geneva	23
1949	Annecy	13
1951	Torquay	38
1956	Geneva	26
1960–61	Geneva	62
1964–67	Geneva–Kennedy Round	62
1973–79	Geneva–Tokyo Round	102
1986–94	Punta Del Esta to Geneva (Uruguay Round)	123

Ministerial conferences (held at least once in two years) are the primary decision making body of WTO. The WTO also has a General Council, which is responsible for overseeing regulatory operations and for acting as a body for the dispute settlement mechanism.

WTO agreements facilitate producers of goods and services, exporters, and importers to conduct their business in the global market. The WTO essentially aims to remove non-tariff barriers in the short-run and to reduce tariff rates on imports in the long-run. The basis of WTO can be described as:

'No prohibitions or restrictions other than duties and taxes whether made effective through quotas, import or export licences or other measures, shall be instituted or maintained by any contracting country on the importation of any product of any other member country.' (GATT 1947)

The WTO generally prohibits quantitative restrictions (QRs) on the importation or exportation of products. QRs are the limits set by countries to restrict imports (or exports). They could be in the form of quotas or licensing (special import licence, restricted list, and canalized list). *Canalizing of imports* refers to the practice of allowing only a few firms to import specific items by the government agency responsible for monitoring the respective sector. QRs are thus measures other than duties taken to restrict imports.

Import tariffs (duties) per se do not prevent the entry of products (Rao 2005). QRs can be more trade restrictive than tariff measures. Therefore, WTO does not permit member countries to impose QRs under normal circumstances, which in turn facilitates international marketing efforts. The customs duty rates have also been brought down by many countries. Needless to say, exports and imports have witnessed a global surge in recent years.

EXPORTING AS AN ENTREPRENEUR—STEPS

In order to succeed in the era of globalization, it makes sense for entrepreneurs to plan for export business as part of their business strategy. For this, a first-time exporter should be aware of the steps involved in export business. These steps are listed here.

Step 1: Selecting the Right Name

Words like 'international' or 'overseas' in the name of the firm (e.g., AMES International) convey the message that the firm is engaged in export/import.

Step 2: Registration

The registration of the organization (partnership or sole proprietorship) is another important step. The firm has to be registered under the country's prevalent law, such as the Company Act.

Step 3: Opening a Bank Account

The firm needs to open an account with a bank dealing in foreign exchange (designated branches). It makes sense to open an account with a branch which directly undertakes export–import documents and converts foreign exchange.

Step 4: Quoting the Permanent Account Number

The permanent account number (PAN) needs to be quoted to apply for the importer-exporter code (IEC) number and to claim tax exemptions and deductions under the IT Act. Details about the IE code number are discussed under Step 6.

Step 5: Registering with the Sales Tax Office

The exporter need not pay sales tax while making purchases for export. To avail this benefit, the firm has to be registered with the Sales Tax Office (Rama Gopal 2006). The exporter needs to give to the seller Form-H, along with a copy of the import letter of credit or the export order.

Step 6: Obtaining the IEC Number

The IEC number is the most important registration required by an exporter/importer. No export or import for commercial purposes shall be made by any person without an IEC number. An IEC number can be obtained through an application to the relevant authority, e.g., the Director General of Foreign Trade (DGFT) in India. A specimen copy of the form is given in Annexure 1. There is no expiry date for the IEC number. The registered/head office of the applicant can apply for the IEC number to the licensing authority—the regional office of the DGFT—in the prescribed format. The application should be accompanied by relevant documents, which are as follows:

- Application form (in duplicate)
- Company profile (in duplicate)
- True copy of income tax PAN A/c number
- True copy of sales tax certificate, if any
- Government fees

- Bank certificate as per format
- Full address of branches in India and abroad, if any
- Three passport size photographs duly signed on the reverse
- SSI registration copy, duly certified, if any
- Declarations in duplicate

Validity and Features of IEC Number

An IEC number allotted to an applicant is valid for all its branches/divisions/units/factories as indicated on the IEC number. Some features of the IEC number are listed here.

1. The IEC number is the first and foremost requirement for exporters and importers.
2. It is a permanent number and has no expiry date.
3. It is valid for imports as well as exports.
4. It is valid for all products.
5. It is a 10-digit number.

Step 7: Registration with Export Promotion Councils

Governments in many countries have set up Export Promotion Councils (EPCs) to provide information and to facilitate exports.

The basic objective of EPCs is to promote and develop the exports of the country. Each Council is responsible for the promotion of a particular group of products, projects, and services. The EPCs keep abreast of the trends and opportunities in international markets for goods and services and assist their members in taking advantage of such opportunities in order to expand and diversify exports

Functions

The major functions of EPCs are:
- to provide commercially useful information and assistance to members in developing and increasing their exports;
- to offer professional advice to members in areas such as technology upgradation, quality and design improvement, standards and specifications, product development, innovation, etc;
- to organize overseas delegations of its members in order to explore global market opportunities;
- to organize participation in trade fairs, exhibitions, and buyer–seller meets; and
- to promote interaction between the exporting community and the government, both at the Centre and state levels.

Nature

Export Promotion Councils are non-profit, autonomous, and professional bodies. They are non-profit organizations registered under the Companies Act or the Societies Registration Act.

The Ministry of Commerce and Industry/Ministry of Textiles of the Government of India, as the case may be, would interact with the managing committee of the councils concerned, twice a year, once for approving their annual plans and budget, and again for a mid-year appraisal and review of their performance.

Registration-cum-Membership

An exporter may, on application, register and become a member of an EPC. On being given membership, the applicant shall be granted forthwith Registration-cum-Membership Certificate (RCMC) of the EPC concerned, subject to certain terms and conditions. Prospective/potential exporters may also, on application, register and become associate members of an EPC.

Step 8: Registration with the Export Credit Guarantee Corporation

Exporters should register with the Export Credit Guarantee Corporation (ECGC) to secure payment against political and commercial risks.

Step 9: Central Excise

Goods are subject to exemption from excise duty on the final product meant for export. Where exemption is not availed, the excise duty paid is refunded after actual export. Secondly, the refund of excise duty is made on inputs used in the manufacture of goods meant for export. Form ARE-1 has to be used in India for this excise clearance.

Step 10: Registration with Chambers of Commerce, Productivity Councils, etc.

It is desirable for a firm to become a member of the local chamber of commerce, productivity council, or trade promotion organization recognized by the Ministry of Commerce. This is helpful in many ways, including obtaining a Certificate of Origin.

Step 11: Registration for Business Identification Number

It is important to obtain a PAN, based on the Business Identification Number (BIN), from the DGFT registration office prior to filing for customs clearance of export goods.

Step 12: Export Licence, if required

Many items are free for export, without any licence, if they do not fall in the negative list. The negative list can consist of items that are:

(a) prohibited (i.e., cannot be exported);

(b) restricted (through licence); or

(c) canalized (a licence can be obtained for a short period through a canalizing agency of the government).

An exporter has to procure a licence, if his item is not listed under the freely exportable items by the government.

ROLE OF GOVERNMENT/SEMI-GOVERNMENT AGENCIES IN EXPORT PROMOTION

There are many organizations and offices in the public sector that aim to facilitate international trade, such as the DGFT, EPCs, etc. Their objectives, broadly, are:

- to stimulate and support export efforts in the country;
- to help exporters develop particular products and commodities for export;
- to establish and develop incentives/schemes to enable self-sustenance in the international market;
- to develop guidelines, principles, and policies; and
- to establish laws for the smooth running of international business.

Ministry of Commerce and Industry (known as Dept. of Commerce in USA)

The Union Ministry of Commerce and Industry is an umbrella organization for the foreign trade of the entire country. It is connected with all foreign commercial matters. It formulates policies related to import/export development. It helps develop commercial relations with other countries.

The Ministry of Commerce in many countries comprises different divisions, each headed by a divisional head. These divisions are:

- Trade Policy Division
- Export Products Division
- Export Services Division
- Economics Division
- Administrative and General Division
- Foreign Trade Division
- Export Industries Division
- Finance Division

Director General of Foreign Trade

The Director General of Foreign Trade (DGFT) was earlier known as the Chief Controller of Imports and Exports. It is the regulatory authority on foreign trade. It is responsible for the execution of the import and export policies of the Government. Besides promoting exports, it facilitates the removal of control and operates through regional offices spread all over the country.

Commodity Boards

Commodity boards, such as the Rubber Board and the Silk Board, are public sector organizations. They are related to specific products in the country and abroad. They deal with the entire range of problems concerning the production, development, and marketing of concerned products. Commodity boards also undertake promotional activities. For instance, they are involved in participation in international trade fairs and exhibitions and sponsorship of delegations for international trade studies.

The Tea Board, Coffee Board, Coir Board, Central Silk Board, All India Handloom and Handicrafts Board, Tobacco Board, Rubber Board, Spices Board, Jute Mills Association, and Sugar Mills Association are some examples of commodity boards in our country.

Export Promotion Councils

The major functions, nature, and registration policies of Export Promotion Councils (EPCs) have already been discussed in the previous section. EPCs have been set up for products such as apparels, basic chemicals, pharmaceuticals and cosmetics, chemicals and allied products, carpets, cashew, cotton textiles, electronics, computer software, engineering, gems and jewellery, handicrafts, handloom, leather, overseas construction, plastics and linoleums, shellac, silk, synthetic and rayon textiles, sports goods, and wools and woollens.

In addition to the functions mentioned in the previous section, they are also responsible for building a database on exports and imports of members and international trade data for members' use. They also keep track of changing trends and opportunities abroad and educate members on country-specific opportunities accordingly.

Exhibit 1.1 provides a list of export promotion councils in India.

Exhibit 1.1	List of Export Promotion Councils

Sl. No.	Name of Export Promotion Council
1.	Agricultural and Processed Food Products Export Development Authority (APEDA)
2.	Apparel Export Promotion Council
3.	Basic Chemicals, Pharmaceuticals & Cosmetics Export Promotion Council
4.	The Cashew Export Promotion Council of India
5.	Carpet Export Promotion Council
6.	Chemicals & Allied Products Export Promotion Council
7.	Coffee Board
8.	Coir Board
9.	The Cotton Textiles Export Promotion Council
10.	Electronic and Computer Software Export Promotion Council (ESC)
11.	Engineering Export Promotion Council
12.	Federation of Indian Export Organisations (FIEO)
13.	The Gem & Jewellery Export Promotion Council
14.	Export Promotion Council for Handicrafts
15.	The Handloom Export Promotion Council
16.	The Indian Silk Export Promotion Council
17.	Council for Leather Exports
18.	The Marine Products Export Development Authority
19.	Overseas Construction Council of India
20.	The Plastics and Linoleums Export Promotion Council
21.	The Rubber Board
22.	Shellac Export Promotion Council
23.	The Sports Goods Export Promotion Council
24.	Spices Board
25.	The Synthetics & Rayon Textiles Export Promotion Council
26.	Tea Board
27.	Tobacco Board
28.	The Powerloom Development and Export Promotion Council (PDEXCIL)
29.	Jute Manufacturers Development Council

Service Institutes

The Ministry of Commerce facilitates foreign trade through service institutes such as the Indian Institute of Foreign Trade (IIFT) and Indian Institute of Packaging (IIP).

The IIFT
- acts as a nucleus of human resource development in the field of foreign trade;
- organizes special training programmes on export–import (EXIM) business;
- conducts research into problems related to EXIM business and undertakes commodity studies and foreign market surveys;
- organizes exchange of trade delegates;
- provides consultancy to export organizations; and
- publishes journals on EXIM business.

Export Inspection Council

The Export Inspection Council (EIC) is a statutory body responsible for the enforcement of quality control and compulsory pre-shipment inspection of exportable goods in the country. It establishes laboratories and testing centres all over the country.

Export Credit Guarantee Corporation

The Export Credit Guarantee Corporation (ECGC) is a wholly owned subsidiary of the Government of India under administrative control of the Ministry of Commerce and Industry with export insurance services. The ECGC
- supports and strengthens export drive;
- covers commercial and political risks of exporters;
- arranges insurance against pre- and post-shipment credit finance to commercial bankers;
- provides guarantee to commercial banks against export credits extended;
- issues overseas investment insurance policies;
- covers exchangse investment risks through forwards and futures; and
- provides guarantees against projects, term loans, export finance, and export performance.

Directorate General of Commercial Intelligence and Statistics

The Directorate General of Commercial Intelligence and Statistics (DGCI&S) has its head office in Kolkata. The DGCI&S
- collects and compiles complete information and disseminates it to trade organizations;
- publishes journals and informative bulletins; and
- helps Indian businessmen with letters of introduction when they are going abroad.

India Trade Promotion Organisation (ITPO)

The ITPO, earlier known as the Trade Fair Authority of India

- organizes trade fairs and other exhibitions in the country and abroad for products;
- sets up showrooms in the country and abroad for the promotion of exports of new items; and
- publishes journals such as the *Journal of Industry and Trade, Udhyog Vyapaar Patrika*, and *The Indian Export Services Bulletin*.

Federation of Indian Exporters' Organization

The Federation of Indian Exporters' Organization (FIEO) is the apex body of various exporters and export promotion organizations. It provides a common coordinating platform for commodity councils, boards, and service institutions.

Export–Import Bank

The Export–Import (EXIM) Bank is an apex organization that finances, facilitates, and promotes exports. Its major function is to arrange loans/funds for exporters, either directly or through other commercial banks. The bank undertakes financing with regional/global development banks, agencies, and other financial institutes. They also arrange pre- and post-bid finance for export projects.

The State Trading Corporation of India Ltd.

The State Trading Corporation of India Ltd (STC) has the following subsidiaries that help promote exports of various commodities:

1. Handicraft and Handloom Export Corporation of India Ltd.
2. Cashew Corporation of India Ltd.
3. Central Cottage Industries Corporation of India Ltd.
4. Tea Trading Corporation of India Ltd.
5. Project and Equipment Corporation of India Ltd.

Government Trade Representatives

Government trade representatives such as embassies, high commissions, commercial counsellors, and commercial secretaries attached to various India houses abroad act as the eyes and ears of the government in sensing trade opportunities. They also help in the settlement of trade disputes.

Freight Investigation Bureau

This Bureau is based at the Office of the Director General Shipping, Mumbai, and it looks into the problems related to ocean freights. It also gives suggestions and settles disputes related to ocean freight.

Customs and Central Excise Department

The Customs and Central Excise Department operates through customs houses in Mumbai, Kolkata, Chennai, New Delhi, and other industrial areas and export zones. The department handles and implements policies related to drawback imposition and recovery of customs and central excise.

SUMMARY

It is worth noting that international trade is increasing by leaps and bounds in the world because of the forces of globalization, such as the World Trade Organization. Member countries of the WTO have lifted quantitative restrictions (non-tariff barriers) on imports and reduced customs duty rates substantially. The competition to capture more market share has intensified in the world. In such a scenario, companies need to formulate their business strategy based on exporting and importing in a systematic way that increases profit and reduces cost.

This chapter discussed the steps involved in starting an export business. Many government and semi-government agencies are involved in export promotion. The Ministry of Commerce and Industry, the DGFT, and EPCs are examples of some such agencies. The activities of these agencies have also been discussed in the chapter.

CONCEPT REVIEW QUESTIONS

1. Discuss the role of the WTO in Export–Import business.
2. Discuss the steps involved in export business, if you have to enter into it as an entrepreneur.
3. Discuss the role of public sector organizations in export promotion activities.

OBJECTIVE QUESTIONS

For each of the following statements, choose the most appropriate option.
1. The WTO is criticized for the following aspects:
   (a) WTO dictates policy
   (b) WTO is tool of powerful lobbies
   (c) WTO destroys jobs and worsens poverty
   (d) WTO only (a) and (b) together
   (e) All (a), (b), and (c) together
2. The main functions of WTO are:
   (a) To handle disputes constructively
   (b) To help promote peace among business community.
   (c) To provide rules that make life easier for all people involved in foreign trade.
   (d) All of the above
3. GATTs cover all internationally traded services. They are:
   (a) Cross-border supply and consumption abroad
   (b) Commercial presences and presences of natural persons
   (c) None of the above
   (d) Both (a) and (b)
4. Agreement on textiles and clothing (ATC) 1995–2004 was a transitional instrument, covering the following elements:
   (a) Encompasses yarns, fabrics, clothing, textiles products
   (b) Establishment of TMB (Textile Monitoring Body)
   (c) Progressive integration of textiles and clothing products into GATT, 1999 rules.
   (d) All of the above.

SELECT REFERENCES

Mahajan, M. I., 2006 *Export Policy – Procedures and Documentation*, Snow White, New Delhi.

Paul, Justin, 2007 *International Business*, third edition, Prentice-Hall of India, New Delhi.

Rama Gopal, C., 2006 *Export-Import Procedures*, New Age International, New Delhi.

Ram, Paras, 2007 *Incoterms – Export Costing and Pricing*, Anupam Publishers, New Delhi.

Rao, P. Krishna, 2005, *WTO-Text and Cases*, Excel Books, New Delhi.

THE MARINE PRODUCTS EXPORT DEVELOPMENT AUTHORITY*

Case
Study
1

Steering the Indian Seafood Industry Ahead

The Marine Products Export Development Authority (MPEDA) was constituted in 1972 under the Marine Product Export Development Authority Act, 1972. The role envisaged for MPEDA under the statute covers fisheries of all kinds, export standards, processing, marketing, and extension and training in various aspects of the industry.

The MPEDA's activities relate mainly to the registration of infrastructure facilities for seafood export trade, collection and dissemination of trade information, projection of Indian marine products in overseas markets by participation in overseas fairs, and organizing international seafood fairs in India.

The other responsibilities of MPEDA include implementing develop-ment measures vital to the industry, such as distribution of insulated fish boxes, building fish landing platforms, improving peeling sheds, and providing financial aid for modernizing the industry *via* upgradation of plate freezers, installation of Individually Quick Frozen (IQF) machinery, generator sets, ice-making machinery, quality control laboratories, etc.

The MPEDA also promotes brackish water aquaculture for the production of prawns for export, deep-sea fishing projects through test fishing, and joint ventures and equity participation. It provides financial support to set up integrated aquaculture projects, seafood processing units, and deep-sea fishing projects.

The MPEDA functions under the Ministry of Commerce and acts as a coordinating agency with different central and state government outfits engaged in fish production and other allied activities.

The development schemes of the Authority are implemented under various major heads, namely, export production, induction of new technology, and modernization of processing facilities and market promotion.

With headquarters at Kochi, the Authority has field centres in all the maritime states of India, a trade promotion office in New Delhi to liaise with Union ministries, and trade promotion offices in New York (USA) and Tokyo (Japan).

*Source: Handbook on Shipping and Ports 2005. Dhanam Publications, Kochi. Reprinted with permission.

The regional offices at Mumbai, Kolkata, Kochi, Chennai, Visakhapatnam, and Veraval, alongwith the sub-regional offices at Kollam, Mangalore, Tuticorin, Goa, and Bhubaneshwar, function to implement the various activities of the Authority.

These offices also promote the export of marine products by providing guidance and assistance to processing units and the export trade.

Address: The Marine Products Export Development Authority, Ministry of Commerce, MPEDA House, Panampilly Avenue, P. B. No.4272, Kochi – 682 036, Tel: 2311979, 2312838 Fax: 2313361, E-mail: mpeda@vsnl.com, Internet: www.mpeda.com.

Question: Discuss the activities of MPEDA

PORT-BASED SPECIAL ECONOMIC ZONE AT KOCHI*

Case Study 2

A Global Manufacturing Hub in the Making

C. UNNIKRISHNAN[†]

From the concept of a closeted public sector enclave focusing on export, Special Economic Zones (SEZs) are now turning into large-scale integrated manufacturing complexes managed by public–private partnerships.

Today, at least 120 countries have established SEZs. With 266 zones, USA alone has generated over 400,000 zone-related jobs. China has created 360,000 employment avenues from its zones. The Philippines generates 67% of its exports from SEZs. As much as 37% of Sri Lanka's exports originates from SEZs, while India could generate only less than 5% of its export from them. The impact of the contribution of SEZs to wealth creation, employment generation, and regional development has not yet been felt in India as it has been in similar economies.

The SEZ in Kerala, the Cochin Export Processing Zone (CEPZ)[#] at Kakkanad, was established in 1986. Realizing the changing image of Kerala as an investment destination and to increase the awareness of its potential, the Ministry of Commerce and Industry recently gave permission to set up India's first Port-Based Special Economic Zone (PBSEZ) in Kochi.

---

*Handbook on Shipping and Ports 2005, Dhanam Publications, Kochi. Reprinted with permission.
[†]The writer is Deputy Secretary, Cochin Port Trust
[#]CEPZ changed to Cochin Special Economic Zone (CSEZ) in 2003.

For the Kochi PBSEZ, the opportunities lie in the accelerating trend of outsourced manufacturing. At present, developed countries confine this outsourcing to basic components. This sector of manufacturing demands higher skills and derives a higher degree of inbuilt margin. The remaining part of manufacturing outsourcing is assembling, which is a semiskilled job requiring a higher proportion of low-cost labour, available in plenty in developing countries.

Outsourced manufacturing of the semiskilled kind can be accommodated at the proposed PBSEZ in Kochi. The PBSEZ will focus upon generating substantial employment. However, through an evolutionary process, the expertise built up in performing semiskilled functions could be enhanced to attempt manufacturing critical components and moved in to higher value markets.

The Kochi Port has earmarked 448 hectares in Vallarpadam and Puthuvypu for developing the PBSEZ. The PBSEZ is proposed to be developed in a public–private partnership format. A major part of the terminal-related activity of the international container terminal will be performed in the SEZ. This aspect will provide a cutting edge to the terminal's performance vis-à-vis competing terminals.

A SEZ in the proximity of the container terminal will have the advantage of imports at the lowest freight rate and minimal transit distance from the port to the manufacturing plants, thereby saving costs.

The international scene is also littered with failures of SEZ projects, that are an eye-opener. Causes of failures of SEZ world-wide can be attributed to business strategies based heavily or solely on tax holidays, imposition of rigid eligibility norms, and poor and suppressed labour relations. Instances of initial over-subsidy, poor maintenance of common facilities, and poor locations spelling doom for SEZs are also not rare.

The key positive trend observed in the success and growth of SEZs is the competitive advantage driven by logistics. The developments in the software sector and the prospects of increased flights from the international airport are some of the factors in favour of the PBSEZ.

The investors in the PBSEZ can take maximum advantage by capitalizing on logistics. With a series of mutually supportive projects also coming up in the vicinity of Kochi Port, opportunities are aplenty.

Question: Discuss the rationale for a PBSEZ.

FORMAT OF IMPORTER–EXPORTER CODE NUMBER

GOVERNMENT OF INDIA
MINISTRY OF COMMERCE AND INDUSTRY
OFFICE OF JT./DY. DIRECTOR GENERAL OF FOREIGN TRADE
(Full Address)
CERTIFICATE OF IMPORTER–EXPORTER CODE (IEC) NUMBER

1. Name _____

2. Address _____

   _____

   _____

   PIN ☐☐☐☐☐☐

3. Address of the Branches/ _____

   Division/Units/Factories, _____

   if any. _____

   PIN ☐☐☐☐☐☐

4. IEC Number _____

5. Date of issue _____

6. PAN Number _____

(Signature of the Issuing Authority) _____

Name _____

Designation _____

(Official Stamp) ☐

Place _____

Date _____

2 Export-Import— Documentation and Steps

Learning Objectives

After studying this chapter, you will be able to understand
- the step-by-step procedures of the export–import business
- the process of starting an EXIM business
- the various aspects of transport and financial documents
- the role of export promotion councils
- the meaning of international commerce terms

The advantages and benefits of being an exporter far outweigh the disadvantages and problems involved.

Like any decision in business, the decision to go in for exporting or importing is motivated by the idea of comparative advantage and achieving international competitiveness.

The prospective advantages of exporting, vis-à-vis being confined to the domestic market, can be specified as follows:

(a) The company becomes globally competitive in all areas of business
(b) Business risk can be spread throughout many markets and countries
(c) Profit and turnover increases
(d) The company gets many incentives

It is essential that a person engaged in international trade be aware of the various procedures involved. The business of exports and imports is heavily document-oriented and one must get acquainted with the entire procedure. Failure to comply with documentary requirement may lead to financial loss and therefore it is advisable for traders to know about all procedures.

STEPS FOR SUCCESSFUL EXPORTING

Most exports take place between two independent companies. The systematic understanding of the various stages and steps in an export transaction would help companies conduct their export businesses successfully.

The steps involved in an export transaction can be listed as follows. The steps mentioned in chapter 1 have been elaborated and classified further.

Step 1

Those interested in Export–Import business need to apply to the Director General of Foreign Trade (DGFT) regional office for getting Importer–Exporter Code (IEC) Number. This is true for any individual or company willing to undertake export or import from India. IE code number is not mandatory in the case of imports for personal use. The DGFT has regional offices in many states. Step 1 is applicable only in the case of first time exporters.

Step 2

The exporter has to register with the concerned export promotion council. For example, in case of garments, it is essential to obtain registration-cum-membership certificate (RCMC) from the Apparel Export Promotion Council (AEPC). Registration is essential in order to obtain various permissible benefits given by the government.

Step 3

The exporter can now go in for procuring orders, by first sending a sample, if required. Both exporter and importer will have to agree upon the terms and conditions of the contract like pricing, documents, freight charges, currency, etc. After this, the importer sends a purchase order.

Step 4

With export orders in hand, the exporter starts manufacturing goods or buying them from other manufacturers.

Step 5

The exporter makes arrangements for quality control and obtains from the inspector of quality control, a certificate confirming the quality of the goods, depending upon the requirement.

Step 6

Exportables are then despatched to ports/airports for transit.

Step 7

The export firm has to apply to an insurance company for marine/air insurance cover. (The exporter asks the importer to take marine/air insurance under cost and freight, free on board etc., terms of contract.)

Step 8

After the completion of these formalities, the exporter contacts the clearing and forwarding agent (C&F agent) for storing the goods in warehouses. (The exporter can also store the goods personally.) The forwarding agent presents a document called the Shipping Bill, which is required for allowing shipment by the Customs Authority.

Step 9

After loading the goods in to the ship, the captain of the ship issues a receipt known as 'Mate's Receipt' to the ship superintendent of the port. The superintendent calculates port charges and handover to exporter/C&F agent.

Step 10

When the port payments are made, the C&F agent or exporter gets the Bills of Lading or Airway Bill from the official agent of the shipping company or the airline.

Step 11

The exporter applies to the relevant Chamber of Commerce for obtaining Certificates of Origin, stating that the goods originated from India. (This is not a mandatory document in all cases.)

Step 12

The exporter also sends a set of documents to the importer, stating the date of shipment, name of vessel, etc. Moreover, it is desirable to send certain documents like the Bills of Lading, Custom Invoice, and Packing List to their foreign counterparts.

Step 13

The exporter now presents all the important documents at his bank. (This has to be done within 21 days after the shipment.) The bank scrutinizes these documents against the original letter of credit/purchase order.

Step 14

The exporter's bank sends these documents to the importer's bank. The importer's bank should make the payment on or before the due date. Although these steps give a clear picture about how to export, some steps are not essential.

EXPORT–IMPORT DOCUMENTATION

An export trade transaction distinguishes itself from a domestic trade transaction in more than one way. One of the most significant variations between the two arises on account of the much more intensive documentation work.

Proforma Invoice

Proforma Invoice, as the name suggests, is a proforma of the invoice. It is prepared by an exporter and sent to the importer for necessary acceptance. When the buyer is ready to purchase the goods, he will request for a proforma invoice. This document suggests to a buyer what the actual invoice would look like if he were to place an order and the goods were to be supplied to him.

Packing List

The Packing List is a consolidated statement in a prescribed format, detailing how the goods have been packed. It is informative and itemizes the material in each individual package, such as a drum, box, or carton. It is a very useful document for customs at the time of examination and for the warehouse keeper of the buyer to maintain a record of inventory and to effect delivery.

The packing list will have many details common to those in an invoice. However, it does not indicate the unit rate and the value of the goods.

Subject to the instructions of the buyer, a specific number of copies of the Packing List are prepared.

Commercial Invoice

An invoice is a fundamental document of prime importance. It contains the names of the exporter, importer, and the consignee, and the description of goods.

It is a requisite for the invoice to be signed by an exporter or his agent. Normally, the invoice is prepared first, and several other documents are then prepared by deriving information from the invoice.

The invoice prepared by an exporter is required to be presented before different authorities for different purposes.

Certificate of Origin

The Certificate of Origin is a very useful document in the export–import trade. This certificate indicates that the goods, which are being exported, are actually manufactured in a specific country mentioned therein. This certificate is sent by the exporter to the importer. It is useful for the clearance of the goods from the customs authority of the importing country. However, it is worth noting that the Certificate of Origin is required by some countries only.

Normally, the Certificate of Origin is issued by the local Chamber of Commerce. The Indian Merchant's Chambers, the Indo Arab Chamber of Commerce, the local Chambers of Commerce at different places like Mumbai are some of the chambers regularly approached by exporters for obtaining the Certificate of Origin. In many cases, a statement of origin printed on the company letterhead will also suffice.

Generalized System of Preference Certificate of Origin

As its name indicates, the Generalized System of Preference (GSP) certificate of origin certifies that the goods being exported have originated/been manufactured in a particular country. It is mainly useful for taking advantage of a preferential duty concession, if available.

When imports from certain countries are favourably treated in the matter of levy of import duties, the Customs authorities of the concerned importer country insist upon some proof of the fact that the goods are genuine products of such countries. For this, the GSP certificate is sent to the importer by the exporter.

Products will be considered to have originated in India if they have been either wholly produced in India or produced there wholly or partly from imported materials, which have undergone sufficient working or processing in India to be regarded as having originated there.

The GSP certificate is normally issued by government-authorized agencies, some of which are:

1. The Directorate General of Foreign Trade and its regional offices.
2. Development Commissioners.
3. Export Promotion Councils.
4. Export Inspection Councils (and its field offices called Export Inspection Agencies).
5. Textile Committee, Mumbai and its field offices.
6. Central Silk Board.

Shipping Bill/Bill of Entry

The Shipping Bill is a requisite for seeking the permission of customs to export goods by sea/air. It contains a description of export goods, number and kind of packages, shipping marks and numbers, value of goods, the name of the vessel, the country of destination, etc.

On the other hand, importers have to submit copies of a document called Bill of Entry for customs clearance. Later, a copy has to be given to the bank for verification.

ARE-1 Form

This form is an application for the removal of excisable goods from the factory premises, for export purposes. For example, if you are exporting a ball-point pen or a magazine, on which there is no excise applicable, you do not need to fill in this form.

The ARE-1 form has multiple copies, which are distributed to different authorities, including Customs, Range office of Excise, Refund office of Excise, etc. Earlier, this form was known as AR-4 or AR-4A.

Mate's Receipt

After the cargo is cleared from the customs examination and other formalities are over, the cargo is handed over to the shipping company for loading. The Mate's Receipt is issued by the captain of the ship. It contains the name of the vessel, shipping line, port of loading, port of discharge, shipping marks and numbers, packing details, description of goods, gross weight, container number, and seal number. The mate's receipt is exchanged for the Bill of Lading.

Exchange Declaration Form (GR/SDF Form)

One of the main functions of the Central Bank is to control and monitor the foreign exchange reserves of the country. Since exports directly relate to the country's foreign exchange earnings it becomes essential for nations to regulate an export transaction.

The Reserve Bank has prescribed a GR form (SDF), a PP form, and SOFTEX forms to declare the export transactions. The GR form contains:
(a) Name and address of the exporter and description of goods.
(b) Name and address of the authorized dealer through whom proceeds of exports have been or will be realized.
(c) Details of commission and discount due to foreign agent or buyer.
(d) The full export value, giving break up of FOB, Freight, Insurance, Discount, and Commission, etc.

Distribution/Disposal of Copies of GR Form

1. GR forms, covering the export of goods, should be completed by the exporter in duplicate, and both copies should be submitted to customs at the time of shipment.

2. Customs will verify all particulars of all goods and the value will be declared in the GR form.
3. After the shipment has been sent, the original of the GR form will be retained by the customs for onward submission to the Reserve Bank of India.
4. The duplicate copy of the GR form will be returned to the exporter through the concerned clearing agent.
5. An exporter is under obligation to submit this duplicate copy of GR, as soon as possible, but not later than 21 days from the date of shipment, to his authorized dealer (Banker).

Statutory Declaration Form

Some offices in the customs department are now computerized. To meet the requirements of electronic data interchange system, the GR form has been replaced online by a new form known as Statutory Declaration Form (SDF). This is prepared in duplicate and submitted to customs at the time of shipment. The SDF bears cross-references of the shipping bill number. Over a period, it is estimated that the GR Form will be completely replaced by the SDF.

Post Parcel Form

When goods are exported by post, then instead of the GR form, the exporter has to fill up a Post Parcel (PP) form in triplicate. This PP form needs to be signed in original by the banker. Therefore, an exporter has to first submit the form to his banker for the necessary counter signature. The bank will return the original form to the exporter for submitting it to the Post Office along with the parcel.

The concerned post office shall forward the PP form to the office of the Reserve Bank of India after the goods have been despatched. The duplicate copy of the PP form will be kept by the authorized dealer to whom the exporter should submit relevant documents for collection/negotiation. The time limit prescribed is 21 days.

SOFTEX Forms

The declaration in form SOFTEX, in respect of export of computer software and audio/video/television software, shall be submitted in triplicate to the designated official of the Department of Electronics of Government of India at the Software Technology Parks of India (STPIs) or at the Free Trade Zones (FTZs) or Export Processing Zones (EPZs) in India.

After certifying all three copies of the SOFTEX form, the designated official shall forward the original directly to the nearest office of the Reserve

Bank and return the duplicate to the exporter. The triplicate shall be retained by the designated official as part of record.

Bills of Exchange

The Bill of Exchange is commonly known as a draft. It is "an instrument in writing, containing an order, signed by the maker, directing a certain person to pay a certain sum of money only to the order of a person to the bearer of the instrument".* It is in the form of a demand. The bill of exchange is a negotiable instrument as per Section 5 of the Negotiable Instruments Act 1881.

There are two types of bills of exchange—Sight Draft and Usance Draft.

Sight Draft

When the drawer, i.e., exporter expects the drawee, i.e., importer to make the payment immediately upon the draft being presented to him, the draft involved is called a Sight Draft. In this case, the buyer cannot take delivery of the goods/documents without making the payment. The corresponding terms of payment is referred to as Delivery against Payment (D/P).

Usance Draft

When the exporter has agreed to give credit to the foreign buyer, he draws the Usance Bills of Exchange. A draft may be drawn according to the period of credit viz. 30 days or 60 days after it is presented to the drawee (importer), who will retire the documents by accepting the draft by writing his signature and date.

On the due date, the importer will make the payment to the bank. The bank will then forward the money to the exporter's bank.

In case where the full payment is received in advance, no Bill of Exchange is required to be drawn.

Inspection Certificate

The Inspection Certificate is required by some importers and countries in order to get the specifications of the goods shipped attested. The attestation is usually performed by a government agency or by independent testing organizations.

Bill of Lading

The Bill of Lading (B/L) is a document issued by the shipping company or

---

*This is a quote from Negotiable Instruments Act, 1881.

its agent. It acknowledges the receipt of the goods mentioned in the bill, for shipment on board of the vessel. It is also an undertaking to deliver the goods in the like order and condition as received, to the consignee or his order, provided the freight and other charges specified in the Bills of Lading have been duly paid. B/L is issued in the standardized aligned document format. For vessels, there are two types of B/L (i) A straight B/L, which is non-negotiable; (ii) a non-negotiable or shipper's order B/L. The latter can be bought, sold, or traded while the goods are in transit. The customer usually needs an original non-negotiable as proof of ownership to take possession of the goods.

The B/L is generally made out in sets of three originals. All originals are duly signed by the master of the ship or the agent of the shipping company and all the originals are equally valid for taking the delivery of the goods. Once any one original is utilized, the other originals become null and void. All the Original B/L should bear the stamp duty.

Utmost care is required to be exercised to ensure that the full set of original B/L is obtained by the exporter from the shipping company and no original copy passes into the wrong hands. Extra copies of B/L marked as 'NON NEGOTIABLE COPY' are also issued for records. These copies cannot be utilized for taking the delivery of goods.

The B/L is the legal document to be referred in case of any dispute over the shipment.

It contains the following information:
- The shipping company's name and address
- The consignee's name and address
- The port of loading and port of discharge
- Shipping marks and particulars
- Number of packages shipped on board with date–rubber stamp
- Description of packages and the goods
- Gross weight and net weight
- Freight details and name of the vessel
- Signature of the shipping company's agent

Airway Bill

The Airway Bill is a contract between the owner of the goods and the carrier or its agent. The receipt issued by an airlines company or its agent for carriage of goods is called an Airway Bill.

The first three digits of the Airway Bill Number normally represent the code, which identifies the carrier.

Here are some examples of airline codes:

125 – British Airways
074 – KLM Royal Dutch Airline
176 – Emirates Airline

The Airway Bill should indicate freight pre-paid or freight to collect. Other charges related to shipment are also mentioned on the Airway Bill.

Insurance Certificate

The Insurance Certificate is used to assure the consignee that insurance will cover the loss or damage to the cargo during transit (marine/air insurance). This can be obtained from the freight forwarder.

Consular Invoice

The Consular Invoice is a document required by certain countries. This invoice is an important document, which needs to be submitted for certification to the embassy of the country concerned.

A Commercial Invoice and sometimes a Certificate of Origin are required to be signed/certified by the consular of the importing country located in the country of export. The main purpose of a Consular Invoice is to enable the importer's country to collect accurate and authenticated information about the value, volume, quantity, source, etc., of the import for assessing import duties and for other statistical purposes. It helps the importer to get goods cleared through customs without any undue delay.

SUMMARY

Learning the step-by-step processes and procedures to be followed in an export contract is a crucial activity in export–import management. All the important steps have been explained. More steps have been given in the text from the point of view of first time exporters. The characteristic features of all the documents and the specimens of major documents are provided in the appendix to help the reader learn scientifically the art of EXIM business.

CONCEPT REVIEW QUESTIONS

1. Discuss the steps involved in an export contract from negotiation to execution?
2. Name the mandatory documents required to be prepared by an exproter? Discuss the salient features of each of these documents?
3. Discuss the role of export promotion councils?

OBJECTIVE QUESTIONS

Specify whether the following statements are True or False.
1. For an importer, sight bill is more convenient than the usance bill.
2. In export business, the parties involved in the contract mutually agree on the applicability of a particular country's law.
3. The exporter draws a usance bill under the documents against payment method.
4. In the documents against acceptance method, the buyer can take possession of the goods without making the payment.
5. Advance payment is the safest method of payment for the importer.

For each of the following statements, choose the most appropriate option.
6. A document that is a receipt for goods delivered to the common carrier for transportation, a contract for the services rendered by the carriers, and a document of title is known as a(n):
   (a) Export licence
   (b) Commercial invoice
   (c) Consular invoice
   (d) Bills of lading
7. The first three digits of the airway bill represent a code, which identifies:
   (a) The country of origin
   (b) Name of the exporter
   (c) Name of the Air carrier
   (d) None of the above.

EXERCISES

Visit your nearest exporter/importer and cross-check the documents his company has prepared with the list of documents mentioned in the chapter. Discuss the reasons for not using one or two specific documents, which you may not see in his office.

SELECT REFERENCES

Branch, Alan, 2000, *Export Practice and Management,* Thomson Learning-Business Press, London.

Mahajan, M.I., 2006, *Export Policy—Procedures and Documentation,* Snow White, New Delhi.

Paul, Justin, 2007, *International Business*, Third Edition, Prentice Hall of India, New Delhi.

Spar L, Debbora, 2005, *Managing Trade and Investment*, Imperial College Press

---

KELKAR AND ALPHA TYRES

Case Study

Mr. Vijay Kelkar has been a successful General Manager with Alpha Tyres Pvt. Ltd., Mumbai. Under Mr. Kelkar's visionary leadership, within 10 years of its inception (since 1997), the company was ranked fifth among the tyre companies in India in terms of market share in the domestic territory. Through international market research, Mr Kelkar obtained an import purchase order from Ace Motors in Thailand. Although Alpha Tyres had obtained IE Code Number from the DGFT office, the executives of the company were not well versed in export procedures and documentation.

Ace Motors had called for certain documents from the exporter, while sending the purchase order. These included one original and three copies of the invoice, an original GSP Certificate of Origin issued by a competent authority, the Sight Bill of Exchange, and an inspection certificate. Mr. Kelkar received the confirmed purchase order on 15th May, and the latest date of shipment was 30th May. Mr. Kelkar and his team had to ship the goods (tyres) within 15 days of getting the contract. The team managed to arrange and send the goods, along with the inspection certificate. The goods were despatched to the C&F agents after collecting the information on the time schedule and rate charged by shipping lines from Mumbai to Bangkok.

However, none of the team members were aware of the importance of the Certificate of Origin. The C&F agent too did not check whether the importer had called for the Certificate of Origin.

The goods were loaded into the ship and the cargo arrived at the importer's port after seven days. Meanwhile, the State Bank of India, the Bankers of Alpha Tyres, sent the export documents to HSBC Bank in Bangkok, as instructed by Alpha Tyres, for collection of the export bill amount of US Dollars 10,000. Upon scrutiny, the HSBC Bank manager, Mr. Chu Lee found that the exporter had not sent the Certificate of Origin alongwith the other documents and duly informed the Vice-President, Imports about this. Subsequently, payment to Alpha Tyres was withheld.

As it happened, Ace Motors had specifically called for the GSP Certificate of Origin with the intention that they would have been in a position to import at nominal customs duty rates from Alpha Tyres, had the exporter sent the document. (As per India's bilateral free trade–preferential trading-agreement with Thailand, companies in Thailand can import from India at preferential duty rates on most commodities.)

Questions

1. What would you suggest to Ace Motors in this case?
2. Do you think that Mr. Kelkar can force Ace Motors to make a payment without delay?

3

Methods and Instruments of Payment and Pricing Incoterms

Learning Objectives

After studying this chapter, you will be able to understand
- the methods and instruments of payment in the export–import business
- the various methods by which exporters and importers can arrange for finance.
- the various aspects of instruments of payment such as the Letter of Credit
- the difference between Incoterms, such as FOB, CIF, and CFR

METHODS OF PAYMENT

It is common practice that an exporting firm offers credit to the importer. The exporter evaluates new customers with care and continuously monitors their old accounts. An export firm may, wisely, decide to decline a customer's request if the risk involved is too great. Instead, the firm may propose an advance payment on a documentary sight draft or irrevocable confirmed letter of credit. On the other hand, if the customer is fully creditworthy, the experienced exporter may allow the customer a month or two to pay (usance facility).

Receiving the entire payment in time is of utmost concern to exporters and the level of risk in extending credit is a major consideration. There are several ways in which an exporter can receive payment when selling products abroad, depending upon how trustworthy he/she considers the buyer. Typically, with domestic sales, sales are made on open account if the buyer has good credit; if not, cash in advance is sought. For export sales, the basic methods of payment in ex-im trade are:

1. Payment in advance
2. Letter of Credit (Import LC)

3. Bill of Exchange
4. Open account

1. Advance Payment (Payment in Advance)

An exporter would prefer payment in advance of the shipment. A telegraphic transfer is commonly used for international remittances.

For the importer, advance payment tends to increase risks. Furthermore, payment in advance is not very common in most countries. Buyers are often concerned that the items may not be sent if payment is made in advance. Those exporters who insist on this method of payment as their sole method of doing business may find themselves losing out to competitors who offer other terms of payment, discussed later in this section.

Many exporters who sell through the e-commerce route accept credit card payments for exports of consumer products, generally of a low value, sold directly to the end user. In the case of international credit card transactions, exporters should be aware of the dangers of fraud. They should take care to determine the validity of transactions.

2. Letter of Credit (Import LC)

A Letter of Credit (LC) is often used to protect the interests of both the buyer and the seller. When importers do not prefer to pay in advance, exporters may ask them to get a Letter of Credit opened by a well-known bank. A Letter of Credit adds a bank's promise to pay the exporter on behalf of the importer provided the exporter has complied with all the terms and conditions of the LC. Thus, the exporter gets an assurance of payment from the LC opening bank, in the eventuality of the importer defaulting the payment.

Since payment by this method is made on the basis of documents, all terms of payment should be clearly specified in the LC in order to avoid confusion.

Banks charge a fee for opening the LC—which is based on a percentage of the amount of payment.

The exporter usually expects the importer to pay the charges for the LC, but some buyers may not agree to this additional cost. In such cases, the exporter has to either absorb the costs of the LC or risk losing that potential sale. LC for smaller amounts can be somewhat expensive since the fee can be high.

Payment under a LC is based on documents and does not take into account the physical condition of the goods. The LC specifies the documents required to be presented by the exporter, such as the Bill of Lading invoice, draft, and an insurance policy. The LC also contains an expiry date. Before payment, the concerned bank verifies that all documents submitted by the exporter conform to the requirements of the LC.

A modification made to a LC after it has been issued is called an amendment. Banks charge a fee for this service as well. The importer should make an effort to get the LC right at the first instance (Taking concurrence from the exporter on the terms to be included in LC).

Importers can request their banks to use wire (telegraphic) transfer to expedite the payment, if required.

3. Drafts/Bills of Exchange

A draft, also called a Bill of Exchange, is an instrument to be submitted by the exporter alongwith other documents to his/her bank. The exporter's bank will send this to the importer's bank. The importer will make the payment on or before the due date, depending upon whether the Bill of Exchange is a Sight Bill or Usance Bill.

Sight Bill

A Sight Bill of Exchange is used when the exporter wishes to get the payment before the importer collects the goods from the port. The corresponding term of payment is Delivery Against Payment (D/P).

In practice, the Bill of Lading is sent by the exporter via the exporter's bank to the buyer's bank. It is accompanied by the Sight Draft, invoices, and other supporting documents specified by the buyer (e.g., packing list, invoice, insurance certificate). The importer's bank notifies him when it has received these documents. As soon as the draft is paid, the importer's bank hands over the Bill of Lading that enables the importer to obtain the shipment.

Usance Bill / (Time Draft)

A Usance Bill of Exchange (time draft) is used when the exporter extends credit and the facility to use the goods to the buyer. The draft states that payment is due by a specific time after the buyer accepts the time draft and receives the goods (e.g., 30 days after acceptance). By signing and writing 'accepted' on the bill, the importer is formally obligated to pay within the stated time. The corresponding payment term is Delivery Against Acceptance (D/A), i.e., the delivery of the transport document by the bank to the importer against acceptance to pay after collecting the goods, within a stipulated time.

4. Open Account

In a foreign trade transaction, an open account can be a convenient method of payment if the importer is reputed and has a long and favourable payment record. With an open account, the exporter simply bills the customer, who is expected to pay under agreed terms at a future date. Some multinational firms make purchases only on an open account, to save the cost of opening a LC.

However, there are risks to an open account sale. The absence of documents and banking channels makes it difficult to pursue the legal enforcement of claims. The exporter might have to pursue collection abroad, which could be difficult. Another problem is that receivables may be harder to finance, since this type of account does not involve drafts (i.e., pre-shipment or post-shipment finance will not be possible). Exporters contemplating a sale on open account terms should thoroughly examine the political, economic, and commercial risks.

FINANCING EXPORTERS AND IMPORTERS

Financing international trade is an important function of commercial banks. Banks extend trade finance products through select branches, designated as 'foreign exchange' specialized branches. With the increase in the volume of foreign trade, many banks have identified 'trade finance' as a focus area. The 'trade finance' functions of a bank can be broadly classified as
1. Financing exporters
2. Financing importers

1. Financing Exporters

Financial assistance to exporters is in the form of
(a) Pre-shipment finance
(b) Post-shipment finance
These topics have been covered in detail in Chapter 6.

2. Financing Importers

A LC is both an instrument for settling trade payments and an arrangement for making payment against documents. Under the arrangement, a bank, at the request of a customer, undertakes to pay a third party by a given date, according to agreed stipulations and against presentation of documents, the counter-value of goods or services shipped. A LC is a commitment on the bank's part to place an agreed sum at the seller's disposal on behalf of the buyer, under precisely defined conditions. The importer knows that the negotiating bank will not effect payment to the seller unless and until the latter tenders the documents strictly in accordance with the terms of the LC. The seller is assured of getting the payment as long as he presents the documents as per LC terms to the negotiating bank.

LCs, also known as Documentary Credits, are governed by provisions of Uniform Customs and Practice for Documentary Credits (UCPDC) framed by the International Chamber of Commerce (ICC), Paris. Steps in an import transaction with LC is given in Figure 3.1.

Parties to LC

The different parties to an LC involved in an import transaction can be:

(a) Applicant—normally, the buyer of the goods

(b) Issuing Bank or Opening Bank—the bank that issues the LC, i.e., the bank that opens the LC and undertakes to make the payment.

(c) Beneficiary (Exporter)—the seller of the goods, who has to receive payment from the applicant. LC is issued in his favour to enable him or his agent to obtain payment on submission of stipulated documents.

(d) Advising Bank—the bank that advises LC to the beneficiary, thereby assuring the genuineness of the LC. It is normally situated in the country/ place of the beneficiary.

(e) Confirming Bank—the bank which adds guarantee to the LC opened by another bank, thereby undertaking the responsibility of payment/ negotiation/acceptance under the credit, in addition to that of the issuing bank. LC confirmation is not mandatory and is desirable in some cases where the parties and the banks are not internationally reputed. For example, sometimes, sellers abroad may not be aware of the standing of the LC opening bank, and hence may ask for the credit to be guaranteed for payment by a bank in his/her own country, against presentation of documents, without recourse.

(f) Reimbursing Bank—the bank authorized to honour the reimbursement claim in settlement of the negotiation/acceptance or payment lodged with it by the paying, negotiating, or accepting bank. It is normally the bank with which the issuing bank has an account, from which the payment is to be made (Nostro account)*

---

*Nostro account refers to 'My Account with you'. For example, the State Bank of India maintains a Nostro Account in US Dollar with the Bank of America, New York and a Nostro Account in Pound Sterling, with the Barclays Bank, London.

The importer concludes a purchase contract for the buying of certain goods.

↓

The importer requests his bank to open a LC in favour of his supplier.

↓

The importer's bank opens a LC as per the application.

↓

The opening bank will forward the original LC to the advising bank.

↓

The advising bank, after satisfying itself about the authenticity of the credit, forwards the same to the exporter.

↓

The exporter scrutinizes the LC to ensure that it conforms to the terms of contract.

↓

In case any terms are not as agreed, the importer will be asked to make the required amendments to the LC.

↓

In case the LC is as required, the exporter proceeds to make arrangement for the goods.

↓

The exporter will effect the shipment of goods.

↓

After the shipment is effected, the exporter will prepare export documents, including Bills of Exchange.

↓

The exporter's bank (negotiating bank) verifies all the documents with the LC.

↓

If the documents are in conformity with the terms of LC and all other conditions are satisfied, the bank will negotiate the bill.

↓

The exporter receives the payment in his bank account.

↓

The LC Opening bank (Importer's Bank) receives the bill and documents from the exporter's bank.

↓

The importer's bank checks the documents and informs the importer. The importer then accepts/pays the bill (This would depend on the terms, Delivery Against Acceptance or Delivery Against Payment). On acceptance/payment, the importer gets the shipping documents covering the goods purchased by him.

↓

The LC issuing bank reimburses the negotiating bank, the amount, if the documents are found in order.

Fig. 3.1 Steps in an import transaction with letter of credit

Source: This is a modified version of the flow chart given in the book *International Business* by Justin Paul, published by Prentice Hall of India.

Types of LC

(i) **Revocable LC**—a revocable LC may be cancelled or amended at any time without prior notice to the beneficiary. Such credits are rarely established.

(ii) **Irrevocable LC**—most commonly used in foreign trade. An irrevocable LC cannot be revoked or amended without the consent of all parties thereto. As per UCPDC, if the LC is silent, it is considered as irrevocable.

(iii) **Revolving LC**—under the terms and conditions of revolving LC, the amount under the revolving LC can revolve in relation to time or value. This type of LC provides for delivery of goods in instalments and at intervals. Such a credit would stipulate a certain ceiling amount in addition to the date of expiry.

(iv) **Transferable LC**—in some cases the seller or beneficiary may not be the actual producer of the goods. In such cases, the seller may request the buyer to open a Transferable Irrevocable LC. On receipt of the same, he will instruct to transfer the credit in favour of the actual supplier.

(v) **Red Clause LC**—it contains a clause providing for payment in advance for purchasing raw materials/processing and/or packing the goods. A LC with a clause enabling the beneficiary to avail advance (before affecting shipment) to the extent stated in the clause is called Red Clause L/C. It is called so, because the referred clause is normally incorporated in red ink.

INSTRUMENTS OF PAYMENT

In import transactions, the most widely used payment instruments in the world are: credit transfers, direct debits, cards, and cheques. Electronic money (e-money) is little used at the moment but has the potential to grow and may become a major payment instrument in the days to come. (e-money is in the form of pre-paid cards or instruments that can be stored on a PC.)

Credit transfers are instructions from the importer to his/her bank to debit his/her bank account and to credit the exporter's bank account. Credit transfers are the most frequently used payment instruments in Europe. They account for around 30% of all non-cash payments.

Direct debits are pre-authorized debits on the importer's bank account that are initiated by the exporter. They are often used for recurring payments. Telegraphic Transfer (TT) is most frequently used to transfer money for making payments.

Payment cards (debit or credit cards) are cards issued by a bank or card company. The debit card indicates that the holder of the card may charge his/her account at the bank and credit card draws on a line of credit up to an authorized limit.

A cheque is a written order from the importer (the drawer) to the exporter (the drawee, normally a bank), requiring the drawee to pay the indicated sum on demand to the drawer or to a third party specified by the drawer. Usage of cheques is still high in some countries (especially in France, Ireland, Portugal). Importers, sometimes, use a Demand Draft (DD) as an instrument for making payment, particularly, when they have to make some payment in advance. DDs are preferred when the bank charges a greater fee for TT of money.

Incoterms

International Commercial Terms, known as Incoterms, are a series of international sales terms widely used and accepted throughout the world. They divide transaction costs and responsibilities between a buyer and seller.

Incoterms are connected to the steps in delivery of the products from the seller to the buyer, such as carriage of products, export and import clearance responsibilities, who pays for which cost, and who faces the risk for the products at different locations in the transport process. Incoterms are always linked with geographical location.

Incoterms were devised and published by the International Chamber of Commerce (ICC) and endorsed by the United Nations Commission on International Trade Law (UNCITRAL).

A list of Incoterms are as follows:

1. EXW (**Ex Works**): export packing, marking crates with shipping marks
2. FCA (**Free Carrier**): first carrier, this could be any mode of transport, example air, rail, road.
3. FAS (**Free Alongside Ship**): the seller gets goods alongside ship. This is used for shipping transport only.
4. FOB (**Free On Board**): dock dues, loading goods on board ship. Preparing shipping documents. This is used for shipping transport only.
5. CFR (**Cost and Freight**): sea freight to bring the goods to the port of destination. This is used for shipping transport only.
6. CIF (**Cost, Insurance and Freight**): marine insurance (port to port). This is used for shipping transport only.

7. DEQ (**Delivered Ex Quay**): landing charges at port.
8. DDP (**Delivered Duty Paid**): import duty.

SUMMARY

It is very important to understand the different modes of payment, such as Advance payment, instruments of payment like Letter of Credit, which enable a manager to take decisions while importing and exporting. Similarly, the meaning and implications of International Commerce Incoterms and its relationship to pricing has also been discussed in this chapter. This information will be useful to the exporters and importers in their discussion while negotiating the terms and conditions as well as in their marketing efforts.

CONCEPT REVIEW QUESTIONS

1. What are the different methods of payment to be made by an importer?
2. If you are an importer, would you prefer to pay in advance? Discuss the pros and cons of advance payment?
3. Discuss the various types of LCs.
4. Elucidate the steps involved in opening a Letter of Credit.
5. Distinguish between FOB, CIF, and C&F Incoterms.

OBJECTIVE QUESTIONS

Specify whether the following statements are True/False.
1. It is necessary to hire a C&F agent in the export/import process.
2. In the business of exports and imports failure to comply with documentary requirements may lead to financial loss.
3. Shipping bill is a document required to seek permission of customs to export goods by sea/air.
4. Ex factory price means the goods delivered to an importer at his country's port.
5. Cost and freight means the price quoted by the seller includes the payment of freight charges.

For each of the following statements, choose the most appropriate option.

6. The characteristic of a Letter of Credit is:
   (a) It is an undertaking of a bank.
   (b) It is an undertaking to make payment.
   (c) It is an undertaking given on behalf of a person.
   (d) All of the above.

7. The most widely used mode of payment by importers is:
   (a) Payment by Letter of Credit
   (b) Documentary collection
   (c) Deferred payment
   (d) Cash in advance

SELECT REFERENCES

Corporation Bank Manual for Importers and Exporters, Corporation Bank, Head Office: Mangalore.

ICC Website, www.iccwbo.org, on 20th November 2007.

Madura, Jeff, 2006, *International Financial Management*, Thomson Learning, New Delhi.

Paul, Justin and P Suresh, 2007, *Banking & Financial Services*, Pearson Education, New Delhi.

Paul, Justin, 2007, *International Business*, Third Edition, Prentice Hall, New Delhi.

UCPDC website www.ucpdc.org on 21st November, 2007.

PRICING—(EXIM INCOTERMS)

Case Study

An importer in Singapore, asks for a quotation for 5000 kg of almonds. You are an exporter in Dubai. You have to take a decision on the amount to be quoted. Assume that the unit price is $2 per kg, the total price for 5000 kg almonds would be $10000 for the goods alone. How do you calculate the additional costs of delivering the goods to the importer?

How is your quotation (price) effected by Incoterms?

If you quote	Price includes	Additional cost ($)	Price ($)
EXW	**Ex works (Dubai)** Export packing, marking crates with shipping marks	400	10,400
FCA	**Free carrier** Delivery to railway station by road transport	100	10,500
FAS	**Free alongside ship** Rail transport to port and getting goods alongside ship	310	10,810
FOB	**Free on board** Dock dues, loading goods on board ship. Preparing shipping documents	100	10,910
CFR (C&F)	**Cost and freight** Sea freight to Singapore	875	11,785
CIF	**Cost, insurance and freight** marine insurance (port to port)	100	11,885
DEQ	**Delivered ex quay** Landing charges at Singapore	90	11,975
DDP	**Delivered Duty paid** Import duty on 5000 kg almond	1,000	12,975

Questions

1. How much does the exporter have to pay as sea freight charges from Dubai to Singapore?
2. What would be the total price to be quoted to the importer, if the marine insurance (port to port) cost is $50, instead of $100?
3. What kind of quotation would you prefer as an exporter?

4 Export–Import Strategies and Practice*

Learning Objectives

After studying this chapter, you will be able to understand
- the export—import strategy of an organization
- the formulation of a successful export strategy
- the major financial issues related to exporting
- how the sourcing (import) strategy works to achieve cost competitiveness

EXPORT—IMPORT BUSINESS PLAN AND STRATEGY

A company decides to enter an international market when motivated by its profit making goals in export business. Whether a company plans to handle international business operations on its own or in collaboration with other firms, entering the global arena requires formulation of strategies. Apart from its objectives and policies, other determinants that influence a company's choice to enter a foreign market are physical and social factors and competitive environment.

Export/import is an important mode for entering the foreign market. Export results in the receipt of or claim on money whereas import results in payment of or claim on money. Nowadays, not only goods but also services are exported (imported) in the global economy. There are several reasons why a company would choose to export. Most companies export primarily to increase their sales revenue; some, such as biotechnology and pharmaceuticals companies, export to boost their economies so that they can spread their R&D expenditure over a large sales area. Export can also be a means of alleviating excess capacities in the domestic market. Many companies export as part of their diversification strategies and sometimes also because of the perceived high risk of operating in a foreign environment.

*This chapter has been co-authored by Dr. Justin Paul, Mr. Amit Gupta, Mr. Vipul Agrawal, Mr. Sumit Joshi, Mr. Rupesh Bhagchandani and Mr. Vijay Rastogi.

Companies import goods and services because they can be supplied to the domestic market at cheaper prices and better quality than competing goods manufactured in the domestic market.

A company can export goods and services to its own branches and subsidiaries, or it can export to independent customers. Sometimes, a company exports final or finished goods, while at other times it exports semi-finished goods to its related companies overseas, which sell the goods and services or use them in the manufacturing process. The export strategy must be aligned with the company's overall strategy. Successful exporting is a complex process. It requires careful planning and preparation, some of the important steps of which are:

- Identifying the goods and services the company wants to sell
- Exploring market opportunities
- Developing a product or service development strategy
- Arranging goods/services
- Determining the best means for transporting the goods and services to the market
- Selling the goods and services and receiving the payment

Compared to other modes like establishing subsidiaries abroad, exporting is a low-risk mode of entry in foreign markets. A company decides on how to enter a foreign market, based upon different factors, such as the ownership advantages of the company, the location advantages of the market, and the internalization advantages that result from integrating transactions within the company.

Ownership advantages are specific assets, international experience, and the ability to develop differentiated products. For example, Boeing capitalizes on its ownership advantage through the development of sophisticated aircraft. Companies that have lower levels of ownership advantage either do not enter the foreign market or use low risk strategies such as exporting. Location advantages of the market are a combination of market potential and investment risks. Internalization advantages are the benefits of holding on to specific assets or skills within the company and integrating them into activities rather than licensing or selling them.

However, the choice of exporting as an entry mode is not just a function of these ownership, location, and internalization advantages but must also fit in with the company's overall strategy. Although, exporting requires a lower level of investments than any other mode, it also offers a corresponding lower risk/return on sales. Exporting allows significant management operational control but does not provide much marketing control because the exporter is removed from the final consumer and must often deal with independent distributors. Companies should prepare their export business plan based on the following questions:

- What does the company want to gain from exporting?
- Would it be possible for the company to opt for direct exporting or should the company depend on agents?
- Is exporting consistent with other goals of the company?
- What demands will export place on its key resources such as management, personnel, production capacity, and financing, and how would these demands be met?
- Are the expected benefits worth the costs or could company resources be better used for developing new domestic business?

A company has to collect information on weather (temperature), time in different countries etc. in order to take proper decisions. Data on average temperature in different cities across the world and the world time are given as annexures to this chapter.

Exhibit 4.1   Export strategy for Dairy products in India

With 198 million cattle and 86 million buffaloes, India has the largest population of milk animals in the world. These livestock constitute more than 50 per cent of the buffaloes and 20 per cent of the cattle in the world. With a well-crafted strategic approach, this huge animal wealth could be utilized in the right perspective for enhancement of milk production without many incremental inputs. In contrast, a small rise in milk production requires intensive inputs and crossing of genetic barriers in advanced countries, where milk animals are utilized to produce milk at their maximum potential. With modest efforts towards managing increased milk production, India could match/exceed the milk productivity of major exporters in dairy commodities. It is this potential that can transform India into a major dairy exporting country on global basis. A nation-wide programme for prevention and control of animal epidemics, and creation of disease free zones coupled with efficient delivery of artificial insemination network can have a tremendous impact on improving the productivity of milk animals. This, in turn, would strengthen India's entry into the global milk products market, as well as improve the quality and visibility of the entire Indian dairy industry, in the world market.

India is located amidst perennially milk deficit countries in Asia and Africa. Major importers of milk and milk products are Bangladesh, China, Hong Kong, Singapore, Thailand, Malaysia, The Philippines, Japan, UAE, Oman, and other gulf countries located in close proximity to India. China, India and Indonesia alone account for more than 40 per cent of the world's six billion-plus population. Economic growth and changes in dietary preferences in the Southeast Asian countries have stimulated consumption of dairy products, even though milk is not a part of their traditional diet.

(Contd.)

Exhibit 4.1 (Contd.)

> Growth of quick service restaurants (QSRs), particularly pizza chains, and growing bakery and other food processing industries also increase the demand for cheese and other dairy products. India, thus, enjoys a strategically advantageous geographical location in terms of international trade of dairy products.
>
> Global opportunities available to the Indian dairy industry arise primarily out of the availability of a large quantity of competitively priced milk. As the Indian dairy sector produces milk without any subsidies, the country stands to gain from the fair implementation of WTO agreements. However, it is sad that quality of milk produced in India falls way below the internationally accepted standards. Development of awareness, mindset and commitment on improving the quality of milk is necessary. Intensive efforts are needed to meet the WTO's Sanitary and Phyto-sanitary (SPS) and Technical Barriers of Trade (TBT) agreements guidelines on quality and safety.

EXPORT STRATEGY FORMULATION

A particular research on the characteristics of exporters had led to two erroneous conclusions:

- The probability of being an exporter increases with the size of the company.
- Export intensity, i.e. the percentage of total revenues originating from the exporter, is not positively correlated with company size.

However, a recent study of Canadian companies showed that firm size was not the most important factor in determining the propensity to export, the number of countries served, and export intensity. Factors such as the risk profile of the management and industry determinants were as important as size. In other words, managers who were more likely to take risks were also likely to engage in exporting. The greater the risk in the export business, the greater is the return.

Export Business—Strategic Plan: Stages

Developing a good export strategy is of paramount importance. Many manufacturing companies begin exporting by accident rather than by design. Therefore, they tend to encounter a number of unforeseen problems. The export strategy has to be prepared as a business plan in the following stages:

Phase-I   Pre-engagement = Market Research (Overseas)
Phase-II   Initial Exporting to one or two clients
Phase-III Regular Exports

Most governments provide several benefits to companies with a good track record of exports (For example, Star Trading House has been given self-certification powers). Hence, it makes sense to enter into the export business.

Formulating an Export Strategy

Formulating a strategy can help managers avoid making certain costly mistakes exporting often entails. A successful export strategy must take each element of the transaction chain into consideration. A transaction chain consists of all the activities involved in the export of goods or services, such as the credit check of the buyer, transportation, financial transaction, etc. A detailed export business plan is an essential element in the implementation of an effective export strategy. To coin a successful export strategy, the management must:

- assess export potential by examining its opportunities and resources.
- determine business risk coverage strategy—inspection, insurance, etc.
- select a market or markets.
- formulate and implement an export strategy.

Exhibit 4.2	Export practices and strategies of Australian biotechnology companies

In the late 1980's, the Australian government's concern about increasing exports was reflected in several official reports that were released seeking to influence government policy in this area (The Hughes Report, 1989; Garnaut Report, 1989; Pappas Carter Report, 1989 on Manufacturing in the 1990's: Global Challenge, submitted to government).

Biotechnology is a key to Australia's industrial future because it can contribute to the economy in a number of ways:

- It is fundamental to maintaining or increasing the competitive edge in existing export-oriented industries, such as agriculture, livestock, forestry, and mining;
- It is central to establish new high value-added exports in other industries or niche product areas.

The Australian biotechnology industry comprises of a diverse group of companies:

1. Those using traditional technologies to manufacture products, such as beer, wine, bread, cheese, etc.
2. 'Dedicated biotechnology companies'—these are firms created specifically to exploit the commercial potential of biotechnology. The main activities of these companies include research, development, application, or manufacture of 'new' biotechnologies.
3. Firms providing specialist services to biotechnology such as legal services, (patent attorneys), technology transfer companies, R&D companies, consultants, and equipment manufacturers.

(Contd.)

Exhibit 4.2 (Contd.)

Further, industrial activity in biotechnology is also expanding rapidly around the world, giving rise to new products and growing world markets. Many of the new biotechnology products are high value-added and low volume, often based upon renewable resources and geared primarily for global markets. It is the commercial opportunities presented by these global markets for novel products, which provided the main rationale for Australian firms investing in biotechnology.

Export Behaviour

Most companies in the biotechnology industry in Australia were found to export a large proportion of their output. In fact, about half of the companies surveyed (47%) export more than 50 per cent of total sales. This is a significant finding, which demonstrates the high level of dependence Australian biotechnology firms have on the export business. As more than half of the sales of these companies are destined for overseas markets, they are oriented towards foreign customers and market conditions. (As reported in the paper by Frederick Frost and Diana Smith.)

Export Destinations

The five major export locations to which the Australian biotechnology industry exports its goods and services, include (in order of importance), Southeast Asia, New Zealand, Europe, USA, and Japan.

Most companies target Southeast Asia because of its geographic proximity to Australia, which facilitates easy distribution and communication. Another attraction is the rapid economic growth and potential of the region.

New Zealand, on the other hand, is targeted not only because of its close proximity to Australia, but also its similarity to the Australian market. New Zealand is perceived as psychologically 'closer' to Australia than other markets; consequently it is viewed as a good starting point for exporting before attempting to enter the more 'distant' markets.

The US and European markets are seen as the largest and most well developed markets, as well as the most lucrative. These 'wealthy' markets have a comparable level of health care and technology with Australia, creating a strong demand for Australia's predominantly 'wealth-driven' biotechnology products. However, Australian firms also view these markets as difficult to enter, legally complicated, and extremely competitive.

While the US and European markets are financially more dependable and have a closer lifestyle to Australian conditions, Australian companies see more of a future in Southeast Asia, China, and Japan.

Export Motives

Australian biotechnology companies export predominantly for proactive reasons, that is, they actively pursue international markets and do not merely react or respond to environmental forces.

(Contd.)

Exhibit 4.2 (Contd.)

Channels of Distribution

The most commonly used mode of entry to overseas markets is through an overseas-based agent. The other modes used are: directly to a wholesaler, an agent in Australia, direct to end-user, own office, joint venture and Licensing Agreement. The use of an overseas-based agent is consistent with the fact that most firms are small and this is perhaps the cheapest and simplest means to enter the overseas market. Larger, more resourceful companies are able to establish their own offices overseas.

Export Planning and Strategy

Most Australian biotechnology companies who export began with a formal export-marketing plan, whilst some have had no formal export strategy. Companies, which do not have an export strategy or plan in place, lack any long-term direction in their exporting effort.

(*Source:* This is a substantially revised write-up on the basis of an article by Dr Frederick A Frost and Diana Wearing Smith.)

EXPORT FINANCING

From the point of view of an exporter, four major issues relate to the financial aspects of exporting:

- The price of the product
- The method of payment
- Financing of receivables
- Insurance

Product Price

Product pricing in export has to be based on certain factors, which managers generally overlook when determining product prices for domestic markets. For example, in export pricing, exchange rates have to be taken into consideration. Other factors, which influence export pricing are:

- Transportation costs
- Duties (Export/Import Duty)
- Insurance costs
- Banking costs

Method of Payment

The importer can pay via advance payment or as sight payment. Alternatively, he or she may avail the Usance Bill facility. Exporters and importers deal in foreign exchange; the transfer of funds from one bank to another across international borders takes place through instruments like

Telegraphic Transfer. The exporter can avail shipment/post-shipment finance facilities from banks. The exporter also gains access to funds through factoring and forfaiting. Factoring is the discounting of a foreign account receivable. Forfaiting is similar to factoring, but usually involves a longer time period and carries a guarantee from a bank in the importer's country.

Financing of Receivables

Exporters get post-shipment finance from banks before the actual realization of the export bill. This type of financing is known as financing the receivable.

Insurance

Two kinds of insurance are used most often in exports. These are:
- Insurance on transportation risks, such as weather or rough handling by carriers.
- Political, commercial, and foreign-exchange risks that might keep the exporter from collecting from the importer.

IMPORT STRATEGY (SOURCING STRATEGY)

There are two basic types of imports:
- Finished goods (consumer and capital goods)
- Intermediate goods and services that are part of a firm's global supply chain

Companies import raw materials, components, and machinery to provide in the domestic market better quality products at cheap prices and also products that are not locally available. For example, petroleum companies in South and East Asia are major importers of crude oil because the demand of crude oil is far greater than the crude produced in those countries. There are three types of importers:
- Importers conducting business with the purpose of importing and selling
- Importers looking for foreign sourcing to get their products at the cheapest price
- Importers using foreign sourcing as part of their global supply chain. (For example, raw materials or components)

The import process is a mirror of the export process. It involves both strategic and procedural issues. The export business plan could easily be adapted into an import business plan. The importer needs to:
- research potential source countries;
- determine the legal ramification of importing products, both in terms of the products and the countries from which they come; and
- deal with parties, such as freight forwarders, banks, shipping lines, etc.

Importing requires a certain degree of expertise in dealing with institutions and documentation. When importing goods into any country, a company must be absolutely familiar with the customs requirements of the importing country. An importer needs to know how to get the goods cleared, what duties to pay, and what special laws exist regarding the importation of products. Customs officials examine the goods to determine whether there are any restrictions on their importation and also calculate the customs duties to be paid by the importer.

An importer also has to learn how to handle a transaction scientifically. A knowledgeable importer minimizes import duties and manages his or her risk by using appropriate risk management tools, some of which are:

- valuing the product in such a way that it qualifies for more favourable duty treatment;
- qualifying for duty refunds through drawbacks provisions;
- availing exemptions from duties by way of entering into export business; and
- limiting liability by properly marking an import's country of origin. (whether preferential or free trade agreements are applicable.)

Ten Steps to become a Successful Exporter/Importer

1. Know well the potential of your product.
2. Learn about the competition in the foreign market and the sales potential of the product.
3. Get into strategic alliances with distributors and agents.
4. Advertise in the local market before going there personally, in order to determine the interest level and build contacts.
5. Work hard and try to gather all relevant information and show your business acumen.
6. Build a strong response base back home and resolve complaints/queries immediately to build trust among business associates.
7. Do not rely on potential representatives to solve problems in the target country. Too much reliance on the representatives shows a lack of understanding of the local environment.
8. Make someone at the home office the single-point contact for representatives to resolve their problems, answer their questions, and also to provide assistance.
9. Learn the customs and business etiquette of the country you are dealing with.
10. Send an authorized representative to make a decision and commitment to the company.

Exhibit 4.3   Hinduja Group as an international trade partner

The diversified, multi-billion dollar Hinduja Group had its origins in trading activities. The Group now trades internationally in practically all products and commodities, except tobacco, meat, and alcohol and offers technical services to several infrastructure sectors.

To simplify the complexities of international trade transactions, most clients require a partner who provides a broad solution to all their trade needs while being sensitive to the unique characteristics of each transaction. The Hinduja Group plays the role of such a partner and provides 'tailor-made' solutions to its clients. Backed by its worldwide network of offices and professionals, the Group has the infrastructure and expertise to structure and execute any type of trade transaction.

Finance/Service

In the world of trade, financial services are becoming as important as conventional services. The Hinduja Group offers alternative forms of financing to suppliers and customers. In addition to handling standard trade practices like documentary credit operations, cash management, disposition of financial means, and hedging against fluctuations in exchange and interest rates, the Group facilitates new methods of financing such as export financing, management of trust accounts, and project financing based on counter-trade in cooperation with international banks. These new financing models are becoming increasingly important and complement traditional trading functions.

Counter-trade

Counter-trade is inherently an ad hoc activity, which varies according to local regulations and requirements, the nature of the goods to be exported, and the current priorities of the parties involved. Counter-trade consists of transactions, which have a basic linkage, between exports and imports of goods or services in addition to, or in place of, financial settlements.

With many years of experience in this activity, the Group can assist large multinationals in fulfilling their counter-trade obligations. The Group uses counter-trade aggressively as a marketing tool and regards offset and counter-purchase as an opportunity (to make money through trading).

Buy-back

The Hinduja Group believes that trading in modern times goes well beyond the traditional activity of direct buying and selling. Trading skills have to keep pace with the changing world of instant communications and the varied requirements of customers for mutual benefit. One such method is to enter into two-way trade with the customer whereby against supply of certain goods to a customer, the customer supplies his own goods in lieu of payment for his purchase.

SUMMARY

It is now clear that both an exporter and an importer have to formulate their strategy and prepare business plans and review their performance. This, in turn, will help their companies to prepare their Vision-Mission statements and set their goals.

CONCEPT REVIEW QUESTIONS

1. Discuss the phases of entering the export business. How does one formulate a business strategy for export?
2. What are the factors one should take into account, while conducting EX-IM business?

SELECT REFERENCES

"Foreign Trade Review", 2006, January-March, IIFT New Delhi.

Joshy, R. M., 2005, *International Marketing*, Oxford University Press, New Delhi.

Journal of International Business Studies, 2007, Academy of International Business, USA.

Mahajan. M. I., 2006, *Export Policy—Procedure and Documentation*, Snow White, New Delhi.

GOLDEN INDUSTRIES

Case Study

Golden Industries, based in the United Kingdom, manufactures laboratory and industrial ovens, furnaces, and heat processing systems. Before Golden Industries got involved in exporting, it experienced problems when one of its customers moved overseas. Initially, the firm continued to supply the customer with furnaces, but this market eventually began to get eroded, as the customer started sourcing locally. The company initially had not considered export proactively and aggressively due to the following reasons:

- The nature of the product: industrial ovens and furnaces are rather large and bulky, and they are also relatively expensive. Further, product sizes make shipping costs high.
- Doubts about its success abroad: Golden was a small business and top management presumed that they would not succeed internationally.

From Local into Export Business

Golden chose to move into the international market because of a combination of factors. First of all, the company had confidence in its products. As its president noted, "Golden's strength is in selling engineered products, using 45 years of expertise to build something for customers".

Further, not only did some of Golden's clients move abroad, but also the company began to experience stiff competition in its number one and two local markets from foreign manufacturers. Additionally, they were having to contend with local competition and high transportation costs.

Thus, the changing scenario helped Golden realize that an international market might not be a bad choice. Consequently, they made efforts to increase their clientele-base abroad to increase sales and also to insulate themselves from fierce competition in one specific market.

Although considered a small company in terms of total sales, the export revenues of Golden are significant and they are the key to its survival. It is now necessary for Golden to maintain its export market share abroad and also its competitive position in the US market.

Export Strategy

After initial hesitation, the executives in Golden finally adopted pro-active approach by selecting Southeast Asia as an area for export development. Golden's Chairman, Mr. Luke, was motivated towards this strategy when he attended a seminar that featured UK's ambassadors to the ASEAN* countries.

Mr. Luke used the information provided by the participants in the seminar for research on the Asian market. In addition, the top executives of Golden worked with a representative from the Export Promotion Council of the UK. Mr. Luke also undertook a trip to Southeast Asia primarily to gauge the market potential and identify possible agents. He decided to export finished products and marketed them through agents/distributors.

The company could have explored licensing its technology to manufacturers in Southeast Asia but preferred to maintain control over its technology and serve Southeast Asia through exports from its own plants in the US. They advertised in leading newspapers in Thailand and Singapore.

Golden's executives quickly learned that they had to cut shipping costs to remain competitive in the Southeast Asian market. So they decided to redesign the packaging of their product, making it more compact. Additionally, they hired/contracted with freight forwarders to find the best rates, which varied depending on the forwarder's experience and relationship with a particular shipping line.

---

* ASEAN stands for Association of Southeast Asian Nations.

Noting that the Southeast Asian customers are very keen upon forming a personal association with the exporter, Mr. Luke learned the importance of visiting potential customers in the region personally rather relying on a sales manager. Another behavioral pattern he noticed among these customers was that they wanted to ensure that the exporter was financially secure and had sufficient funding to continue work with them for a long period. Thus, he used this knowledge to strengthen trust with his Southeast Asian clients and find his company a strong foothold in the export business.

Questions
1. Why did Golden Industries start exporting?
2. Discuss the export strategy formulated by Mr. Luke?

Average Temperature (in Celsius) in Major Cities around the world

Sl. No.	City	January	April	July	October
1	Adelaide	24	19	11	17
2	Amsterdam	3	9	17	11
3	Athens	9	15	27	20
4	Auckland	20	16	11	14
5	Bangkok	26	30	28	27
6	Beijing	5	14	26	13
7	Berlin	0	9	18	9
8	Brisbane	28	21	15	23
9	Brussels	2	8	18	10
10	Cairo	13	21	28	24
11	Chennai	29	35	35	32
12	Colombo	26	28	27	27
13	Copenhagen	0	7	18	9
14	Darwin	28	26	25	29
15	Delhi	14	29	31	26
16	Dhahran	17	25	33	28
17	Dhaka	19	28	29	27
18	Dubai	18	25	35	27
19	Frankfurt	1	10	16	9
20	Hong Kong	15	22	29	25
21	Istanbul	5	12	24	16
22	Jakarta	26	28	27	27
23	Karachi	15	22	29	24
24	Kathmandu	10	19	24	20
25	Kolkata	20	29	31	26
26	Kuala Lumpur	27	28	27	27
27	London	5	9	18	11
28	Los Angeles	13	16	22	20
29	Male	28	29	28	28

(Contd.)

(*Contd.*)

30	Manchester	4	8	16	10
31	Manila	26	29	28	27
32	Mauritius	25	24	20	22
33	Medan	27	28	27	27
34	Melbourne	20	16	10	15
35	Mumbai	24	28	27	28
36	Osaka	3	13	25	1
37	Paris	3	11	19	11
38	Penang	27	28	28	27
39	Perth	23	19	13	16
40	Port Moresby	28	26	23	25
41	Rome	8	14	25	18
42	San Francisco	10	13	15	16
43	Seoul	4	13	24	13
44	Shanghai	10	19	27	23
45	Singapore	27	27	28	27
46	Sydney	22	19	12	18
47	Taipei	17	25	30	30
48	Tokyo	3	13	25	17
49	Vancouver	3	9	17	10
50	Vienna	1	12	21	11

Source: Adapted from Dun and Bradstreet Diary, USA; Compiled by Dr. Justin Paul.

ANNEXURE 2

World time
Hours fast (+) or slow (−) Greenwich Mean Time

Sl. No.	Country	Time
1	Afganistan	+ 04.30
2	Algeria	+ 01.00
3	Argentina	− 03.00
4	Australia:	
	— New South Wales	+ 10.00
	— Western Australia	+ 08.00
5	Austraia	+ 01.00
6	Bahamas	− 05.00
7	Bangladesh	+ 06.00
8	Bahrain	+ 03.00
9	Belgium	+ 01.00
10	Bermuda	− 04.00
11	Brazil:	
	— East	− 03.00
	— West	− 04.00
12	Myanmar	+ 06.30
13	Canada:	
	— Atlantic	− 04.00
	— Pacific	− 08.00
14	Chile	− 04.00
15	Beijing	+ 08.00
16	Colombia	− 05.00
17	Costa Rica	− 06.00
18	Cyprus	+ 02.00
19	Czech and Slovak	+ 01.00
20	Denmark	+ 01.00
21	Ecuador	− 05.00
22	Egypt	+ 02.00
23	Ethiopia	+ 03.00

(Contd.)

(*Contd.*)

24	Finland	+ 02.00
25	France	+ 01.00
26	Germany	+ 01.00
27	Ghana	GMT
28	Gibraltar	+ 01.00
29	Greece	+ 02.00
30	Hong Kong	+ 08.00
31	Hungary	+ 01.00
32	India	+ 05.30
33	Indonesia, Java	+ 07.00
34	Iran	+ 03.30
35	Iraq	+ 03.00
36	Ireland	GMT
37	Italy	+ 01.00
38	Jamaica	− 05.00
39	Japan	+ 09.00
40	Jordan	+ 02.00
41	Kenya	+ 03.00
42	Korea, South	+ 09.00
43	Kuwait	+ 03.00
44	Lebanon	+02.00
45	Libya	+ 01.00
46	Malaysia:	
	— West	+ 07.30
	— Sabah, Sarawak	+ 08.00
47	Malta	+ 01.00
48	Mauritius	+ 04.00
49	Mexico City	− 06.00
50	Morocco	GMT
51	Nepal	+ 05.20
52	The Netherlands	+ 01.00
53	New Zealand	+ 12.00
54	Nigeria	+ 01.00
55	Norway	+ 01.00
56	Oman	+ 04.00
57	Pakistan	+ 05.00
58	Panama	− 05.00

(*Contd.*)

(Contd.)

59	The Philippines	+ 08.00
60	Poland	+ 01.00
61	Portugal	GMT
62	Qatar	+ 03.00
63	Romania	+ 02.00
64	Saudi Arabia	+ 03.00
65	Singapore	+ 08.00
66	South Africa	+ 02.00
67	Spain	+ 01.00
68	Sri Lanka	+ 06.00
69	Sudan	+ 02.00
70	Sweden	+ 01.00
71	Switzerland	+ 01.00
72	Syria	+ 02.00
73	Tanzania	+ 03.00
74	Thailand	+ 07.00
75	Trinidad and Tobago	− 04.00
76	Tunisia	+ 01.00
77	Turkey	+ 02.00
78	UAE	+ 04.00
79	UK	GMT
80	USA:	
	— Eastern	− 05.00
	— Central	− 06.00
	— Mountain	− 07.00
	— Pacific	− 08.00

Source: Adapted from Dun and Bradstreet Diary 2007.

Export Marketing*

*This chapter has been co-authored by Dr Justin Paul with Mayur Udermani.

Learning Objectives

After studying this chapter, you will be able to understand
- the newly emerged concept of marketing post globalization and deregulation of economies
- the nature and scope of international marketing activities
- Globalization the role of free trade blocks, WTO, etc. in export marketing activities

MARKETING—THE CONCEPT

Marketing, in the simplest of terms, might be defined as the process which profitably meets the need for products.

The more formal definition of marketing[1] is that it is an organizational function and a set of processes for creating, communicating, and delivering value to customers and for managing customer relationships in ways that benefit the organization and its stakeholders.

A related concept is marketing management, which deals with the choosing of target markets and the management of customers through creating, delivering, and communicating superior customer value.

The concept of marketing that we now see emerged as a result of the industrial revolution. Before this, marketing as a function had been at a nascent stage. During the pre-industrial revolution era, the environment was essentially that of scarcity with sellers dominating the market. But after the advent of mass production, the chasm between supply and demand grew increasingly narrower and hence arose the need for marketing. The concept of marketing differed from the prevailing concepts of product, production, and selling in that the main focus shifted from the product to the consumer.

---

*This chapter has been co-authored by Dr Justin Paul with Mayur Udermani.
[1]Definition as prescribed by American Marketing Association, *Source:* Philip Kotler and Kevin Lane Keller, 2006, *Marketing Management*, 12/e, Pearson Education, Pg. 6

During the last decade, the business environment has changed drastically, such that the holistic marketing concept, based on development, design, and implementation of marketing programmes and processes, has taken centre stage. This concept also accommodates other important dimensions, such as internal marketing, integrated marketing, relationship marketing, and socially responsible marketing. Some of the key drivers of this radical change in the concept of marketing are:

- Globalization
- Deregulation of economies
- Customer empowerment
- Increased competition
- Emergence of big retail players
- Convergence of various industries

Marketing activities have been traditionally depicted in terms of a marketing mix, which can be defined as the set of marketing tools needed to pursue marketing objectives. The marketing mix consists of four broad groups, popularly referred to as the four Ps of marketing. These are

- Product
- Price
- Place
- Promotion

This marketing mix is typically from the seller's point of view whereas the mix corresponding to the customer is based on

- Customer solution
- Customer cost
- Convenience
- Communication

Successful companies are those which can change their marketing strategy in tune with changing marketplaces and spaces.

INTERNATIONAL MARKETING

Simply put, in the era of decreasing trade barriers between countries and decreasing transportation costs, marketing of goods (and services) across international barriers is called international marketing.

Philip R. Cateora and John L. Graham in their book *International Marketing*, define it as the performance of business activities designed to plan, price, promote, and direct the flow of a company's goods and services to consumers or users in more than one nation for a profit.

Marketing as a concept is universal, but the markets and behaviour of consumers vary across countries and can be quite different. This makes it essential for any student of international marketing to gain knowledge in three critical areas:

- Cross-cultural knowledge
- Country/regional knowledge
- Cross-border transactions knowledge

In general, the different stages in any firm's international transition are:
1. No direct foreign marketing
2. Infrequent export marketing
3. Regular foreign marketing
4. International marketing
5. Global management

In the above mentioned stage one, a firm does not undertake direct export business. After achieving some profit from the local market, in the second stage, it enters into export marketing, but not frequently. This can also be called occassional exports. In the third stage, exporting becomes a regular activity. Thereafter the firm stabilizes in export business and gets into international marketing with other modes of entries too, in the next two stages.

EXPORT MARKETING—GOING GLOBAL

This section addresses the all-important question: Why should a firm enter the international market? Some of the more obvious reasons for firms to enter overseas markets are:
1. Profitability
2. Growth
3. Achieving economies of scale
4. Risk spread
5. Access to imported inputs
6. Uniqueness of products and services
7. Marketing opportunities due to life cycle
8. Spreading R&D costs

Exhibit 5.1 Internationalization of Tata Steel

For long, steel has been known to be the one industry where economies of scale operate to a maximum. Steel is a cyclical industry with marked ebullient and depressed phases. The economies of scale help in increased margins in up cycles and reduced losses in case of a down cycle.

With the liberalization of India, Tata Steel, the country's leader in steel production perceived a threat from the world's largest steel producers, such as Arcelor-Mittal and POSCO, who were showing interest in India.

(Contd.)

Exhibit 5.21 (Contd.)

To overcome the challenge and to reap benefits of larger operations, Tata Steel bought NatSteel in Singapore and Corus in Europe.

Tata Steel now benefits from the lower operational costs of Tata Steel and NatSteel in Asia, and the captive Iron Ore and Coal Mines and the high margin business of Corus in Europe.

GLOBALIZATION

Trade, in the present context, is marked by two important concepts of globalization. One is the rise of international agreements like the General Agreement on Tariff and Trade or GATT (replaced by the World Trade Organization or WTO, which now comprises GATT for international trade, General Agreement on Trade of Services or GATS for services, and Trade Related Intellectual Property Rights or TRIPS for intellectual property). The second is the creation of regional trade blocks and their evolution.

History of GATT and WTO

The United States and 22 other countries signed GATT after World War II. GATT was a landmark in terms of the large scale launching of international business. The salient objectives of GATT were:

- Non-discriminatory trade between countries
- Protection through custom tariffs, not through commercial measures like quotas
- Consultation to solve trade issues

WTO is an institution, formed in January 1995, which governs trade between its 132 member countries by issuing binding decisions (unlike the GATT). The WTO was specifically set up to overcome the deficiencies of GATT. It also includes services and intellectual property related issues. Thus, the WTO can be simplistically represented as:

$$ \text{WTO} \quad = \quad \text{GATT} \quad + \quad \text{GATS} \quad + \quad \text{TRIPS} $$

The rise in trade through the WTO and the International Monetary Fund or IMF raised concern in many countries about job losses, dumping of cheap exports by foreign countries, and the destruction of indigenous industry. All these led to the creation of a parallel administration in the form of multinational market regions starting with the Regional Cooperation Groups (RCG). RCGs are explained in the next section.

Understanding Different Levels of International Integration

This section outlines the various multinational market groups based on their degree of cooperation and interrelationship.

- **Regional Cooperation Groups**
  - Exhibit the most basic level of integration
  - Governments participate jointly in RCGs to develop mutually beneficial projects

Example, India and Bangladesh working together on the Ganges and several other rivers to avoid floods.

- **Free Trade Areas**
  - Involve more cooperation than do the RCGs.
  - Custom duties and non-tariff trade barriers are different among partners while maintaining standard rules for others.

For example, North American Free Trade Agreement or NAFTA between Canada, the USA and Mexico, SAARC or South Asian Association for Regional Co-operation in the Indian subcontinent.

- **Customs Unions**
  - Involve reduced or non trade barriers like a FTA and common tariff for other external countries.
  - Do not allow free movement of labour between member countries, but allow free movement of capital.

- **Common Markets**
  - Involve elimination of all tariffs and restrictions on internal trade.
  - Allow free movement of all factors of production (capital, labour).
  - Provide common marketplace for all goods and services produced elsewhere in the marketplace.

For example, European Economic Community (EEC), Southern Cone Common Market (MERCOSUR), etc

- **Political Unions**
  - Signify the final step of integration in regional cooperation.
  - Provide a common marketplace and common central bank.
  - Involve common fiscal and monetary policies.

For example, European Union (EU), Commonwealth of Independent States (CIS) of the former USSR

Exhibit 5.2   European Union

During the 20th century, two world wars were fought on European soil. The end of World War II saw the rise of two superpowers, the US and the USSR, the latter actually a political union of a number of states, which later disintegrated.

(Contd.)

Exhibit 5.2 (Contd.)

With the end of World War II, Europeans lost their status as the superpowers of the world. However, setting aside their differences, the European countries came together to form the European Union or the EU which began as a free trade area of eight European countries and then underwent the transition from a customs union and common market to (almost a weak) political union with a single currency, the Euro, which re-established the power of the European states on the world map.

DIFFERENT FORMS OF INTERNATIONAL TRADE

The various alternatives in international trade and marketing that a company can pursue as a long-term or intermediate strategy for expansion are:

Export–Import of Goods

This is the most basic form of business expansion internationally. It involves search for marketplaces in foreign countries (export) and search for raw materials in foreign countries (import). For example, Arvind Mills exports a significant proportion of its production to American supermarket chains like Wal-Mart.

Subsidiaries

Setting up a subsidiary of the company in another country is another form of business expansion overseas. The subsidiary is a registered company in foreign land. For example, Coca Cola sales operations in India are handled by a wholly owned subsidiary called Hindustan Coca-Cola Beverages Private Limited.

Joint Ventures

One can also join hands with another company in a foreign country. This way it benefits from local knowledge and culture. Capital to be employed reduces, but so does a proportion of the upside, which is to be shared with the Joint Venture or the JV Partner. For example, Mahindra-Ugine, a specialty steel producer for automotive uses, is a JV between the Mahindra Group of India and the Ugine Group of Europe.

Franchises

Another form of international expansion is when the technology or the process is patented/protected but its implementation is outsourced. Local Franchises then implement policies, and produce and sell goods. For example, McDonalds has patented processes, but sells its famous eatables through thousands of franchised outlets.

> **Exhibit 5.3   Coca-Cola in India: Franchise or Private Subsidiary?**
>
> Coca-Cola re-entered India by buying out an Indian Carbonated Soft Drinks Division (CSD) manufacturer, which operated through a number of franchisees. The franchisees of the erstwhile Group were reluctant to put in any fresh investment in expansion or technology, because they were badly hit by the ongoing battle between the Coca-Cola Group and Pepsi for supremacy in the Indian market. Coca-Cola, then had to invest in a wholly owned subsidiary, Hindustan Coca-Cola Beverages Private Limited (HCCBPL) and invest to grow in size as well as to bring in new technology.
>
> This case illustrates that there is always a tradeoff; franchises increase scope with lower capital from the company, but will not always invest in newer technology or upgradation, as the company will.

International Consumer Behaviour

Marketing, in the international context, is complicated by varying consumer behaviour, which itself is governed by a number of factors that are sometimes uncontrollable.

The first step, therefore, is to classify the factors as controllable and uncontrollable. The controllable factors must be taken care of in any international marketing assignment, and there should be continuous tracking of the uncontrollable factors in order to judge early the impact of those factors, especially when they turn unfavourable.

The uncontrollable factors affecting international marketing decisions and success are:

- Political environment
- Legal environment
- Consumer behaviour determined by cultural factors
- Level of infrastructure and technology affecting distribution and manufacturing
- The geography and climate of the country

The list is not exhaustive, but these are some of the more important determinants that affect marketing decisions.

The behaviour of consumers in any country can be understood largely by its culture.

Culture is affected by a number of elements, including:

- History of the region
- Social institutions like family, schools etc
- Regional, political, and economic stability
- Effect of Peers (Peer Pressure)

Consumer behaviour manifests itself in the values, rituals, thought processes, beliefs, symbols, and other expressions.

Hofstede* studied the cultural differences between 90,000 people in 66 countries and arrived at the conclusion that variations in market and consumer behaviour across various countries mainly exist due to fundamental differences in their cultural values. His study further recognized four major dimensions based on which, these cultural differences and peculiarities could be assessed. These dimensions are now known as Hofstede's dimensions and form an important part of the study of international consumer behaviour, which helps in localizing marketing content to a particular region.

Hofstede's dimensions are:

1. **Individual/Collectivism Index (IDV)** refers to the preference to promote one's own self interest or that of the group.
2. **Power Distance Index (PDI)** refers to the tolerance of power inequality between superior and subordinates.
3. **Uncertainty Avoidance Index (UDI)** measures the comfort level with ambiguity and uncertainty among members.
4. **Masculinity/Femininity Index (MAS)** determines whether assertiveness and achievement are taken as focus areas for success.

Hofstede's dimensions and the understanding of consumer behaviour in general is very helpful in formulating national and regional strategies for Multinational Companies (MNCs) that operate in cultural contexts very different from their own.

Selecting Markets for Exporting

Target markets should be selected after careful consideration of various factors like political embargo, sales scope of the exporter's selected product, demand stability, preferential treatment to products from developing countries, market penetration by competitive countries and products, distance of potential market, transport problems, language problems, tariff and non-tariff barriers, distribution infrastructure, size of demand in the market, expected life span of market and product requirements, and sales and distribution channels. For this purpose, one must collect adequate market information before selecting one or more target markets. The information can be collected from various sources like Export Promotion Council (EPCs)/ Commodity Boards, Federation of Indian Export Organisation (FIEO), Indian Institute of Foreign Trade (IIFT), India Trade Promotion Organisation (ITPO), Indian Embassies abroad, Foreign Embassies in India, Import Promotion Institutions abroad, Overseas Chambers of Commerce and Industries, various directories, journals, and market survey reports*.

---

*Hofstede Geert, 2001 Culture's Consequences, 2nd Edition, Thousand Oaks, California.
* *Source: How to Import and Export,* Nabhi Publications.

Selecting Channels of Distribution

The following channels of distribution are generally utilized while exporting to overseas markets :
- Exports through consortia
- Export through canalizing agencies
- Export through other established merchant exporters or export houses, or trading houses
- Direct Exports
- Export through overseas sales agencies

Selecting Prospective Buyers

The addresses of the prospective buyers of the commodity can be collected from the following sources:
- Enquiries from friends and relatives or other acquaintances residing in foreign countries.
- Visiting/participating in International Trade Fairs and exhibitions in India and abroad. Contacting the Export Promotion Councils, Commodity Boards and other government agencies.
- Consulting the *International Yellow Pages* (a publication from New York by Dun & Bradstreet, USA) or other Yellow Pages of different countries, such as Japan, UAE, etc.
- Collecting addresses from various Indian directories available at Jain Book Agency, C-9, Connaught Place, New Delhi-1. (Tel. 3355686, Fax. 3731117).
- Collecting information from international trade directories/ journals/ periodicals available in the libraries of the Directorate General of Commercial Intelligence and Statistics, IIFT, Export Promotion Councils, ITPO, etc.
- Making contacts with trade representatives of overseas governments in India and Indian trade and other representatives/international trade development authorities abroad.

SUMMARY

Marketing is a universal concept. Though the basics of marketing remain the same across various countries, complications arise in international marketing because of two fundamental reasons:
1. The differences in the cultural context between the originating country and the target country.

2. The presence of uncontrollable factors in the foreign regions that might hinder the success of otherwise foolproof international marketing strategies.

Further, local regional blocs and WTO are the two opposing trends in international business and trade.

CONCEPT REVIEW QUESTIONS

1. Discuss the various aspects of export marketing.
2. Why does a company opt for export business?
3. Compare the characteristic features of conducting business in countries like India and any other foreign country.
4. How does an exporter get information about markets abroad?
5. Discuss the international marketing strategy of Tata Steel.

SELECT REFERENCES

Cateora, Philip R. and Graham, John L. *International Marketing*, Twelfth Edition, McGraw-Hill, USA.

Hill, Charles W. L., 2004, *International Business*, Fifth Edition, McGraw-Hill, New Delhi.

Hofstede, Geert *Culture's Consequences*, Second Edition, California, USA.

Kotler, Philip, 2005, *Marketing Management*, Twelfth Edition, Pearson Education, New Delhi.

Paul, Justin, 2007, *International Business*, Third Edition, Prentice Hall of India, New Delhi.

Paul, Justin and Kapoor, Ramneek, 2008 *International Marketing*, McGraw-Hill, New Delhi.

www.wikipedia.com last accessed on 30th October, 2007.

www.wto.org last accessed on 31st December, 2007.

6 Methods of Financing Exporters

Learning Objectives

After studying this chapter, you will be able to understand
- the basics of export finance (pre-shipment finance, post-shipment finance)
- about financing in foreign currency and domestic currency, factoring
- business risk coverage through insurance; role of ECGC.

Exporters require money from banks both at pre-shipment and post-shipment stage. Export finance offered by banks can be classified as pre-shipment finance and post-shipment finance.

PRE-SHIPMENT FINANCE

Financial assistance extended to the exporter before the shipment of goods, is termed pre-shipment finance.

An exporter can avail pre-shipment finance either in the form of
(a) packing credit in local currency (e.g., packing credit in rupees), or
(b) as pre-shipment credit for foreign currency (PCFC).

Packing Credit in Domestic Currency

When exporter takes pre-shipment finance in currency, it is known as packing credit in domestic currency.

Purpose of the Packing Credit

The purpose of packing credit is to enable the exporter to purchase raw materials, process or manufacture the same, and make it ready for export. The credit granted by a bank to an exporter enables him/her to make the goods ready for export. This is known as a short-term working capital advance.

Documents to be given to Bank by Exporter

Packing credit loan is sanctioned only against a confirmed export order or proforma invoice or irrevocable letter of credit.

The following persons are eligible for packing credit:

1. All exporters submitting the above documents to the bank. Export houses with star status get this facility on running account basis.
2. The supporting manufacturer of the export house who has not received the export contract directly but would be executing the contract through the export house. In such an event, the manufacturer has to produce the letter from the export house/exporter indicating the details of the order received, such as description of goods, quantity, and value, along with an undertaking that the export house/exporter will not avail the packing credit to the extent mentioned in the letter.

Form of Finance

The forms of finance can be classified as

1. *Fund based advance* It is in the form of domestic currency or a foreign currency. The packing credit in foreign currency is generally given by banks on the basis of the track record of the exporter, in the foreign currency in which the export earnings are expected to be received.
2. *Non-fund based advance* It is in the form of a Letter of Credit (LC), domestic as well as import, for the purchase of raw materials etc., which an exporter can avail, if required.

Quantum of Finance

Generally 90% of the export order or LC value is given as pre-shipment advance.

Period of Finance and Interest Rate

The interest rate for the first 90 days is the lowest, and increases herewith for every successive 90-day period. Banks normally approve additional period of loan subject to production of revalidated export order or Letter of Credit (LC) by the exporter. The interest rate of the bank has to be lower than its prime lending rate. Banks are not allowed to charge any other service charges other than those stipulated by the Foreign Exchange Dealers' Association.

Procedure

The procedure to be followed by the exporter for getting the packing credit limit by the bank is as follows:

(a) The exporter has to submit formal application along with necessary documentary proof.

(b) The exporter should be aware that the credit may be sanctioned once, or a regular packing credit limit is set, based on the assessment by the bank.

(c) For every export order, a separate packing credit loan account is opened for appropriate monitoring.

(d) While sanctioning a loan, the bank obtains an undertaking from the exporter that the documents covering shipment of goods, for which packing credit is sanctioned, will be negotiated through the concerned bank and the packing credit account will be closed with the trade proceeds.

Closure of Packing Credit Loan

There are two important points an exporter should be aware of, regarding the closure of packing credit loan. The exporter can close the loan either

(a) out of realization of sale proceeds of export order; or

(b) if the exporter is not able to export, for one reason or another, the bank charges higher rate of interest on such a loan.

Running Account Facility

Banks have the autonomy to sanction running account facility even in the absence of a confirmed purchase order/letter of credit, subject to the following conditions:

(a) A need for running account facility has to be established by the exporter, to the satisfaction of the bank.

(b) Banks extend this facility only to those exporters who have a good track record.

(c) The concessional credit facility, available to the exporter, should not exceed 180 days.

Pre-shipment Credit in Foreign Currency

The pre-shipment credit facility is analogous to that of packing credit in domestic currency. An exporter with a proven track record can avail this type of credit. The exporter can repay using the export earnings in foreign currency. Exporters compare the interest rates on domestic currency vis-a-vis, foreign currency and decide on which loan to avail.

The foreign currency loans granted to exporters by the banks are known as PCFC. The salient features of PCFC are given below:

(a) PCFC is available only for cash exports, in foreign currency.

(b) There is a cap on the interest rate a bank can charge over and above the London Interbank Offered Rate (LIBOR), in the case of PCFC. For example, Reserve Bank of India (RBI) had fixed a cap that the interest rate shall not exceed one per cent above 6 months. LIBOR for the initial period of 180 days. Even though the interest rate is lower in PCFC, compared to that of Packing Credit in Rupees, exporters may not prefer PCFC when they expect a fall in the value of the Rupee. For example, if the Rupee depreciates against the US Dollar subsequent to availing of PCFC, say, from 1 USD = Rs 43 to Rs 48, the exporter will not get the benefit of such a depreciation as the export proceeds in USD will be adjusted against the Packing Credit (PC) already accounted for, in Dollars. The exporter will get the benefit of the depreciation, only if the PC was availed of in Rupees, as the bank will convert the export proceeds in Dollars to Rupee @ 1 US dollar = Rs 48, for adjusting the PC outstanding and crediting the balance to the party's account.

(c) For lending under the PCFC scheme, banks can use the foreign currency balances available with them, in Exchange Earners Foreign Currency (EEFC) account/Resident Foreign Currency (RFC) accounts, and Foreign Currency Non-Resident (FCNR) deposits*, etc.

(d) PCFCs can be maintained as running accounts.

(e) PCFC is self-liquidating in nature and is liquidated by purchasing/discounting of bills.

POST-SHIPMENT EXPORT ADVANCE

Banks give short-term finance to the exporters against the exports receivable up to 120 days. The following are the primary types of advances.

(a) Exports Bills Negotiation

(b) Exports Bills Purchase

(c) Exports against Bills sent for collection

Post-shipment finance is available at concessional rate to the exporters. The above mentioned types of post-shipment finance can be elaborated as follows.

Negotiation of Export Documents under Letters of Credit

Exporters are required to submit the bills and documents after shipment to a bank. If an exporter requests for immediate credit, The bank will scrutinize all the documents required under LC. These are presented and are drawn in conformity to the terms of the LC. Only when the documents are in order and comply absolutely with all the terms of the letter of credit, does the negotiating bank make the payment to the exporter. Even if there is a

---

*FCNR deposit refers to the deposits denominated in foreign currencies with the bank accounts maintained by non-residents.

slightest deviation from the terms of the LC or there is a minor discrepancy in the documents, the negotiating bank does not make the payment to the exporter. If the documents are not in order, even after the negotiating bank has made payments to the exporter, the LC opening bank does not reimburse the negotiating bank (exporter's bank).

Purchase/Discount of Foreign Bills

When the exporter does not possess the LC from the importer, he/she requests the bank to purchase/discount documents for receiving immediate payment. The bill may be drawn on D/A (Documents against Acceptance)* or D/P (Documents against Payment) basis, depending on the terms of the export contract. When the exporter enjoys the sanctioned limit for purchase/ discount of bills, the exporter can get the funds immediately. When it is a D/P bill, the bank purchases it. The exporter gets concessional rate of interest from the banker. When the payment term is D/A, post-shipment finance is termed a discount.

The bank may insist that the exporter takes ECGC (Export Credit Guarantee Corporation of India Ltd) policy in his/her favour and assigns the policy in favour of the bank. Under the policy, the ECGC may fix payment terms and limits to individual buyers and the bank ensure that the limits are not exceeded while purchasing the bills. More so, banks can also take guarantee from ECGC regarding the post-shipment finance, either on selective or whole turnover basis. If the importers are new, banks may also obtain credit reports about them before purchasing the bills, drawn on them.

Advance against Export Bills sent on Collection

Exporters send bills drawn on importers, on collection basis through a bank when:
(a) the documents drawn under LC contain minor discrepancies but the bank is confident that the buyer will retire documents.
(b) the bill purchase limit of the exporter is exhausted and bank is not willing to sanction additional amount.

Under the above circumstances, banks may finance a part of the total bill amount as advance. As and when the bill is realised, the advance will be liquidated and the bank will pay the balance to the exporter. This advance carries the same rate of interest, applicable to post-shipment finance.

---

*D/A = Delivery of Transport Document by importer's bank to importer, against acceptance which would enable importer to collect goods from the port. D/P = Delivery of Transport Document against payment, to importer.

Advance against Export Incentives

Advances against export incentives can be sanctioned by the bank both at pre-shipment and post-shipment stages. Advance under this category is sanctioned when the exporter has to receive the duty draw-back incentive from the government and refunds from customs and excise duty. Exporters can get refund from customs department for import of capital goods/raw materials, if they are importing such items for manufacturing exportable products. Similarly, manufacturers can get excise duty refund if the items are exported. Export items are, in general, either free from excise duty or eligible for refund.

Normally, in such a case the bank gets the power of attorney executed by the exporter in favour of the bank and registers with the concerned authority such as Director General of Foreign Trade, Commissioner of Customs, etc. The bank sanctions this type of advance only when it also grants other facilities to the same exporter.

Post-shipment Credit

The exporter has the option of availing the post-shipment credit in domestic currency or in foreign currency. When the exporter opts to avail the credit in foreign currency, the interest rate will be linked to LIBOR. The credit has to be liquidated in foreign currency.

FACTORING

When an exporter ships goods before receiving payment, he can consider 'factoring' his export bill. The exporter is taking the risk of financing the entire process, unless he/she has taken a loan from the bank. The exporter has to closely monitor the entire proceedings. There is also the risk that the importer or buyer may not make payment for the goods exported. In this situation, the exporter may consider selling the account receivable to a third party, who is called factor.

The factor then assumes all administrative responsibility of collecting the dues from the buyer and associated credit risk. The factor conducts his/her own investigation of the importer before purchasing the receivable. In return, the factor purchases the receivable at a discount and collects a processing fee as well, i.e., post-shipment finance without recourse* to the exporter can be termed as factoring. (In ordinary post-shipment finance cases, as discussed earlier under the Letter of Credit/Purchase or Discount, the bank has got recourse to the exporter.)

---

*Finance without recourse refers to providing advance to the exporter at the sole responsibility of the lender (factor in this case). Exporter will not pay back in case the export bill does not get realized.

The advantage to the exporter is that he is relieved from the burden of collecting the receivables, the creditworthiness of the importers and receives immediate cash, which improves his cash flow.

INSURANCE

The Export Credit Guarantee Corporation of India Limited (ECGC) provides credit insurance support to exporters and banks in India. The risks covered by ECGC are as follows:

1. The risk of payment defaults by importers, due to both commercial and political reasons, from the date of shipment.
2. Financial guarantees are issued to banks to protect them from risks of loss involved in their credit to exporters. Some of these guarantees are:
   - Whole Turnover Packing Credit Guarantee (WTPCG)
   - Whole Turnover Post-shipment Guarantee (WTPSG)
   - Export Production Finance Guarantee (EPFG)

Risks covered by standard policies offered by ECGC fall into the following categories:

1. Commercial risks arising out of insolvency of the buyer, default in payment, failure of the importer to accept the goods.
2. Political risks, which include, restriction of the buyers' country on the remittance of sale proceeds, war or civil disturbances in the importer's country, change in the government policy of the importer's country, etc.

The following risks are generally not covered:

1. Commercial disputes including the quality disputes raised by the buyer.
2. Insolvency of the collecting bankers, agents, or the exporters themselves.
3. Losses, which can be covered through commercial insurance.
4. Exchange rate fluctuations.

SUMMARY

It is important to understand how an exporter can avail finance and get insurance to cover capital requirements and manage risks. Experienced exporters always look at the interest rate before deciding on whether to avail finance in local currency or foreign currency. It makes sense to plan strategically as per the alternatives available, such as pre-shipment or post-shipment finance depending on the cost of the capital. Those who compare the cost of loans in this case can leverage opportunities arising out of interest rate and exchange rate fluctuations.

CONCEPT REVIEW QUESTIONS

1. Discuss between Packing Credit in domestic currency and foreign currency.
2. Discuss the rationale for an exporter to avail pre-shipment finance.
3. What is meant by post-shipment finance?
4. Distinguish between negotiation, purchase, and discount.

EXERCISES

1. *Pre-shipment Finance* An exporter has the requirement of Rs. 2,40,000 to meet his expenditure at the pre-shipment stage. He has a choice of availing Packing credit in Indian Rupees or a PCFC in US Dollars. He is planning to apply for the loan on 1st January. Assume that the exchange rate is Rs 48= 1 US Dollar. He gets an offer from his bank for PCFC of USD 5000 (equivalent of Rs 2,40,000/- FOR 6 MONTHS AT LIBOR + 120 basis points (LIBOR on USD=2.5%) on 1st January. He has to pay 8.5% interest rate, if he has to avail pre-shipment loan in Indian Rupees. How much does he have to pay back, if he avails Rs 2,40,000 as Rupee loan? Calculate his repayment liability, if he goes for FCL, IF EXCHANGE RATE becomes 1USD=Rs 50. State which one would be profitable for him? What would be his liability, if he gets a forward contract @ 1 USD=49.50 for repayment?
2. *Post-shipment Finance* Exchange Rate of Swiss Franc against Indian Rupees (CHF/INR) in the Inter-bank market is 26.8967/9235. An exporter requests bank to purchase a bill for CHF 3,50,000. (A)What rate bank quotes the exporter, if the bank requires an exchange margin of 0.20%. (B) Interest on Export Finance to be recovered from exporter, if the transit period of the export bill is 25 days and the rate of interest is 8%. (C) Rupee amount payable to the exporter.

OBJECTIVE QUESTIONS

Specify whether the following statements are True or False.
1. The Two Way Exchange Rate Quotation (Buying & Selling Rates) is used in most countries for dealings between banks and their customers.
2. Banks have discretionary power to determine FCL period.
3. LIBOR stands for London Inter-bank Offer Rate.

For each of the following statements, choose the most appropriate option.
4. When a customer takes a FCL,
    (a) he cannot repay the loan before the agreed time period.
    (b) he can repay the loan before the agreed time period.
    (c) he can repay the loan before the agreed time period with a penalty.
    (d) he can repay the loan after the time period without any penalty.

SELECT REFERENCES

Mahajan, M.I., 2005, *Export Policy, Procedure and Documentation*, Snow White, New Delhi.

Paul, Justin, 2006, *International Business*, Third Edition, Prentice Hall of India, New Delhi.

Ramgopal C., 2006, *Export-Import Procedures*, New Age International, New Delhi.

ANSWERS TO EXERCISES

1.(a) Money, he has to pay back, if he takes PC in Rupees to be calculated.

Interest amount for 6 months $= 2{,}40{,}000 \times \dfrac{8.5}{100} \times 0.5$

$$= 20{,}400 \times 0.5 = 10{,}200$$

Principal + Interest $= 2{,}40{,}000 + 10{,}200 = 2{,}50{,}200$

(b) Interest rate for FCL can be calculated as LIBOR + Margin %
i.e., LIBOR 2.50% + Margin 1.20% = 3.70% = .037
Interest amount for Foreign Currency Loan (6 months)
$= 5000 \times .037 \times 0.5 = 92.5$ dollar
\Repayment Liability = USD 5000 + 92.5 = 5,092.5
If the exchange rate is steady @48, liability $= 5{,}092.5 \times 48$
$$= \text{Rs.}2{,}44{,}440$$
If the exchange rate becomes @ Rs.50 = 1 USD, Liability
$$= 5{,}092.5 \times 50 = \text{Rs.}2{,}54{,}625$$

(c) If 1USD becomes Rs.50/- Rupee Loan would be profitable for the exporter. Otherwise, FCL would be profitable.

(d) If he books forward contract liability would be = Rs.2,52,078.75

2.(a) Rate at which Global Bank can sell CHF in the interbank market
= 26.8967 (Buying rate of price maker banks) Rate at which Global Bank quotes to the exporter, provided bank requires an exchange profit of 0.20%

$$= 26.8967 \times \frac{.20}{100} = 26.8967 \times 0.002 = 0.0538, 26.8967 - 0.0538$$
$$= 26.8429$$

(b) Interest amount on Export Finance $= 3,50,000 \times 26.8429 \times .08 \times \frac{25}{365}$
$= 93,95,015 \times .08 \times .06849 = $ Rs.51,480

(c) Rupee amount payable to the exporter i.e.,
$3,50,000 \times 26.8429 - 51,480 = 93,95,015 - 51,480 = $ Rs.93,43,535

7 Business Risk Management and Coverage

Learning Objectives

After studying this chapter, you will be able to understand
- the types of risks involved in Export–Import business
- how to manage the risks
- the quality aspect in international trade

RISK MANAGEMENT IN EXPORT-IMPORT BUSINESS

Risk is an aspect of any organization's operation. When it is recognized, understood, and managed, risk itself can set the stage for sustainable growth. Companies need to identify risks within their operations and plan a systematic approach to manage them. However, identifying and minimizing market, financial, and operational risks while pursuing a high growth strategy is a difficult task. A risk management process can help companies balance their risk/return objectives and mitigate obstacles to achieve strategic goals.

Risk is inherent in every business, more so in the international arena. Success in business depends, largely, on careful evaluation of risks and their subsequent minimization. Eradicating all risks is, of course not possible, but an efficient risk management system can help combat risks to a great extent.

TYPES OF RISKS

The different types of risks are as follows:
- Commercial risk
- Political risk
- Risks arising out of foreign laws
- Cargo risk
- Credit risk
- Foreign exchange risk

Commercial Risk

The general causes for commercial risks are:
- Lack of knowledge about foreign markets
- Inadaptability of the product
- Longer transit time
- Varying situations, such as, change in preferences and fashion
- Competition

Commercial risks can be minimized by using forecasting techniques and by keeping a careful watch on the changing business scenario in the concerned country, in particular, and the world economy, in general. Exporters have to be prepared to face any eventuality; wisdom lies in forecasting, anticipating, and of course, finally, speedily responding, at the earliest hour.

Political Risk

Some of the common causes for political risks are:
- Changes in political power and hence policies
- Coups, civil wars, and rebellion
- Wars between countries
- Capture of cargo during war

Political risks can be avoided to a certain extent by judicious selection of countries to which goods are exported. Insurance companies can agree to cover risks, if paid some additional premium. ECGC also covers some of these risks.

Risks Arising Out of Foreign Laws

Risks arising out of foreign laws due to
- Different laws as operating in domestic country
- Expensive and complex litigation

In case of any disputes arising out of contracts, these risks can be avoided by the appointment of an arbitrator at the time of contract.

Cargo Risk

Most goods are transported by sea. Transit risks such as storms, leakage, fire, explosion, etc., can be classified under cargo risk. It is possible to transfer the financial losses resulting from perils of sea and perils in transit to professional risk bearers (Ramgopal 2005), i.e., cargo risks can be covered by taking an insurance policy. Risks are termed as perils in marine-related literature.

The various kinds of perils are:

Marine Perils

These are natural occurrences or manmade mishaps. Natural occurrences include earthquakes, storms, lightning, entry of sea water into the vessel, among others. Fire, smoke, collisions etc., are examples of manmade mishaps.

Extraneous Perils

These are incidental perils. These perils are caused due to falls in loading, carrying, and unloading.

War Perils

These perils relate to losses due to war, including civil war.

Credit Risk

Selling on credit is becoming a common phenomenon. As there are many exporters competing for the cake of international trade, importers are much sought after. So it is but natural that importers dictate terms. At the same time, insolvency rates are on the rise and many countries are suffering from balance of payment difficulties.

Two issues of prime importance in relation to credit risk are

1. The exporter must have sufficient funds to offer credit to the buyers abroad.
2. The exporter should be prepared to take credit risks.

Meaning of Credit Risk

Once goods are sold on credit, risks arising in realizing the sale proceeds are known as credit risks. Risks may arise due to the inability of the buyers to pay on the due date. Or, even if the buyer makes the payment, situations may change in the buyer's country such that funds do not reach the exporter. An outbreak of civil war, war, a coup, or an insurrection may block or delay the payment for goods exported. However, this can be avoided by using the services of an insurance agency.

Organizations Covering Credit Risk

Almost all countries have public sector organizations to cover the credit risk for exporters. In India, the Export Risks Insurance Corporation (ERIC) was set up in 1957 in order to provide export credit insurance support to Indian exporters. ERIC was renamed Export Credit & Guarantee Corporation Limited (ECGC) in 1964. The Corporation's name was again modified to the present Export Credit Guarantee Corporation of India Limited in 1983. ECGC functions under the Ministry of Commerce and has a Board of Directors representing Government, Banking, Insurance, and Industry.

Types of Cover Issued by ECGC

Standard policies: They are ideally suited to exporters in order to cover payment risks.

The ECGC has designed four types of policies for shipment made on short-term credit*:

- Shipments (Comprehensive risks) policy
- Shipments (Political risks) policy
- Contracts (Comprehensive risks) policy
- Contracts (Political risks) policy

They cover political and commercial risks.

Commercial risks include Insolvency in the buyer; Protracted default in payment; as also the buyer's failure to accept the goods despite there being no fault, per se, on the part of the exporter, under special circumstances specified in the policy.

Political risks result from the imposition of restriction in the buyer's country by the government for remittance of the sale proceeds, which may block or delay payment to the exporter. These include, war, revolution, or civil disturbance in the buyer's country; New import restrictions in the buyer's country; and cancellation of valid export licence or imposition of a new licensing restriction after the date of contract, applicable under the contract's policy.

But the ECGC does not cover risks arising from contractual disputes or due to causes inherent to the nature of goods.

Specific policies: These are specifically designed to protect Indian exporters from risks involved in

(a) exports on deferred payment contracts;
(b) services rendered to foreign parties; and
(c) construction works and turnkey projects undertaken abroad.

Financial guarantee: A financial guarantee is issued to a bank for covering risks in extending credit at pre-shipment as well as post-shipment stages.

Foreign Exchange Risk

Foreign exchange risks occur when the invoice is prepared in foreign currency. If the foreign currency depreciates in terms of rupees, the exporter

---

*Sourced from the website of ECGC.

will receive lesser amount in rupees and vice-versa. If the export bill is purchased or negotiated under a letter of credit and the foreign currency undergoes fluctuation, the bank will bear the risk. If there is an intervening difference in the exchange rate between the date of giving the bill for collection and date of realization, the exporter stands to lose or gain, depending on the trend in fluctuation. Foreign Exchange risk can be hedged by using forward contracts. The risk can also be avoided by invoicing in the Indian rupee.

Transfering risks to third party

The exporter may manage to transfer some of the risks to third parties, which specialize in the same. These parties are termed as insurance agencies. The various agencies and risks covered by them are given in Table 7.1:

Table 7.1   Risks covered by various agencies

	Category of risk	Agency
1	Credit risk	ECGC
2	Physical risk	General insurance company
3	Product liability risk	General insurance company
4	Foreign Exchange risk	Commercial Bank

Source: Rama Gopal, 2006, *Export-Import Procedures*, New Age International, New Delhi.

We have discussed in detail in the previous section on how an exporter can transfer credit risk to ECGC. Similarly, the exporter can take a policy by paying premium from General insurance companies to cover physical risk and product liability risk. Exporters can transfer the foreign exchange risk to a bank by booking forward contract or option contract.

QUALITY AND PRE-SHIPMENT INSPECTION

Quality assumes highest importance in penetrating, capturing, and sustaining share in the international market. The international market is highly competitive and the quality of produce an important determinant in export business. One of the critical problems faced by developing countries is quality or rather the lack of it. Therefore, improvement of quality is one of the prerequisites in driving exports.

Quality Control

Quality control (QC) is a set of procedures intended to ensure that a product or service adheres to defined quality criteria or meets the requirements of the client.

As part of an effective QC programme, an enterprise must first decide which specific standards the product or service must meet. Then the extent of QC precautionary actions should be undertaken (for example, the percentage of units to be tested from each lot). Next, real-world data must be collected based on past performance/experience (for example, the percentage of units that fail). After this, corrective action must be taken. If too many unit failures or instances of poor service occur, a plan must be devised to improve the production or service process. Finally, the QC process must be ongoing to ensure that remedial efforts, if required, have produced satisfactory results.

Pre-shipment Inspection

Pre-shipment inspection is carried out by specialized agencies/councils as per the buyer's specifications, and quantity of exports. In many countries, governments insist that exportable items (if the item falls under the list of items placed for compulsory inspection category) should be subjected to pre-shipment inspection as part of attempts to ensure quality of the items originated in those countries. However, exporters with good track record (e.g., with export house status) have been empowered to carry out such inspection on self-certification basis.

Advantages of Pre-shipment Inspection

Pre-shipment inspection facilitates transparency in trading activities. It ensures that goods conform to contract specifications. It provides the government the effective means of overseeing and controlling foreign trade through accurate statistics.

Mechanism for Enforcement of Quality

Enforcement of quality promotes exports as per international standards. It involves the inspection of the majority of goods. An example of such a mechanism is the Export Inspection Council (EIC) under the government. The Export Act, 1965 deals with quality control and inspection.

Methods of Quality Control and Pre-shipment Inspection

There are primarily three methods for quality control and pre-shipment inspection. These are discussed as follows.

Consignment-wise Inspection

Each actual consignment in packed condition is inspected by export inspection agencies. The agencies conduct inspection on the basis of statistical sampling plans. Certificates are awarded after passing quality checks.

Certificates carry a validity period before which the item should be shipped. Most of the items undergo these inspections, except those which have in-house quality control process.

In-process Quality Control

In-process quality control deals with continuous process industries, such as paints, ceramics, printing ink, etc. To become an approved "export-worthy" unit, a company should possess the requisite infrastructure. Export units get inspection certificates, based on self-declaration.

Self Certification

It is a recent introduction to the compulsory inspection scheme. Manufacturing units having in-built responsibility for quality control have the freedom to self-certify their products.

Procedures of Quality Control and Pre-shipment Inspection

The detailed procedures involved in the given quality-control and inspection mechanisms are given in the following sections.

Consignment-wise Inspection*

Procedure of consignment-wise inspection includes

1. Application to Export Inspection Agency EIA: The exporter has to apply in the prescribed "Intimation for inspection" well in advance of the date of shipment to avoid delays, along with the following documents:
   - Copy of export contract
   - Copy of letter of credit
   - Details of packing specifications
   - Commercial invoice giving evidence of Free On Board (FOB) value of export consignment
   - Crossed cheque/DD in favour of EIA towards inspection fees
   - Declaration regarding importer's technical specification
2. Deputation of inspector: After receiving the "Intimation for inspection", EIA deputes an inspector to conduct an inspection of the consignment at the factory/warehouse of the exporter.
3. Inspection and testing: The inspector conducts the inspection on a random basis. He conducts the inspection with reference to the agreed specifications, which should not be inferior to the notified specifications. Samples may be drawn and sent to the laboratory, if required.

---

*Sourced and compiled from the website of Export Inspection Council of India.

4. Packing and sealing of goods: If the inspector is satisfied with the quality of the goods, he issues instructions for packing of goods in his presence. After packing, the consignment is marked and sealed with the official seal of EIA.

5. Submission of report to EIA and issue of inspection certificate: Based on the field inspection report, the deputy director of the EIA issues, in triplicate, the inspection certificate to the exporter.

6. Issue of rejection note: If the inspection report is not favourable, the deputy director issues a "Rejection note".

7. Appeal against rejection note: The exporter can file an appeal against the order. The appeal is to be made within 10 days from the issue of the "Rejection Note". On receipt of the appeal, EIA arranges to convene a meeting of the Appellate panel which reviews the report and rechecks the consignment. Their decision is final and binding on both the exporter and the Export Inspection Agency.

In-process Quality Control

Manufacturing units, having continuous processing systems, are given an option to become "export-worthy" status units so that they get the inspection certificate on the basis of their own declaration. These units are highly quality-conscious and conduct thorough quality control at each and every stage of production, including

- raw materials,
- process control,
- product control, and
- packing and packaging control.

Self Certification

Certain manufacturing units are given the freedom to certify their own inspection certificates. The theory behind this scheme is that manufacturing units with proven track record of maintenance of quality deserve to enjoy the freedom to issue pre-shipment inspection certificate themselves. The essential condition for this module is that the unit should not have received a single complaint during the last three years.

Inspection Agencies

A list of various inspection agencies is given in Exhibit 7.1.

Exhibit 7.1   Various Inspection Agencies

Government Inspection Agencies

- United States Food and Drug Administration (USFDA)
- Australian Quarantine and Inspection Service (AQIS)
- Sri Lanka Standards Institute (SLSI)
- Korea Food and Drug Administration (KFDA)
- Turkish Customs Authorities (TCA)
- Japan Health Authorities
- General Administration of Quality Supervision, China

Private Inspection Agencies (with offices in India)

- Trinity International Forwarders
- Global Resources—leather and furniture
- ACE Testing and Allied Services—textile
- Mari-Tech Surveyors—containerized cargo
- Toyosha Industrial Co. (Taiwan)—chemicals

Inspection Agencies in India

- Export Inspection Council of India (EIC)
- Export Inspection Agency (EIA)
- National Accreditation Board for Testing and Calibration Laboratories (NABL)
- Rites Limited—metals
- Bharat Agro—agricultural products
- Internal quality departments
- External auditors
- Environmental agencies

Export Inspection Council of India

The Export Inspection Council (EIC) was set up by the Indian Government under the Export (Quality Control and Inspection) Act, 1963, as an apex body to provide a platform for export trade through quality control and pre-shipment inspection. Under the council, there are Export Inspection Agencies (EIAs) with offices at Chennai, Kochi, Kolkata, Delhi, and Mumbai and with a network of 38 sub-offices and laboratories to back up pre-shipment inspection and certification activity.

Although the liberalization of the trade regime has taken place, the role of EIAs is important. Although, it has become voluntary for many items, certification for exports remains mandatory for items such as, fish and fishery products, dairy products, poultry products, meat and meat products, and honey. EIAs also provide support, by way of training and awareness, to the trade and industry for overall upgradation of their quality and knowledge systems in order to meet the international requirements.

Exemption from Inspection

The following are exempted from export inspection in India:
- Export House, Trading House, Super Trading House, and Super Star Trading House
- 100% Export oriented units set up in the Export Processing Zones (EPZs) or Free Trade Zones (FTZs)
- Products bearing ISI/AGMARK for exports (when the overseas buyer does not want a pre-shipment inspection certificate).

SUMMARY

Exporting, although more profitable than domestic business, in most cases, involves various risks. Therefore, an exporting enterprise has to be handled carefully and developed step by step. Companies need to handle export/import consignments with due importance and seriousness with the intention of covering risks effectively. Inspection and insurance are two important activities in an export transaction. It is also important to appoint knowledgeable and experienced professionals in an exporting/importing organization to manage risks related to logistics, foreign exchange, quality, and packaging.

CONCEPT REVIEW QUESTIONS

1. Discuss the reasons for mandatory inspection requirement of some commodities, while exporting.
2. Why does an importer ask for an Inspection Certificate from an exporter?
3. Distinguish between various types of risks involved while exporting.
4. Discuss how an exporter covers payment related risks?
5. Discuss how an exporter manages risks pertaining to quality?

OBJECTIVE QUESTIONS

For each of the following statements, choose the most appropriate option.
1. The exporter gets his payment as soon as he/she
    (a) books the consignment

   (b) ships the goods.

   (c) ships the goods and produces necessary documents in compliance.

   (d) when the consignment is received by the importer.

2. Extra copies of bills of lading marked as non-negotiable copy

   (a) cannot be used for taking delivery of goods.

   (b) can be used for taking delivery of goods.

   (c) may be used for taking delivery of goods.

   (d) none of the above.

3. An ISO 9000/BIS 14000 certification holder company is exempted from

   (a) Customs Duty.

   (b) Compulsory pre-shipment inspection.

   (c) Letter of credit.

   (d) All of the above.

4. The inspection under which every consignment is checked before it is allowed for export is

   (a) Self-Certification scheme.

   (b) Exemption.

   (c) Consignment basis.

   (d) None of the above.

5. The validity of IEC (Importer-Exporter Code Number) is

   a. 1 year.

   b. 2 years.

   c. 5 years.

   d. Permanent number with no expiry.

SELECT REFERENCES

Branch, Alan, 2000, *Export Practices and Management*, Thomson Learning, London.

How to Import and Export?, Nabhi Publishers, New Delhi.

Kapoor D. C., 2003, *Export Management*, Vikas Publishers, New Delhi.

Paul, Justin, 2006, *International Business*, Third edition, Prentice Hall

Rama Gopal, 2005, *Export-Import Procedures and Documentation*, New Age International, New Delhi

Website of Export Credit Guarantee Corporation, www.ecgc.in accessed on 10th June, 2007.

Website of Export Inspection Council, www.eicindia.org accessed on 10th June, 2007.

8 Customs Clearance of Import and Export Cargo

Learning Objectives

After studying this chapter, you will be able to understand
- the import cargo clearance mechanism
- the export cargo clearance mechanism
- the role of Electronic Data Interchange in customs clearance of cargo
- various types of customs duties levied
- the basis of customs valuation
- the concept of Carnet
- the new developments in customs clearance procedures

Countries across the globe follow a certain set of procedures for customs clearance of import and export cargo. The following are the objectives for working according to these procedures:

1. To determine if the goods offered for examination are allowed for import or export as per the customs laws of the country.
2. To determine if the owner of the goods has the permission / licence from the relevant authorities to import or export the goods.
3. To determine if proper documentation for customs clearance has been carried out.
4. To determine if any customs duty is leviable on the import or export cargo. In case a duty is leviable, the customs department collects the duty before giving clearance to the cargo. In every country, customs duty is an important source of the government's revenues.
5. Following the correct procedures helps the government gather statistical data of all the goods imported into and exported from the country.

While subjecting the cargo to customs examination, it is to be ensured that cargo owners are suitably guided regarding the procedures in order to avoid delay and inconvenience. This helps in a fair assessment of the value of the cargo by the customs authorities for calculation of the duty. Whereas some of the procedures may differ from country to country, most countries follow a standard set of procedures for the convenience of cargo owners and their agents operating in a global environment.

CLEARANCE OF IMPORT CARGO

As per the customs manual, goods imported in a vessel/aircraft have to cross the customs barrier in the country of import, complete the customs clearance procedure, and pay applicable customs duty. This procedure is not applicable if the goods are not meant for customs clearance at the port / airport of arrival by a particular vessel / aircraft and are intended for transit by the same vessel / aircraft or transhipment to another customs station or to any place outside India. Detailed customs clearance formalities of the landed goods have to be followed by the importer. It is, therefore, clear that customs duty is applicable on all the goods entering in the country, unless these goods are in transit (e.g. under transhipment) to another country or to another customs station. As per the Customs Act, customs station and customs authorities effectively have the same meaning. Customs station means customs port (for ships), customs airport (for aircrafts) or land customs station (for trucks or motor vehicles). For containerized cargo, the customs formalities can also be completed at Inland Container Depots (ICDs) or Special Economic Zones (SEZs) set up by the government or approved by the government. In case the goods are being taken to a customs bonded warehouse, the customs clearance formalities can be completed and applicable duty can be paid by the importer at the time of taking delivery of the cargo at the warehouse.

The basic document required for customs clearance is called the Bill of Entry (B/E). Every importer must file a B/E as per Section 46 of the Customs Act, for home consumption or warehousing, in a prescribed form. The B/E comprises different copies meant for different purposes. In case of goods for domestic consumption, the importer has to file the B/E in four copies. The customs department retains the original and duplicate copies; the third copy is meant for the importer and the fourth copy for submission to the bank for making remittances to the foreign supplier.

The following documents have to be submitted by the importer for customs clearance of import cargo:
1. Overseas supplier's invoice, duly signed
2. Packing list
3. Bill of lading / Airway bill
4. The General Agreement on Tariffs and Trade (GATT) declaration form
5. Importer's / Custom House Agent's (CHA's) declaration

6. Import licence, if necessary
7. Copy of letter of credit / purchase order bank draft
8. Insurance policy
9. Industrial licence, if required
10. Test reports, if required
11. Exemption order, if applicable
12. Duty Exemption Entitlement Certificate (DEEC) / Duty Entitlement Pass Book (DEPB) book in original
13. Product catalogue / technical details, wherever relevant
14. Separate values of machineries, spares, components, wherever relevant
15. Certificate of Origin, in case preferential duty is sought
16. No commission declaration

The importer or the customs house agent has to fill in various details in the B/E, such as description of goods, their value, etc. Along with these details, a declaration also needs to be signed to certify the correctness of the details provided in the B/E. This declaration is in the form at the bottom of the B/E. In case of incorrect declaration or false declaration, the importer has to face legal action. As such, utmost precaution is recommended while filling-in the B/E and signing the declaration.

Various Stages of Processing a Bill of Entry

Manual Procedure

Figure 8.1 illustrates the various stages in the manual import clearance process. The stages are discussed in detail as follows.

Stage I It comprises submission of B/E and other shipping documents to the customs house for noting of B/E according to the Import General Manifest (IGM) filed by the ship carrying the import cargo. The importer has to get the B/E noted for getting the consignment checked by the concerned unit. A B/E number is generated and printed on all copies of the bill of entry.

Stage II The duly noted B/E is sent to the appraisal section of the customs house for assessing the value of the goods, computing the duty, etc. Different groups in the assessment wing of the customs house work on different commodities under different chapter headings of the customs tariff. At this stage, the import permissibility of the cargo is also scrutinized, such as the need for permission/ licence/ permit, etc. For the assessment of duty, the proper classification of goods, under Harmonised System (HS) code is essential. Also, the correct valuation of goods is necessary if the goods are to be assessed on ad valorem basis. The assessing officer also takes into consideration the invoice value and other declarations, to determine whether to accept it for the assessment of duty. Under the Customs Act, the assessment officer can redetermine the value of the goods as per the case law, various notifications and contemporaneous values, and other information available with the customs house. In case of any doubt about the description or the classification of goods, the assessment officer gives an examination order on the reverse of original copy of bill of lading B/L. If necessary, the samples are drawn for conducting tests before the final assessment of value is carried out.

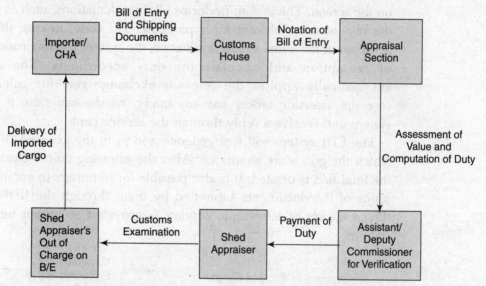

Fig. 8.1 Non Electronic Data Interchange (Manual Import Clearance Process)

Stage III On the basis of the examination report, the appraising officer in the group assesses the B/E. The officer indicates various applicable duties such as basic, countervailing, anti-dumping, safeguard duties, etc. Depending on the value of goods, the B/E is then sent to Assistant Commissioner / Deputy Commissioner for verification. After this, the actual duty is computed taking into consideration exchange rates on the given date.

Stage IV The importer / CHA pays the duty at the nominated bank.

Stage V In case the importer is not satisfied with the classification, valuation or rate of duty applied to the cargo, the importer can appeal against the assessment order within the prescribed time limit.

Stage VI After the payment of duty, the documents are handed over to the shed appraiser, who after customs examination will release the cargo for delivery to the importer or the concerned agent.

EDI Procedure

Today, a number of major ports and international airports are linked with CHAs, shipping lines, and their representatives through Electronic Data Interchange (EDI). Electronic processing of documents, depicted in Fig. 8.2, speeds up the customs clearance process.

In the EDI system the importer has to file a cargo declaration giving the necessary details of the cargo. The computer system then generates a B/E electronically. The assessing officer examines the consignment related details on the screen. The system performs all the calculations, such as determining the rate of duty relevant for a particular HS code; in case the goods are accepted under some exemption notice, the system will determine the extent of exemption and calculate the duty accordingly. The system also automatically applies the relevant exchange rate for calculations. In case the assessing officer has any query, he/she can raise it through the system and receive a reply through the service centre.

The EDI system will first generate and print the assessed B/E, based on which the goods are examined. After the assessing officer clears the goods, the final B/E is printed. It is also possible for importers to enquire about the status of the documents submitted by them through the EDI system. For this, a facility of telephonic enquiry is provided at certain major customs stations.

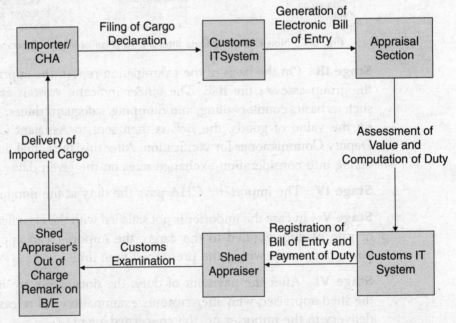

Fig. 8.2 Import Clearance Process (EDI)

Examination of Import Cargo

Physical examination of goods is normally done on random basis, as it is physically not possible to examine entire consignments. In many cases, where the importer does not have full details of the cargo, he/she can request examination of goods before the assessment. This is called the *First Appraisement*, for which the importer has to make a specific request at the time of filing the B/E, or at data entry stage. It is expected that a suitable reason be given for conducting first appraisement. Based on the findings of examination of cargo by the shed appraiser, the assessing officer assesses the duty. It is also possible to conduct the customs examination after the assessment and payment of duty. This is called *Second Appraisement*. In most cases, the consignments are cleared on second appraisement.

Under the EDI system, the B/E has to be registered at the registration counter after the assessment by the group or first appraisement. After this, the shed appraiser examines the goods, based on the bill of entry and other documents presented by the CHA. The appraiser also verifies the importer's declaration for correctness of entries and genuineness of the original documents. If the goods are cleared, the shed appraiser either gives 'out of charge' (in case of already assessed bills of entry), or enters his/her findings in the system and transfers the first appraisement B/E to the group. The B/E and order of clearance carrying the examination report, order of clearance number, and name of shed appraiser are printed in triplicate. Two copies each, duly signed by the appraiser of the B/E and the other order are given to the importer/CHA while one copy is retained by the shed appraiser.

Special Provisions

The following are certain special provisions.

1. In many cases, importers are given various facilities/concessions by the government by virtue of their status, or under special schemes or notification. For example, in case of duty free imports or imports under concessional rates, the importer has to execute a bond in prescribed forms. This bond, along with the bank guarantee, has to be submitted to assessing officer.
2. Similarly, regular importers with good track record are given the green channel clearance facility. It enables importers to clear the goods without routine examination. For this, an importer has to submit a declaration form along with B/E. The value appraisal is conducted as usual, but there is no physical examination of the goods.

3. The importer can pay the import duty through designated banks.
4. In case of transhipment cargo, where the importer does not know the details of feeder vessel at the time of the advance noting of the B/E, the importer can write the name of mother vessel as per the B/L. The B/E can be later amended to mention names of both the mother vessel and the feeder vessel.
5. Amending the B/E is possible with the approval of deputy/assistant commissioner of customs, in case of any error in the details provided in the B/E.
6. In case the imported goods are to be transferred to a custom bonded warehouse, a separate B/E is filed. The B/E is assessed as usual, but the duty is paid at the time of clearance of goods from the bonded warehouse. The rate of duty applied for clearance from the warehouse is the rate prevailing on the date of removal of goods from the warehouse.

CLEARANCE OF EXPORT CARGO

Every consignment leaving Indian shores by sea, air, or land has to undergo a prescribed procedure of customs clearance. This can be done by an exporter in person or by his/her CHA.

Registration Procedure

Every exporter must have a Permanent Account Number (PAN) given by the relevant income tax authority. Against PAN, Director General of Foreign Trade (DGFT) issues a Business Identification Number (BIN) to the exporter. The BIN is sent electronically by the DGFT to the customs. The exporting company must open a current account in a designated bank and register the authorized foreign exchange dealer code, through which export proceeds will be realised and export incentives credited. All airlines, shipping lines, airports, and ports handling export-import cargo must also register with the customs system. These registrations are useful for correlating the various details of the consignment in case of EDI based customs clearance. Exporters availing export promotion schemes must also get their licences/ DEEC books registered with the customs station from where the export goods are to be cleared.

Processing of a Shipping Bill

A shipping bill is required for customs clearance of cargo being exported by sea/air. Similarly, a bill of export is required if the cargo is being exported by land transportation. Shipping bill/bill of exports has different copies for export of dutiable goods, duty free goods, and for goods eligible for duty drawback.

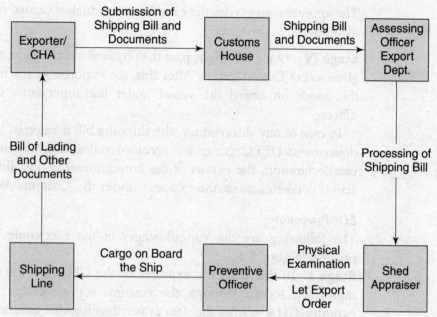

Fig. 8.3 Non EDI (Manual Export Clearance Process)

Manual Procedure

The various stages in getting the export consignment cleared are illustrated in Figure 8.3. The details of the Manual Export Clearance Process are discussed as under:

Stage I The following documents are required to be submitted by the exporter along with the shipping bill to the customs house.
1. Invoice
2. Packing List
3. Guaranteed Remittance (GR) Form
4. Application for Removal of Excisable Goods (ARE) Form for excise clearance
5. Pre-shipment inspection certificate issued by export inspection agency

Stage II The assessing officer will check the value of goods, duty drawback classification (if applicable), rate of export duty (if applicable), etc. The officer will also check if the cargo under assessment is allowed to be exported under the prevailing EXIM Policy. There is a separate group for assessing DEEC/DEPB policy shipping bills. The assessing officer tallies the description of goods in invoice and DEEC shipping bill with the DEEC book. Samples can be drawn and a thorough test conducted by the assessing officer to establish the authenticity of goods.

Stage III After the shipping bill is passed by the export department, the cargo is presented to the shed appraiser (export) for physical examination.

The appraiser supervises the examination, which is carried out by the customs examiner.

Stage IV Once the goods pass the physical examination, the shed appraiser gives a 'Let Export' order. After this, the exporter or his/her agent can load the goods on board the vessel under the supervision of the preventive officer.

In case of any discrepancy, the shipping bill is referred back to the export department/DEEC group for reconsideration/amendment, etc. In case of mis-declaration, the export of the consignment is not allowed and suitable action is taken against the exporter under the Customs Act 1962.

EDI Procedure

The following are the various stages in the Electronic Data Interchange process (Figure 8.4).

Stage I In this case, the exporter or the CHA fills the declaration in the prescribed format through the customs service centre (IT system). The exporter/CHA verifies the data as per the checklist generated by the system. If the data is correct, the system generates a shipping bill number endorsed on the printed checklist and this is given back to the exporter/CHA. In case of dutiable items, the exporter pays the duty along with TR-6 challan generated by the system.

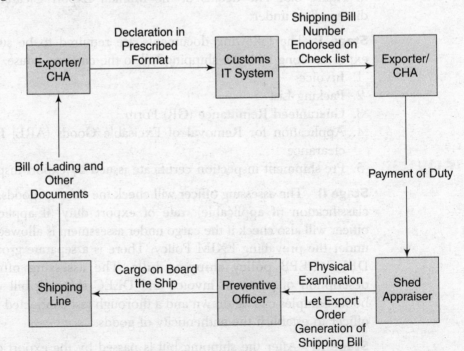

Fig. 8.4 Export Clearance Process (EDI)

Stage II At this stage, the exporter is not given any copy of the shipping bill. The goods are allowed to enter the dock on the strength of the checklist endorsed with the shipping bill number. The exporter/CHA submits this checklist with original invoice, packing list, GR forms, ARE forms, etc. to the customs officer, who verifies the documents against the received goods and hands over all original documents to the shed appraiser, for a physical examination of the cargo.

Stage III The customs officer designated by the shed appraiser conducts a physical examination of cargo, enters his/her observations into the system, and returns all the original documents to the shed appraiser.

Stage IV If the shed appraiser is satisfied with the report submitted by the customs officer regarding the quantity and description declared by the exporter, he/she may issue a 'Let Export' order. The shipping bill is generated by the system in two copies only after the 'Let Export' order is given by the customs. One copy is for customs and the second copy is for exporter. One more copy that is third copy is generated after the submission of Export General Manifest (EGM). It is mandatory for the shipping lines to electronically submit the shipping billwise EGM to the customs, within seven days of sailing of ship.

Stage V The exporter/CHA submits exporter's copy of shipping bill duly signed by the dock appraiser to the preventive officer for allowing the cargo to be loaded on board the ship. In case of containerized cargo, the preventive officer supervises stuffing of container at the docks. The officer also ensures that the container is properly sealed. He/she enters the container number; the seal number and endorses the shipper's copy of shipping bill, before allowing the container to be loaded on board the ship. The officer may also stamp a 'shipped on board' seal on the shipping bill.

CUSTOMS VALUATION

When an import consignment reaches Indian shores, it has to clear the customs barrier, where the goods are assessed for their value and a suitable import tariff is imposed. The importer or agent has to pay the duty before the goods are cleared by the customs. A tariff is a schedule of duties. It is also the duty or tax imposed by a country and the duty or tax within the tariff schedule. As a tax, it is placed on goods as they cross the border between two countries (Nelson, 2000).

Import and export duties are levied either at specific rates or on ad valorem basis. In case of ad valorem duties, the value of the goods becomes the basis for calculation of duties. Section 14 of the Customs Act, 1962 lays down the basis for valuation of import and export cargo in India.

The Customs Act of 1962 empowers the central government to fix tariff value for any product. Ad valorem duties are calculated on the basis of tariff value, if they are already fixed. The criteria for fixing the tariff value for any class of import or export goods is based on trend of value of such or similar goods. Once the tariff value of a certain commodity is fixed, it is notified in the official gazette.

In case no tariff value is fixed for imported/export goods, as per subsection (1) of Section 14 of Customs Act, the value of such goods shall be deemed to be 'the price at which such or like goods are ordinarily sold, or offered for sale, for delivery at the time and place of import as the case may be, in the course of international trade, where the seller and the buyer have no interest in the business of each other and the price is the sole consideration for the sale or offer for sale. In simple terms it means that for valuation purpose, fair price of the commodity, which is prevailing at the time of import or export is taken as the basis.

India being a member of the World Trade Organisation (WTO) also follows the method of valuation prescribed in the WTO customs valuation agreement. Accordingly the importer is required to truthfully declare the value in the B/E and also provide a copy of the invoice and file a valuation declaration in the prescribed form to facilitate correct and expeditious determination of value for assessment purposes.

Methods of Valuation

When an importer brings goods in India from a foreign country, he/she declares the value of the goods in the B/E. For the purpose of valuation, the customs department considers transaction value of the goods as the basis of calculation of duties subject to certain terms and conditions. Transaction value is the price actually paid or payable by the importer for the goods when sold for export to India. If the customs authorities have any doubts regarding the truthfulness of the value declared by the importer, they can evaluate the goods in the following order:

1. **Comparative value method** Comparison with transaction value of identical goods (Rule 5 of Customs Valuation Rules, 1988)

2. **Comparative value method** Comparison with transaction value of similar goods (Rule 6)

3. **Deductive value method** Based on sale price in the importing country (Rule 7); or computed value method based on cost of materials, cost of manufacturing and profit in the country of origin of goods (Rule 7A)

4. Fall back method   Based on previous methods with flexibility (Rule 8)

Factors of Valuation

There are two types of factors of valuation. The first type is dutiable factors, which includes commissions and brokerages, cost of containers and packing, the value of various goods and services supplied free of charge or at reduced cost but whose value has not been included in the price paid or payable. For example, material, components, tools, dies, moulds, royalties payable on the sale of goods, advance payments, freight charges up to place of import, loading, unloading and insurance, etc. The second type is non-dutiable factors, such as interest charges for deferred payment, post-importation charges, such as inland transportation charges, installation and commissioning charges, etc.

Types of Customs Duties

The Customs Tariff Act of 1975 defines the rates of customs duty. The types of duties are:

1. Basic Customs Duty

This duty is levied as a percentage of value determined under Section 14(1). The range of applicable rates is 5%, 15%, 25%, and 30% for different commodities. The government has imposed an education cess on imported goods with effect from 9th July 2004 at the rate of 2% of aggregate duty of customs.

2. Additional Customs Duty

This is also called counter vailing duty (CVD). This duty is equal to excise duty levied on an identical product manufactured in India. If the identical product is not manufactured in India, the base is the excise duty that would be leviable if the article had been produced in India. The CVD is payable on the value plus basic customs duty. A Special Additional Duty (SAD) is levied under Section 3(1) of the Customs Tariff Act.

Example: Let us assume that an importer imports an article with assessable value of Rs. 1 lakh into India. The rates of various duties on this article are:

Customs duty	25%
CVD	16%
SAD	4%
Educational cess	2%

The duty calculation would be as given in Table 8.1

Table 8.1

Serial No.	Duty Component	Value
A	Assessable value	Rs. 1,00,000
B	Customs duty @ 25%	Rs. 25,000
C	Sub-total for calculating CVD (A+B)	Rs. 1,25,000
D	CVD @ 16% of Rs. 1,25,000	Rs. 20,000
E	Sub-total for calculating SAD (C+D)	Rs. 1,45,000
F	SAD @ 4% of Rs. 1,45,000	Rs. 5,800
G	Sub-total for calculating cess (B+D+F)	Rs. 50,800
H	Educational cess @2% of Rs. 50,800	Rs. 1,016

Hence the total duty payable is-

Customs duty	Rs. 25,000
CVD	Rs. 20,000
SAD	Rs. 5,800
Education cess	Rs. 1,016
Total	Rs. 51,816

Note As explained in the example above, CVD is charged on assessable value of the goods, plus basic duty chargeable on the imported article. The following facts need to be noted carefully.

- Though the CVD is payable at effective rate of excise duty on similar goods manufactured in India, CVD is not excise duty.
- CVD is payable even if similar goods are not manufactured in India.
- An importer can claim Central Value Added Tax (CENVAT) credit against the amount of CVD paid, as per the relevant CENVAT rules.
- Special additional duty is leviable on assessable value of goods plus customs duty, plus CVD.

3. Additional Duty under Section 3(3)

This duty is in addition to CVD, which can be levied by the central government. This is to counter balance excise duty leviable on raw materials, components, etc, similar to those used in production of such articles. Whereas the CVD is applicable to all goods, additional duty under section 3(3) is applied only on a case to case basis, as determined by the central government.

4. Protective Duty

This duty is imposed on those goods, which are perceived to threaten the interests of the Indian industry. This duty can be rescinded, reduced or increased with suitable notification by the Tariff Commission established under the Tariff Commission Act 1951.

5. Counter Vailing Duty on Subsidized Goods

If a country is found to subsidise its goods for exporting to India, the central government can impose counter-vailing duty equivalent to the amount of such subsidy. In case it is not possible to ascertain the extent of subsidy, a provisional duty is imposed till the amount of subsidy is ascertained.

6. Anti-dumping Duty on Dumped Articles

There are instances when a foreign manufacturer starts exporting its products to India at very low prices compared to prices in his/her domestic market. Such tactics, referred to as 'dumping', are used either to get rid of unsold or excessive stock or to cause injury to domestic industry in India. To nullify the impact of dumping, the central government can impose anti-dumping duty equivalent to the margin of dumping.

This duty is compatible with WTO agreements, which permit imposition of such duty if the act of dumping is proven. However, this duty can be imposed only if an Indian industry is producing similar articles.

7. Safeguard Duty

This duty can be imposed by the central government if it is convinced that certain goods are being imported into India in large quantities and are causing, or may cause serious injury to the domestic industry.

The above discussion amply proves that the objectives of various types of customs duties levied are

1. to collect revenues from import-export trade,
2. to create a level playing field in the Indian market for international and domestic manufacturers to compete with each other on equal and fair terms,
3. to protect the Indian industry from the unfair business practices adopted by foreign manufacturers,
4. to generate revenues for a social cause; for example, education cess contributes towards the education sector in India,
5. to prevent banned items from entering the country and ensuring that safety and security of the country is not compromised, and
6. to ensure that India conforms to all international conventions and complies with its various international obligations such as WTO agreements.

THE HARMONIZED SYSTEM

The Harmonized Commodity Description and Coding System, better known as the Harmonized system or the HS, is one of the most successful instruments developed by the World Customs Organisation (WCO). There are 121 Contracting Parties to the HS Conventions who use it as the basis for their Customs tariffs and international trade statistics. HS is called the "language of international trade" since it is also used in many areas, such as trade policy, rules of origin, the monitoring of controlled goods, internal taxation, transport tariffs, statistics, quota controls, and economic studies and analyses. As of March 2006, more than 200 countries and economic or customs unions, that account for almost 98% of world trade, were using the HS.

Importance of HS Nomenclature

The importance of the HS nomenclature can be highlighted by the fact that it has enabled the harmonization of customs and trade procedures, and non-documentary trade data interchange. The HS code employs the same numeric code on a worldwide basis for a given commodity. This helps reduction in the international trading costs. Other benefits of this system are:
- Accuracy in the calculation of customs duty
- Fewer disputes between shippers and customs authorities
- Reduction in customs clearance time
- Reduction in transaction costs
- Easier trade negotiations
- Simplification of trade data analyses
- Better supply chain security

It can therefore be concluded that in the era of computerization, HS coding has significantly helped international trade. Considering the increasing volumes of exports and imports across the world, HS Nomenclature is proving to be a blessing for all stakeholders in international trade.

CARNETS

A carnet or ATA (*admission temporaire*) carnet is an international customs document issued by more than 87 countries. It is presented when entering a carnet country with merchandise or equipment that will be re-exported within 12 months.

When an importer presents the carnet, he/she is permitted to clear customs without the payment of duties and taxes on equipment or merchandise. The carnet guarantees that the merchandise or equipment will be re-exported within a year. Thus, the use of a carnet is a way of temporarily importing into foreign countries, without payment of duties and taxes.

The ATA carnet is a standard international customs document used to obtain duty-free temporary admission of certain goods into countries that are signatory to the ATA convention. Under this convention it is possible for a commercial and professional traveller to take commercial samples, tools of the trade, advertising material, and cinematographic, audio-visual, medical, and scientific or other professional equipment into member countries temporarily, without paying customs duties and taxes or giving a bond at the border of each country to be visited (Nelson 2000).

An ATA carnet is valid for one year from the date of its issuance. Merchandise listed on an ATA carnet can be imported to and exported from any of the member countries as many times as needed during the one-year validity of the carnet.

If the holder of an ATA carnet sells, donates, or otherwise disposes of any of the goods listed on the carnet, the issuing organization will be required to pay liquidated damages equal to 100 per cent of the import duties and taxes. That organization in turn will attempt to collect these moneys from the holder of the carnet who violated the terms of the contract. In some cases, the country where the violation occurred will hold both the organization that issued the carnet and the importer equally responsible.

ATA carnets can be used in the following countries.

Algeria	Iceland	Poland
Andorra	India	Portugal
Australia	Ireland	Puerto Rico
Austria	Isle of Man	Reunion Island
Balearic Isles	Israel	Romania
Belgium	Italy	St. Barthelemy
Botswana	Ivory Coast	St. Martin (French part)
Bulgaria	Japan	St. Pierre
Canada	Jersey	Senegal
Canary Islands	Korea (Rep. of)	Singapore
Ceuta	Lebanon	Slovakia
China	Lesotho	Slovenia
Corsica	Liechtenstein	South Africa
Croatia	Luxembourg	Spain
Cyprus	Macedonia	Sri Lanka
Czechoslovakia	Macao	Swaziland
Denmark	Malaysia	Sweden
Estonia	Malta	Switzerland
European Union	Martinique	Tahiti
Finland	Mauritius	Tasmania
France	Mayotte	Taiwan
French Guiana	Melilla	Thailand
French Polynesia	Miguelon	The Netherlands
Germany	Monaco	Tunisia
Gibraltar	Morocco	Turkey
Greece	Namibia	United Kingdom
Guadeloupe Bailiwick	New Caledonia	United States
of Guernsey	New Zealand	Wallis &
Hong Kong	Norway	Futuna Islands
Hungary		

US CUSTOMS 24-HOUR ADVANCE MANIFEST REGULATIONS

Nobody can forget the terrorist attack on the twin towers of the World Trade Center in New York on September 11, 2001. Investigations into this incident revealed that the attack was the result of security lapses at various points including US ports and airports. The US has already adopted a tight immigration policy and has tightened visa rules to ensure that visa is granted to a foreign visitor only after ensuring his or her credentials. Similarly, on arrival at US airports, the passengers are again thoroughly interviewed before being allowed on US soil.

US security agencies are also apprehensive about the cargo that lands in the country on board ocean carriers from across the world. It is feared that for future attacks terrorists may bring in arms and ammunition through shipping containers. Various steps have been undertaken in order to prevent this. Effective from 2nd December, 2002, US customs regulations were amended and the rule regarding 24-hour advance manifest policy was published in the Customs Federal Register (CFR). Under this requirement, manifest information must be provided 24 hours prior to a US-bound shipping container being loaded onto the vessel in a foreign port. The US-bound Customs and Border Protection (CBP) may deny the loading of high-risk cargo, while the vessel is still overseas. The rule requires all ocean carriers or non vessel operating common carriers (NVOCCs) to submit a complete cargo manifest to US customs at least 24 hours prior to cargo loading, if that vessel is calling a US port directly.

Any vessel that began its entire voyage to the US on or after 2nd December 2002 has to comply with the 24-hour manifest rule. US customs coordinates with foreign governments to perform examination of shipments deemed to be high-risk.

As a part of compliance, ports across the world issue 'do not load messages' to the carriers/NVOCCs in case of clear violation of the 24-hour rule. If the cargo description is clearly in violation of the 24-hour rule, ports will issue a 'do not load message' on these shipments. Some examples of the descriptions considered to be a clear violation of the rule are as follows:

(a) Consolidated cargo
(b) FAK (Freight All Kinds) with no other description
(c) General merchandise
(d) Machinery
(e) 25 pallets
(f) Various retail merchandise

The correct and specific description of cargo on manifest is now mandatory. The names and addresses of all shippers and consignees are required to be noted in full form. NVOCCs using Automatic Manifest System (AMS) to transmit data to U.S. customs will be treated as ocean carriers and will be liable for any errors, omissions, or untimely information. All NVOCCs and forwarders are encouraged to register with an AMS service provider.

US customs have the power to reject the loading of cargo that does not meet the designated regulations; 'do not load messages' will be issued to ocean carriers or NVOCCs in clear violation of the rule. This message is sent on phone and/or fax or by e-mail. Once the ports have issued the 'do not load message', the cargo should not make its originally planned voyage. If the cargo is loaded without prior approval by customs, the container is denied the permission to unload its cargo at any US port.

Exhibit 8.1 highlights the need to inspect the cargo of dangerous goods.

Exhibit 8.1	**Dangerous Goods Incidents a Growing Menace: TT Club**

With the share of world container cargo made up of dangerous goods going upwards from 10 per cent, transporter insurance provider TT Club has urged regulatory bodies of nation states to step up provisions to police the transport of such cargo that poses great risks.

The TT Club has suffered an estimated $ 100 million loss in the explosion and fire aboard the Hyundai Fortune in the Gulf of Aden on the Far East to Europe run.

If nation states do not conduct safety compliance inspections, then the industry itself—carriers, terminals, forwarders—must take on inspection themselves, remarked TT Club risk management director, Peregrine Storrs-Fox.

Source: The Economic Times, 7 May 2007

NEW DEVELOPMENTS IN CUSTOMS CLEARANCE PROCEDURES

There is a general consensus among customs boards as well as the trade and industry that the present customs clearance procedure is cumbersome and creates bottlenecks in the movement of cargo in and out of India. In the last few decades there have been three major reasons for increase in World Trade.

1. Formation of WTO and resultant breaking down of trade barriers.
2. Application of information technology, which has made the communication and transfer of information and data faster than ever before.
3. Advancement in transportation sector; such as containerization of cargo, development of air freight carriers, faster and bigger ships, superior material handling systems, better port, road and rail infrastructure, etc.

These new developments have increased the volumes of imports and exports in India. Hence, there is an urgent need for a faster customs clearance procedure. In September 2001, the Customs Board has approved in principle the concept of the customs business process reengineering. It is expected that there will be more emphasis on system appraisal for a larger number of importers/commodities than at present.

Also, the best practices for customs clearance adopted by other countries based on self-assessment, selective examination of cargo, and post-clearance audits for specific categories of importers are also being studied. This exercise may result in a risk management based customs clearance mechanism, with the following potential benefits:

1. Smooth and speedy flow of goods without hindrance.
2. Minimal personal interaction between importers and departmental officers.
3. Reduction in transaction costs, there by achieving better competitiveness in world markets.
4. Scrutiny of larger volumes of cargo with better efficiency.

The International Convention on the Simplification and Harmonization of Customs Procedures (Kyoto Convention) entered into force in 1974. The WCO council adopted the revised Kyoto Convention in June 1999 as the blueprint for modern and efficient customs procedures in the 21st century. The General Annex to the revised convention recommends the following principles that a modern customs administration should implement:

- Standard, simplified procedures
- Continuous development and improvement of customs control techniques
- Maximum use of information technology
- A partnership approach between customs and trade.

The key elements within the revised Kyoto Convention to be applied by modern customs administrations are:

- The maximum use of automated systems
- Risk management techniques (including risk assessment and selectivity of controls)
- The use of pre-arrival information to drive programmes of selectivity
- The use of electronic funds transfer
- Coordinated interventions with other agencies
- Making information on customs requirements, laws, rules and regulations easily available to anyone
- Providing a system of appeals in customs matters
- Formal consultative relationships with the trade

India is a signatory to the international convention, also known as Kyoto Convention, on the simplification and harmonization of customs procedures, which entered into effect from 3rd February, 2006.

SUMMARY

Over the last decade, the world has moved its focus from logistics to supply chain management. It is, therefore, important that the supply chains are freed from bottlenecks. As the supply chains have crossed national boundaries, it is imperative for customs departments all over the world to play an important role in the expeditious clearance of cargo. This because they are a vital link in the global supply chains. The Kyoto Convention is a step in the direction of making customs clearance procedure easier than before. However, customs officers in different parts of the world have to keep a keen eye on illegal trafficking of arms, explosives, drugs, and other banned items. This is a tough balancing act. In the process, they have to use latest technology and have also come up with tougher laws to keep a vigilant eye on the flow of goods across the continents. Information technology in the form of Electronic Data Interchange is being widely used for speedy processing of shipping bills, bills of entry, and other documents. This has eased the load of paperwork in the customs department. The concept of the carnet has further helped trade as well as enforcement authorities clear small consignments, which are sent as commercial samples, tools of trade, etc. Hence, the role of the customs department is that of an enforcer of law as well as a facilitator of trade.

CONCEPT REVIEW QUESTIONS

1. What are the objectives for subjecting imported and export goods to customs examination?
2. What is the importance of the Bill of Entry in an import operation? Discuss the manual as well as EDI procedures for processing B/E for import cargo.
3. Customs clearance procedure of export cargo creates bottlenecks for Indian exporters. Do you agree or disagree with this statement? Give reasons in support of your answer.
4. Why is there an increasing demand for simplified customs clearance procedures for export and import cargo? What will be the advantages and disadvantages of a simplified procedure?
5. Discuss the differences between manual customs clearance procedure and EDI based procedure.
6. What is the importance and basis of valuation of import-export cargo?

7. What are the different types of customs duties imposed in India? Discuss the reasons for levying each type of duty.
8. Explain the US Customs Advance Manifest Regulation. What is its impact on:
   (a) Global Supply Chains
   (b) Port procedures
9. What are the new developments in customs clearance procedures. How will they help shippers and other stakeholders in international trade? Give your suggestions for further improvements.
10. Write short notes on Harmonized System and Carnets.

OBJECTIVE QUESTIONS

For the following questions, choose the most appropriate option.

1. Which of the following is NOT the objective of levying customs duties in India:
   (a) To create a level playing field in Indian market for the international and domestic manufacturers to compete with each other on equal and fair terms.
   (b) To protect Indian industry from the unfair business practices adopted by the foreign manufacturers.
   (c) To prevent the foreign goods from entering into Indian market.
   (d) To collect revenues from import-export trade.

2. Which of the following is the purpose for demanding Certificate of Origin for customs clearance:
   (a) To know the port of despatch of goods
   (b) To assess the value of the goods
   (c) To know if the country is member of ATA Carnet
   (d) To claim preferential duty

3. Which of the following documents is required for duty free clearance of import cargo:
   (a) Copy of letter of credit/bank draft
   (b) A bond with bank guarantee
   (c) Copy of industrial licence
   (d) Product catalogue/samples

4. Which of the following is the potential benefit of risk management based customs clearance mechanism:
   (a) Reduction in transaction cost
   (b) Reduction in risks of handling dangerous cargo

(c) Reduction in the possibility of theft, damage, and pilferage of the cargo

(d) Increase in the security at the ports/airports

5. Which of the following is NOT the objective of conducting customs examination of goods:

(a) To create trade barrier for the export-import business

(b) To determine if proper documentation for customs clearance has been coducted.

(c) To help the government gather statistical data of all the goods imported into and exported from the country.

State whether the following statements are True or False.

6. EDI procedure of customs clearance is time consuming and tedious.

7. Manual procedure of customs clearance is followed at most of the Indian ports because it is easy to understand.

8. In case of containerized cargo, customs clearance can be completed at ICD/SEZ.

9. In case of transhipment cargo, where the importer does not know the details of feeder vessel at the time of advance noting of bill of entry, the name of mother vessel is provisionally accepted.

10. India is a member of the ATA carnet.

EXERCISES

1. Visit the website of World Trade Organisation (WTO) and prepare a note on WTO Customs Valuation Agreement.

2. Mark on a map of India ports with EDI facilities.

3. Suppose you are travelling to the US on a business trip along with samples of your product. How will you find out if these samples are covered under carnet or not? What preparations would you make to ensure that your samples are allowed entry in to the USA without payment of duty?

4. Visit an importing organization and collect samples of all the documents required for customs clearance of import cargo.

5. Visit the websites of Jawaharlal Nehru Port in India and Jebel Ali Port in Dubai and compare the customs clearance procedures of the two ports.

SELECT REFERENCES

Nelson Carl A., 2000, *Import Export-How to get started in International Trade*, 3rd edition, McGraw Hill, New York.
www.atacarnet.com, last accessed on 4th October 2007
www.cbec.gov.in, last accessed on 15th July 2007
www.customs.gov/xp/cgov/home.xml, last accessed on 10th October 2007
www.oocl.com, last accessed on 11th October 2007
www.wcoomd.org, last accessed on 4th October 2007

SECURITY VS. SUPPLY CHAIN

Case Study

Rohit Sharma, a leading Mumbai based garment exporter is a worried man today. The source of his worry is a news item, which has appeared in newspapers regarding US customs advance manifest regulations. According to this new rule, ocean carriers and/or automated NVOCCs are required to submit a cargo declaration 24 hours before the cargo is loaded on board a vessel.

The US is the main market for Sharma's company, Tulip Garments, which exports more than 50 per cent of its production to American buyers. For Sharma, meeting stringent delivery schedules of his overseas buyers was itself an uphill task on a daily basis. He was faced with acute power-cuts (for which a new diesel generating set has been ordered) and labour unrest. The timely delivery of fabrics, which is his raw material, is also a constant source of worry. Added to this is the news about the new customs regulation in US.

Sharma is particularly concerned because his established way of conducting business will be seriously affected by the 24-hour rule. Most of the deliveries made by Tulip Garments are on a just-in-time (JIT) basis. This means that a consignment despatched from his factory on Friday evening could still be loaded on a vessel due to sail on Saturday. With the new rule, this has all changed. Mahesh Shinde, the forwarding agent of Tulip Garments has informed Sharma that now he will have to get his consignment ready at least 48 hours earlier. That is, instead of 1700 hours on Friday, now the consignment has to be despatched by 1700 hours on Wednesday. This will give ample time to Shinde to submit data via AMS to US Customs. This is particularly true for less-than-containerload (LCL) cargo, which needs consolidation. Full-container load (FCL) cargo, though, is not much affected.

Sharma is now thinking how to trim 48 hours from his production cycle from fabric to garment? He realizes that he himself follows in the JIT system •of inventory management and is dependent on the daily arrival of fabrics from mills, which are his suppliers. The smallest delay in arrival of fabric will disturb his own delivery schedule. To Sharma's mind, the solution could be to keep the raw material inventory in stock. For converting fabrics into garments, Sharma depends on manual labour and is already facing problems related to absenteeism. Even one tailor's absence, stretches his delivery schedule to limits. He is wondering, how he would slash those 48 hours? Will automation help him solve this problem? But he realizes that every solution to his new problem demands new investments. If Sharma keeps raw material in stock, his capital is locked in inventory. If he employs more people, he adds to his work force and ends up paying more salaries, and adding to his existing problem of labour unrest. If he decides to invest in automation, he will have to raise funds on loan from his bank and add to his interest burden. Shinde has also informed Sharma that he would have to bear an additional surcharge of US$ 20 per B/L towards meeting the operational cost of data transmission to the US customs using AMS.

Sharma calculated his additional costs with each alternative and finds that his already wafer-thin profit margin is being swallowed by just one change in the US customs rule.

Questions

1. Is the US government justified in putting their own security concerns ahead of business interest of thousands of small entrepreneurs like Sharma? Could they have devised any other way to add security without hurting small enterprises?
2. Should Sharma be made to pay operational cost of data transmission to US Customs? Alternatively, please suggest who in your opinion should bear this cost?
3. Offer your suggestions to Rohit Sharma to overcome his various problems stemming out of the US customs 24-hours manifest rule.

9 Logistics and Characteristics of Modes of Transportation

Learning Objectives

After studying this chapter, you will be able to understand
- the importance of physical distribution system
- the benefits of an efficient logistics system
- the critical elements of a logistics system
- the international transport system
- how to choose the best mode of transportation

Marketing can be defined as a system of business activities designed to plan, price, promote, and distribute satisfying products to a target market in order to achieve organizational objectives (Stanton, Etzel and Walker, 1994). This definition assigns equal importance to manufacturing, advertising/publicity, and distribution of goods. Any marketing activity is incomplete if a well-manufactured product of the right quality, produced at the right cost and which is well promoted, does not reach the consumers at the right time. For example, if woollen garments do not reach the market well before winter, they have no value. Similarly, if they reach the customers well past the season, they have no value. The manufacturer, therefore, has to ensure that his/her product reaches the market in time, neither too early nor too late. If the goods reach the market too early, they lose their freshness and a higher inventory carrying cost is incurred. If the goods reach too late, the customers may not be interested in buying them.

This underlines the importance of distribution in the entire marketing activity. Product distribution involves systems and procedures for physically moving the products and services from the point of origin to the point of consumption. The system and procedures involved in distribution of products and services is termed logistics.

In a modern industry, logistics functions are central to success in the marketplace. In the past, logistics was not a defined function. The task of purchase, material receipt, transportation, warehousing, despatch, and documentation was handled by different people, working under different departmental heads. These people learnt their skills on the job and rose in the hierarchy according to the level of their competence. Today, the scenario has changed completely. A logistics manager has to typically deal with a number of agencies, which are sub-sectors of logistics functions.

The concept of logistics has also changed significantly. Evolution of logistics can be divided into three stages.

Stage 1   In the 1960s and 1970s, the concept of logistics was confined to the physical distribution of goods or outbound logistics. Related activities included transportation, distribution, warehousing, packaging, material handling, and so on. The logistics manager had to deal only with outbound traffic.

Stage 2   In the 1980s, the concept of integrated logistics management was developed. This concept combined outbound logistics (physical distribution) with inbound logistics (materials management). Companies leveraged their inbound and outbound traffic with transport companies, warehouses, and others to obtain competitive rates. Also, the logistics manager had to deal with both inbound and outbound traffic. In other words, the logistics manager was responsible for efficiency in materials management as well as physical distribution of finished goods.

Stage 3   From the late 1980s onwards, organizations started thinking beyond the efficiency of their own logistics operations and expanded the concept of logistics to include all the firms involved—suppliers and sub-suppliers on the one hand and customers on the other. They jointly tied up with logistics service providers such as transporters, warehouse operators, and others to create a strong supply chain. The era of supply chain management thus began. This multiplied the responsibilities and the scope of work of a logistics manager manifold. To cope with these additional responsibilities, a logistics manager must be technology savvy, and possess new skills and knowledge of modern management practices. In recent years, globalization and advancement in Information Technology (IT) have added new dimensions to logistics operations.

PLANNING PHYSICAL DISTRIBUTION

An effective physical distribution system needs careful planning. In order to plan, the objectives of the distribution system should be clearly defined. For example, an objective could be, all the export orders to be executed within eight weeks of receipt of purchase order/letter of credit. The objective also could be to bring down the total distribution cost, or to ensure minimum damage or loss of goods. Once the objectives are defined, important decisions regarding inventory levels, mode of transportation, warehousing and number of distributors, etc., can be taken.

Planning Process

Given below are the five steps in the planning process.

Step 1 To start with, a customer's needs and expectations from the products and services must be determined. Sometimes the customer wants to buy the product off the shelf, as in case of cosmetics, confectionary, grains, vegetable oils, and FMCG (Fast Moving Consumer Goods) products. In such cases, the distribution system should be agile and prompt. Sometimes the customer is willing to wait for the product, as in the case of cars, two wheelers, machinery, and consumer durables. These being high-value products with very competitive markets; the distribution system should also be cost competitive and ensure the safety of the products. In either case a different approach is required.

Step 2 Improved customer service comes at a cost. The next step is to determine the cost at which the company can fulfill the customer's expectations. Prompt deliveries are always appreciated, but extra costs are not.

Step 3 A balance needs to be struck between improved service and additional cost. For example, by deciding to airfreight the material, the objective of speedy services to the customer is achieved, but the additional cost could be exorbitant. Or, deciding to increase the frequency of replenishment of stocks at the warehouse may make the response to the customer's demand agile, but will burden the product with additional costs. Hence this step involves an examination of the entire distribution system to identify the locations where the goods can be made available at a reasonable cost.

Step 4 An assessment of the competitor's quality of service vis-à-vis the cost is necessary. Keeping an eye on the best practices adopted by competitors can help the organization to redefine its distribution strategy.

Step 5 There should be a regular evaluation of the physical distribution system, keeping in mind the change in technology in the areas of production, promotion, and distribution. The system should always be in line with the available technology. For example, the use of Electronic Data Interchange

(EDI) or Radio Frequency Identification (RFID) system can make the tracking of cargo on high seas or elsewhere possible. The physical distribution system should be flexible enough to adopt new technology.

BENEFITS OF AN EFFICIENT LOGISTICS SYSTEM

In the age of universal globalization, the World Trade Organization (WTO) is working towards reducing tariff barriers and eliminating all non-tariff barriers. Tariff levels the world over are also being brought down. The mantra of free trade is spreading fast and manufacturers and service providers are now exploring global opportunities. The need to physically carry the goods from one country to another has highlighted the importance of a sound logistics system. It is now being realized that the desired efficiency of a logistics system is directly proportional to the distance travelled by the cargo. The longer the distance to be travelled, the higher is the efficiency demanded of a logistics system. Integrated logistics, which takes into account fast-paced technological changes and the forces of globalization, works as a strategic weapon for business. Strategy guru Michael Porter acknowledges the importance of logistics by assigning in-bound logistics (spanning sourcing and procurement) and out-bound logistics (covering post manufacturing deliveries) two out of five links on the value chain from which companies can derive their competitive advantage.

The following are the various benefits of an efficient logistics system.

Increased Operational Efficiency

The primary objective of any logistics system is to make optimum use of resources available so that in-bound raw materials, components and sub-assemblies as well as finished products are delivered in the right quantity, at the right place, and at the right time. This helps the supply chain become more responsive to the ever-changing market demands at minimum cost and time. In international business, the choice of mode of transportation such as road, rail, sea, river, or air is critical. The choice is made depending on the nature of the cargo, delivery commitment, and the cost of transportation. Other considerations include prevention of damages, theft, and pilferage. Transnational companies with multiple locations of manufacturing plants and warehouses must devise a system that enables them to deliver the goods to the market using the shortest routes, keeping the minimum inventories, and avoiding duplication. A logistics system can be designed to increase operational efficiency and help the company respond to market demands and service customers better than competitors. In other words efficient logistics means an edge over the competitors.

Channellization of Resources

A company invests its resources for providing the service to the customer. While devising a logistics system, the company assesses the value of this service to the customer. In other words, how much the customer could be willing to pay determines the efficiency of the logistics system. For example, the frequency of a visit of a delivery van to a small town will depend on the product sale and profit margins. Hence, a retailer who offers higher margins and guaranteed sales is serviced more frequently than the retailer who has an erratic demand. A company with a limited number of delivery vans will, therefore, schedule the visits of these vans to various towns and cities depending upon the profitability of such operations. Thus, while devising a system a logistics manager studies the availability of vans, their routes, and the profitability on each route. Thus, logistics helps make the optimum use of available resources.

Improved Customer Service

In every organization, depending on individual functions, each department has its own priorities. For example, the production department would want all inputs and consumables to be always available in inventory, whereas the purchase and planning department may want to keep the inventory levels low. The sales and marketing department may insist on well-stocked retail outlets, irrespective of demands. This may lead to a stockpile of finished goods inventory. The primary focus of the logistics system should be to provide a better customer service than the competitors. In other words, it means on-time delivery without mistakes, defects, and breakages. In addition, if the company provides personalized service and communicates clearly or directly with the customers, it adds to customer delight.

For example, the global fast food chain McDonald's aimed at customer satisfaction and created a logistics system, which converts data on daily orders into accurate forecasts of future weeks. This helps them cut down the lead-time between order and delivery to as low as possible. The efficiency of customer service can be appreciated by the speed at which ordered food items are delivered at any McDonald's outlet across the world. It means that a smart logistics system helps companies serve their customers better.

Inventory Control

A sound logistics system helps the company to keep not only the inventory under control, but also improves the overall gains to the company. A marketing executive of such a company can commit ambitious delivery schedules to the customer because he/she is sure that the company is capable of backing the deals with on-time deliveries without cost overruns. A reputed tyre manufacturing company managed to halve its inventory of finished goods from 50 days to 25, thanks to the use of logistics. This company used to overstock products due to the long distance between its despatch centres and selling points. The logistics solution was to ensure the supply at a short notice by creating despatch centres at various strategic locations, which were accessible to 125 selling points within 48 hours. Hence, the logistics system helps a company tailor its inventory exactly to customer demand.

In a fiercely competitive marketplace where along with the price, the quality of customer services too decides the fortunes of a business, more and more companies are relying on logistics solutions to provide them a cutting edge over their competitors. Large MNCs have their own logistics departments headed by senior managers with several years of experience. Many companies outsource their logistics operations to the logistics management companies who specialize in this field. These companies cater to a number of clients and can provide an entire range of value added services. Their services range from customs clearance to storage, from physical distribution to material handling, and from transportation to packaging. This helps companies concentrate on their core areas of expertise such as manufacturing, marketing, etc. They need not waste their resources in creating the service infrastructure, which can be provided more efficiently at competitive rates by logistics management companies. Some of the leading companies offering logistics solutions in India are Federal Express, Blue Dart Express, DHL Logistics, Maersk Logistics, Safe Express, Geologistics, and Miebach Logistics. The presence of so many companies providing specialized solutions is an ample testimony of the importance of logistics management.

MARKETING LOGISTICS SYSTEM: THE CONCEPT

Logistics is defined by the Council of Supply Chain Management Professionals, Ohio USA, as the process of planning, implementing, and controlling the efficient, cost effective flow and storage of raw materials, in-process inventory, finished goods, and related information from point of origin to point of usage. More simply, the objective of a logistics system is that the right products reach the right place in the right quantity and at the right time to satisfy customer demand.

Logistics is also defined as the design and operation of the physical, managerial, and informational systems needed to allow goods to overcome time and space. Logistics encompasses all the activities, which move the goods from raw material to finished stage, store and sort them to facilitate distribution process, deliver the products to the customers as per their requirements, and provide spares for after sales service to customers. Logistics is the flow of material, information, and money between customer and supplier, whereas global logistics is the flow of material, information, and money between countries (Frazelle).

The UK-based Chartered Institute of Logistics and Transport define Logistics as the time related positioning of resources. Logistics is also defined as the management of inventory in motion and at rest.

Logistics Process

The various steps involved in setting up an effective logistics system are discussed as follows.

Planning

This is the first step towards an effective logistics system. The system can be effective if the geographical locations and the distance between the point of origin of goods and the point of consumption are kept in mind. Depending upon the distance and geographical hurdles such as, oceans, mountains, rivers, and the various difficult terrains involved, different modes of transportation can be considered. Also, the nature of the product plays an important role. Physical attributes such as weight, volume, perishability, and fragility play an important role in the logistics planning process.

Implementing

This is the second step of an effective logistics system. Theory aside, in a real life situation it is found that even the best-laid plans go haywire due to unforeseen circumstances. Therefore, contingency plans should also be in place in case of need. Implementation of a logistics plan is a group process, where different agencies and people located in different geographical locations have to coordinate their activities with each other. Precise instructions, quick communication, and mutual understanding are the key ingredients of the successful implementation of a logistics plan.

Controlling

The third step of an effective logistics system is controlling the flow of goods. The timely arrival of cargo at the destination is very important. Sometimes if the goods arrive too early, they incur demurrages on ports or warehouses or else they simply perish. On the other hand, if the goods arrive late, it leads to customer dissatisfaction and loss of opportunity. Therefore, an effective logistics system is one, which ensures the timely and safe delivery of goods at the most economical cost. This can be achieved only through keeping a tight control on the passage of goods from the point of origin to the destination.

The scope of marketing logistics includes warehousing, distribution, and information management. It is also part of international supply chain management and added value/pre-retailing services.

The flow diagram in Figure 9.1 illustrates the journey made by the goods from vendors' shops in raw material form till they reach the end customer in their final, and finished form.

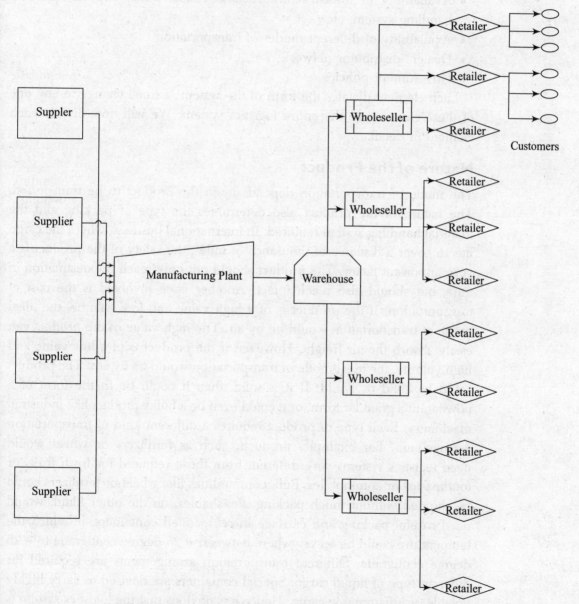

Fig. 9.1 Supply Chain—from raw material supplier to end customer

CRITICAL ELEMENTS OF A LOGISTICS SYSTEM

The following critical elements decide the structure of the entire logistics system.

- Nature of the product
- Location of the manufacturing plant
- Availability of infrastructure such as roads, ports, airports, material handling system, etc.
- Availability of different modes of transportation
- Dealer/ distributor network
- Government policies

Each element dictates the form of the system; a small change in any one of these can change the entire logistics system. We will now discuss each element in detail.

Nature of the Product

The mode of transportation depends upon the product to be transported. The nature of the product also determines the type of packing and the material handling system required. In international business, where the cargo has to cover a distance of thousands of miles, the safety of the product is a very important factor. The product should not only reach the destination in time, but should also reach intact. Another issue involved is the cost of transportation. If the product is of a high value and low volume, the ideal mode of transportation would be by air. The high value of the product can easily absorb the air freight. However, if the product is of a low value and high volume, the ideal mode of transportation would be by sea. The product could be solid or liquid. If it is solid, then it could be in the form of a powder, in a granular form, or it could even be a bulky product like industrial machinery. Each type of product requires a different kind of transportation arrangement. For example, products, such as fertilizers or wheat would need logistics systems very different from those required for fresh fruits or toothpastes or automobiles. Bulk commodities like wheat or fertilizers could be shipped without much packing. Perishables, on the other hand, would need careful packing and carriage in refrigerated containers, in which the temperature could be set anywhere between + 25 degree centigrade to – 25 degree centigrade. Different transportation arrangements are required for different type of liquid cargo. Special containers are devised to carry highly volatile or inflammable cargo. Hence it is obvious that the logistics system is highly product dependent.

Location of Manufacturing Plant

Normally, manufacturing plants are located either close to the source of raw materials or close to the markets to which the company caters. Another criterion for choosing the plant location is government subsidies available at the location. In India, the government offers various tax holidays to plants located in economically backward regions. Nowadays the survival of manufacturers depends not only on the domestic markets but also, increasingly, on export markets. It would be more convenient for an export-oriented manufacturing plant to be located near the port or airport; the proximity would make the movement of material easy. If the plant is situated far away, then the availability of good roads becomes critical. In a country like India, this is a very important issue because very often a truck carrying very tall cargo has to travel extra miles due to obstructions, such as railway bridges with low heights, low hanging electric or telephone wires, etc. The timely delivery of the cargo at the port/airport is important because of the adherence to conditions of purchase order/letter of credit. Hence the location of the plant in relation to the port is an important element of the logistics system. Nowadays, many countries are very consciously developing free trade zones, which are close to seaports or international airports. Jebel Ali Free Trade Zone (FTZ) near Dubai and Shenzen Special Economic Zone (SEZ) in China are good examples of this strategy. The proximity to a port helps the manufacturer to devise an efficient logistics system, thereby providing better service to the overseas customer. Many manufacturers nowdays prefer to have their manufacturing units in such FTZs/SEZs.

Availability of Infrastructure

Infrastructure is the backbone of industry in any country. If the infrastructure of a country is strong, its industry can prosper. The success of the Chinese industry in exports can be attributed to the strong infrastructure the Chinese government has created over the last ten years. This includes good roads, railways, air transport and inland waterways systems, efficient telecommunication system, and modern ports with the capability to handle all types of containerized and break-bulk commodities. Good road conditions help speedy movement of cargo. Also, good port facilities with suitable material handling systems help the cargo move without wastage of time. In many developed countries land transport, such as trains are used to carry bulky or voluminous materials. For such a cargo, the roads and the entire infrastructure have to be excellent. Many ports in developing countries lack adequate warehousing and material handling facilities. In India too, poor infrastructure is one of the obstacles restricting the growth of exports. Indian exporters have to keep in mind various possibilities of delays during transit due to lack of good infrastructure while designing their logistics systems. On the other hand, ports in many developed countries are equipped with excellent facilities, which ensure speedy despatches. Modern airports are also designed keeping in mind the necessity of the smooth movement of cargo.

Availability of Different Modes of Transportation

Nowadays, the export cargo moves on various modes of transportation. Containerization has revolutionized the concept of multi-modal transport. If the air service is available to an exporter of flowers or vegetables, his/her products can reach the desired overseas markets in fresh condition and in time. However, in the absence of air service, the exporter would have to depend upon refrigerated containers to carry the cargo to the nearest port. This would delay arrival of the cargo at the destination. Because it is now possible to transport cargo through various modes of transportation, the absence of any mode of transportation becomes a weak link in the entire logistics system. Efficiency of the logistics system depends upon the availability of different modes of transportation. In India, the air feeder system at various locations in the hinterland could help the exporters meet their overseas commitments more efficiently.

Location of Warehouse

Today, every customer prefers off-the-shelf delivery. This is the result of the 'Just-In-Time' concept of inventory adopted by many companies. No company wants to keep their capital locked in inventories. Warehouses help the industries keep the stock of goods, which can be lifted at the time of consumption. The location of the warehouse is important because it helps solve distribution problems. Besides offering storage facilities, modern warehouses offer many more services to the exporters and importers, which includes bar coding, assembly, custom-bonding, etc. Automobile giants such as General Motors, Ford Motor Company, BMW, and Mercedes prefer those automobile component suppliers who can keep their stock ready close to their assembly plant locations. The Engineering Export Promotion Council (EEPC) of India has established warehouses at various locations around the world to help exporters keep their stocks in the overseas markets ready. Availability of such warehousing facilities cuts down the response time of the exporters and makes their logistics system more efficient.

Dealer and Distribution Network

This is an important component of the product mix of any company. A company may have an excellent product, which is attractively priced and aggressively promoted, but if it does not have an efficient distribution system, its success in the market will be doubtful. A dealer or a distributor is the vital link between a manufacturer and a customer. A customer prefers the product that is available next door. An extensive network of dealers and distributors makes it possible for a company to reach the nook and cranny of each market. A classic example is Coca Cola, which has a very impressive network of outlets all over the world. A strategically located dealer brings more business for the company; however, if the dealer or the distributor is not conveniently located, it can lead to a loss of business opportunity. A distributor who is willing to keep adequate stocks of the product makes the logistics system more effective.

Government Policies

The logistics system needs to be designed to conform to the policies of governments of exporting countries as well as the importing country. Government policies related to sales tax, excise duty, Octroi, MODVAT, Motor Vehicle Act, etc., in India affect the critical elements of any logistics system. For example, due to regulations related to Octroi and Motor Vehicle Act, many companies prefer to have their warehouse outside city limits. In international business, where many developed countries offer access to the products of developing countries under a Generalized System of Preference (GSP), the exporter can avail of the benefit of lower or zero import duty if his/her products have already reached the host country and been kept in customs bonded warehouse from where they can be cleared without any delay. Speed in such cases is very important because such benefits are provided in many cases on first come first served basis.

In a nutshell, whereas each of the above elements affects the logistics system, they also affect each other considerably. Each element of a logistics system is important individually as well as collectively. Hence, exporters and importers have to give due importance to all these elements while targeting an overseas market.

INTERNATIONAL TRANSPORT SYSTEM

Transportation refers to the movement of product from one location to another as it makes its way from the beginning of the supply chain to the consumer's hands. Transportation plays a key role in every supply chain because products are rarely produced and consumed in the same location (Chopra and Meindl, 2004). Transportation is an integral part of logistics. In case of international business where the supplier of the goods and his/her customers are situated far apart, transportation is a vital link in the entire supply chain. Transportation doesn't merely provide movement to the goods, but a high quality transport system adds value to the goods. In the age of just-in-time inventory system, efficient transport systems keep the assembly lines of manufacturing companies continuously fed with raw materials, spare parts, and components. Any fault in the transport system brings the entire manufacturing process to a grinding halt. Therefore, the choice of mode of transportation is a strategic decision for anybody involved in international business. Due to technological advancement, a variety of options are available for transporting the goods. Many a time a single mode of transportation is not adequate for the speedy and efficient movement of cargo. In such a case, the cargo has to use multiple modes of transportation. Some of the popular modes of transportation are as follows:

Air Transport

Air transport is resorted to only in case of absolute necessity or urgency. Two factors are responsible for the infrequent use of air transportation in India. First is the cost of air freighting which is very high compared to other modes of transport. The second factor is the lack of connectivity by air to international and domestic destinations. India has 60 airports, including 11 international airports. This still leaves a large part of the country unconnected by air. Exporters of perishables such as fruits, vegetables, flowers, etc., suffer due to lack of air connectivity. Large quantities of food products perish in India every year, which if exported could bring in precious foreign exchange for the country. The absence of necessary infrastructure is costing the nation heavily.

The biggest advantage of air transportation is speed. Modern commercial aircraft travel at high-speed. But the average speed of the journey between one airport to another is somewhat less than the flying speed due to lower speeds during taxiing on the runway and the ascent and descent of the aircraft. In addition to this there is 'cooling off' period up to 72 hours before the cargo is loaded on board the aircraft. This period is mandatory at many airports across the world due to terrorist threats of planting bombs and detonators in the air cargo. The cooling off period is expected to defuse explosive devices, after which the cargo is considered safe for stacking on board the aircraft. All these factors bring down the average airport to airport speed of an aircraft. In fact, for shorter distances it is easier and quicker to send the cargo by surface transport instead of air.

Air service however depends on various factors, such as mechanical breakdowns, weather conditions and traffic congestion at the airports. Due to these factors the reliability of air transport often comes under question. Also, the physical dimensions and the load carrying capacities of an aircraft put constraints on the utility of air transport in many cases. For example, Boeing 747 'jumbo jets' and Lockheed 500 aircraft can handle 125 to 150 tons of cargo.

One of the attractions of air transportation is lesser incidence of loss or damage during transit. It is a fact that the claims against loss and damage during air transit are much less than surface transport, such as ships, trains, or trucks. Due to this air cargo needs less protective and therefore less expensive packaging. Insurance companies also consider air cargo less risky as compared to cargo travelling by surface transport and, therefore, they charge lesser premiums on air cargo.

Ocean Transport

Since antiquity, sea routes are being used for transportation of cargo from one continent or country to another. More than 95 per cent of international trade is conducted by sea routes. Maritime transport, a key constituent to the trade and economic growth in India, contributes 90 per cent in terms of volume and 77 per cent in terms of value. India has 12 major and 184 minor / intermediate ports spread across its vast coastline of 7517 km (Chandrasekharan and Kumar, 2006). Coastal shipping is also used for transporting cargo from one port within the country to another. For example, in India, the cargo can be transported from Chennai port to Visakhapatnam port using the coastal shipping route.

Sea routes are used for carrying bulk commodities, such as coking and thermal coal, ores, grains, fertilizers, rock phosphate, etc., and liquid cargo, such as crude oil, ammonia, and acids, among others. Ideally, goods with high volume and low value are suited for ocean transport. In the era of containerization even high value cargo can be safely transported within containers over long distances. Technology has enabled the cargo carrying capacities of ships to increase manifold. In 1956, the first containerized ship belonging to Sea Land Corp. carried 58 20-feet containers; modern ships have the capacity to carry 7000 such containers. One of the biggest ships owned by Maersk-Sea Land is 1,138 feet long from end to end and 140 feet wide at midship. Such ships are called post-Panamax ships.

Table 9.1 shows growth in the volume of cargo handled by major Indian ports.

Table 9.1   Cargo Handled by Major Indian Ports (in million tons)

Port	1997–98	1998–99	1999–2000	2000–01	2001–02	2002–03
Kolkata	7.95	9.16	10.31	7.15	5.37	36.00
Haldia	20.20	20.21	20.69	22.84	25.01	
Paradip	13.30	13.10	13.63	19.90	21.13	24.00
Visakhapatnam	36.01	35.65	39.10	44.68	44.34	46.00
Chennai	35.53	35.20	37.44	41.22	36.11	34.00
Tuticorrin	9.97	10.15	9.99	12.28	13.01	13.00
Cochin	12.17	12.68	12.79	13.11	12.05	13.00
New Mangalore	15.28	14.20	17.60	17.89	17.50	21.00
Mormugao	21.18	18.02	18.22	19.62	22.92	23.00
Mumbai	32.09	30.96	30.38	27.06	26.43	27.00
JNPT, Navi Mumbai	8.89	11.72	14.97	18.57	22.52	27.00
Kandla	38.90	40.63	46.30	36.74	37.72	41.00
TOTAL	251.47	251.68	271.42	281.06	284.11	305.00
% Growth Rate over Previous Year		0.08	7.84	3.55	1.09	7.35

Source: Indian Ports Association

At present, the major Indian shipping lines are the Shipping Corporation of India (SCI), Essar Shipping, and Great Eastern Shipping, each with a capacity in excess of 1 million DWT (Dead Weight Tonnage). All these companies carry bulk commodities and liquid cargo, with only SCI involved in the carriage of containerized cargo. SCI's present fleet stands at 80 vessels aggregating about 2.75 million GT (Gross Tonnage) (4.79 million DWT) consisting of cellular container vessels, crude oil tankers (including combination carrier), product tankers, bulk carriers, LPG/ammonia carriers, acid carriers, passenger vessels, and offshore supply vessels.

SCI provides fully containerized cellular liner services to USA, Europe, West Asia Gulf, and Far East Asia; through a mix of three owned and five chartered vessels. Table 9.2 gives the comparative shipping data of various countries, including India.

Table 9.2 The 35 most important maritime countries and territories as of 1 January 2006[a]

Country of domicile[b]	Number of vessels			Deadweight tonnage				
	National flag[c]	Foreign flag	Total	National flag	Foreign flag	Total	Foreign flag as a percentage of total	Total as a percentage of world total
Greece	709	2318	3027	47466	115928	163394	70.95	18.02
Japan	707	2384	3091	11763	119940	131703	91.07	14.52
Germany	420	2366	2786	13120	58397	71516	81.66	7.89
China	1763	1130	2893	29832	35656	65488	54.45	7.22
United States	625	1054	1679	10172	36755	46927	78.32	5.18
Norway	732	933	1665	13658	31738	45397	69.91	5.01
Hong Kong, China	292	371	663	17973	25870	43843	59.01	4.84
Republic of Korea	638	355	993	12696	16977	29672	57.21	3.27
Tiwan Province of China	109	444	553	4772	19618	24389	80.44	2.69
Singapore	467	287	754	14695	8285	22980	36.05	2.53
United Kingdom	370	409	779	8961	12334	21295	57.92	2.35
Denmark	316	428	744	9.228	10328	19556	52.81	2.16
Russian Federation	1670	487	2157	6803	9889	16692	59.25	1.84
Italy	543	159	702	10192	4297	14490	29.66	1.60
India	366	40	406	12511	1264	16774	9.17	1.52
Switzerland	26	346	372	791	10968	11759	93.28	1.30
Belgium	69	134	203	5902	5657	11559	48.94	1.27
Saudi Arabia	60	74	134	977	10387	11364	91.40	1.25
Turkey	436	365	801	6793	3497	10290	33.98	1.13
Iran (Islamic Replubic of)	156	23	179	8894	936	9830	9.52	1.08
Malaysia	249	76	325	5454	4179	9633	43.38	1.06
Netherlands	515	207	722	4520	4288	8808	48.69	0.97
Canada	216	140	356	2540	4007	6548	61.20	0.72
Sweden	159	183	342	1692	4684	6375	73.47	0.70
Indonesia	591	120	711	3822	2408	6231	38.65	0.69
Kuwait	40	29	69	3682	1361	5043	26.99	0.56
Philippines	275	37	312	4052	971	5023	19.33	0.55
France	164	126	290	2208	2655	4863	54.60	0.54
Brazil	135	12	147	2590	2164	4755	45.52	0.52
United Arab Emirates	46	140	186	557	3942	4499	87.62	0.50
Spain	75	235	310	871	3225	4096	7873	0.45
Thailand	278	40	318	2741	457	3198	14.30	0.35

(Contd.)

(Contd.)

Israel	20	52	72	868	1828	2697	67.80	0.30
Croatia	73	37	110	1684	979	2663	36.77	0.29
Australia	45	35	80	1375	1253	2628	47.68	0.29
Total (35 countries)	13355	15576	28931	285855	577123	862978	66.88	95.17
World Total	15576	17238	32814	303768	602985	906753	66.50	100.00

Source: Compiled by the UNCTAD secretariat on the basis of data supplied by Lloyd's Register Fairplay.

[a]Vessels of 1,000 grt and above, excluding the US Reserve Fleet and the US and Canadian Great Lakes fleets.

[b]The country of domicile indicates where the controlling interest (i.e. parent company) of the fleet is located. In several cases, determining this has required making certain judgements. Thus, for instance, Greece is shown as the country of domicile for vessels owned by a Greek owner with representative offices in New York, London and Piracus, although the owner may be domiciled in the United States.

[c]Includes vessels flying the national flag but registered in territorial dependencies or associated self-governing territories. For the United Kingdom, British flag vessels are included under the national flag, except for Bermuda (listed in Table 17 as an open registry territory)

The popularity of ocean transport over other means of transportation is due to the various advantages ocean transport offers. The biggest advantage of this mode is the ability of a ship to carry a very large volume of cargo. Technology has enabled gigantic ships to travel faster than ever before. Also, the increased efficiency at various ports translates into fast turnaround time for the ships.

The costs arising from loss and damage from sea transport is low as compared to other modes of transport. As far as low value cargo is concerned, damage and delays are not serious concerns for the shippers. Information technology also helps trace and track services for the cargo ships, due to which a shipper can closely monitor the cargo during transit.

The major disadvantage of sea transport, however, is the relatively higher percentage of losses to high value cargo. Also the cost of packaging of sea cargo is high due to the possibility of damages during loading and unloading operations at the port. For similar reasons, the insurance premium for sea cargo is also higher than other modes of transportation. Due to longer voyage time and longer transit time in warehouses the cost of carrying the inventory is also high.

Rail Transport

Rail transport is basically suitable for carrying raw materials, bulk commodities such as coal, grains, petroleum products, timber, ores, chemicals etc. over long distances. It is estimated that more than 70 per cent of goods carried by the Indian Railways belong to state-owned enterprises, major amongst these being Coal India Ltd., Food Corporation of India Ltd., Fertilizer Corporation of India Ltd., etc. For the past 20 years, freight trains have run at an average speed of 23 km per hour; with electrification and modern locomotives the average speed should have increased to 40–45 km per hour.

The relatively slow speed and the shorter distance travelled by a railway wagon is due to the time spent in loading and unloading operations, the shunting of wagons within the station premises for assembling wagons into trains, or sometimes giving way to more important passenger trains. Out of the total transit time of a railway wagon between the point of origin and destination, more than 80 per cent is spent in these activities. Yet, railways is the most favoured mode of transportation for majority of the privately owned enterprises, including exporters and importers in India. These companies look for speedy movement of cargo with guaranteed arrivals and departures. Unfortunately, the Indian Railways does not provide such services. Some of the other disadvantages that rail transport suffers from are:

- Railway freights are not always the cheapest.
- The cargo has to be delivered to and collected from railway stations, which needs an additional road transport facility.
- Additional material handling is required during transportation by railways. This is cumbersome as well expensive.
- Various formalities and approvals are needed to get a railway siding, which is not always easy and is time consuming as also tiring for an enterprise.

In many countries, the railways provide professional services to their customers along with excellent links to ports and road networks. Such linkages encourage exporters and importers to opt for transportation of their cargo by railways.

Exhibit 9.1 Improving efficiency of Indian Railways

Freight Traffic Movements

The Indian Railways is a massive 63,465 route-kilometre network that plays a significant role in the transportation and economic scenario of India. It is a known fact that there is a positive correlation between a country's economic development and the demand for a transportation network. As the country develops, demand on the network increases. When technology advances, the network continues upgrading its systems to take advantage of the latest features and applications. In this context, Indian Railways paid close attention to upgrade its freight movements, wagon turnaround time, maintenance, quality control and cost-efficiency, since these factors play an important and integral role in the efficient operation of the railways.

In 2005–06, Indian Railways carried 666.5 million tonnes of revenue earned cargo and witnessed a growth rate of 10.7 per cent against the

(Contd.)

Exhibit 9.1 (Contd.)

previous year 2004–05. At the same time the increase in railway freight has posted a compound annual growth rate (CAGR) of 7.1 per cent during 2001–02 to 2005–06. Factors like higher economic growth, increasing industrial activities, increasing consumer spending, and robust trade growth (both internal and external) have driven a higher growth in Indian railway freight traffic. Apart from these, improved wagon turnaround time also contributed to the growth in freight traffic.

Currently, the Indian Railways is on the verge of a major change. Now, the railways is looking forward to improve its market share in both bulk and non-bulk freight traffic by improving its efficiency and providing better services with reduction in transit time and reliability.

Source: CII Logistics & Freight News Dt. 10.5.2007

Road Transport

Semi-finished and finished products of medium and small sizes and weights are ideally suited for transportation by trucks. The best advantage of sending goods by trucks is the door-to-door services provided by them. Hence, once the cargo is loaded at the point of origin, it is unloaded directly at the destination. This saves time and money and also prevents damage resulting from the repeated handling of cargo. This is a distinct advantage of road transport over other modes of transport. Another advantage of road transport is that the trucks can be hired on exclusive contract by shippers for their dedicated service. This facility of exclusivity is not available with other modes of transportation. Thirdly, road transport offers reasonably fast and dependable service for small consignments. Lastly, a shipper needs only 10 to 12 tonnes of cargo to fill the truck. A railway wagon on the other hand demands more tonnage to be filled and will move only when the entire goods train is fully loaded with cargo.

India has an extensive road network of 3.2 million km. It comprises national highways (124,300 km), district roads, rural roads, urban roads and special purpose roads (for military, ports, etc.). Though the geographic coverage of India's highway network, of 0.66 km of highway per square km of land, compares favourably with that of USA (0.65), the condition of Indian roads is very poor in terms of surface quality and lane capacity.

Exhibit 9.2 Fragmentation of trucking industry in India

The trucking industry contributes over 75 per cent of total cargo movement in India and plays a crucial role in the economy. Indian trucking industry has increased its contribution to freight movement from around 20 per cent in the 1950s to an estimated 75 per cent in 2006.

(Contd.)

Exhibit 9.2 (Contd.)

The industry in India, however, is largely unorganized and extremely fragmented. As per the Transport Corporation of India, the trucking industry employs around 20 million people in various segments of the sector. There has been a rapid increase in the number of goods vehicles in India from 82,000 in 1951 to 4.04 million (estimated) in 2005. The road freight sector in India is highly fragmented as 86 per cent of the sector is unorganized and is estimated to have grossed revenues around Rs 370.2 billion in 2005. Whereas, the organized sector's revenue was around Rs 60 billion, with a market share of 16 per cent. The road freight industry is largely in the hands of the private sector, mostly dominated by small fleet operators. Basically, the industry operates through brokers who arrange load for small fleet owners from the shippers.

Source: CII Logistics & Freight News dated 14 December 2006

Inland Waterways

The commercial utility of transportation by inland waterways in India is limited, basically because either the shipper must be located on the waterway or he/she has to transport the cargo at the water head by other means of transport. Another limitation posed by inland waterways is the average speed of water service, which is 6 to 10 km per hour, that is among the lowest. This speed further reduces if the vessel travels against the direction of water flow. Weather also affects the water services; for example, during monsoon season, when the rivers are flooded, it is not safe to ply boats on the waterways, and during summer when the water level depletes, the waterways cannot be used by boats laden with cargo. The river ports are also not as well equipped in terms of material handling equipment and other infrastructure as seaports. All these factors severely limit the use of inland waterways in the country.

Considering the variety of modes of transportation available, each with its unique advantages and disadvantages, it is necessary for shippers to analyse various factors and choose the most appropriate mode of transportation for their cargo.

Selecting the Right Mode of Transportation

It is a challenge to every logistics manager to decide the most suitable mode of transportation or transportation mix which will best serve organizational objectives as well as the interest of the customer. The manager has to ensure that the cargo reaches the destination safely at the most economical cost possible, without any delays in the transit. The task of the manager becomes even more challenging in case of an overseas customer. This is because the manager has to choose the most appropriate mode of transport from the various choices available. He/she can also consult the freight forwarder concerned for expert advice while making this decision.

Example 1   An exporter who deals with cutting tools in India can send his/her cargo to Bangladesh either by truck, or by sea, or even by air. While choosing the mode of transportation, the exporter has to keep in mind the cost and the delivery commitment to the customer. If the exporter is located in Central India, he/she may choose to send the cargo by road because of economy and also the speed. If he chooses the sea route, the cargo will first have to cover a long journey to the nearest port of despatch on truck. Then only can the cargo travel by sea. However, if the exporter is located near a port from where there is a direct shipping service to Bangladesh, he/she may choose to send the cargo by sea and still enjoy the benefits of cost and speed.

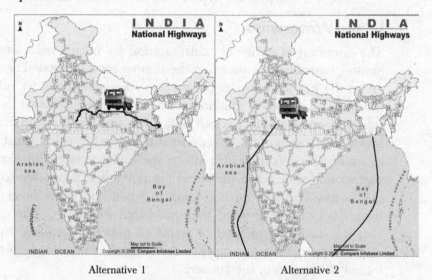

Alternative 1   Alternative 2

Fig. 9.2   Selecting the right mode of transportation

Example 2   An exporter of cut flowers based near Bengaluru in Karnataka has an export order from Dubai. The exporter has only one choice, which is to send cargo by refrigerated container to the Bengaluru airport and from there by flight to Dubai. In this case, because of the nature of the product, the choice of mode of transportation is limited to only air.

Example 3   An exporter of heavy machinery in Delhi has to execute an order for a customer in Malaysia. The exporter will load the machinery weighing 10 tonnes in a container and send it by truck to the Local Inland Container Depot in Tughalakabad. From there the container can travel to Jawaharlal Nehru Port in Mumbai by rail or by road. From Mumbai, this container can be loaded on to a ship bound for Malaysia.

Example 4 An exporter of readymade garments from China receives an order from a customer in Germany. This order has to be executed on an urgent basis and must reach Germany within eight weeks to meet the heavy demand during Christmas season. The manufacturing time required by the exporter for this consignment is four weeks. The transit time between Shanghai port and Hamburg port is eight weeks by sea. Hence, the total delivery period needed is 12 weeks if the cargo is sent by sea. If the cargo is sent by air, it will be very expensive. The exporter consults the freight forwarder who advises the exporter to send the cargo from Shanghai to Jebel Ali port in Dubai by sea, and from Dubai to Germany by air. This will enable the exporter to economize on the freight charges, and to meet his delivery commitment also.

The above examples highlight that different situations demand different logistics solutions. Often, the logistics managers can apply their own experience and knowledge to find a suitable solution. Sometimes they may have to seek expert advice from a professional like a freight forwarder. The variables which make the difference are the nature of the product, urgency or, geographical locations of buyer and seller, proximity to a port or international airport, and last but not the least the cost of transportation.

Logistics managers use the total cost approach to coordinate logistics, materials management, and physical distribution in a cost-effective manner. This approach is built on the premise that all relevant activities in moving and storing products should be considered as a whole (i.e., their total cost), not individually (Murphy and Wood 2004).

Example 5 Sunshine International, a Chennai based electronic goods manufacturer, exports its products generally by sea to its customers in Singapore. The sea freight works out to $ 500 and the transit time is 10 days. For an urgent consignment, Sunshine invited from an airline a quotation, which worked out to $ 1400; the goods would reach the customer the next day. Sunshine also knew that the cost of carrying the in-transit inventory is $ 120 per day for these goods. The logistics manager of Sunshine calculated the logistics costs as shown in Table 9.3.

Table 9.3

Cost Element	Freight	Inventory Carrying Cost	Total Cost
Mode of Transportation			
Sea	$ 500	$ 1200	$ 1700
Air	$ 1400	$ 120	$ 1520

It is obvious that in this case, the choice of mode of transportation would be air, because it is faster and also works out to be cheaper. It is normally assumed that air transportation is more expensive than any other mode of transportation. This is in fact, true in most cases. However, with the total cost approach, an organization can enjoy the benefits of speed as well as economy in a number of cases. Hence it is the duty of a logistics manager as well as the freight forwarder to ascertain which mode of transportation provides the total cost benefit.

SUMMARY

Marketing activities in the era of globalization are no more confined to the domestic market alone. There is an ever-increasing demand for good quality products at competitive prices all over the world. This has also resulted in an increase in the demand for high quality global logistics services, which is the flow of material, information, and money from one country to the other. Any organization, which is involved in global trade, wants to strengthen its supply chains in order to achieve complete customer satisfaction. The new competitive paradigm is that supply chain competes with supply chain and the success of any one company will depend upon how well it manages its supply chain relationships (Christopher 1998). This new paradigm highlights the importance of an efficient logistics system, which translates into competitiveness between prices of globally marketed products. However, there are a number of variables on which the design, performance, and efficiency of a logistics system depends. There are certain factors, which an organization can control, such as choosing the right location for manufacturing or warehousing, or choosing the right mode of transportation for the product. However, there are also some uncontrollable factors, such as government policies, to which the logistics system must comply with.

Indian exporters and importers have been historically handicapped by poor quality of infrastructure in the country. They also have to take infrastructure into account while taking vital decisions about their logistics needs. Today, there is greater awareness about the need for improving infrastructure and the Indian government has taken various steps to improve the quality of ports, airports, and road and rail services in the country. India ranks 15th as a maritime nation in terms of number of vessels owned and dead weight tonnage carried. A considerable amount of foreign exchange can be saved and cost competitiveness be achieved by building a larger fleet of ships for carrying cargo to and from India. This will reduce the dependence of Indian shippers on foreign shipping lines.

For transportation of products from one country to another, there is a choice of modes of transportation available with the shipper. However, he must be aware of the various advantages and disadvantages of using each mode of transportation. Following a thumb rule all the time is not a good strategy for a logistics manager. While deciding about the transportation mode, the manager must consider the nature of the product, urgency of delivery, cost of transportation as well as other costs, such as cost of warehousing, inventory carrying cost, etc., before taking the final decision.

CONCEPT REVIEW QUESTIONS

1. Define logistics and explain its importance in the marketing process.
2. Planned physical distribution is the key to success in a competitive marketplace. Do you agree or disagree with this statement. Give reasons in support of your answer.
3. What are the five steps of planning a physical distribution system? Discuss with examples.
4. What are the various benefits of an efficient marketing system? Explain with examples.
5. Define logistics and discuss the various critical elements of an efficient logistics system.
6. Discuss the following factors which influence the effectiveness of a logistics system:
   (a) Product movement
   (b) Flow of information
   (c) Punctuality
   (d) Service charges
   (e) Team work
7. What are the various modes of transportation available in international transport system? Explain the advantages and disadvantages of each mode of transportation.
8. Write short notes on:
   (a) Air transport
   (b) Sea transport
   (c) Rail transport
   (d) Road transport
9. Explain how a logistics system helps optimize the utilization of resources to the organization's benefit?
10. How will you select a particular mode of transport for export?

OBJECTIVE QUESTIONS

In the following questions choose the correct option.

1. Which of the following is the benefit of an efficient logistics system:
   (a) Lower advertising costs
   (b) Improved product quality
   (c) Better utilization of resource
   (d) None of the above

2. Which of the following is NOT a part of definition of logistics:
   (a) Flow of the material
   (b) Flow of human resources
   (c) Flow of information
   (d) Flow of money

3. Which of the following is NOT an element of logistics system:
   (a) Nature of product
   (b) Availability of infrastructure
   (c) Quality of product
   (d) Government policies

4. Which of the following products is NOT suitable for sea transportation:
   (a) Timber
   (b) Hazardous cargo
   (c) Gems and jewellery
   (d) Automobiles

5. Which of the following products is suitable for air transportation:
   (a) Heavy machinery
   (b) Oil
   (c) Fertilisers
   (d) None of the above

State whether the following statements are True or False.

6. The systems and procedures involved in distribution of products and services is termed as logistics.

7. Location of a manufacturing plant is not an important factor in designing a logistics system.

8. India is among the top five maritime countries in the world.

9. An exporter can seek the help of his/her freight forwarder while selecting the mode of transportation.

10. The commercial utility of inland waterways in India is limited.

EXERCISES

1. Visit the website of the Council of Supply Chain Management Professionals, Ohio USA, and The Chartered Institute of Logistics and Transport, UK, and list the various certified professional courses offered by them.
2. Prepare a chart showing various modes of transportation and their characteristics and display the same in your classroom.
3. Visit a manufacturing organization to study their logistics system. Offer your suggestions for improvement in the system.
4. Prepare a logistics plan for a manufacturer who wants to ship his/her liquid pharmaceutical products from India to Belgium.
5. Mark the various major ports on the map of India.

SELECT REFERENCES

Chandrasekharan, N and Mohan Kumar, 2006, *Seaports: Challenges and Issues in India, A white paper of sea ports*, CII Institute of Logistics.

Chopra, Sunil and Meindl Peter, 2004, *Supply Chain–Strategy, Planning and Operation*, Second edition, Prentice Hall of India, Delhi.

Christopher M., 1998, *Logistics and Supply Chain Management*, Pitman Publishing, London.

Frazelle Edward H, 2005, *Supply Chain Strategies*, Tata McGraw-Hill, New Delhi.

Murphy, Paul R. and Wood, Donald F., 2004, *Contemporary Logistics*, Pearson Prentice Hall, New Jersey.

William Stanton, Michael Etzel, and Bruce Walker, 1994, *Fundamentals of Marketing*, McGraw Hill, New York.

World Bank Main Report, 2002, *India's Transport Sector: The challenges ahead*, Vol. 1.

www.cilt-international.com last accessed on 10th June 2007.

www.cscmp.org last accessed on 7th June 2007.

www.shipindia.com last accessed in July 2007.

www.worldbank.org/in last accessed on 13th December 2006.

10 | Characteristics of Shipping Industry

Learning Objectives

After studying this chapter, you will be able to understand
- the history of the shipping industry
- the characteristics of the shipping industry
- the role of intermediaries in the shipping industry
- latest trends in logistics operations
- ocean freight structure

HISTORY OF THE SHIPPING INDUSTRY

The movement of cargo can be achieved by deploying various means of transportation. The world shipping industry has evolved from manually operated sea ships that would take a long time to traverse short distances to large cargo carriers, which cover long distances only in a matter of days. Europeans can be credited with developing the ship building industry and inventing navigational systems. This initial interest encouraged explorers, such as Christopher Columbus, Marco Polo, and Vasco da Gama to plan voyages to Asia in general, and to India in particular, the latter at that time being known for its wealth and prosperity all over the world. Whereas Marco Polo and Vasco da Gama were successful in discovering sea routes to Asia, Columbus ended up discovering the route to America. The knowledge of sea routes encouraged the Europeans to build superior ships, which would not only carry the adventurous seafarers, but would also have cargo carrying capacities. Soon enough, the Europeans realized that the quickest way to earn wealth was to initially trade with Asian countries and eventually, colonize them. What started as a trickle of trade in spices, timber, and minerals got converted into massive transfer of wealth from Asia to Europe. With each successive conquest, the Europeans needed to develop better and larger ships with sophisticated navigational and cargo carrying and cargo handling facilities. The Portuguese, the Spanish, the British, the

French, and the Scandinavians were at the forefront of the development of the shipping industry.

Even today, the developed countries control the shipping industry in the world. Their technological edge has contributed largely to their superiority in this field. They have adapted to the changing needs of the global trade. Earlier, the ships were built for safe passage of cargo, but later, speed became vital. As the volume of global business grew, the cargo carrying capacities were also enhanced. But these ships were suited only for carrying the break-bulk cargo. With the advent of containerization, ships were redesigned to carry containers. Also, ports, roads, and other infrastructure were geared up to handle the containerized cargo. Nowadays, some ships are exclusively designed to carry specialized cargo, such as oil, mineral ores, fertilizers, and timber, etc. Keeping up with the pace of the changing shipping industry, the developed nations have built large cargo carrying capacities and have thus captured about 92 per cent of the industry share. On the other hand, the developing countries, which account for about 65 per cent of the tonnage loaded, own only about 8 per cent of world fleet. Ships are technically sophisticated high value assets (the largest hi-tech vessels can cost over US $150 million to build) and the operations of merchant ships generate an estimated annual income approaching US $500 billion in freight rates, representing about 5 per cent of the total global economy.

The following factors contribute to the disparity in the global shipping industry share:

(a) Non-availability of long term finances for developing countries to expand their fleet. It is estimated that developing countries would need US $15 to 20 billion to achieve 10 per cent of the total world dead weight tonnage (dwt).

(b) International financial institutions prefer to finance only infrastructural projects. They do not offer credit to buy ships.

(c) Commercial credits, being very expensive, are not suitable.

(d) For developing countries with scarce financial resources, building a fleet of ships in not the priority. They would rather invest in infrastructure, education, job-oriented industries that would create employment, etc. The result is that the shipping industry has to take a backseat, and due to this, the gap between the cargo carrying capacities of the developing and developed countries is forever widening.

However, the developing countries can procure export credit finance from ship builders and this presently is the most popular mode of financing. Such credit is normally 70 per cent of the total cost, the remaining 30 per cent has to be invested by the buyers. The prevalent rate of interest is minimum 8 per cent per annum. Also, such finances are available for buying only new ships. The purchase of second hand ships has to be self-financed. Thus, developing countries need more avenues for obtaining soft loans so that they can increase the size of their fleet and thereby increase their share in the global shipping industry.

SHIPPING INDUSTRY CHARACTERISTICS

The shipping industry has some unique characteristics, which it has acquired over a period of time. The most important of these are discussed below:

Open Registry System

This is a characteristic peculiar to the shipping industry. The open registry system allows the shipowners of developed countries to register their ships in specified less developed countries, such as Cyprus, Malta, and Liberia, etc., to the benefit of both, the shipowners as well as the host countries where the ships are registered. Shipowners can have their tax burden reduced because the host countries levy lesser tax on the profits earned as compared to the country of origin of the shipowners. Also, shipowners can avail local and cheap labour of the host country. The host country benefits on account of revenue it earns by levying a moderate tax. Also, this ensures employment for its citizens. A ship registered under the open registry system can cite the flag of the host country. When the owner, who lives in one nation chooses to register his/her vessel in a second nation and have the ship fly the second nation's flag, he is said to be flying a "Flag of Convenience" (FOC) (Wood and Murphy, 2002).

There are 32 countries, which are identified as "Flag of Convenience" by the International Transport Worker's Federation (ITF). They are:

Antigua and Barbuda	German International Ship Register (GIS)
Bahamas	Georgia
Barbados	Gibraltar (UK)
Belize	Honduras
Bermuda (UK)	Jamaica
Bolivia	Lebanon
Cambodia	Liberia
Cayman Islands	Malta
Comoros	Marshall Islands (USA)
Cyprus	Mauritius
Equatorial Guinea	Mongolia
French International Ship	Myanmar
Register (FIS)	Netherlands Antilles

North Korea	Sri Lanka
Panama	Tonga
Sao Tome and Príncipe	Vanuatu
St Vincent	

Some of the benefits offered by a host country, such as Cyprus to the shipowners are as follows:

- Nominal or no tax on profits from the operations of a Cypriot registered vessel or on dividends received from a shipowning company.
- Double tax treaty with 26 countries.
- No capital gains tax on sale or transfer of a Cypriot registered vessel or the shares of a ship owning company.
- No estate duty on the inheritance of shares in a shipowning company.
- No income tax on the emoluments of officers and crew.
- No stamp duty on ship mortgage deeds or other security documents.
- Extensive network of bilateral agreements through which Cypriot ships receive either national or favoured nation treatment in the ports of other countries.
- Competitive ship registration costs and annual tonnage taxes.
- Favourable tax regime for ship management and other offshore enterprises.
- Low set up and operating costs.
- Availability of excellent telecommunication channels and easy access by air and sea.
- Availability of highly qualified managerial and technical staff.

The listed incentives are designed to attract shipowners to register their ships in Cyprus. In 1982, Cyprus ranked 32nd on the list of leading maritime nations. It now ranks fourth with around 2,650 ships totalling over 5 million gross tonnage. The island's maritime policy aims to develop an integrated shipping infrastructure by granting appropriate incentives. Similar incentives are also provided by other host countries. In fact, the open registry system is quite old and has been in practice in many countries for several decades.

Exhibit 10.1   Issues before the Indian Shipping Industry

The domestic shipping industry plays an important role in the Indian economy. India has 12 major and 187 minor/intermediate ports along its coastline of around 7,517 kms. It is estimated that approximately 95 per cent of India's international trade by volume and 70 per cent by value is seaborne. Indian shipping companies collectively owned about 721 vessels

(Contd.)

Exhibit 10.1 (Contd.)

with 8.3 million Gross Registered Tonnage (GRT) or around 13.75 million deadweight tonnage in 2005–06. India holds the 15th position in the world by flag of registry forming about 1.5 per cent of the total world tonnage. As of December 2005, India had a fleet strength of 721 ships aggregating 8.24 m GRT, marking an addition of 52 vessels with 0.54 m GRT compared to 2004.

There are certain bottlenecks, which stand as roadblocks in the way of Indian shipping companies' competition with their foreign counterparts.

Insurance

Indian shipowners are statutorily required to insure their fleet for hull and machinery with Indian insurance companies. The premium rates (fixed by the tariff advisory committee) have traditionally been much higher than those prevailing internationally.

Depreciation

The rate of depreciation as applicable to the shipping industry is 25 per cent. By contrast, vehicles such as trucks and cars are permitted a 40 per cent rate of depreciation. There is a strong case for removing this inequity by raising the depreciation rate to 40 per cent, as it would help companies to build up reserves to finance fleet replacement and growth.

Manpower related issues

Indian shipping industry officers are some of the best-trained in the world and their demand has been increasing over the years. However, the Indian taxation regime for both companies and ship personnel imposes additional costs, making careers in Indian ships unattractive. Indian officers and crew employed on Indian flagged vessels (for a period of less than 183 days) are subject to income tax. No such taxation requirement is imposed on foreign flags, making employment on these flags more attractive. This means that Indian shipping companies are not able to retain quality manpower in India. These disadvantages deprive the Indian shipping industry of a level playing field in the global market.

Therefore, the government should look into these aspects to make the Indian shipping industry more competitive in terms of employment opportunity.

Source: CII Logistics & Freight News dated 22.2.2007

Registration of Ships

The host country requires shipowners who wish to register their ships to incorporate a company in the host country. The main types of vessel registration are 'provisional,' 'permanent,' and 'parallel'. Both cargo vessel and passenger ships can be registered. The conditions of registration of the ship depends on its age. The older the ship, the stricter are the conditions of registration. Every ship has to undergo a special inspection and only if it is found sea worthy, it can be registered, provided the shipowner fulfills all the other conditions under the local laws. Special inspections are carried out by the surveyors of the department of Merchant Shipping in the host country at the expense of the shipowners. This inspection may take place within six months prior to, on, or after the provisional registration of the vessel. But it must be done before the vessel is registered permanently. All recommendations arising out of this inspection have to be implemented prior to the permanent registration of the vessel.

Downside of Flag of Convenience (FOC) System

Though there are a number of stated benefits of FOC system, there are also a number of detracting issues, which have been addressed by the International Transport Worker's Federation (ITF), a UK based organization, which is campaigning against flags of convenience and substandard shipping.

The ITF is of the firm view that there should be a genuine link between the real owner of a vessel and the flag the vessel flies, in accordance with the UN Convention on the Law of the Sea (UNCLOS). There is no 'genuine link' in the case of FOC registries. According to ITF, some of these registers (countries) have poor safety and training standards and place no restriction on the nationality of the crew. Sometimes, because of language differences, seafarers are not able to communicate effectively with each other, putting the safety and the efficient operation of the ship at risk. In many cases, these flags are not even run from the country concerned. Once a ship is registered under a FOC, many shipowners then recruit the cheapest labour they can find, pay minimal wages, and cut costs by lowering the standards of living and working conditions for the crew.

Due to increased competition in the shipping market, each new FOC tries to be competitive by offering the lowest possible fee and the minimal regulations. Similarly, shipowners are forced to look for the cheapest and least regulated ways of running their vessels in order to compete, and FOCs seem to be the best solution around.

ITF has also pointed out the disparity in the wages of the personnel on the basis of nationality. For example, a vessel Captain from Norway earned four times more than a Captain from the Philippines. An able-bodied seaman from England earned 24 times more than an able-bodied seaman from Bangladesh, according to an ITF report.

The ITF has been campaigning for better working conditions of seafarers for the past 55 years, as a result of which they have a network of inspectors to check the suspect ships. They have often found that that seafarers are routinely exploited by FOC vessels by way of

- very low wages;
- poor on-board conditions;
- inadequate food and clean drinking water;
- long periods of work without proper rest leading to stress and fatigue.

They have also reported that many FOC vessels are very old and unsafe for undertaking sea voyages. Such vessels have higher casualty rates than non-FOC vessels, with more than 2000 deaths at sea every year.

Another reason to be concerned over FOC vessels is that they are susceptible to being used for illegal activities, such as smuggling in arms and narcotics, and even human trafficking. After the recent spate of terrorist attacks in many parts of the world, there is a need for more vigilance on FOC vessels.

Transchart

In the pre-liberalization era, government policies were driven by the need to conserve foreign exchange. As per the existing policy of the Indian government, all import contracts are to be finalized on FOB (Free on Board)/ FAS (Free Alongside Ship) basis in respect of government owned/controlled cargoes on behalf of Central Government Departments, State Government Departments, and Public Sector Undertakings concerned. In case of any departure there from, prior permission is required from the Chartering Wing of the Ministry of Shipping on a case-to-case basis. Shipping arrangements are centralized in the Chartering Wing of the Ministry of Shipping (popularly known by its telegraphic address Transchart in shipping circles). For exports, government departments/Public Sector Undertakings are free to finalize contracts on C&F/CIF basis without obtaining prior permission from Transchart. It was established in 1957 for liasoning between the department of transport and various other ministries.

In order to give the maximum benefit of government and public sector cargoes to Indian vessels, a Shipping Coordination Committee (SCC) was set up subsequent to a Cabinet Directive in December 1957. A Chartering Committee was set up under the SCC in 1960, which is known as Transchart to handle bulk cargoes, which move in chartered ships. The job of Transchart is to engage ships at internationally competitive rates. Transchart circulates cargo details to Indian shipowners as well as to shipbrokers who represent empanelled shipping lines. If the freight rates of Indian owned ships are not found competitive, foreign vessels are hired.

However, during the last few years it has been found that Transchart is often bypassed by various PSUs and government organizations and C&F

imports, and FOB exports have taken place without permission of Transchart. The reasons are:

1. Transchart has no mechanism to keep itself informed about breach of policy. Earlier, due to tighter control of RBI on foreign exchange, it was possible to find out the payments in foreign exchange made to foreign shipping lines for which authorization of Director General, Shipping was required. Ever since the rupee has been made freely convertible on the trade account, this mechanism has ceased to be effective.

2. The size of the fleet of the Shipping Corporation of India (SCI) has shrunk since 1985 onwards, and the ships chartered by SCI have not always been at competitive rates. Hence the economy expected from the function of Transchart could not be achieved.

3. Some PSUs complained that Transchart could not offer them lower freights than they were offered in composite C&F contracts for imports.

4. In May 1994, a committee of secretaries recommended some procedural modifications to increase the efficiency of Transchart.

Although, the quantum of cargo carried by Indian flagships has risen from 21.39 million tonnes in 2003 to 24.13 million tonnes in 2004, the percentage of cargo transported by domestic vessels has remained the same–36.23 million tonnes in 2003 and 36.31 million tonnes in 2004.

The Shippers' Association

The policies and practices relating to fixation of freight rates, provisions of services, etc., concern not only shippers, but also various governments. As a result, it is increasingly perceived by the shipper community that they should be actively involved in freight negotiations. Also, governments may feel that conferences should pay due regard to the policies of host countries and should protect the interest of the shipper community. But individually, a shipper has no bargaining strength against conferences. This is how the idea of a shipper's association took shape and today in many countries such associations have been established on a voluntary basis.

These Associations are modelled differently in each country, depending upon the attitude, policies, and the interest of the government. For example, in case of many European countries, very strong Shipper's Associations are formed on voluntary basis without the involvement of the government. These associations have enough bargaining power and are capable of protecting their own interests. In Australia, the government has given authority to its Shipper's Association through legislative measures to negotiate with the shipping conferences. The government's backing grants Australian shippers a lot of strength and they are in a position to leverage favourable terms from shipping conferences.

In the US, the government is actively involved in all matters related to the shipping conferences. The government has established a Federal Maritime Commission under the Shipping Act to monitor and regulate the activities of US and the foreign shipping lines. The primary objective and concern of the commission is to protect the interest of exporters and importers against the monopolistic practices of the shipping conferences. Federal Maritime Commission monitors activities of ocean common carriers, marine terminal operators, conferences, ports, and Ocean Transportation Intermediaries (OTIs) who operate in the U.S. foreign commerce to ensure they maintain just and reasonable practices. In USA, it is legally mandatory for every shipping conference to comply with the following regulations.

1. All tariffs to be kept open to public scrutiny.
2. All the agreements including conference agreements have to be approved by the Federal Maritime Commission. In case a shipper has any grievances, he can approach the commission and the commission can disapprove any freight rates or such matters, which are against the interest of the US trade.
3. Federal Maritime Commission expects complete transparency in all the policy matters and decisions of the conferences operating out of USA.

A regulatory body such as Federal Maritime Commission does every thing to ensure a fair deal to the shipper community and does not allow shipping conferences to dominate the shipping industry.

On the other hand, in India, no state regulatory body exists to keep the shipping conferences in check. Shippers are expected to guard their own interests against the monopoly of shipping conferences. Unfortunately, in India the shipper community is not united and has not been able to establish a cohesive force, which can negotiate with shipping conferences on equal terms. The Indian government, despite being a major partner in international trade, has done very little to encourage the formation of a Shipper's Association. Bodies like All India Shipper's Council and Standing Committee on Promotion of Exports by Sea (SCOPE) do exist, but they too lack the support of shippers and as a result can do little to protect the interest of shippers.

ROLE OF INTERMEDIARES IN SHIPPING INDUSTRY

Intermediaries have an important role to play in the shipping industry. They provide various vital services to shipping lines as well as shippers and are an important link between the two. Intermediaries exist because they improve the efficiency of marketing channels (Wood and Murphy, 2002). These days, intermediaries have global operations and because of their specialized infrastructure and superior contacts, many organizations outsource a variety of services to these intermediaries. The most important among these are discussed as follows:

Clearing and Forwarding (C&F) Agents

Clearing and Forwarding (C&F) agents are an important link between the exporter and various other agencies. Activities of a C&F agent are as follows:

1. A C&F agent works closely with the shipper right from the offer stage. He/She provides freight rates to various destinations and also informs the shipper about the most economical modes of transportation. The agent also provides the most cost effective routing advice for the destination.
2. Once the order is received by a shipper, the C&F agent books a ship keeping in mind the last date of shipment on the letter of credit (L/C).
3. As the despatch deadline approaches, the C&F agent estimates the transit time between the factory and the port of shipment as mentioned in the L/C. The C&F agent advises the despatch date from the factory to the shipper so that the cargo reaches the port in time. If the cargo reaches too early, it attracts demurrage charges. On the other hand, if the cargo reaches late, it may miss the ship, thereby causing delay. Such delays are inconvenient and expensive to both the importer as well as exporter.
4. Once the goods are despatched from the factory, the C&F agent intimates the shipping line regarding the expected arrival schedule of the goods at the port, along with the mode of inland transportation. He/she also completes the octroi formalities (wherever necessary) so that the export goods are not subjected to octroi duty.
5. The C&F agent then applies for and secures port permit so that the goods can enter the port premises. At the same time, the export declaration dispalying the names of shipper and consignee, value of the goods, and commodity classification number, etc. are prepared.
6. After this, the C&F agent prepares the B/L in compliance with the terms and conditions of the sale/L/C.
7. After this, the B/L is submitted to the shipping company and the cargo is loaded on board the vessel. The shipping company's representative examines the cargo for its condition & signs the B/L accordingly. In case of C&F and CIF contracts the ocean freight is also paid at this stage and the "Freight Prepaid" seal is obtained on the B/L.

8. Then the C&F agent collects all the documents such as bill of lading, custom's certified invoice, consular invoice, certificate of origin etc. from the respective authorities and sends them to the shipper for further negotiations of documents as per L/C conditions.

The activities described ensure that the shipper can effect shipments in time and in the most efficient manner possible, as facilitated through various services and advice provided by his/her C&F agents. The C&F agent plays a vital role in fulfilling the various delivery commitments made by the shipper to the importer abroad, thereby ensuring repeat orders and growth in business for the shipper.

Freight Forwarders

For the movement of international cargo, the exporter needs an expert with knowledge of various formalities and contacts with various agencies, such as shipping lines, port authorities, customs, warehouses, etc. The freight forwarder possesses such contacts and knowledge for the benefit of the shipper. A freight forwarder is a private service company licenced to support shippers and the movement of their goods. This specialist in international physical distribution acts as an agent for the exporter (shipper) in moving cargo to international destination (Nelson, 2000). Normally, the freight forwarder prepares the shipping documents on behalf of the shipper. With the advent of containerization and the new developments in the shipping industry, many freight forwarders now offer extended services such as transport operators for inland transportation as well as multi-modal inland and ocean bound transportation. These freight forwarders are as also known as non-vessel operating common carriers (NVOCCs) and are authorized to issue transport documents. Freight forwarders perform the following functions:

- Arrange transport services and prepare documentation.
- Advise shippers on the best and the most economical mode/s of transportation.
- As a multi-modal transport operator (MTO), the freight forwarder assumes the direct responsibility for the carriage of goods on door-to-door basis. Forwarders are liable also for those segments of transit where they themselves may not be operators.
- The forwarder provides other specialist services such as packing, container stuffing/destuffing, customs clearance, etc.

Third Party Logistics Operators

A Third Party Logistics (3PL) is a division of an asset-based company that provides transport, warehousing, forwarding, information technology, other logistics, or supply chain management related services. A 3PL is seen by the parent company (a shipping line) as a way to develop more business while using the services of the parent company.

A Logistics Service Provider (LSP), on the other hand, has no parent company to provide any transport or other service. The LSP can make use of various services available in the market, which suit the requirement of the customer.

Today, globalization has created a high-pressure international market place, where time is the most precious commodity. Customers demand a reliable and speedy door-to-door service. Although the C&F agent helps with the despatch of cargo, preparation of shipping documents, and the transportation arrangements of the cargo and works as a link between the exporters and various agencies, a shipper, at times, needs a more comprehensive service. The shipper requires an agency, which can lift the cargo from his/her doorstep and deliver the same at the customer's doorstep abroad. Logistics companies provide such efficient and reliable services to the shippers, the details of which are as follows.

Road Transportation

Logistics companies provide an effective road service network to deliver the goods in a cost effective manner. In the intensely competitive global marketplace, companies try to cut costs wherever possible. Cost-cutting could be achieved by way of slashing the inventory levels and reducing the order cycles. As a consequence, cost-cutting methods demand punctual deliveries from the logistics companies, which are ensured by an efficient road transportation service. The logistics companies schedule their trucking operations such that the time in transit for the cargo is minimized. High quality overland feeder services are an important activity for logistics companies. The door-to-door concept means that every inter-continental consignment inevitably involves road transport at some point of time.

Sea Freight

Logistics companies transport the cargo by sea. These companies enjoy exclusive agreements of cooperation with global shipping conglomerates and have a world wide dedicated network of offices and agents at major ports like New York, Hamburg, Rotterdam, Hong Kong, and Singapore, etc. which enables them to offer an effective integrated forwarding system in sea freight.

Air Freight Services

Logistics companies offer air freight services for cargo in order to expedite the arrival at overseas destinations. Fast deliveries are instrumental in improving performance and ensure that the exporter enjoys a competitive edge. Air freight companies have offices all over the world and an extensive network, which includes the well-trained and dedicated assistance of their experienced specialist staff. Companies have their space reserved on the world's leading cargo and commercial airlines and provide maximum flight flexibility as per the requirements of the customer. They can also arrange for chartered cargo planes. Logistics companies offer airport-to-airport and door-to-door service options and can arrange for time sensitive, full load, and out of gauge cargo. They also provide expertise in custom's procedures and formalities at every stage.

Project Forwarding

Project exporters have to move large quantities of material and machines to their project sites in all parts of the world, including remote places. This is an activity in which logistics companies often specialize. They employ qualified and experienced staff and approved sub-contractors to provide complex transport services. Quite often their services are outside the conventional forwarding field. The 3PL companies have special material handling equipment, engineers, technicians, and transport equipment to handle such complex jobs. Many a time they undertake the dismantling of a complete factory in one country and its reinstallation–piece by piece–in another country.

Oil and Energy

Many logistics companies nowdays provide dedicated services to the oil industry. These services include the supply of equipment and global logistics management apart from value added services like procurement, support, and material base management. They also act as shipping agents for freighters, tankers, supply vessels, and drilling rigs.

Warehousing and Distribution

3PL companies also offer warehousing and allied services to their clients. Such services are customized and containerized freight stations, warehouse management technology, depot management, and associated transportation. They provide distribution centres located at strategic points across the country, which serve as nodal centres connecting the client's manufacturing facilities and depots. State of the art technology, aided by modern material handling systems and real time information processors help minimize inventory costs and maximize profits.

Due to escalating costs, companies around the world are reorganizing themselves and in the process they sub-contract non-core activities, including warehousing and distribution to a third party specialist. Logistics companies are well equipped to offer such specialized services. These companies have fully computerized dedicated distribution centres all over the world, manned by professionals trained in all relevant areas ranging from picking to packing to light assembly.

The following warehousing and inventory services are provided by logistics companies:

- Bar coding and labelling
- Bonded warehouse facilities (for duty deferment)
- Inventory control
- Accounting
- Storage
- Pick and pack
- Documentation
- Light manufacturing
  - Assembly
  - Customizing orders
  - Local sourcing
- Order processing
- Reverse logistics
  - Return and repairs

The listed services provided by logistics companies reduce the burden of shippers to a great extent. Logistics companies provide these services at a price which easily works out to be far more economical for the shippers, compared to what it would be were they handling all these activities themselves.

In addition to the C&F agents and logistics companies, freight brokers and shipping agents at every port work on behalf of shipping companies as well as shippers to book ship space and provide various services. With the advent of the internet and e-commerce, the role of freight brokers and shipping agents is fast-diminishing; technology is making middlemen redundant.

When a shipper engages the services of a logistics company and hands over his/her cargo to it, the shipper is given a secure user ID, which gives him the freedom to track and query shipment data by purchase order number, item number, container number, or by containers sailing or arriving within the specified date range or calendar month. This data can be easily printed directly from the website or downloaded in the user's personal desktop as text files. Such a logistics information system gives total global visibility to the users for their cargo anywhere in the world.

Customs Clearance Services

Countries all over the world wish to prohibit the entry of undesirable cargo into their territories. Also, they wish to maximize their revenues by way of import duties in order to support their economies. Under the WTO, these issues have become sensitive and advice of experts is continuously sought both by governments as well as shippers. As a result, importers and exporters are becoming increasingly accountable for the accuracy and correctness of their customs declarations. A critical part of the international distribution process is the skilled and experienced customs clearance of shipment across international border barriers.

Logistics companies are experienced in customs compliance, duty and tax structures, and procedures and documentation. Sometimes they even have online links to customs agencies, which enables them to expedite the movement of shipment all over the world.

Information Technology

These days, logistics companies have their own in-house logistics information system, to provide accurate and timely information. The shippers expect cost effective and profitable business solutions, which are delivered by the logistics companies through their global networks and supplemented by the use of the internet. Shippers can track their cargo anywhere in the world, enabling them to assess the arrival time of their cargo. Thus, they can accordingly plan their inventories. This information system supports ocean transportation, trucking operations, and airfreights. As such all the modes of transportation are adequately covered.

LATEST TRENDS IN LOGISTICS OPERATIONS

The various operations involved in the logistics process are the same, globally. However, different countries wield different degrees of sophistication in Supply Chain Management. For example, in Europe or in the US, the logistics companies provide "one stop solutions" for the supply chains of their clients. On the other hand, in Asian countries the logistics companies specialize only in certain areas, such as multimodal services, warehousing operations, inbound sourcing, etc. Some 3PL providers specialize in serving specific industries such as automobile, pharmaceuticals, agro-products, processed foods, etc. Each of these sectors is unique and needs very specialized transportation, material handling, and warehousing facilities.

Figure 10.1 illustrates the entire supply chain in international business.

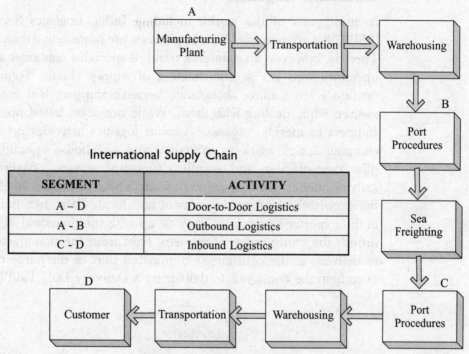

International Supply Chain

SEGMENT	ACTIVITY
A – D	Door-to-Door Logistics
A - B	Outbound Logistics
C - D	Inbound Logistics

Fig. 10.1   International Supply Chain

Door-to-door Logistics

Door-to-door logistics covers the entire chain of activities related to logistics right from the manufacturer's doorstep to the doorstep of the customer. Some of the prominent 3PL providers who operate on worldwide basis and provide door-to-door services through the chain of their offices, warehouses, vehicles, and trained personnel are Maersk Logistics, Schenker, APL Logistics, P & O Nedlloyds, Panalpina, etc.

Many renowned automobile companies like General Motors (GM), Ford, and BMW etc. have located their manufacturing plants in Southern Thailand near Port Laem Chabang. Schenker Logistics has established a specialized warehouse near Port Laem Chabang, and offers services to a number of European vendors of these automobile companies. Suppliers from Europe ship Full Container Load (FCL) cargo from European consolidation centres to Laem Chabang; Schenker clears the containers and arranges delivery to its own warehouse where cargo is quality-checked, sorted, bar-coded, labelled, and then stored in a racking system. As and when GM or Ford or BMW requires any one of the hundreds of components, Schenker arranges to send it to the respective factories on Just-In-Time (JIT) basis.

Outbound Logistics

In most parts of the world, including India, Logistics Service Providers (LSPs), that are non-asset based operators, are more active than 3PL providers. There is, however, an emerging trend of specialist container and warehouse operators who act as coordinators of supply chains (Figure 10.2). Such operators are gaining acceptance because shippers feel more secure and assured while dealing with them. While non-asset based operators seem to shippers to merely 'organize' various logistics activities on a global basis, charging a high mark-up, container and warehouse operators, conversely, offer cost-effective and seamless logistical services, covering all export activities under one management team. These operators, in effect, take over the exporter's shipping department and locate their own trained personnel at the exporter's premises. They tie-up with multinational 3PL providers to furnish the entire range of services, right from the manufacturing plant up to delivery at the consignee's nominated port of discharge overseas. They even help the consignor to deliver on a Delivery Duty Paid (DDP) basis.

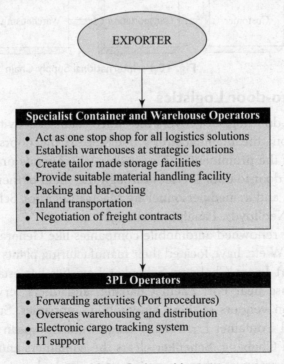

Fig. 10.2 Outbound Logistics

Such arrangements suit the large manufacturers of fabricated/semi-fabricated products, chemicals, etc., who have unique outbound warehousing needs and would like to keep the stocks of finished goods ready for despatch at short notice.

Secondary Distribution (Inbound Logistics)

Inbound logistics (Figure 10.3) is one of the fastest growing segments of Supply Chain Management (SCM). The growth is largely due to very specialized personal services the LSP is expected to offer, and which are rare to find.

A secondary distribution system aims at feeding assembly lines and retail outlets on JIT basis. It includes warehousing, picking, subassembly, and delivery to manufacturing plants. A secondary distributor can supply not just big batch orders, but also the individual components in small batch orders. The larger LSPs are not interested in undertaking such jobs and often subcontract the secondary distribution to small players. Information technology (IT) plays an important role in secondary distribution. IT tools are available to track the cargo right from the time a shipment is booked till it is delivered to the customer. It is also possible to access the current shipment data as well as historical data. Secondary distribution is gaining popularity because there are many customers who do not require the entire range of Supply Chain Management (SCM) services. They prefer separate agencies to handle deep-sea traffic and secondary distribution.

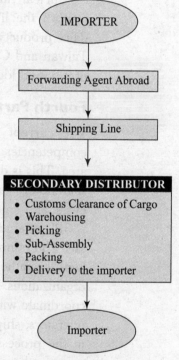

Fig. 10.3 Inbound Logistics

Suppliers often complain that they do not get personalized services from large companies, which provide all solutions under one roof. This system results in dealing with different persons within the organization for solving a typical problem. It amounts to duplication of communication and makes it virtually impossible to pin the responsibility specifically upon someone. A secondary distributor on the other hand is more accessible and can provide immediate solution to the problems faced by the shipper. Typically, a secondary distributor providing logistics support should not only have technical know-how, but should also possess the following skills:

- Good contacts and working relationship with various agencies, such as customs, central excise, port authorities, shipping lines, etc.
- Flexible operations and adaptability to the changing requirements of the customers.
- In-depth understanding of the local laws and working culture.
- Experienced and dedicated staff retained over a period of time, who have established a good rapport with customers and understand their specific needs.
- Ability to work under adverse conditions, inadequate infrastructure, and unclear rules and regulations.

With the liberalization of the Indian economy, fruits, vegetables and dairy products from Australia and New Zealand and electronic goods from Taiwan and China are entering the domestic market, mostly with the help of inbound logistics support.

Fourth Party Logistics Operators

The current trend is that organizations want to focus on their core competencies and tend to outsource activities, which are not in their focus area. This is due to the need to keep the organization lean and fit, increase shareholder value, stay ahead of competition, increase the speed of inventory cycle, and enjoy better return on investment.

3PL operations have enjoyed limited support from the organizations so far. Their limited success can be attributed to their priority to manage logistics, rather than to the supply chains for their clients, which are shipping organizations. As a part of their logistics management services, 3PL companies coordinate with various components of the logistics chain, such as transport operators, shipping lines, warehouse operators, freight forwarders, etc. but in the process they tend to ignore the real need of the customer, i.e. to manage the customer's supply chains in parts of the world. Multinationals like General Motors, Toyota, Samsung, Siemens, Procter and Gamble, Wal Mart, etc., are sourcing their requirements from all over the world. They wish to exercise a tighter control on their entire supply chains in order to function smoothly. Such MNCs do not wish to be bothered about chasing individual shipments based on container number or B/L given to them by their 3PL operator. They would prefer an online, real time information based on their purchase order numbers to ensure that their orders are executed in time, every time.

This is where Fourth Party Logistics (LIPL) operators step in and provide a complete Business Process Outsourcing (BPO) solution to their customers.

IT plays a significant role in 4PL operations. The important elements of 4PL operations are people, process, and technology.

For example, let us say a US-based retail chain is sourcing its products from 500 different suppliers from China, India, Japan, Malaysia, Sri Lanka, Thailand, etc. The competitiveness of this retailer is based on the efficiency of its supply chain. Its experience with a 3PL operator has not yielded the desired results in terms of in-time deliveries and cost competitive logistics solutions. It is perceived that the 3PL operator was too focused on individual shipments rather than on effectively coordinating with 500 suppliers spread throughout Asia. Hence, the clients themselves kept a track of incoming inventories by continuously following up with all the suppliers as well as following up with the 3PL operator. Communication and transmission of documents through conventional emails and fax messages was also proving to be tedious and time consuming.

This is where the idea of engaging the services of a 4PL enters. The solutions provided by 4PL are based on business process re-engineering and technology with a human interface provided in terms of strategically placed personnel to have a seamless integration of process, people, and technology. The focus is to manage supplies from diverse locations and to support the client by providing complete solutions, rather than giving piece meal alternatives to the problems on a case-to-case basis (Fig. 10.4).

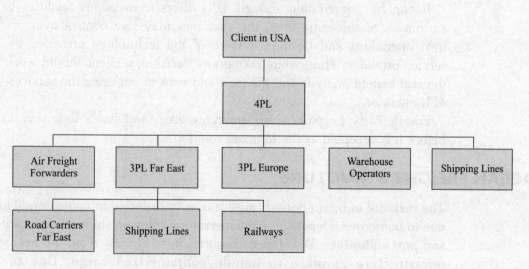

Fig. 10.4 Fourth Party Logistics

A Fourth Party Logistics operator typically, offers to provide the following services:

1. Study the entire operation of a retail chain in terms of the location of the retail outlets, sources of its supplies, and the 3PL services it is availing at present.

2. Redesign the entire process, create benchmarks for the performance of every link in the supply chain, monitor the performance, and take corrective action where necessary.

3. Develop an online solution for the client right from tracking the inventories in retailer's warehouses in the US, automatically generating purchase orders if the inventory falls below a certain defined level, and coordinating with 3PL operators or transport companies to ship the material in time from the suppliers. This online solution will have the facility of operations in different languages for the convenience of overseas suppliers and service providers

4. Provide EDI based data transmission and communication tools to give a common platform for various participants in the supply chain.

5. Place its representatives in different countries to coordinate with suppliers as well as service providers.

As a result of a 4PL arrangement, the retail chain now has a complete visibility of its supply chain. It has to co-ordinate only with one agency, i.e. the 4PL operator for all its logistics needs.

It can be argued that though 4PL offers tremendous facilities to its customers, at the same time, the customer may lose control over his/her own operations and become a slave of the technology provided by the service provider. Thus, while taking any decision, a client should work out the cost benefit analysis and the pros and cons of engaging the services of a 4PL operator.

Fourth Party Logistics is an emerging area; and has a long way to go before it is accepted as the ultimate solution.

OCEAN FREIGHT STRUCTURE

The majority of ocean bound cargo is now transported in containers. This is due to numerous advantages cointanerization offers to shippers, shipowners, and port authorities. Developed countries have already fixed the necessary infrastructure in place to handle containerized cargo. Due to the overwhelming wave of globalization and the establishment of WTO, the volume of world trade is expected to increase manifold in the years to come. In anticipation of a boom, major ports are now gearing up to handle cargo in excess of 1 million Twenty-feet Equivalent Units (TEU), annually.

Even developing countries like China, India, The Philippines, and Indonesia, etc., are investing heavily in the enhancement of the cargo-handling capacities of their existing ports. They are also adding new ports equipped to handle larger volumes of containerized cargo.

In light of these developments, it will be prudent to discuss only the freight structure of the containerized cargo.

If we consider the voyage undertaken by the containerized cargo, we find that it is carried from the point of origin to its destination abroad by different modes of transportation. For example, cargo is packed in containers in a factory premises, which could be hundreds of miles away from the nearest port. This distance is covered by the container on a truck or on a railway wagon. In India, the preferred mode of transportation is truck. This, despite the poor road conditions, multiple octroi and other checkpoints, cumbersome documentation, and the dilapidated condition of the trucks. The reason is that in spite of all these handicaps the transit time on road is less than on rail. Also, road transporters can guarantee the delivery of the cargo at the desired port; however, in railways offer no such guarantee. In addition, the cargo on rail is subjected to multiple handling at different locations. This is due to the fact that in India, though there is an excellent railway network, there are no dedicated railway tracks for cargo movement; the freight trains have to share tracks with passenger trains and in the process they do not get due priority.

Thus, irrespective of the distance, shippers prefer to send their cargo to the ports by road. This may sound contrary to the logic that longer the distance to be covered lower is the rail freight. But international trade is a business of commitments and if one has to honour their commitments to overseas buyers, he/she cannot afford to be late with their despatches. Hence, road haulage remains the first choice of shippers in India, because it offers better reliability as compared to rail haulage.

Freight Structure

A Multi-modal Transport Operator (MTO) has to consider both inland freight as well as ocean freight while calculating the tariffs of the containerized cargo. Ideally, an MTO should be in a position to offer the services of an entire transport chain on both land and on sea. In USA, a shipping company either owns or leases the trucking services, and the inland freight charges are governed by the Interstate Commerce Commission.

However in India, the situation is very different. The shipper arranges for the road transport to carry the cargo from the point of origin to the port. In some cases, the shipper sends the cargo in break-bulk condition by truck to

ICD, where it is stuffed in the containers under the supervision of Central Excise and Customs Department. This cargo is further sent by Container Corporation of India Ltd. CONCOR to the port, either by rail or road transport.

It would therefore be worthwhile to look into both inland as well as ocean freight tariff structures.

Inland Freight Tariffs

The containers are mostly carried to the port by trucks. The truck operators have their own criteria for fixing tariffs, which largely depend upon the distance to be covered, and/or the weight of the cargo to be carried in a 20-feet or 40-feet container. Other factors which are considered while fixing the tariff are road conditions, the duration of the journey, the number of state border crossings and octroi check posts to be crossed, the nature of cargo, special fixtures, if required to hold the cargo, etc. The Motor Vehicles Act of India governs the rules and regulation of trucking operations. The Indian road transport industry is largely in the hands of private truck operators who do not have different norms for domestic and export cargo. Their practices and tariffs are generally decided by Truck Owner's Unions. The mechanism of determination of tariffs may also include the cost of truck, depreciation charges, maintenance charges, fuel cost, staff salary, overheads, etc. The shippers normally negotiate the freight with the truck operators and arrive at mutually satisfactory tariffs.

Basic Principles of Ocean Tariffs

Ocean freight is the major component of the tariff of sea borne containerized cargo charged by an MTO. Basically, ocean freight is the price charged by a shipping line for the transport service rendered to the shipper.

The criteria to determine the freight of a liner ship and a tramp ship are different. This is due to the difference in their inherent nature of operation. The tramps do not follow any schedule and undertake a voyage exclusively for a shipper who would pay the tramp operator maximum freight.

On the other hand, liners have a fixed schedule of arrival and departure and they do not wait for cargo or for the highest bidder. They carry whatever cargo is available at the time of sailing. Since maximum cargo is carried by the organized sector of the industry, i.e., liner ships, we will confine our discussions mainly to the freight structure of liner operations. Most of the liner operators are conference members and are not forthcoming with their formula of arriving at liner ocean freight. However, the following components are broadly considered while computing tariffs:

Organization Overheads

These remain fixed and include
1. Depreciation,
2. Interest on borrowed capital,
3. Administrative costs.

Voyage or Operation Overheads

These remain fixed for a liner vessel but are variable for a tramp ship. They include the following:
1. Fuel,
2. Wages for the staff and crew members,
3. Insurance premium,
4. Canal toll charges,
5. Port charges.

Voyage Variable Costs

These depend upon the nature of the cargo and mainly include cargo handling charges. It constitutes a large component of the tariff.

It is interesting to note here that the larger component of cost for a liner ship is fixed, whereas for a tramp ship, the larger component is variable. Also the components mentioned above give us an idea about various costs involved in a ship operation.

Ocean tariffs are normally based on the following three basic principles:

The Cost of Service Principle

A liner operator offers continuous and regular service and in return expects to recover the above-mentioned cost components and even earn a profit. This sets the lower limit of the freight below which the operator does not wish revenues to fall. In short, according to this principle,

Ocean freight = Organizational overheads + Voyage or operational overheads
+ Voyage variable costs + Profit.

Value of Service Principle

In many cases, the shipper is willing to pay a higher freight rate for the quality of service provided by the liner ship. This quality could be in terms of lesser transit time, i.e., faster deliveries at the destination, better storage and handling facilities on the ship, etc. For such services, the shipping line charges a premium, but this premium should not be so high that the goods become uncompetitive in the overseas market. As such, the value of service principle sets the higher limit of ocean freight.

What the Traffic can Bear

Every cargo has a defined capacity to bear freight charges. If the freight exceeds this limit, the shipper will not be able to sell his/her products in the overseas markets. In such a case, the shipping line charges higher freight rate on high value cargo and a lower freight rate on low value cargo, e.g., grains are charged a freight rate below cost, whereas expensive carpets can be charged premium freight rates. It means that carpets would subsidize grains.

Other Important Factors

The three principles as mentioned above only provide the thumb rules for deciding the ocean freight rates. In reality, computing the ocean freight rates is a complex process. The following factors are normally considered while deciding the freight rates:

- Character of cargo
- Volume of cargo
- Availability of cargo
- Susceptibility of damage
- Susceptibility to pilferage
- Value of goods
- Packing
- Storage
- Relationship of weight and measurement (whether heavy or light cargo)
- Heavy lifts
- Extra lengths
- Competition with goods coming from other sources/countries
- Cargo via competitive ports
- Competition from other carriers
- Direct cost of operation
- Distance
- Cost of handling
- Special deliveries
- Fixed charges
- Insurance
- Port facilities
- Port charges and dues
- Canal tolls
- Port location
- Possibility of securing return cargoes

In addition to the factors listed above, the shipping lines are concerned with the following questions:

1. What is the rate at which the shipper would be attracted to ship a particular commodity, and
2. Can the shipping line afford to carry the cargo at this rate?

The shipping lines and shippers are dependent on each other and hence, it is in their mutual interest to arrive at a freight rate, which is conducive to mutual growth.

The Government of India has established a Freight Investigation Bureau as a part of the Directorate General of Shipping with branches at major ports in India. The shippers who have any freight related problems are advised to contact the freight investigation bureau; which then takes up genuine grievances with the concerned shipping conference to sort out the matter.

SUMMARY

Historically, the shipping industry has been dominated by developed countries. Some of the practices in this industry, such as open registry system and the shipping conference system are age-old. However, such practices are now being opposed all over the world. Organizations like the International Transport Worker's Federation (ITF) are trying to change this situation so that developing countries can get a fair deal and exploitation of labour can be stopped. Similarly, Shipper's Associations and other agencies are trying to contain the monopoly of shipping conferences. The major change witnessed in this industry in the recent past has been the changing role of intermediaries between shippers and shipping lines. Instead of fragmented services, such as, transportation, port procedures, warehousing, customs clearance, and documentation offered by different agencies, today there is a trend towards consolidation of services under one roof. Also, shippers have started outsourcing various services to logistics service providers. This has given rise to the popularity of 3PL & 4PL LSPs. 3PL companies are being considered as one-stop shops for logistics services. 4PL operations, which provide people, process, and technology driven logistics solutions to the shippers are a step ahead and provide more comprehensive services than 3PL operators. The need to be more competitive is the prime reason for this evolution.

The shipping industry facilitates the flow of goods from one country to another. Freight rates are determined by various factors, one of the most important among which is the ability of a commodity to bear freight. Some commodities can absorb higher freights without losing their share in overseas markets. Other commodities are very freight sensitive. Hence shipping lines have to consider all these factors while fixing ocean freight rates for various commodities.

CONCEPT REVIEW QUESTIONS

1. Explain the reasons for the dominance of developed countries in the global shipping industry. What measures should the developing countries adopt to overcome their weaknesses?
2. Open registry system is a necessary evil for the shipping industry. Do you agree with this statement? Give reasons in support of your answer.
3. Write short notes on
   (a) Open registry system
   (b) Shippers association
   (c) Transchart
4. Explain the differences between the functions of a C&F agent and a freight forwarder.
5. What is third party logistics (3PL)? What are the various services provided by the 3PL service providers?
6. Discuss the latest trends in logistics operations.
7. In what ways are the third party logistics operations different from fourth party logistics operations?
8. Write a short essay on the role of intermediaries in shipping industry.
9. What are the various principles on which ocean freight is based?
10. Explain the various costs incurred by an ocean carrier.
11. Write short notes on the following principles on which ocean tariff is based.
    (a) The cost of service principle
    (b) The value of service principle

OBJECTIVE QUESTIONS

Choose the correct option in the following questions.

1. Which of the following is a reason for the dominance of developed countries in shipping industry?
   (a) Availability of credit to developed countries from commercial banks.
   (b) Historical maritime superiority

(c) Non-availability of long-term finances for developing countries to expand their fleet.

(d) Lack of ship building expertise in developing countries.

2. Which of the following is NOT a benefit of the open registry system?
    (a) Employment generation in developing countries
    (b) Low taxation for shipowners in host countries
    (c) Transfer of technology from developed to developing countries
    (d) Availability of highly qualified managerial and technical staff

3. Which of the following is the reason for the failure of the Transchart system?
    (a) Adequate number of ships available with Indian Shipping Lines
    (b) Disinvestment process initiated by the government
    (c) Lack of support from foreign shipping lines
    (d) Lack of support from Public Sector Undertakings (PSUs)

4. Which of the following services are NOT offered by a C&F agent to shippers?
    (a) Coordination with shippers and shipping lines
    (b) Storing the cargo in his own warehouse at the port
    (c) Securing port permit for the cargo
    (d) Completing the customs formalities at the port on behalf of shippers

5. Which of the following is NOT a voyage or operational overhead?
    (a) Port charges
    (b) Canal toll charges
    (c) Fuel charges
    (d) Interest on borrowed capital

State whether the following statements are True or False.

6. Under the open registry system, shipowners register their ship in their home country as well as the Flag of Convenience country.

7. International Transport Workers Federation opposes the open registry system because of the disparity in wages on the basis of nationality.

8. The Shipper's Associations have successfully countered the monopoly of shipping conferences.

9. Fourth party logistics companies provide process-based solutions to the shippers.

10. The cost of service principle sets the higher limit of ocean freight.

EXERCISES

1. Visit the nearest office of the Shipping Corporation of India and gather information about their existing capacities and future plans.

2. Visit the website of Federal Maritime Commission USA and find out how they protect the interests of shippers in their country.
3. List the names, addresses, and websites of important Third Party Logistics Operators and Fourth Party Logistics Operators in India.
4. Find out the important shipping industry events such as exhibitions, seminars and conferences in India and prepare a calendar of the same. The information can be gathered from news papers and websites.

SELECT REFERENCES

Nelson Carl A., 2000, *Import Export—How to get started in International Trade*, Third edition, McGraw Hill Publication, New York.

Wood, Donald F., Anthony Barone, Paul Murphy and Daniel Wardlow, 2002, *International Logistics*, Second edition, AMACOM Publication.

www.flagsofconvenience.com last accessed on 22nd May 2007.

www.fmc.gov last accessed on 29th May 2007.

www.itfglobal.org last accessed on 22nd May 2007.

www.marisec.org last accessed on 20th May 2007.

www.shipping.nic.in last accessed on 25th May 2007.

FREIGHT RATE TRICKS

Case Study

Shippers know that the ocean freight rates are stable on most of the trade routes. However, those shippers who have time, expertise, and patience can still save shipping costs by seeking price and service quotations from a number of freight operators before selecting the most appropriate offer.

In this exercise, quotations were requested by e-mail in the name of a company called Kitchen Home, for a shipment of three 20 ft. dry cargo containers from Coventry, UK to New Delhi, India. The contents were described as "Kitchen Appliances packed in cartons on pallets."

The freight operators were asked to quote the UK haulage, terminal, and documentation costs, and the ocean freight and Indian inland transportation charges. The cost of marine insurance and customs clearance (charges and duties/taxes in India) were asked to be excluded. Also, the following information was requested:

1. Sailing frequency from UK
2. UK loading port
3. Total approximate transit time
4. Whether shipment would be direct to an Indian port or would involve trans-shipment over a Middle East Gulf port
5. Validity period of the offer

Around 20 quotation requests were e-mailed, mostly to serving UK-India Trade, but also to a few forwarders and NVOCCs. Replies were received from 14 freight operators. The following facts emerged from the quotations received:

(a) Although all the respondents gave segment wise rate/cost, none of them gave overall cost from collection in Coventry to delivery in New Delhi.

(b) Various charges in almost all quotations were quoted in three currencies:

   (i) UK charges, involving collection, inland transportation, terminal handling, and documentation were quoted in Pound Sterling.

   (ii) Ocean freight and Bunkerage Adjustment Factor (BAF) was quoted in US dollars.

   (iii) Inland transportation charges within India were quoted in Indian rupees.

It was therefore necessary to calculate final cost of shipment by first converting the currency in Pounds Sterling and US Dollars to Indian Rupees and then adding them to arrive at the total freight per container.

It is interesting to note the great variations in the total freight amount quoted by each shipping line.

The lowest quotation was US $4907 for three containers @ $1636 per container from Allied Shipping. The highest was $6229 for three containers @2076 per container from Aqua Charter Line. Hence, the highest quotation was 26.9 per cent higher than the lowest. Interestingly, both operators quoted the same ocean freight.

Also, different operators quoted different Bunker Adjustment Factor, which varied from $70 to $80 per container. However, it was clarified that BAF would be charged as applicable at the time of shipment.

Overall, it was apparent that the fastest service was not the cheapest. For example, Northern Container Line port-to-port transit time of 19 days, which was the fastest, quoted $1839 per container, which was on a higher side. On the other hand, Allied Shipping with a lowest offer of US $1636 per container quoted a total transit time of 33 days from Coventry to New Delhi.

Only two operators, namely Northern Container Liner and Daniel Thorpe indicated involvement of a transshipment over a port in the Middle East.

Most of the operators advised only port-to-port transit time, with two days added for haulage in UK and three days for transit from Nhava Sheva Port to ICD, Tughlakabad near Delhi.

The major issue of concern was the validity of offers received. At the enquiry stage it was clearly mentioned that the shipment was likely to take place in February 2007. In spite of this, a number of quotations had validity only upto 31 December 2006 with a clause that after this date the rates would be reviewed. Others had quoted validity till end of February or even end of March, which was just adequate to cover the anticipated shipment period.

A shipper has to submit an export quotation at least two to three months in advance and can do so only on the basis of firm shipping costs. Ocean carriers, on the other hand, might well argue that their costs are liable to change at any time. But so are the costs of other inputs, which an exporter is expected to absorb. The question is that if the exporter can absorb the increased cost of his/her inputs, then why cannot the liner industry absorb theirs.

The time has surely come when it is expected from the liner industry to guarantee prices beyond limited periods. As shippers often state, perhaps the liner industry has not yet noticed, but we are now living in the 21st century.

Questions

1. Prepare a quotation covering a voyage between Coventry in UK to ICD Tughlakabad near New Delhi via Nhava Sheva in Mumbai. The contents are 'kitchen appliances' as mentioned in the case. The quotation should be shipper-friendly and without various lacunae as mentioned in the case.
2. What are the reasons, in your opinion, for the different ways in which, ocean carriers submit quotations to the shipper?
3. List and discuss different variations in quotations received by M/s Kitchen Home.
4. List down various queries, which a shipper must incorporate in his/her request for quotation to the ocean carriers, in order to get an accurate offer that meets all requirements.

11 World Shipping

Learning Objectives

After studying this chapter, you will be able to understand
- the importance of ports in maritime industry
- the working of shipping conferences
- the freight practices of shipping conferences
- the difference between liner and tramp vessels
- identify and describe the various types of ocean cargo carrying vessels

The shipping industry is an important part of the international transportation system. More than 95 per cent of the world trade is conducted through sea. Therefore, the knowledge of this industry is important for all those who are connected to international trade, directly or indirectly.

The stakeholders in this industry are ports, shipping lines, shippers, intermediaries, various types of service providers, banks, insurance companies, etc. In this chapter, the focus of our discussions would be on shipping lines and ports, because they are the most vital stakeholders in this industry. There have been numerous changes in the shipping industry over the last few decades. Historically, ports have played a dominant role in the shipping industry because ports make up the infrastructure available for shipping lines to conduct their business. Most ports were government owned traditionally, and used to enjoy monopoly status. Shipping lines had to comply with very tough rules and regulations imposed upon them by port authorities. But, the scenario has changed radically today. Privately-owned ports are now a reality and there is open competition among them to attract shipping lines. Nations are pumping in billions of dollars to create modern infrastructure at ports so that the turnaround time of the ships is minimal. This is to attract the shipping lines which own mega ships to avail the state-of-the-art port facilities. The latest trend is that of large port operators like DP World of Dubai to operate the ports in different parts of the world. DP

World is one of the largest terminal operators globally and has the widest network of 51 terminals spanning 24 countries and five continents (Wood and Murphy, 2002). They have a global capacity of more than 50 million TEUs and a dedicated, experienced, and professional team of around 34,000.

It is important for the students as well as practicing managers in the logistics industry to understand the evolution of the shipping industry from its early days to the modern times.

OVERVIEW OF PORTS

In the era of globalization the importance of shipping industry in world economy has increased manifold. Since 1995, when the World Trade Organization was born, tariff and non-tariff barriers across the world have been brought down significantly. This has resulted in a quantum leap in the volume of world trade. More and more raw materials, consumables, capital goods, consumer goods, luxury items, etc. are being traded on global basis. Also, foreign direct investment (FDI) from developed countries to developing countries has increased significantly; resulting in the creation of new manufacturing units in automobile, electronics, and consumer goods sectors in the emerging markets in developing countries. The increased volumes of imports and exports is applying a tremendous pressure on the ports as well as other infrastructure, such as airports, roads, railways, telecommunication services, warehousing facilities, etc., around the world. To meet these new challenges, new ports are being constructed with modern infrastructure to handle containerized as well as break-bulk cargo.

Table 11.1 World Exports of Merchandise and Commercial Services, 2000–2005

(Million Dollars and Percentage)

	Value	Annual Percentage Change				
	2005	2000–05	2002	2003	2004	2005
Merchandise	10159	10	5	17	22	13
Agriculture	852	9	6	16	15	8
Fuels & Mining Products	1748	15	–1	24	33	36
Manufactures	7312	9	5	16	21	10
Commercial Services	2415	10	7	14	20	10
Transportation	570	10	5	13	24	12
Travel	685	7	5	10	18	8
Other Commercial Services	1160	12	10	18	18	11

Source: WTO

Although the term *port* is often used generically, ports can be classified as sea, lake, river, and canal, depending on the type of business that is transacted there.

As the sea ports are more commonly used for international trade, all the discussions in this chapter would pertain to sea ports only.

Port Operations

The sequences of various operations right from arrival of a ship at a port till its departure are as follows:

1. Shipping line submits its Import General Manifest (IGM), which is a document giving the description of the ship's cargo to the customs authorities at the port of destination of the cargo. IGM is submitted in advance of the arrival of the ship.
2. The ship announces its arrival to the port authorities.
3. Port authorities request the ship to wait on high seas until a vacant berth is available at the port to receive it.
4. A pilot vessel is sent by the port authorities to high seas to escort the visiting ship to the vacant berth.
5. Shipping or cargo agents complete the paper formalities for the unloading of import cargo and loading of export cargo.
6. Unloading and loading operations begin. Import cargo is unloaded and stacked at the designated area in the port premises for custom's examination and further formalities.
7. Export cargo, which is customs cleared, is loaded on board the ship.
8. After the port operations are complete, the pilot vessel escorts the ship out of the port back on the high seas.

SHIPPING CONFERENCES

A shipping conference is a group of ocean freight carriers that voluntarily come together for the purpose of limiting and regulating competition among themselves. Variously called liner conferences, shipping conferences, and ocean shipping conferences, they are formal agreements between liner shipping lines on a route, always setting (possibly discriminatory) prices, and sometimes pooling profits or revenues, managing capacity, allocating routes, and offering loyalty discounts (Loninson, 2006). There are two types of shipping conferences, 'closed type' and 'open type'. Closed conferences reserve the right to refuse membership to a shipping line. It is like an exclusive club, the membership to which is restricted. On the other hand, an open conference is one in which there are no restrictions upon membership other than ability and willingness to serve the trade. In the

United States an approval of the Federal Maritime Commission is required for the establishment of a shipping conference. US law requires all the conferences serving the US to be open.

Conferences have a strict code of conduct and operate either on oral understanding or written agreements. Once a liner is accepted as a member of a shipping conference, it has to assign an amount as deposit. The member is expected to follow all the rules and regulations of the conference. Failure to comply with the rules and regulation can lead to penalties and forfeiture of the deposit. On the one hand, conferences rule the shipping industry due to their monopolistic nature; while on the other they also try to win the patronage of the shippers by offering them loyalty contracts. Under such contracts, deferred freight rates are offered to the shippers, who regularly patronize the shipping services offered by the conferences. This helps the conferences meet the competition from non-member shipping lines.

Shippers prefer the regular services offered by the shipping conferences, because the export import business largely depends upon reliability and commitments. The exporter can make a firm commitment about the delivery of the cargo at the destination, depending upon the commitment he receives from the shipping line. He does not mind paying the freight charges demanded by the shipping line for such a committed service and remains loyal to the shipping line. The members of the shipping conference eliminate the internal competition by agreeing amongst themselves to charge uniform freight rates. If any member violates this agreement, he is suitably penalized. Member shipping lines pool their services and earnings on particular trade routes.

Shipping conferences operate on the democratic system of one member one vote basis. This is irrespective of the size of operation or the volume of tonnage possessed by the member. However, those members with large fleets and larger resources have more say and weightage in the policies and the running of the shipping conference.

Origins of the Conference System

During the British occupation of India and other parts of Asia, huge shipping traffic existed between Indian ports and British ports. Large quantities of raw materials, minerals, etc. were sent from India to UK and the finished goods were sent from UK to India. During the course of time, shipping lines built up large fleets to carry the cargoes to and fro. The ships would travel via the Cape of Good Hope in South Africa, which was a very long route.

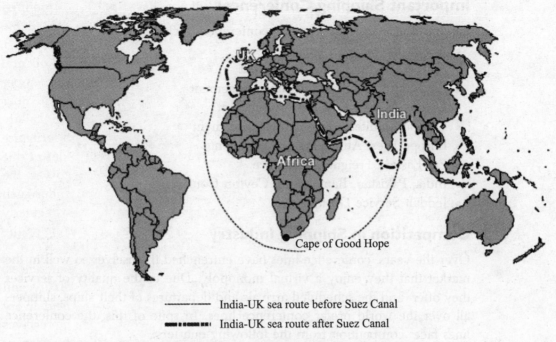

Fig. 11.1 History of Shipping Conference

Due to the opening of the Suez Canal in 1869, the distance between India and UK ports was shortened by approximately 4000 miles and as a consequence the voyage time was also considerably shortened. The drastic reduction in the voyage time resulted in excess shipping capacity, due to which the freight rates started falling steeply. In order to contain the fall in the freight rates, the shipping lines operating on the UK–Calcutta route formed the first shipping conference in 1875 and decided not to compete amongst themselves and to charge uniform freight rates. This was a successful strategy for the lines, but the shippers were annoyed with the monopolistic attitude of shipping conferences. Gradually, shippers started favouring non-conference lines which were offering more competitive freight rates. This was a setback for the conferences and in order to win back the business, they started offering deferred freight rates to the shipper. The more a shipper patronized a conference line, the better freight rates he/she received. Also, conferences started offering committed departures and arrivals and better services. The first shipping conference to operate on sea routes was the India, Pakistan, Bangladesh, Ceylon Conference. The shippers appreciated this and the conference system was not only accepted on UK–Calcutta route, but was also initiated in various trade routes all over the world. There are roughly 150 conferences in operation worldwide as of 2001, ranging in membership from two to 40 lines.

Important Shipping Conferences

Some of the important shipping conferences include the following.

- Aqaba Rate Agreement
- Asia Westbound Rate Agreement
- Eastbound Management Rate Agreement
- Europe Middle East Rate Agreement
- Europe Mediterranean Trade Agreement
- Europe West Africa Trade Agreement
- Far Eastern Freight Conference
- India, Pakistan, Bangladesh, Ceylon Conference
- Jeddah Service Group

Competition in Shipping Industry

Over the years, conference lines have entrenched themselves so well in the market that they enjoy a virtual monopoly. Due to the quality of services they offer and the scheduled arrivals and departures of their ships, shippers all over the world prefer conference lines. In spite of this, the conference lines face competition from the following quarters:

- Tramp competition
- Competition from non-conference lines
- Commodity competition

We shall discuss Tramp Competition later in this chapter under Liners versus Tramps.

Competition from Non-conference Lines

Conference lines face competition from non-conference lines, which offer services similar to conferences. They have their own tariff schedules, sailing schedules, contracts with shippers, etc. A number of freight forwarders also offer their services for non-conference lines and book the cargo on these lines. However, despite similarity of operations, non-conference lines are unable to match the quality of services offered by conference lines due to lack of resources. Conference lines are much stronger than non-conference lines, which still manage to get a small share of the market in the shipping industry.

Commodity Competition

Commodity competition is peculiar in nature and occurs when more than one country exports a product to a third country. For example, India, China, and Brazil export steel tubes to the United States. Out of this, India has the largest share of the market. As the export of steel tubes from India to the US increases, the conference might be tempted to increase the ocean freight. Due to this, the proportion of ocean freight in relation to the FOB price of the commodity, i.e., steel tubes in this case, increases substantially. This would lead to a rise in the price of Indian steel tubes in the US market, thereby making them incompetitive as compared to Chinese and Brazilian tubes. Indian tubes could thus start losing their market share and in extreme cases the export of tubes from India to US could also cease altogether. As such, a conference cannot afford to charge higher freight than other conferences, otherwise the export of that particular commodity will cease and the shipping conference will lose business.

It should be always kept in mind that shippers are not forced to deal with conferences. Shippers can, and do, negotiate with individual conference members.

SHIPPING CONFERENCES AND THEIR FREIGHTING METHODS

All liner companies, irrespective of whether they are operators of container ships, conventional vessels, or roll-on and roll off (Ro-Ro) ferries, fall into two categories: those which are members of liner conference and those which are not the members of any conference. As mentioned earlier, a shipping conference is a group of ocean freight carriers, who voluntarily come together for the purpose of limiting and regulating competition among themselves.

For conferences, this means that they do not have to compete with member lines in the conference. In order to ward off competition from non-conference lines, the conferences have formulated ways of maintaining the loyalty of shippers. The most common methods are discussed as follows:

Deferred Rebates

Deferred rebates are offered to shippers who regularly patronize a particular shipping line. The rate of discount on the ocean freight rates goes on increasing with each subsequent shipment up to a certain limit. For example, if the ocean freight to a particular destination is USD 100 per cubic feet, then the shipper has to pay this amount in full for the first time. The second time round, the shipper will be charged USD 99 per cubic feet, and so on. The progressive discount can go up to say USD 95 per cubic feet. This motivates the shipper to patronize a particular shipping line on a regular basis.

Loyalty Contract

The shipper and the conference shipping line enter into a contract, whereby the shipper commits to patronize the shipping line on a continuous basis for a particular period of time. In return, the shipping line charges specially discounted rates to the shipper.

Service Contract

Under a service contract, a shipper engages the shipping line to carry their cargo for a particular project or for a fixed duration against specially negotiated rates. For example, Reliance Industries may enter into a service contract with a shipping line to carry in all the equipment and machinery imported for its projects in India. The shipping line receives bulk business from a major Indian business house. In turn, it offers attractive ocean freight rates to the shipper.

Volume Related Discounts

In this case the discount increases with the volume of business received from a shipper up to a maximum limit.

Liner Tariff

The tariff schedule of a liner contains the following details:
1. Name of Conference and a list of the member lines
2. The geographical area covered
3. An index to the tariff classes
4. Measurement rules
5. Pallet rules
6. Heavy lift charges
7. Additional charges for long length cargo
8. Currency of tariff

1. Member List

All the shipping lines, which are members of a shipping conference, are listed in the tariff schedule. These members are those which have agreed to charge the tariffs mentioned in the schedule.

2. Area Covered

The geographical area covered by each conference is part of the tariff schedule.

3. Tariff Classes

Each commodity is listed in alphabetical order and each is placed in a category (known as a class) corresponding to rate of freight. The list includes several hundred commodities. Different classes of commodities attract different freight rates. Their charges are based on the varying risks, which the shipping lines undertake when they carry the goods with a wide range of values, shapes, sizes, and susceptibility to damage.

Shipments on less than container load (LCL) and break-bulk basis are generally charged per tonne (1000 kilograms) or per cubic meter; whichever is more profitable to the shipping line. Full Container Load (FCL) rates are normally per 20-feet general-purpose container. Normally, freight rates for 40-feet containers are double the rates of 20-feet containers. If the goods require shipment in a special container, such as a reefer (refrigerated) container or a flatbed container, then an additional charge may apply. The list of special containers, along with the related charges, appears in the tariff schedule.

Liner tariffs should, as a matter of rule, contain as many commodities as possible. But because of the numerous products traded, a particular commodity or variation may not coincide with any tariff entry. To provide for such eventuality, tariffs have additional categories, known as Enumerated, Not Otherwise Specified (NOS), and Not Otherwise Enumerated (NOE).

4. Measurement Rules

Shipping lines measure the goods according to the rules they devise. For example, volumes are measured when the freight rate is payable per cubic metre, or weight is measured if the freight is charged according to weight, say per tonne.

5. Pallet Rules

In case pallets are used, shipping lines follow certain rules:
(a) The dimensions and weight of the pallets are not added to the weight of cargo while calculating the freight, or
(b) A pallet allowance is provided which is an amount per tonne or cubic meter, to the shipper by means of a reduction in the freight.

6. Heavy Lift Charges

For carrying heavy pieces (e.g., over 5,000 kg or 10,000 kgs), most shipping lines charge an additional amount. This is because additional material handling equipment such as mobile crane, heavy-duty wall ropes, and chains, etc. have to be hired at extra cost.

7. Long Cargoes

Sometimes the cargo exceeds a stipulated length and requires special handling, including use of spreader bars. Due to its length, such cargo takes a longer time to load and unload. This involves extra costs, which are charged to the shipper.

8. Currency of Tariff

Usually, the ocean freight is quoted and charged in US Dollars. This is because the US Dollar is the most accepted and stable currency in the world. People all over the world feel comfortable if the dealing is in US Dollars. However, for the sake of convenience to the shippers, shipping lines accept the freight in equivalent local currencies. For example, an Indian shipper pays Indian Rupees to the shipping lines towards the freight even if the shipping line quotes the freight rate in US Dollars. With the emergence of the Euro, many shipping lines have also started quoting their freight rates in Euros.

Basis for Freight Calculation and Freight Tariff Terms

Sea freight is calculated by the liners on the basis of the weight or measurement of the cargo; the expression weight/measurement (W/M) is applied here. For high value cargo, value rates or a scale of value or ad valour, W/M is applied.

The shipping lines calculate the freight either on per 1,000 kilo grams or per cubic metre basis, depending upon which will earn the highest amount for the liner company. For calculating the freight, the decimal system is used as illustrated in the following examples-

$$1,000 \text{ kilograms} = 1.000 \text{ tonne}$$
$$1 \text{ m}^3 \text{ (cum)} = 1.000 \text{ m}^3$$

Example 1 For a box of consumer durables weighing 1,000 kilograms = 1.000 tonne and the measurement is 0.650 cubic meters, **the freight is calculated on weight basis.**

Example 2 For a box of electronic items, that weighs 1,000 kilograms = 1.000 tonne and the measurement is 1.85 cubic meters, **the freight is calculated on volume basis.**

General Rates Increase

Ocean freights are increased by a shipping line or conference; such an increase is known as General Rate Increase (GRI). The frequency of GRI depends upon the market conditions, ability of the shippers to absorb extra freight burden, and the level of competition in the international market. Normally, adequate notice is given to shippers before the introduction of GRI. The notice period may vary from situation to situation.

Such notices are published in popular newspapers, shipping journals, and other publications. These notices indicate the amount of increase in the freight rate and the date from which the freight hike takes effect. Shippers' associations are also given advance notice of GRI. In many countries, the conference holds consultations with shipper's council to justify the increase in freight rates. The United Nations code of conduct for liner conferences prescribes consultation with shippers' associations before a conference decides to increase the freight rates.

Loyalty

The shipping conferences offer various incentives to shippers to remain loyal and to deter them from patronizing the competitors. If a shipper uses the services of a conference to ship his goods to all the destination ports served by the conference lines, he/she can avail a rebate of 10% on freight charges. The rebate applies to shipments made over a specific period of time. Rebate is applicable only on the basic rate and not on surcharge.

If the shipper uses the services of a competitor during the specified time, the conferences forefeit the accumulated rebate amount. This way the shipper remains loyal to the conference till he/she has availed of the rebate due. In exceptional cases the conferences allow the shipper to use the services of a competitor, in which case the shipper is still considered loyal and gets the rebate.

Special Rates

Under certain circumstances such as poor market conditions or the inability of the cargo to bear freight, the shipping conferences allow special discounted rates. To avail these rates, shippers must submit the following information in support of their case.
(a) Port or place of shipment
(b) Port or place of delivery or discharge
(c) Full details of the commodity for which special rate is requested
(d) Dimensions of the pieces to be shipped and details of packing
(e) Period of shipment
(f) Type and size of container needed
(g) Reason why a special rate is required and the rate requested
(h) Quantity to be shipped and the frequency of shipment

The shipping conference may allow discounted rates in order to support the shipper to enter a new market or overcome a difficult market situation if it is convinced about the genuineness of the shipper's request.

Project exporters often tie up with a shipping conference to ship the entire project material through the member lines. Such projects continue over a long period of time, sometimes even years. Once an agreement is reached, shippers start writing the name of the project on their documents for the conference lines to identify and apply special negotiated rates for the project consignments.

Sometimes the shipping conference enters into volume related rate contract with the shipper. This is a flexible arrangement, which does not necessarily bind the shipper with the conference. The shipper can avail lower freight rates merely by shipping more volumes.

Additional Charges

The shipper has to pay a variety of additional charges over and above the normal ocean freight. These surcharges are levied against various heads for the additional expenses borne by the shipping line. Some important surcharges levied by conference lines are as follows:

Currency Adjustment Factor

Shipping lines always quote their freight rates in US Dollars; however they incur the expenses in various currencies. In case of fluctuations in the value of currencies against the US Dollar, the shipping lines may face losses. To compensate for such losses, the currency adjustment factor or the CAF is introduced, so that there is no change in the freight revenues for the ship owner in spite of the currency fluctuation.

Bunker Surcharge

Many a time, there is a sudden and heavy rise in bunker prices. As bunker adjustment factor, a bunker surcharge is then charged to the ship owner to compensate for the raise.. This practice has been followed by all shipping conferences since 1973 when there was a great surge in bunker prices. Bunker surcharge is levied as a percentage of general freight rate or as an amount per freight tonne. The bunker surcharge calculation takes into account the percentage increase in bunker prices (this is an average of bunker prices prevailing throughout the trade route under consideration) and also the share of bunker cost as a percentage of total cost. The volume of cargo movement also becomes important, if the bunker surcharge is to be expressed in terms of amount per freight tonne.

Exhibit 11.1   Rates and Surcharges

Member lines of the India Pakistan Bangladesh Ceylon Conference will apply a currency adjustment factor (CAF) of 10.28% from 1–31 March. Furthermore, the lines will implement the following bunker surcharge from 1 March: to/from Great Britain, the Northwest continent, the Mediterranean, and Scandinavia (excluding Baltic Sea Port): USD 165/TEU Caps or USD 16.50 W/M, and +46% (break bulk). TO/from Baltic ports: USD 170/TEU or USD 17.00 W/M and +46% (break bulk).

Source: www.conconf.org

Port Congestion Surcharge

Many ports all around the world are notorious for their inefficiency and high turn-around time. Due to this, ships have to wait for a long time on high seas before they get a berth on the port. Port congestion surcharge is levied by shipping lines to compensate themselves for the losses incurred due to port-congestion and the consequent long delays. This surcharge is expressed either in terms of percentage of a general rate level or as an amount per freight tonne. Sometimes the ships have to deviate from their normal route to visit a minor port. At such times a port additional charge is also levied. If the cargo is heavy, long or has an odd shape, special material handling equipment is used, for which heavy lift/long length additional charges are levied to compensate the ship owners towards additional cost involved in handling such awkward cargo.

Shipping journals and publications publish all types of surcharges on a regular basis to make the shippers aware of the prevailing rates.

Shipping conferences are regarded as loose cartels, which decide freight rates and other charges in order to eliminate any competition. Such monopolistic practices are resented by shippers across the world. However, the concerted efforts of shippers in the form of shipper's associations have yielded limited results to reduce the strength of shipping conferences. The European Union (EU) will be the first to take the lead in doing away with the conferences in their present form to make way for free competition enabling shipping lines to quote their tariffs. The EU has given liner conferences on routes to and from the EU, two years "cooling time" till 2008. After that, the conferences could exist, but will not be allowed to discuss or decide on common freight rates.

UNITED NATIONS CODE OF CONDUCT FOR LINER CONFERENCES

The need to govern the conduct of shipping conferences was felt for a very long time. Post World War II events led to a rapid expansion of world trade and growing influence of shipping conferences over the sea borne trade. The shippers' associations have had a very limited influence on deterring the conferences from using monopolistic practices. This influence was limited only to developed countries. For example, in the US, the Federal Maritime Commission could protect the interest of shipper community to a great extent. But developing nations were still prone to exploitation by the shipping conferences.

The developing nations demanded a code of conduct for shipping conferences under the aegis of the United Nations Convention of Trade and

Development (UNCTAD). The convention proved to be a major achievement of the UNCTAD, which helped in the growth of trade and the economic development of the developing countries. This convention was adopted on 7 April, 1974 and India ratified it in 1978. The objectives and principles and definitions as stated in the convention are given in Exhibit 11.2.

Exhibit 11.2   United Nations Code of Conduct for Liner Conferences

Objectives and Principles

DESIRING to improve the liner conference system,

RECOGNIZING the need for a universally acceptable code of conduct for liner conferences,

TAKING into account the special needs and problems of developing countries with respect to the activities of liner conferences serving their foreign trade,

AGREEING to reflect in the Code the following fundamental objectives and basic principles:

(a) The objective to facilitate the orderly expansion of world sea-borne trade;

(b) The objective to stimulate the development of regular and efficient liner services adequate to the requirements of the trade concerned;

(c) The objective to ensure a balance of interests between suppliers and users of liner shipping services;

(d) The principle that conference practices should not involve any discrimination against the ship owners, shippers, or the foreign trade of any country;

(e) The principle that conferences hold meaningful consultations with shippers' organizations, shippers' representatives and shippers on matters of common interest, with, upon request, the participation of appropriate authorities;

(f) The principle that conferences should make available to interested parties pertinent information about their activities which are relevant to those parties and should publish meaningful information on their activities.

Definitions (as stated in the convention)

Liner conference or conference A group of two or more vessel-operating carriers, which provides international liner services for the carriage of cargo on a particular route or routes within specified geographical limits and which has an agreement or arrangement, whatever its nature, within the framework of which they operate under uniform or common freight rates and any other agreed conditions with respect to the provision of liner services.

(Contd)

Exhibit 11.2 (Contd)

National shipping line   A national shipping line of any given country is a vessel-operating carrier which has its head office of management and its effective control in that country and is recognized as such by an appropriate authority of that country or under the law of that country.

Lines belonging to and operated by a joint venture involving two or more countries and in whose equity the national interests, public and/or private, of those countries have a substantial share and whose head office of management and whose effective control is in one of those countries can be recognized as a national line by the appropriate authorities of those countries.

Third-country shipping line   A vessel-operating carrier in its operations between two countries of which it is not a national shipping line.

Shipper   A person or entity who has entered into, or who demonstrates an intention to enter into, a contractual or other arrangement with a conference or shipping line for the shipment of goods in which he has a beneficial interest.

Shipper's organization   An association or equivalent body which promotes, represents, and protects the interests of shippers and, if those authorities so desire, is recognized in that capacity by the appropriate authority or authorities of the country whose shippers it represents.

Goods carried by the conference   Cargo transported by shipping lines to members of a conference in accordance with the conference agreement.

Appropriate authority   Either a government or a body designated by a government or by national legislation to perform any of the functions ascribed to such authority by the provisions of this Code.

Promotional freight rate   A rate instituted for promoting the carriage of non-traditional exports of the country concerned.

Special freight rate   A preferential freight rate, other than a promotional freight rate, which may be negotiated between the parties concerned.

LINERS AND TRAMP OPERATIONS

Cargo ships can be categorized as liner ships and tramp ships. Due to their fixed schedules of arrival and departure, pre-determined voyages and trade routes and published ocean freight rates, liner ships represent the organized sector of the shipping industry. Liner shipping is dominated by shipping conferences and offers the following advantages to shippers:

- Regular sailings to scheduled ports of call.

- Stable freight rates for a long period of time, which helps the shipper to quote C&F prices with confidence.
- Uniform rates for all shippers.
- Coverage of wide range of ports.
- Rebates of freight rates based on loyalty agreements.

Tramp ships, on the other hand, have the following characteristics:

1. They are free to move anywhere on the high seas at their will.
2. Their voyage routes and schedules are flexible.
3. They travel from one port to another port on various trade routes looking for cargo and carrying the same to various destinations around the world.
4. They arrive or depart without a fixed route or schedule.
5. They fix their voyages according to availability of cargo and as per the requirement of the shippers.
6. The freight rates of tramp ships depend upon the demand and supply conditions in the shipping industry. If there is a glut of shipping space, the tramp freight rates plummet. Whereas in case of shortage of shipping space, the tramp freight rates shoot up.
7. The cargo space on the tramps is generally booked by brokers located in major port cities like New York, London, Rotterdam, Hamburg, Singapore, and Hong Kong, etc. They work as a link between tramp operators and shippers.
8. Tramps normally carry homogeneous cargo like grains, ores, coal, timber, fertilizers, etc.

Cargoes with the following characteristics are ideally suited for tramp operations:

- Bulky and heavy cargo.
- Cargo with low value, which has no urgency to reach the destination.
- Cargoes, which do not require protective covers and any special material handling facilities.
- Cargoes, which are normally shipped in large quantities.

Tramp vessels, as distinct from liners, are usually chartered in some form by a shipper to carry a full shipload of cargo. Firms offering shipping services, either liner or tramp, are called carriers. Their customers are called shippers (Branch, 1994).

Liners vs Tramp Ships

From the discussion above it is clear that the liner ships represent the organized sector of the shipping industry due to their fixed schedules and fixed freight rates policy. On the other hand, tramps, being the masters of their own will, have flexible schedules of arrival and departure. Also, their freight rates vary according to the situation. Due to their unique way of operations, they do not offer a direct competition to the liners. Liners are mainly involved in carrying the general cargo, which requires punctual, regular, and continuous service. Also, the freight rates of the liners are fixed and shippers know them in advance in order to plan their shipments. All these requirements do not conform to the style of operations of tramps. As such there is no direct and regular competition in the area of general cargo between tramps and liners. However, they do cooperate with each other in a situation where business is booming and there is a dearth of shipping space on some routes. In such cases, liner companies charter tramp vessels in order to meet the increasing demand from the market. Liners and tramps compete with each other under the following circumstances:

- As the volume of world trade grows, shipping companies are buying larger ships in order to carry more and more cargo in a single voyage. But sometimes when the market is depressed, large ships do not find general cargo and there is a possibility of the shipping space remaining empty. In such a situation, liner companies may undercut tramps to carry bulk cargo.
- Tramps are normally hired for one-way movement of cargo. They do not often get any suitable cargo for their return voyage. In such cases, they compete with liners by under-cutting the rates and try to get cargo for their return voyage.
- Specialized ships, such as refrigerated vessels and oil carriers may not get suitable return cargo and may carry just about any cargo during the return voyage, just in order to meet operational overheads.

TYPES OF SHIPS AND INTERNATIONAL TRADE

About 5000 million tonnes of cargo is transported by sea every year from one part of the globe to another. This cargo is composed of general cargo, which is packed in boxes, drums, gunny bags, PP bags, cartons, etc. This type of cargo generally comprises of manufactured and semi manufactured goods. The other type of cargo is bulk cargo, which is mostly raw material. This can be dry cargo like sugar, grains, fertilizers, chemicals, etc. or liquid cargo like edible oils, chemicals, petrochemicals, etc.

Various types of ships carry these cargoes; some of the ships are:

General Cargo Ships

General cargo ships vary in size from 8,000 to 21,000 Dead Weight Tonnage (DWT). There are five hatches or holds and twin decks. For carriage of perishable cargo there is also a facility of refrigerated containers, popularly known as reefer containers. The temperature inside the reefer containers can be maintained to suit the cargo. Such containres are particularly suitable for fresh fruits, vegetables, processed foods, etc. Also, tanks are available on board the ships to carry limited quantity of dry or liquid bulk cargo. Winches/ derricks (cranes) are fitted on to the ships to carry a variety of cargoes. These cranes have different load carrying capacities.

General cargo ships can sail at 20 or 22 knots per hour (knot is 6080 feet or nautical mile). The average speed is 15 or 16 knots, which helps to maintain fuel economy and to deliver the cargo on schedule. Higher the speed of the ship, more the fuel it consumes.

Bulk Carriers

These are large ships ranging from capacities 25,000 to 2,50,000 DWT, having 5 to 9 hatches/holds according to size. They normally travel at a speed of thirteen knots. In modern bulk carriers there are generally no cargo handling equipment such as cranes, winches, etc. on board the ship; instead they use the material handling which is available on port terminals. Bulk carriers are used to carry coal, grain, phosphates, and other "loose" cargo. They are almost always employed in tramp service. That is, they often work on a contract basis rather than carrying cargo on a regular, established route.

Tankers

Tankers are ideally suited to carry liquid cargo. They vary in size from 25,000 to 555,000 DWT, having five to nine tanks according to size, speeding at 12 or 13 knots. Tankers are fitted with in-laid pipelines, with cleaning and cooling arrangements. Oil terminals and refineries are connected by submarine pipelines through which oil is pumped in or out. As such, for filling and pumping out operations, ships need not enter the ports. These operations can be carried out away from the ports. All ships, particularly tankers, now have pollution control arrangements due to greater awareness and concern about the safety of marine ecology.

Specialized Ships

With a view to saving time and costs, many new types of ships have comes into being. They are described as follows:

Container Ships

Cellular container ships were developed in the late 1950s. Today, the vessels may be up to 50,000 DWT in size and can achieve a speed of up to 33

Exhibit 11.2 World's largest container vessel delivered

Maersk Line has taken delivery of EMMA MAERSK built by Odense Steel Shipyard. Measuring 397 meters long and 56 meters wide, the EMMA MAERSK is able to carry 11,000 twenty-foot containers (TEU) and is one of the most environmentally friendly container vessels ever built.

Source: The Supply Chain & Logistics Link, Issue 14/ 2006

---

knots. Initially, container vessels were all equipped with their own cargo handling systems. But now with large scale port development, the ports have installed their own cranes. Hence more and more vessels are built without cargo handling equipment. This reduces the investment and at the same time increases the cargo carrying capacity. However, a small number of container vessels are built with some form of cargo handling equipment even today. The holds of cellular container vessels are divided into individual "cells" or compartments, each capable of accommodating one container. The containers are loaded and discharged vertically by means of cranes. The vessels can also carry a number of containers on deck in several tiers. The capacity of a container vessel is given in the number of TEUs it can carry. Although cellular container vessels were originally designed to carry only containers, many enterprising operators have managed to carry in such vessels a limited quantity of other commodities also.

The advantages of container vessels are their high speed and very quick turn-around. This reduces the cost per tonne-mile per unit of cargo carried. The disadvantages of this type of ship include very high initial investment, its dependence on special shore facilities, and the limited number of routes, which carry sufficient cargo volume to justify the introduction of such highly capital intensive but efficient vessels. The container ships are also called Lift On/Lift Off (LO/LO) ships as they facilitate lifting of containerized cargo by cranes.

Roll-On/Roll-Off (Ro/Ro) Ships

As the name suggests, these ships are ideally suited for the cargo, which can be horizontally rolled on board the ship. Such cargo includes all wheeled vehicles, which can be driven on board the ship, such as tractors, buses, and trucks, or oversized cargo loaded on special flatbed, mafi, or lowboy trailers. For the non-wheel cargo, specially designed material handling equipment needs to be employed. Such equipment is expensive, but their utility more than compensates for their high price. These equipment can put non-wheeled cargo such as pallets, bundled goods, pre-slung bags, and containers on board the ship. The concept of Ro/Ro ships was adopted from small sea ferries, which used to cover short distances with their passengers and cargoes. With technological advancements Ro/Ro ships are now plying on major trade routes throughout the world. The most important feature of an Ro/Ro ship is that it has a flat continuous deck without any obstruction, which helps the cargo to be rolled horizontally on board the ship.

Advantages of Ro/Ro

- It is the safest and most inexpensive way to handle and transport oversized or special project cargo.
- Shipments often move as one piece using specialized trailers from port of origin to port to destination.
- It involves less physical handling and there is no need for costly dismantling and reassembly.
- There is no exposure to water or the elements because the cargo is always secured in ship's garage decks for the entire voyage.

Barge Systems

Barges are floating units of different sizes, which can be towed or pushed by tugs in ports and inland waterways and which can be hoisted aboard special barge carriers with the help of special material handling equipment for sea voyage. No international standards have been fixed for barges.

There are different designs of barges to carry different commodities. Following are the main advantages of barge systems over other transport systems

1. Faster turn-around time, due to the large capacity of barges.
2. Barge systems are independent of port infrastructure.
3. Barges are generally very large and carry their own cargo handling equipment. They are therefore not dependent on on-shore facilities.

Barges are taken on board by floating them on to an elevator at the stern of the vessel, lifting them to assigned deck levels, and then transporting them horizontally onto rollers or rails onto their cell. Alternatively, the barges are lifted on board with a gantry crane, which is also located at the stern and lowered into the cell.

Multipurpose Vessels

Multipurpose vessels tend to be more expensive than conventional general cargo but cheaper than container ships, Ro-Ro vessels, or barge carriers. These vessels can be classified into four main categories.

1. General cargo/liner type vessels These vessels are capable of accommodating a number of containers. They are designed to allow efficient carriage of certain bulk commodities as well. They do not achieve the cargo handling speed of container vessels, but they are considered more competitive than the general cargo vessel or the liner in many trade routes to and from developing countries.

2. Combination of bulk carriers and container vessels These vessels may have their own cargo handling gear or rely on shore facilities. The flexibility of vessels of this type allows them to be used on different routes; for example, as bulk carriers on the outward leg and container vessels on the homeward leg, or as a combination of both. This may make balancing of the trade simpler.

3. Combination of container and RO/RO vessels Vessels of this type aim at covering the entire spectrum of multimodal transport. They generally carry containers on deck and in the front holds, while cargoes are loaded rolling through ramps often located in the stern. Vessels of this type have very specialized equipment.

4. Bo-Ro vessel There are ships, which can carry Ro/Ro cargo and containers on one leg of the voyage and bulk cargo on the return trip, while achieving fast turnarounds. Ro-Ro cargo and containers are carried on the upper decks and the lower holds have tanks or space for bulk cargo.

Other Special Types of Ships

Reefer/fruit carriers These ships specialize in carrying refrigerated containers. They provide reefer points to connect the containers with a source of power supply. Reefer carriers are designed to preserve the freshness of cargo at the most stable temperatures.

Oil/Bulk/Ore (OBO carriers) are vessels that can carry both oil, bulk and ore cargoes. They function as tankers when required and as bulk carriers otherwise.

Chemical tankers are ships designed with tanks of stainless steel, or of other materials, capable of containing chemicals.

Live stock carriers are large ships designed to transport sheep, cattle and goats over a long distance. While in transit, the animals are kept in pens, which are protected from adverse weather conditions.

Auto transporters are the car shipping services who specialize in moving large number of vehicles from one place to another.

Oil rig supply boats are ships catering to the needs of oil rigs on the high seas.

Oil drilling and production ships have the facility to drill through a hole in the hull. These are specialized ships used in oil exploration.

Tug boats are small, strongly built vessels, used to guide large ocean-going ships into and out of port and to tow barges, dredging and salvage equipment, and disabled vessels.

Cable laying ships are used to lay submarine cables.

Combi or Multi-purpose vessel As the name suggests, they are multi-purpose vessels.

SUMMARY

The discussion in this chapter has made it clear that ports and shipping industry are complementary to each other. Governments too have an important role to play by formulating the policies, which are conducive to maritime industry. For example, the governments of Singapore and Dubai have invested in their ports and have created an infrastructure and environment where shipping lines, freight forwarders, and shippers find it easy to operate. They have simplified customs and border procedures as well as import duties and tax structure. They have implemented best e-commerce practices, which facilitate easy customs clearance and paperless trade. The government machinery helps to boost the trade and does not create bureaucratic delays. This results in quick turnaround of the ships, encouraging big shipping lines to make these ports their hubs of operations. Whereas various governments are trying to create a business-friendly environment, shipping lines are still practicing their monopoly driven policies of shipping conferences. There is a very feeble resistance to this monopoly from shippers' side. But recently, the European Union (EU) has voiced its intention to contain the monopoly of shipping conferences. The EU statement says, "Existing liner conferences will be able to continue operating on routes to and from Europe until October 2008. After that date, conference activities and in particular price fixing and capacity regulation will no longer be permitted." This is a welcome sign and all the regional trading blocks as well as World Trade Organization should join hands to eliminate such an unfair trade practice in shipping industry.

Advancement in technology is making it possible for ships to travel faster and carry more cargo than ever. Also, ships are being built for specific cargo such as bulk cargo, containerised cargo, refrigerated cargo, automobiles, liquid cargo, etc. The number of such specialized ships is fast growing, thanks to the boom in world trade. The next decade promises further growth for the shipping industry as more and more countries remove trade barriers for international business.

CONCEPT REVIEW QUESTIONS

1. How did the Conference System begin in the Shipping industry? Explain the working of shipping conferences in detail.
2. A Shipping Conference is a monopolistic organization, which kills competition in the shipping industry. Do you agree or disagree with this statement? Give reasons in support of your answer.
3. What is the difference between liner ships and tramp ships? In what ways are liner ships more reliable than tramp ships.
4. Write short notes on
   (a) Commodity competition
   (b) United Nation's Code of Conduct for Liner Conferences
5. Write a note on the competition in shipping industry.
6. List the contents of tariff schedules of a Liner Ship and explain them briefly. Discuss the role of United Nations in restricting the monopoly of shipping conference.
7. Discuss various types of ships offering their specialized services to the shippers.

OBJECTIVE QUESTIONS

In the following questions, choose the correct option
1. The first shipping conference was established in
   (a) 1957
   (b) 1990
   (c) 1852
   (d) 1875
2. The first shipping conference to operate on sea routes is
   (a) Aqaba Rate Agreement
   (b) India, Pakistan, Bangladesh, Ceylon Conference
   (c) Europe Mediterranean Trade Agreement
   (b) Europe West Africa Trade Agreement
3. Which of the following does not help to maintain the loyalty of shippers with conference lines?
   (a) Deferred rebates
   (b) Priority loading of the cargo

(c) Service contracts

(d) Volume related discounts

4. Which of the following is the major advantage offered by conference lines to shippers?

   (a) Door to door services

   (b) Competitive freight rates

   (c) Offices all over the world

   (d) Regular sailings to scheduled ports of call

5. Which of the following is not an advantage offered by Ro-Ro ships?

   (a) Shipments often move as one piece using specialized trailers from origin to port to destination.

   (b) It involves less physical handling and there is no need for costly dismantling and reassembly.

   (c) They have facilities for carrying perishable cargo in reefer containers.

   (d) There is no exposure to water or the elements because the cargo is always secured in ship's RoRo/Containership's garage decks for the entire voyage.

State whether the following are True or False

6. The Import General Manifest is submitted by the shipping line to the customs after the arrival of ship at the port.

7. Shipping conferences work on the democratic system of one-member one-vote basis.

8. Shipping conferences are established to remove monopoly practices in shipping industry.

9. Non-conference liners offer services similar to conference lines.

10. Tramp ships offer regular sailings to scheduled ports of call.

EXERCISES

1. Draw a flow chart of port operations from the time of arrival of a ship till its departure from the port.

2. Find out the list of members of the India, Pakistan, Bangladesh, Ceylon Conference and the trade routes covered by them.

3. Write a short essay on "Advantages and Disadvantages of Conference System".

4. Write an enquiry letter to freight forwarders in your area and get quotations for shipment of a metal cutting machine weighing 10 tonnes from Mumbai port to Singapore port. Prepare a comparative statement of the rates quoted by them.

5. Prepare a wall chart depicting major sea trade routes on world map and various types of ships described in this chapter.

SELECT REFERENCES

Sjostrom William, 1992, 'Price discrimination by shipping conferences', *Logistics and Transportation Review*, pp. 207-215.

Wood, Donald F., Anthony Barone, Paul Murphy and Damiel Wardlow, 2002, *International Logistics*, Second edition, AMACOM Publication.

www.cmptp.com, last accessed on 7th October 2007.

www.dpa.co.ae, last accessed on 1st September 2007.

www.oecd.org, last accessed on 8th September 2007.

SHIPPING CONFERENCE VS SHIPPER'S COUNCIL

Case Study

The Chairman of Western India Shipper's Council (WISC) Pradeep Suri does not like the monopoly of shipping conferences. In fact, recently he argued against the concept of shipping conferences generally, and, the Asia Pacific Trade Agreement (APTA) in particular, because that is the largest conference with which he has dealings. Far from the aggressive reputation he has won in recent years in his fight against conferences, in person Suri is well-reasoned in his arguments and unexpectedly mild in his approach. Suri himself runs a successful import, warehousing, and distribution business. He works with the Shipper's Council and is also the president of the local chamber of commerce and industry as 'just a hobby'. Suri has raised the question why should the shipping lines be allowed to get away with their monopoly practices, when he has to constantly stive for his business to remain competitive in the market.

He has, however, a different approach from many other shipper's councils. Instead of confronting shipping conferences in courts, which takes a lot of time, Suri prefers procedures of negotiation. This is despite the fact that conferences do not seem to be open to negotiations. Peter Watkins, Chairman of APTA acknowledges the discussions with WISC but has also stated that both the parties do not always reach an agreement.

Suri concedes that he does not expect the shipping lines to charge rates, which result in losses. If the rates are too low, some of the shipping lines would disappear, resulting in a decrease in frequency and reliability of shipping services. Such a situation is not in the best interest of the shippers too.

Watkins responds to this by saying that it is the conference system, which prevents this from happening. Stability in both, the rates and services levels is maintained by ironing out the highs and lows. During the periods of high volumes, rates cannot be increased. Similarly, in the times of low volume of business, the rates cannot be reduced. Watkins emphasizes that in fact conferences lend stability to the business of shippers by offering them constant and predictable rates. Watkins also denies the suggestion of overcharging by citing the freight rates of APTA.

Questions

1. Do you agree with the non-confrontational approach of Suri? Give reasons in support of your answer.
2. What is your opinion about APTA? Do they appear to be reasonable in their discussions with WISC?
3. Suggest a course of action that is beneficial to both, WISC and APTA in the long run.

12 Containerization and Leasing Practices

Learning Objectives

After studying this chapter, you will be able to understand
- the concept of containerization
- the history of containerization
- about the different types of containers
- the benefits of containerization
- the chartering practices in the container business
- the concept of inland container depots

Cargo carrying containers are now an integral part of the modern maritime transportation business. Containerization facilitates both the unitization and carriage of cargo through different modes of transportation. It is due to these advantages that the share of containerized cargo in world trade is increasing every year. More and more countries are building infrastructure for easy movement of containerized cargo. This includes building highways to carry large heavy-duty containers, running special trains to exclusively carry containerized cargo, modernizing ports to handle different types of containers, creating warehousing facilities to accommodate containerized cargo, and building ships, trucks and other modes of transportation to carry the containers across continents. In fact, containerization has revolutionized the transportation industry. The term *intermodalism* is, now, nearly synonymous with *containerization*, with the container holding the cargo being exchanged between modes (Wood and Wardlow 2002).

CONTAINERIZATION—CONCEPT AND OPERATION

Containerization is a shipping system based on large up to 48 feet long cargo-carrying containers that can be easily interchanged between trucks, trains, and ships without rehandling the contents.

A container is a single, rigidly sealed, reusable metal box in which merchandise is shipped by vessel, truck or rail. A freight container is defined as an article of transport equipment with the following characteristics:

1. It is strong enough for repeated use.
2. In is specially designed to facilitate the carriage of goods by one or more modes of transport, without intermediate reloading.
3. It is fitted with devices permitting its ready handling, particularly its transfer from one mode of transport to another.
4. It is designed for easy filling and emptying.
5. It has an internal volume of at least 1 m^3 (35.3 cu. ft.) or more.

In other words, a freight container is a rectangular weather-proof article of transportation equipment for transporting and storing a number of unit loads packages of bulk material, which confines and protects the contents from loss or damage and which can be handled as a unit load and transhipped without rehandling its contents.

Containers are made of various types of materials such as steel, aluminium, plywood, fibreglass, etc. A steel container has a steel frame and steel cladding, but can also get rusted after four to five years of use. Aluminium containers have steel frame and aluminium cladding. They are light-weight and rust free, but have a shorter life as a result of erosion of metal due to frequent contact with sea water. Non-metallic containers like plywood or fibreglass containers have steel frame, but their walls, doors, and roof tops made of plywood with fibre glass coating. These containers have good insulation properties, but are very difficult to repair and expensive to manufacture.

HISTORY OF CONTAINERIZATION

Logistics experts had been trying for a very long time to devise a unit load of cargo. A variety of methods to devise unit loads were tried which would improve the efficiency of transport operations. The idea was that the cargo should not only be protected from the vagaries of nature, but also from all the risk it might encounter during long voyages, such as theft, pilferage, damage, etc. In addition, the unit load should be easy to handle and transport across all modes of transport, such as truck, rail, ship, etc.

Malcolm McLean, often called "the father of containerization," first conceived the idea of using the entire truck trailer to load onto and off a ship. He was in the transportation business and was familiar with both land transportation and shipping operations. In 1956, McLean adopted a ship for carrying containers. His first attempts to directly transfer containerized cargo from trucks to ships were successful. McLean later established a very successful multi-modal transportation company called Sea Land Inc. By

1961, regular container services were in operation between New York, Los Angeles, and San Francisco. In 1966, the company started its first Trans-Atlantic Container service between American and European Ports with a capacity of 1000 to 1500 TEUs and service speed of 20 to 30 knots. During the 1970s, most of the ships were built with dimensions to just pass through the Panama Canal, which limited the ship length to 289.5 meter and 32.3-meter beam. These ships were named as Panamax ships and had capacities from 1500 to 3000 TEUs. By the early 1970s, cellular container vessels were operational on most trade routes between America, Europe, Japan, and Australia. During the 1980s, Panamax ships of 4000 TEUs capacity were introduced. By the 1990s, larger post-Panamax ships with 4400 TEUs were being manufactured. Nowadays most shipping lines, such as APL, Maersk, Hyundai, NYK, and Hanjin own ships with a capacity of more than 6000 TEUs and service speed of 25 knots. It is expected that ships with 10,000 to 15,000 TEUs capacity will be built in the next few years.

To cope up with the containerized cargo traffic, ports all around the world are being modernized. Container berths are being deepened to maintain a draft of about 52 feet, which is required to receive 8000 TEUs or bigger ships. Port authorities are also increasing container-handling facilities by increasing the number of container berths, installing suitable material handling equipment and state-of-the art technology. During 2001, ports around the world handled more than 200 million TEUs of container traffic, which by 2012 is expected to touch 500 million TEUs. A number of transhipment centres are also coming up to serve as load centres for the smaller ports.

Indian ports, in comparison to ports in other developed countries, are lagging far behind. During 2000–01, Indian ports handled only 2.7 million TEUs, out of which more than half was handled by (Jawaharlal Nehru Port Trust) JNPT.

Containerization has ultimately provided an ideal unit load, which meets all the logistical requirements. It not only eliminates conventional time consuming methods of cargo handling, but also benefits substantially ship owners, shippers, and port authorities. The added advantage is that containerization simplifies the procedures and documentation related to transportation of cargo. Due to the various benefits offered by containerization, developed countries, such as the USA, UK, Japan, and Germany quickly improved their infrastructure for efficient handling of containerized traffic. They improved their highways, port facilities, and material handling facilities, to meet the challenges of containerization. Countries like Singapore, Hong

Kong, and Dubai also sensed the business opportunities and created excellent and highly efficient ports and made themselves the hub of regional traffic.

Discussing just transport efficiency, however, hardly begins to capture the economic impact of containerization. A container not only lowers freight bills, it saves time. Quicker handling and less time in storage translates into faster transit from the manufacturer to customer and reduction in the cost of financing inventories sitting unproductively on railway sidings or in pier side warehouses awaiting a ship. The container, combined with the computer, makes it practical for companies like Toyota and Honda to develop just-in-time manufacturing, in which a supplier manufactures the goods only as the customer needs them and then ships them, in containers, to arrive at a specified time (Levinson 2006).

There are several other ways of unitizing the load for easy handling. Unitization is combining small units of load into a single large unit, by strapping or binding them together.

Unitization could also be accomplished with the help of pallet (a platform). The cargo contained in wooden boxes or bags could be strapped to the pallet. The pallet could be easily lifted on the twin forks of a forklift truck. The supporters of palletization wanted the pallet to be a world wide standard of unit load. To that extent, some of the ships had even been adapted to carry pallet loads. However, in the long run, the container proved itself safer for the cargo and easier to handle.

Containerization is the most advanced form of unitization. It fulfils all the challenging requirements that repeated sea voyages and the safe carriage of cargo on each journey involve. Modern containers are 20, 40, and 45 feet long. The load carrying capacity of a ship is measured in terms of number of containers of TEUS it can carry. A TEU represents a 20-feet equivalent unit of a container.

TYPES OF CONTAINERS

Different types of containers are available for different applications. Also, containers are available in different sizes with different load-carrying capacities. The standard sizes of containers the world over are 20 feet and 40 feet (Fig. 12.1 and Tables 12.1 and 12.2). Following are the different types of containers.

Most common types of containers are as follows:
1. Open top containers (Fig. 12.2 and Table 12.3)
2. Reefer containers (Fig. 12.3 and Table 12.4)
3. Flat rack containers (Fig. 12.4 and Table 12.5)
4. Platform containers (Fig. 12.5 and Table 12.6)

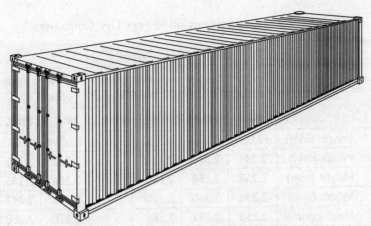

Fig. 12.1 20 feet and 40 feet Dry Container

Some other types of containers include half-height containers, side-door containers, ventilated containers, bulk containers (Fig. 12.6), insulated containers, collapsible containers, and tank containers.

Table 12.1 Specifications of 20-Feet Dry Containers

		Aluminium		Steel			
		Specifications for 20,320 kg		Specifications for 20,320 kg		Specifications for 24,000 kg	
		Min.	Max.	Min.	Max.	Min.	Max.
	Length (mm)	5,926	5,932	5,883	5,926	5,893	5,905
Inside Measurement	Width (mm)	2,343	2,345	2,335	2,352	2,350	2,352
	Height (mm)	2,217	2,416	2,375	2,408	2,376	2,393
Door Opening	Width (mm)	2,330	2,344	2,320	2,345	2,337	2,343
	Height (mm)	2,119	2,308	2,267	2,280	2,267	2,283
Load Capacity (M3)		30.8	33.7	32.9	33.4	32.9	33.4
Container Weight (kg)		1,680	2,000	2,150	2,370	1,960	2,300
Maximum Loading Weight (kg)		18,320	18,640	17,950	18,170	21,700	22,040

Dry Containers:

1. These containers are suitable for general cargo.

2. Forklift pockets are provided on containers.

3. Lashing devices are provided on the top and bottom longitudinal rails and the corner posts.

Table 12.2   Specifications of 40-Feet Dry Containers

	Aluminium				Steel			
	Specifications for 8'6"		Specifications for 9'6"		Specifications for 8'6"		Specifications for 9'6"	
	Min.	Max.	Min.	Max.	Min.	Max.	Min.	Max.
Length (mm)	12,058	12,066	12,062		12,024	12,033	12,033	12,035
Inside Measurement Width (mm)	2,344	2,345	2,350		2,352	2,352	2,350	2,352
Height (mm)	2,258	2,398	2,690		2,386	2,395	2,694	2,700
Door Opening Width (mm)	2,292	2,350	2,350		2,340	2,343	2,338	2,340
Height (mm)	2,258	2,292	2,589		2,270	2,280	2,581	2,585
Load Capacity (M3)	63.8	68.1	76.2		67.5	67.7	76.2	76.4
Container Weight (kg)	2,870	3,300	3,050		3,710	3,810	3,900	4,120
Maximum Loading Weight (kg)	27,180	27,160	27,430		26,270	26,770	26,360	27,580

Table 12.3   Specifications of Open Top Containers

	20-Feet				40-Feet			
	Specifications for 20,320 kg		Specifications for 24,000 kg		Aluminium		Steel	
	Min.	Max.	Min.	Max.	Min.	Max.	Min.	Max.
Length (mm)	5,895	5,922	5,892	5,900	12,056	12,069	12,021	12,056
Inside Measurement Width (mm)	2,345	2,351	2,334	2,348	2,344	2,358	2,334	2,352
Height (mm)	2,184	2,308	2,308	2,350	2,230	2,324	2,321	2,354
Rear Door Opening Width (mm)	22,340	2,340	2,322	2,340	2,340	2,344	2,322	2,340
Height (mm)	2,147	2,222	2,229	2,270	2,230	2,292	2,235	2,284
Roof Header Opening Width (mm)	1,578	1,818	1,860	1,940	1,450	1,922	1,415	1,940
Roof Opening Width (mm)	4,876	5,733	5,581	5,738	11,573	11,699	11,699	11,841
Length (mm)	1,850	2,214	2,214	2,225	2,080	2,180	2,080	2,132
Load Capacity (M3)	30.4	32.0	31.9	32.3	60.8	67.3	65.4	66.6
Container Weight (kg)	1,960	2,500	2,185	2,590	3,670	3,850	3,850	4,050
Maximum Loading Weight (kg)	17,820	18,360	21,410	21,815	26,630	26,810	26,430	26,630

Open top containers:

1. These containers are suitable for cargo with extra height, which can be loaded from topside with Craina crane

2. The top can be covered with tarpauline if required.

3. Suitable forklift pockets, lashing devices, and corner posts are provided.

4. Ideal Cargo: Agricultural and construction machinery, ingots, logs, scrap, rolls of plastic sheets, project cargo, marble slabs, and castings.

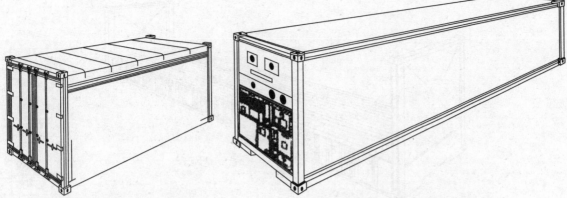

Fig. 12.2   Open Top Container   **Fig. 12.3**   Refrigerated Container

Table 12.4   Specifications of a Refrigerated Container

	20–Feet (8'6")		40–Feet					
	Specifications for 20,320 kg		Specifications for 24,000 kg		Specifications for 8'6"		Specifications for 9'6"	
	Min.	Max.	Min.	Max.	Min.	Max.	Min.	Max.
Length (mm)	5,365	5,477	5,365	5,546	11,460	11,674	11,674	11,674
Inside Measurement Width (mm)	2,225	2,254	2,236	2,286	2,226	2,286	2,286	2,286
Height (mm)	2,087	2,264	2,077	2,256	2,204	2,235	2,509	2,509
Door Opening Width (mm)	2,225	2,286	2,236	2,286	2,226	2,336	2,286	2,286
Height (mm)	2,025	2,202	2,174	2,190	2,121	2,163	2,444	2,444
Side Opening Width (mm)	—	—	—	—	—	—	—	—
Roof Opening Width (mm)	—	—	—	—	—	—	—	—
Length (mm)	—	—	—	—	—	—	—	—
Load Capacity (M3)	25.3	27.5	25.3	28.6	56.5	58.8	66.9	66.9
Container Weight (kg)	2,520	3,460	2,890	3,300	4,330	5,612	4,500	4,500
Maximum Loading Weight (kg)	16,860	17,800	20,700	21,110	24,868	26,150	25,980	25,980

Reefer containers:

1. These containers are suitable for cargo that constantly needs temperature above and below freezing point, such as fruits, vegetables, and other perishables.

2. It is possible to get fresh air supply within the containers in the quantity required to keep the product inside safe.

3. The insulating material, polyurethene foam is sandwiched between two walls of the container.

4. The temperatures can be set between +25 degree C and –25 degree C.

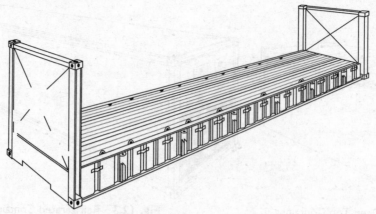

Fig. 12.4 Flat Rack Container

Table 12.5 Specifications of a Flat Rack Container

		20-Feet (8'6") Specifications for 20,320 kg		40-Feet Specifications for 24,000 kg		Specifications for 80,480 kg	
		Min.	Max.	Min.	Max.	Min.	Max.
Inside Measurement	Length (mm)	5,899	5,930	5,702	5,926	11,836	12,062
	Width (mm)	2,238	2,428	2,256	2,256	2,242	2,256
	Height (mm)	2,116	2,325	2,244	2,290	1,964	1,976
Door Opening	Width (mm)	—	—	—	—	—	—
Side Opening	Height (mm)	2,173	2,325	2,244	2,290	1,854	1,976
	Length (mm)	5,424	5,702	5,338	5,608	11,472	11,816
Roof Opening	Width (mm)	2,260	2,260	2,114	2,114	2,018	2,256
Length (mm)		5,836	5,836	5,602	5,702	11,836	11,950
Load Capacity (M3)	27.9	31.2	28.8	29.5	52.6	53.8	
Container Weight (kg)		2,440	3,620	3,150	3,600	4,700	5,900
Maximum Loading Weight (kg)		16,700	17,880	20,400	20,580	24,580	25,780

Flat Rack Containers:

1. These containers are suitable for heavy loads and extra wide cargo.
2. The bottom has strong construction.
3. Fixed end walls allow bracing, lashing, and stacking.
4. Ideal Cargo: air conditioners, boilers, construction machinery, electric generators, newsprint

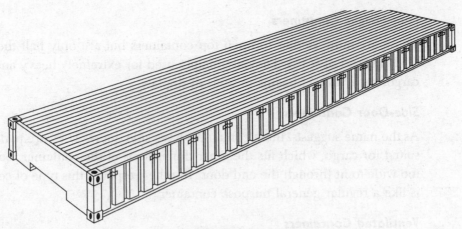

Fig. 12.5 Platform Container

Table 12.6 Specifications of a Platform Container

Platform Dimensions						20'
Construction	**Dimensions**			**Weights**		
	Length mm ft	Width mm ft	Height of bottom mm ft	Max Gross kg lbs	Tare kg lbs	Max payload kg lbs
1'1 1/4" high						
Steel frame with softwood floor	6,058	2,438	335	24,000	2,100	21,900
	20'	8'	1'1 1/4"	52,910	4,630	48,280
Platform Dimensions						40'
Construction	**Dimensions**			**Weights**		
	Length mm ft	Width mm ft	Height of bottom mm ft	Max Gross kg lbs	Tare kg lbs	Max payload kg lbs
2' high						
Steel frame with softwood floor	12,192	2,438	610	45,000	4,200	40,800
	40'	8'	2'	99,210"	9,260	89,950

Platform containers:
1. Platforms are most suitable for heavy loads and oversized cargo.
2. The bottom has strong construction.
3. Ideal Cargo: over- length, and over- height items, pipes, rods, plywood sheets, large irregularly-shaped items, and steel beans.

Half-Height Containers

These are quite similar to open top containers but are only half the height (4′ 3″ instead of 8′ 6″). They are mainly used for extremely heavy and dense cargo, such as steel beams or coils of tinplate.

Side-Door Containers

As the name suggests, these containers have side doors. They are particularly suited for cargo, which fits the inner dimensions of the container, but still is too wide to fit through the end door. In other respects, this type of container is like a regular general purpose container.

Ventilated Containers

These containers are suitable for cargo that needs ventilation, such as coffee or cocoa. They have small openings at each corner that lets fresh air into/out of the container, but to block the entry of rain and sea water.

Bulk Containers

Bulk containers (shown in Fig. 12.6) are ideally suitable for the carriage of dry bulk cargo. Three equivalent manholes are provided for top loading. Forklift pockets and lashing devices are provided. Ideal cargo for bulk containers would be grains, granules, sand, nuts, beans, malt, sugar, dry chemicals, etc.

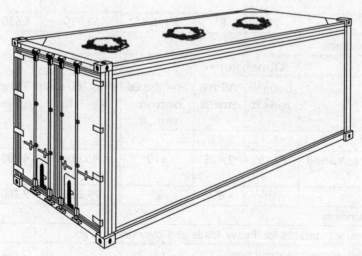

Fig. 12.6   Bulk Container

Insulated Containers

These are normal box containers with insulating material in the walls, top, and bottom. As a result, there is minimum temperature fluctuation inside.

Insulated containers are also attached to a separate temperature control device (Temperature Control Containers).

Collapsible Containers

These are like normal box containers, but the box can be collapsed completely. These containers are used on routes where there is very little return cargo and containers routinely return empty. $4 \times 20'$ collapsible containers in their collapsed form have exactly the same dimensions as $1 \times 20'$ regular box. There is a substantial space savings on returning empties.

Tank Containers

These containers are suitable for chemical products, such as flammables, oxidizing agents, toxic substances, and corrosives. These are also suitable for food products, such as, alcohols, fruit juices, edible oils, and food additives.

BENEFITS OF CONTAINERIZATION

Containerization has brought about enormous benefits to the shipping industry. It has revolutionized the concept of cargo management by bringing about major changes in the areas of land transportation, shipping, procedures and documentation, excise and customs rules, etc. These changes have benefitted shippers, ship owners, as well as port authorities.

Benefits to Shippers

One of the major beneficiaries of containerization is the shipper who sends valuable cargo across the seas. The shipper's business depends upon the speedy and safe passage of cargo to the destination abroad. The following are the benefits of containerization enjoyed by shippers:

Reduction in Transportation Costs

There is a major saving in transportation cost because for the same volume, the ocean freight for containerized cargo is less than break bulk cargo. Shipping lines are in a position to offer very attractive rates for containerized cargo because they can pass on the various cost saving benefits to their customers, i.e., shippers. Also, ship owners and shippers are entering into global contracts, where multi national corporations are using their global volumes to get price discounts from shipping lines.

Saving in Port Charges

Port authorities charge less tariffs for containerized cargo on account of ease of handling. It is much more facile to handle containerized cargo as compared to break bulk cargo. Overhead cranes and forklift trucks can very easily and quickly handle containerized cargo.

Reduction in Warehousing and Inventory Costs

The containerized cargo has to spend less time in warehouses and in transit, which substantially brings down the warehousing and inventory costs. This saving results in better competitiveness and larger market share for export products.

Reduction in Packing Cost

One of the most important features of a container is that it provides a protective metallic cover to the cargo. The container protects the cargo from theft, pilferage, and also to an extent, damage from oil, water, etc. The shipper need not use a very expensive packing material, because the container provides protection from most of the hazards of an ocean voyage.

Reduction in Insurance Premium

The insurance companies charge lower premium rates for containerized cargo because of the better protection provided by the container to the cargo inside. Since there are lesser chances of damage, theft and pilferage in containers, insurance companies perceive containerized cargo as more safe and secure than the general cargo; thus, they charge lesser premium. Consequently, the shipper can offer more competitive prices to the importer abroad on account of lower insurance premium.

More Convenience

Containerization of cargo enables door-to-door delivery of cargo. Once the cargo is stuffed in the container at the factory, the entire responsibility of its carriage is borne by a multi-modal transportation company. The formalities of central excise and customs are also completed at the time of stuffing the cargo. Since most of the formalities are completed prior to despatch of the cargo from the factory, containerization offers greater convenience to the shipper.

Better Acceptance

Ports all around the developed world prefer containerized cargo. Since developed countries are the most attractive markets for the goods from developing countries, shippers who offer to send their cargo in containers find better acceptance in the markets of developed countries.

Emergence of New Markets

The ocean freight cost today is much less as compared to that 10, 15, or even 20 years ago; cheaper transport now enables the shipper to peneterate newer markets. Also, new technological developments like Electronic Date Interchange (EDI) have reduced the transaction cost. All these factors have made global trading more attractive to an increasing number of companies.

In conclusion, it can be said that the shipper can save a substantial amount of money in transportation if the cargo is sent in a container. The savings in cost of warehousing and inventory, packaging, port charges, and insurance help the shipper to offer more attractive prices to the buyer abroad. Better prices result in more business for the shipper and finally for the entire shipping industry.

Benefits to Ship Owners

The following are the major benefits of containerization to ship owners:

Reduction in Turn Around Time

Containerization has speeded up cargo handling on the ports. Container ports and container terminals have to employ efficient material handling systems for quick loading and unloading of containers. Due to this, ships calling on the container ports have to spend less time on the ports. This results in the reduction in the turn-around time of the ships.

More Cargo Carrying Capacity

A containerized ship can carry more cargo as compared to general cargo ships. In addition, higher operating speeds enable the ships to complete the voyage relatively quickly. As such the cargo carried per voyage has increased alongwith the number of voyages made by a ship on a particular trade route. In the early nineties the average capacity of a container ship was 3000 TEUs but now the ships of 6000-TEU capacity are being built. Lesser time spent on the ports means more time spent on the sea. For a ship owner the time spent on the port is idle time. A general cargo ship has to spend around 50 per cent of its total voyage time on various ports. In comparison a containerised cargo ship spends relatively lesser time on the port. This improves the productivity of a ship tremendously.

Higher Return on Investment

Inspite of the higher purchasing price of a container ship, the ship owner finds the return on investment very attractive due to the higher returns they achieve.

Global Contracts

The ship owners and shippers are now entering into global contracts with multi national corporations like Procter & Gamble, General Motors, and Nestle. These MNCs use their global volumes to get discounts on the ocean freight. The shipping lines use these large volumes as their base cargo to make their voyages more profitable.

Higher Profitability

The cost of a large, modern container ship exceeds US$ 75 million and also the high operating cost of a container vessel being up to US$ 50,000 per day, means each day saved at port adds to the profitability of the shipping line.

Inland Operations

Containerization has motivated the ship owners to consider undertaking inland movement of containers. Inland operations also add to the revenues of the shipping lines.

Benefits to Port Authorities

Containerization is beneficial to the Port Authorities in the following ways:

Less Port Congestion

Containerization has substantially reduced the time spent by a ship at a port. In other words, the "turn around time" of the ships has reduced due to faster loading and unloading of containerized cargo. As a result of containerization and the resultant increase in sea borne trade, the governments have recognized ports as a major source of revenue and have created good road, rail, inland transport and feeder links. Ports have thus become hubs of international trade. Singapore, Hong Kong, and Dubai ports have created world-class cargo handling and warehousing facilities and have emerged as major trans shipment points. These ports are generating thousands of jobs for the local people.

Time Saving

Each container has a unique serial number, which helps in easy its recognition and the cargo within. With the advent of computerization, the serial number of the container is fed into a computer, which helps in quickly locating it on sprawling container ports. This saves a lot of time for the port authorities.

Fast and Convenient Loading and Unloading

Easy identification of containers also helps in the quick loading and unloading of the cargo at the port. In comparison, it is much more difficult to locate, load and unload break bulk cargo (general cargo).

Less Marketing Efforts

In the pre-containerization days, the strategy of the shipping line was to "follow the cargo". It means that the shipping line would chase the cargo. However due to containerization, the cargo follows the container ship. The reason is that the shippers prefer to select those ports where there are excellent container handling and storing facilities. Such ports are also the preferred ports of call of container ships. The ports with such traffic concentration have become regional container load centres. Hence the shipping lines need not chase the shippers for marketing their services.

Rationalization of Cargo Handling Charges

The port terminals could charge cargo handling charges in a less complex and easy to understand method as compared to the complex and detailed tariffs of the break bulk era.

GLOBAL TRADE AND CONTAINERIZATION

The process of globalization and containerization are irrevocably linked; one without the other is barely imaginable. Wherever industry locates and produces, containerization follows (Baird, 1997).

We are living today in a world where consumer needs are getting increasingly homogenized. As a result, the successful global organization must treat the whole world as their market. Global corporations, such as McDonald's, Coca-Cola, and Levi Strauss sell virtually the same products in the same way everywhere. For such corporations, the ideal business strategy is to export the standardized product from their plants, which manufacture on global scale. A distribution network to cater to various markets across the globe can be worked out in consultation with logistics experts (Levitt, 1983).

For shipping lines, these global corporations are important customers. Shipping lines lift the cargo from the manufacturing plants of global corporations and ship them to various corners of the world where the markets exist. Large multinational corporations, such as Toyota, Procter & Gamble, Nestle, Ford, and Daewoo are tying up with shipping lines and entering into global contracts with them. Under such contracts, the shipping lines offer special discounted freight rates to the MNC against the large volumes of cargo they get to carry from the various plant locations across the world to hundreds of markets where the corporation's products are sold.

As per door-to-door contracts, MNCs expect competitive freight rates, minimum transit time, and high-quality services from shipping lines. Global carriers have to be more responsive to the needs of their customers and offer them high quality of service at the lowest price. Shipping lines can cut costs by employing bigger ships, and catering to selected major ports. The global carriers should also be in a position to forecast the business strategies of their customers in order to respond quickly to emerging market needs. For example, if a shipping line knows that a MNC is going to start a new manufacturing plant in India, the shipping line may decide to open an office in India to mark their presence in the Indian market and to begin marketing efforts towards getting future business from the MNC.

World Container Trade

The containerization of world trade has grown dramatically in the last few decades. The total world container traffic in 1980 was only 39 million TEU (Twenty feet equivalent units) and it is growing rapidly as Asian countries, particularly China, is expanding the throughput of its container ports rapidly.

Global Container Service Operators

The shipping industry is dominated by 20 major container service operators, as shown in the following table. Between them, these operators carry 4.27 million TEU of shipboard capacity, which is almost 50 per cent of the world's total shipboard capacity. Interestingly, out of these 20 container lines, nine are Asian, and the remaining are either European or American. Considering this trend and also in view of plans to increase the tonnage, Asian lines are likely to dominate the markets in the near future. The present leader in terms of total TEU capacity is the Denmark based AP Moller, which has almost double the capacity of its nearest rival P&O Ned Lloyd.

Top Ten Container Service Operators

Top 10 container service operators on the basis of TEU deployed (October 2005) is given in Table 12.7.

Table 12.7 Top Ten Container Service Operators

Rank 2005	Rank 2004	Carrier	TEU in service	Vessels in service	TEU on order	Vessels on order	Projected TEU	Projected vessels
1	1	AP Moller Group	1,523,347	570	714,184	135	2,237,531	705
2	2	MSC	736,301	268	271,316	36	1,007,617	304
3	3	Evergreen Group	470,234	155	152,583	25	622,817	180
4	5	CMA CGM	424,494	188	363,594	67	788,088	255
5	8	APL	326,291	106	89,908	26	416,199	132
6	17	CSCL	317,541	111	154,160	21	471,701	132
7	7	COSCO	308,223	123	220,583	26	528,806	149
8	9	NYK	292,304	110	146,600	25	438,904	135
9	6	HANJIN	291,207	75	74,365	11	365,572	86
10	10	MOL	240,391	79	90,400	14	330,791	93

Source: Containerization International Yearbook 2006

The number of vessels on order suggests that the top 10 container service operators are in an expansion mode. These expansion plans in capacity are the result of expected increase in world trade volumes in the near future. The Chinese and Indian economies are growing at a rapid pace, fuelling the need for imports and increasing the exports every year. The new vessels ordered are likely to cater to the needs of increased movement of cargo.

Although it remains at the top slot in terms of fleet capacity, the AP Möller-Maersk Group comes at the eighth position for market share growth, a rank achieved thanks to the 2005 purchase of Royal P&O Nedlloyd, which allowed it to boost its market share from 12.5 per cent to 18 per cent overnight, corresponding to an increase of 51 per cent compared with that in January 2000 (Salle).

The economic life of containers is around 10 years. Container service operators try to maintain a relatively new fleet of containers and avoid increasing maintenance and repair costs associated with ageing containers. As such, the old used containers are sold globally to second hand container buyers. Such second hand buyers are generally small time container leasing firms, NVOCC, and merchants.

Major Container Ports

The ports with an annual throughput exceeding 1 million TEU can be categorized as a major container port. Most of these ports act as trans-shipment ports or hub ports. These ports attract direct calls by large mother vessels, which in turn are serviced by smaller feeder vessels which then carry the cargo to smaller ports. At present, the higest number of large container ports is in Asia with at least 15 of them exceeding an annual throughput of 1 million TEU (see Table 12.8)

Table 12.8 Top Twenty Container Ports July/August 2007

2006 Ranking	2005 Ranking	Port	Country	Throughput 2006 TEUs	Throughput 2007 TEUs	Variation	% Change
1	1	Singapore	Singapore	24,792,400	23,199,252	1,600,748	7
2	2	Hong Kong	China	23,539,000	22,480,000	1,059,000	5
3	3	Shanghai	China	21,710,000	18,080,000	3,630,000	20
4	4	Shenzhen	China	18,468,890	16,197,000	2,271,890	14
5	5	Busan	South Korea	12,030,000	11,840,000	190,000	2
6	6	Kaohsiung	Taiwan	9,774,670	9,470,000	305,000	3
7	7	Rotterdam	Netherlands	9,603,000	9,286,757	316,243	3
8	9	Dubai	UAE	8,923,465	7,619,000	1,304,000	17
9	8	Hamburg	Germany	8,861,545	8,087,545	774,455	10
10	10	Los Angeles	USA	8,469,853	7,484,624	985,229	13
11	13	Qingdao	China	7,702,000	6,307,000	1,395,000	22
12	11	Long Beach	USA	7,289,365	6,709,818	579,547	9
13	15	Ningbo-Zhousan	China	7,068,000	5,208,000	1,860,000	36
14	12	Antwerp	Belgium	7,018,799	6,488,029	530,770	8
15	18	Guangzhou	China	6,600,000	4,684,000	1,916,000	41
16	14	Port Klang	Malaysia	6,300,000	5,540,000	760,000	14
17	16	Tianjin	China	5,950,000	4,801,000	1,149,000	24
18	17	New York/New Jersey	USA	5,092,806	4,785,318	307,488	6
19	19	Tanjung Pelapas	Malaysia	4,770,000	4,177,000	593,000	14
20	21	Bremerhaven	Germany	4,400,000	3,735,574	664,426	18

Source: Container Management, July/August 2007

The Jawaharlal Nehru Port at Nhava Sheva near Mumbai is India's biggest port. However, its world ranking was 33rd with a 2.58 million TEU throughput achieved in the year 2005. In 2004, the port was ranked 32nd; thus, it slipped in its ranking in 2005 in the fast developing world of container ports.

Exhibit 12.1   JNPT improves global ranking in box handling

The country's premier container port, the Jawaharlal Nehru Port has improved its global ranking by jumping to the 28th position during the calendar year 2006 from its earlier position at 32. The port improved its global ranking by handling 3.08 million TEUs during the calendar year 2006 as against 2.58 million TEUs the previous calendar year.

The international ranking of container handling ports is done on the basis of throughput handled during a particular calendar year.

During the financial year 2006-07, JN Port handled 3.30 million TEUs, which constitutes 60.67 per cent of total container handling by all Major Ports in India and remaining No. I port in India. The port handled 44.82 million tones of cargo during the financial year 2006-07 as against 37.84 million tones of cargo handled during the last financial year 2005-06. The port crossed 3 million TEUs mark in container handling during the year.

Source: The Economic Times, 23 April 2007

There is a keen competition among ports to attract big shipping lines. The shipping lines now have more bargaining power while negotiating with the ports. More direct service obviously means more benefits to ports. However, the decision to provide direct service to a port is exclusively the shipping line's call. The port authorities can do very little to influence the decision of the shipping line except to improve their performance. With globalization and increasing world trade, the demand for additional port capacity and new ports is also increasing. Some of the new ports which have recently commenced or are likely to commence operations are Subic Bay Philippines (Cap.1 million TEU), Batam Island Indonesia (25 million TEU), Shenzen, China (3 million TEU), and Gioia Tauro Italy (2 million TEU). The new ports offer the following advantages:

- Excellent facilities in terms of water depth, large cranes, and sufficient storage capacity.
- New ports are generally located near shipping lanes, therefore require minimum deviation time.
- Good roads, rail, inland transport, and feeder links.
- Located far from main city areas, they do not suffer from problems, which are faced by ports located in large cities.

At present the number of ports with capacity over 1 million TEUs is about 80.

CONTAINER LEASING PRACTICES

Containers are largely owned by shipping lines and by some of the leading freight forwarding organizations around the world. Additionally, some companies owning containers lease them out to ship-owners, forwarders, or sometimes even directly to shippers for certain time periods.

The practice of leasing containers is important because there is a constant fluctuation in the shipping business. Sometimes the trade volumes in the world markets are very low. During this time, the containers remain idle in different parts of the world. During other periods, there is an upsurge in the shipping volumes and a corresponding shortage of containers. Containers being very expensive, the shipping lines do not own beyond a certain number of them. In case of need, shipping lines would lease from the leasing companies to meet the temporary demand. Another reason for the popularity of leasing is that on Trans-Atlantic route, for example, a liner operator must own for each of its vessels a minimum of three sets of containers, one in Europe, one in North America, and one on the high seas. The shipping lines in such cases resort to short-term or long-term leasing.

Types of Leases

Different types of leases available for containerization are discussed as follows.

1. One-Way Lease

In this case, the container is leased only for outward journey. For example, if a container is leased for a trip from Chennai port to Dubai, the container is leased in Chennai and returned empty and clean to the leaser's depot in Dubai.

2. Round Trip

In this case, the container is leased for both outward as well as inward journeys. This is used when either the shipper has bothways movement of cargo, or when there is no return depot at the port of destination.

3. Short Lease

A short lease implies that the container is leased for 60 or 90 days.

4. Long Lease

In a long lease, the container is leased for two, three, or more years.

5. Master Lease

In this case, shipping lines enter into a master lease contract with leasing companies.

Whenever a leased container is returned, the owner makes receipt (known as the EIR or Equipment Interchange Receipt) in which the following information appears:

1. Date/place of pick-up
2. Name and other details of lessee
3. Full identification of container
4. Condition of container when leased and when returned

Most leased containers are covered by a Damage Protection Plan (DPP); however, the cost of normal wear and tear, i.e., rust holes, etc, need not be borne by the lessee.

Leasing companies are helping the process of containerization in many innovative ways. In developing countries, they assist in building up container services by leasing container ships and container cranes to regional operators. The leading players in the container leasing business are—CTI, ICCU, NIC, CS, XTRA, UNIFLEX, INTERPOOL, TOL, CONTRANS, SEACONTAINERS, ITEL, GENSTAR, etc.

Advantages of Leasing

Advantages of leasing include the following.

1. It is possible to lease a container at a short notice in case of a sudden surge in demand for the containers.
2. Containers can be returned to the leasing company as soon as the demand of the shipping line is over.
3. Leasing saves shipping lines from blocking their capital (which would happen if the lines were to own the containers). Most shipping lines have a policy regarding the percentage of containers owned against percentage leased.
4. The newly formed shipping lines can start off with leased containers, without investing their capital in the ownership of containers.
5. At many places, the leasing companies waive off drop-off and pick-up charges when there is a slump in the demand for containers.
6. The entire business of Non-Vessel Operating Common Carriers (NVOCCs) is built on leased equipment.

INLAND CONTAINER DEPOTS

The container base forms an important part of an integrated international transport system designed to link with inland centers the container terminals where ships are handled. This is achieved through a rail system or road haulage distribution network (Branch). Such bases are called Inland Ports or Inland Container Depots (ICD).

An inland port is a site located away from traditional land, air, and coastal borders. It facilitates and processes international trade through strategic investments in multimodal transportation assets and by promoting value added services as goods move through supply chain.

Inland Container Depots play a significant role in international supply chains. They are now an integral part of global logistics and are established in different parts of the world to

1. provide transportation logistics services for export-import as well as domestic cargo in containers;
2. facilitate trade to and from the industries based in the hinterland (i.e., areas far from the sea ports and international airports);
3. reduce the bottlenecks at sea-ports by freeing up storage space in container yards; and
4. to create employment opportunities and development in rural areas.

The ICD performs the same functions as a port, except for the loading and unloading of ships (the stevedoring operation). In this way, a container will bypass the port container depot and be processed nearer the consignee or shipper. Inland container depots are also called dry ports, since they have all the facilities, which a normal port has for handling the export-import cargo. An ICD is a large enclosed/secure area where cargo-carrying

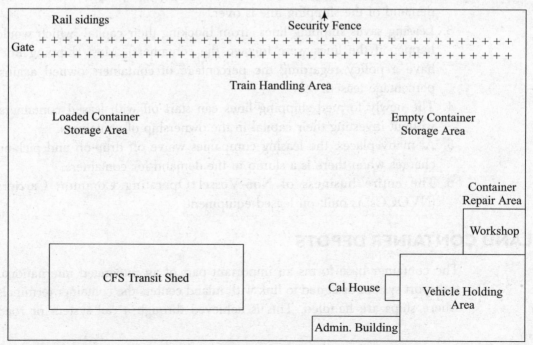

Source: Handbook on the Management and Operation of Dry Ports, UNCTAD, 1991.

containers are stored under customs bond. The ICDs are connected to seaports by rail or by road or both and such movements are carried out under customs bond. ICDs also store empty containers before they are sent off for stuffing.

Prior to the creation of ICDs, import containers were transported from seaports to importer's factory/warehouse in the hinterland. After de-stuffing of cargo, the empty container would return to the seaport. Similarly for export cargo, the empty containers had to be called from the seaport. This was a wasteful exercise in terms of time and money. After the creation of ICDs, the shippers can save time and money by calling the containers from a nearby ICD; the excise and customs clearance can take place at either the shipper's premises or at ICD; and documentation is simplified. Freight Forwarders help in handling ICD related work for and on behalf of customers.

Duties and Responsibilities of an ICD

The various duties and responsibilities of an ICD are as follows.

Gate-in Check

All containers entering the ICDs are checked for damage or contamination. Empty containers are examined both internally as well as externally. The stuffed containers are examined only externally on arrival. Damages are reported to the container owner so that repairs can be carried out either at the ICD or any other repair facility of the owner's choice.

Gate-out Check

Normally, all the containers are checked for their condition on their way out of ICDs. Damaged empty containers are not sent for stuffing. In such a case, the owner is informed and his/her instructions are sought.

Documentation

An Equipment Interchange Receipt (EIR) is issued every time equipment is interchanged between two parties. The EIR contains details, such as the names of the parties involved, container number, seal number (for stuffed containers), name of the transporter, vehicle number, etc.

Reporting

All the movements of containers in and out of an ICD is notified to the owner of the containers. The communication is carried out through e-mail, fax, and where ever it is available, through Electronic Data Interchange (EDI).

Repairs and Maintenance

Any repair work undertaken at an ICD must conform to customs approval standards. The International Institute of Container Leasers (IICL), which is based in the United States, has developed these standards, which are the best-known standards in the industry. In case of reefer containers, the routine maintenance of refrigeration equipment is essential. Before the cargo is loaded, the thermostats are set to maintain the right temperature and other equipment are suitably calibrated.

Storage

ICDs have to make suitable arrangements for safe storage of containers. Empty containers are stacked one on top of the other. ICDs must have suitable material handling equipment for moving the containers within the premises.

Despatch

ICDs arrange for road and rail transportation of the cargo to the ports. They also undertake stuffing and de-stuffing operations, if required.

Miscellaneous Duties and Responsibilities

These include sealing the containers, lashing, securing and bracing odd size cargo, conducting container conditioning surveys, etc.

Container Corporation of India

In India, the Container Corporation of India (CONCOR) has established a network of ICDs in the different parts of the country. CONCOR was established in March 1988 under the Ministry of Railways. The company was set up with the objective of developing multimodal logistics support for India's international and domestic containerized cargo and trade. The task was to provide customers the advantages of direct interaction and door-to-door services that formed the backbone of road transport, while capitalizing on the robust and more economical option of rail movement on the Indian Railways network.

Objectives

CONCOR provides logistics services and support for both international and domestic cargo industry and is currently the only means by which shippers may obtain containerized freight transportation by rail in India. The objectives of CONCOR are to

1. provide transportation logistics services for export-import as well as domestic cargo in containers.
2. expand CONCOR's terminal network in the country so as to enhance its market share in the container business.
3. bring back less than trainload general goods cargo from road to rail in containers through extensive marketing efforts.
4. provide multimodal transportation logistics consultancy services to potential operators who would help CONCOR grow its business.

CONCOR's Core Business

Three distinct categories of CONCOR's core business are as follows.

CONCOR as Carrier CONCOR provides the rail or road link between ports and terminals. It is the sole provider of containerized rail transport in India. Some of the terminals like Pithampur (Indore), Malanpur, Mulund, and Milavittan, etc., are linked to the ports by road. But the majority of ICDs and Container Freight Stations (CFSs) are linked by rail. The rails freight is almost 20% cheaper than road freight. CONCOR passes on this cost advantage to its customers. Indian Railways also provide leased land for container operations and railway wagons and operational support to CONCOR. The rail link reduces the dependence of the exporters on road transport and also helps reduce traffic congestion on roads.

CONCOR as Terminal and Warehouse Operator CONCOR began its operations in November 1989 with seven ICDs. Today, it has a network of 51 terminals of which 44 are export-import container depots, and seven are exclusively domestic container depots. While most of the depots have rail links, seven container depots are connected only by roads. A CONCOR terminal provides all the facilities of a dry port to the shippers, including customs clearance. Other facilities include warehousing, container storage and repairs, etc. These terminals are categorized as deep and medium hinterland, portside and within port terminals. Each category serves a different segment of clients who have differing needs.

CONCOR as CFS Operator   In its role as CFS operator, CONCOR provides value added services by offering transit-warehousing facility to import/export cargo. The shippers can also enjoy the benefits of CONCOR's bonded warehouse from where they seek partial releases of their cargo, thereby deferring duty payment. As CFS operator, CONCOR provides the following services:

- Transit warehousing for import and export cargo.
- Bonded warehousing that enables shippers to seek partial release of their cargo, thereby deferring duty payment.

- Consolidation of Less than Container Load (LCL) cargo.
- Clearance of air cargo using bonded trucking.

SUMMARY

Containerization has changed the face of world trade. The concept of unitization of load was introduced by Malcolm McLean for facilitating the loading of cargo on board a ship. He could not have imagined that this concept would change everything from port infrastructure to shipping documentation. Modern ports are being built specifically to handle containerized cargo. These ports rely more on heavy cranes and other material handling equipment and less on manual labour. Container ships are being designed to carry more and more cargo in order to achieve better economies of scale. The *Emma Maersk*, the largest container ship ever built has a length of 398 meters and can carry 11,000 to 15,000 TEUs. Large ships typically have a lower cost per TEU-mile hour than a smaller unit with the same load factor (Simhan 2006). Roads are being built with container-carrying trucks in mind. Railway tracks are being laid exclusively for single-stack and double-stack container trains.

Warehouses are equipped to handle and store containerized cargo. Customs authorities across the world are geared to examine increasing volumes of containerized cargo. In fact, the customs laws are being amended to ease the clearance of containerized cargo. Information technology is helping shippers track their containers on high seas. In short, the innovation of Malcolm McLean has come a long way and changed the maritime sector. The reason for this change is that it has benefited all the stakeholders.

CONCEPT REVIEW QUESTIONS

1. What are the characteristics of a container? Explain the history of containerization.
2. Discuss the various types of containers and their utilities.
3. What are the benefits of containerization to
   (a) Shippers
   (b) Ship owners
   (c) Port authorities
4. Write an essay on the impact of containerization on world trade.

5. Explain the container leasing operations. What are the benefits of leasing to the various segments of shipping industry?
6. Write a short note on Inland Container Depots.
7. What are the functions of an ICD? Discuss their duties and responsibilities towards the shipping industry.
8. Discuss the role-played by CONCOR in promotion of multimodal transport in India.

OBJECTIVE QUESTIONS

In the following questions, choose the correct option.
1. Which of the following statements is NOT true?
   (a) Containers are strong enough for repeated use.
   (b) Containers are specially designed to facilitate the carriage of goods by only one mode of transport.
   (c) Containers are fitted with devices permitting its ready handling particularity its transfer from one mode of transport to another.
   (d) Containers are designed for easy filling and emptying.
2. The concept of containerization was first introduced by
   (a) Captain Cook
   (b) Christopher Columbus
   (c) Malcom Mclean
   (d) Marco Polo
3. What does TEU stand for?
   (a) Ton Equivalent Unit
   (b) Twelve Equal Units
   (c) Ten Feet Equivalent Units
   (d) Twenty Feet Equivalent Units
4. Which of the following is NOT among the top FIVE container ports in the world:
   (a) Singapore
   (b) Hong Kong
   (c) Shanghai
   (d) Dubai
   (e) Shenzen
5. Which of the following is NOT a benefit of containerization:
   (a) Big container ports dominating the shipping industry
   (b) More cargo carrying capacity on a ship

(c) Higher return on investment

(d) Less port congestion

State whether the following statements are True or False.

6. Jawaharlal Nehru Port is among the top 20 container ports in the world.

7. AP Moeller Group is the top container service provider in the world.

8. Tank containers can be used for carrying perishable cargo.

9. Containers being expensive, shipping lines would rather lease the containers than buy them.

10. CONCOR is a large shipping line.

EXERCISES

1. Mark the locations of the top five container ports on a world map.

2. Mark the locations of Inland Container Depots on the map of India

3. Visit the websites of Singapore port and Jawaharlal Nehru Port and compare the infrastructure of these two ports.

4. Visit the nearest Inland Container Depot to your place and write a short report on your visit.

5. List down the material handling equipment typically used at a container port.

SELECT REFERENCES

Baird Alfred, 1997, 'Globalization, Container Shipping and the emergence of new port network', *Tenth World Productivity Congress Paper Chile.*

Barry Rogliano Sales Report, January 2006, *Alphaliner report,* 11-05

Branch Alan, 1994, *Export Practice and Management,* Thomson Learning

Levinson Mark, 2006, *The Box: How the shipping container made the world smaller and world economy bigger,* Princeton University Press, New Jersey.

Levitt T., 1983, 'The Globalisation of Markets', *Harvard Business Review,* May-June (3) 92-102

Raja Simhan T.G, 2006, 'India must think big on Ports', *The Hindu* dated 16th October 2006.

Wood, Barnes and Murphy, Wardlow, 2002, *International Logistics,* AMACOM Publication, New York

www.concorindia.com, last accessed on 14th September 2007.

www.lectlaw.com, last accessed on 10th September 2007.

www.tti.tamu.edu, last accessed on 14th September 2007

DOWNSIDE OF CONTAINERIZATION Case Study

It is a known fact that the members of shipping conferences enjoy a monopoly in the shipping industry. This monopoly is a continuous source of conflict between some large carriers and the shippers. This is mainly because the conferences do not consult shippers while deciding their pricing policies. It seems that shipping conferences are only interested in maximizing their revenues, irrespective of the hardships faced by the shipper. This problem is particularly acute in developing countries where the regulatory bodies are not strong enough to challenge the conferences.

Today, the shippers have to pay a variety of charges in addition to freight costs. For example, today the cost of sea borne transportation could be

Transport cost = Freight + Terminal Handling Charges (THC) + Bunkarage Adjustment Factor (BAF)+ Currency Adjustment Factor (CAF) + Peak Season Surcharge + Destination Delivery Charges (DDC) + Bill of Lading or documentation fees + War risk surcharge

This is a long list of charges, which seems endless. One of the acrimonious issues is the ever-increasing terminal handling charge (THC). This is a tool used to generate extra revenue for the carriers. THC is an unfair pricing mechanism based on an 18th century principle known as the ship's rail costing (hook-to-hook). However, this is no longer applicable, as after the containerization of cargo was introduced in the 1960s, the method of handing over goods to ship or receiving goods from the ship has changed. Technically, it is only on the basis of break bulk cargo that the original Free On Board (FOB) point remains demarcated at the ship's rail.

Prior to containerization, the shipper was responsible for handing over/ picking up the cargo along side ship (quay), so that the ship's hook (crane) would unload/load cargo (alongside). This system justified the cost of port charges to be borne by the shipper, as he/she was responsible for bringing cargo alongside the ship on the quay. However, with the introduction of the containers, cargo is not only stuffed at the manufacturer's door, but it is also handed over to the ocean carrier in the container yard within port premises. Hence it is clear that today the shipper's responsibility ends with handing over the cargo in the container yard. The shipper no longer moves the cargo alongside ship. This is also the point where the carrier takes responsibility (in case of exports) or hands over the responsibility (in case of imports) to and from the shipper.

This change in technology means that the responsibility of cargo is now transferred at container yard and not at ship's rails. Interestingly, the THC is not charged at every port. For example, ports in the Middle East and in New Zealand do not levy THC. In Asia and the Indian subcontinent, shippers have to pay THC.

Questions

1. Do you agree that the THC is an unfair pricing mechanism, which should be abolished? Suggest a suitable tariff schedule, which is acceptable to both shippers as well as ocean carriers.
2. What are your suggestions to shippers who have to bear various unreasonable charges at the port?
3. Containerization has brought about advantages as well as disadvantages to shippers. Do you agree or disagree with this statement? Give reasons in support of your answer.

13 Export Procedures and Documents

Learning Objectives

After studying this chapter, you will be able to understand
- how to search for an overseas buyer
- the essential components of an offer/quotation
- export procedures
- negotiation of export documents

In Chapter 2, we covered the various steps involved in the execution of an export order, right from the registration of an exporter with the Director General of Foreign Trade (DGFT) and Export Promotion Councils (EPCs) to the despatch of export documents to the concerned bank. The chapter also discussed various export documents and their importance. This chapter will cover the complete procedure of processing an export order, keeping particularly in view the actual process involved in generating an enquiry, aspects of documentation during and after the manufacture of goods, details of excise formalities to be completed while despatching the goods, and the negotiation of documents with the exporter's bank.

THE SEARCH FOR AN OVERSEAS BUYER

An export organization is on the constant look-out for new overseas markets, where there is a demand for their products and the profit margins are attractive. There are various ways in which overseas customers can be located. Some of the effective ways of searching for these customers are discussed in the following sections.

Conduct Market Research

Market research involves desk research to gather secondary data from various journals, magazines, publications, and the internet. This could be followed by a personal visit to the target market for gathering primary data, after meeting the potential customers, distribution channels, government agencies, etc. Personal visits help assess the market demand, profitability, and risks involved.

Participate in an International Exhibition

Several specialized trade exhibitions are held regularly the world over. The exhibition calendar of the Indian Trade Promotion Organisation (ITPO) can help the exporter determine the most appropriate exhibition to participate in India or abroad. ITPO can also help the participant by way of space booking, stand construction, shipment of exhibits, exhibition ground facilities, etc.

Internet

The internet too is a powerful tool to get in touch with potential overseas buyers. Exporters can either launch their own websites to advertise their products or use internet search engines to locate buyers.

Export Promotion Councils and Commodity Boards

EPCs and commodity boards help their members through their offices abroad, customer databases, buyer-seller meets, exhibitions, etc.

The export market being very competitive, exporters have to ensure high quality presentation of their goods by way of an introductory letter, along with attractive leaflets providing organization and product details, samples of quality goods with export worthy packing, and competitive pricing. If the exporter does not create a good 'first impression' it is unlikely that he/she would get a second chance with potential customers. Therefore, before venturing into the export market, careful preparation with an eye for detail is absolutely imperative. A professional attitude can add a touch of class to the product and can help establish a positive image and credibility in the minds of potential buyers. Exhibit 13.1 gives a sample letter of introduction. It gives an idea about the details, which need to be included to initiate correspondence with an overseas buyer.

Once the buyer indicates an interest, he/she will ask the seller to submit an offer/quotation. Due care is needed while preparing the offer, which should include

(a) Names of the buyer and seller
(b) Reference number of offer and date
(c) Enquiry number of offer and date
(d) Product details including technical specifications, where required
(e) Quantity of goods offered
(f) Prices on ex works/FOB/C&F/CIF basis in international currency, such as US Dollar, Euro, Japanese Yen, Pound Sterling, etc.

Exhibit 13.1 Sample introductory letter

Ref. No. X/USA/121/06-07   Date: 16th March 2007

Nouvelle International
Merchandise Division
New York
United States of America

Dear Sir/ Madam,

Sub.: Cotton shirts

We are pleased to introduce our 'Columbus' brand of shirts. We are a leading manufacturer of Cotton Shirts in India. Our integrated state-of-the-art plant located near Mumbai employs the most advanced machinery imported from Europe. A well-trained and motivated staff of about 150 employees ensures that our quality meets the stringent norms demanded by our customers in the European Union and Australian markets. We are an ISO 9000 company, having won a number of prestigious national and international awards for our achievements.

We are now launching a new brand and our advertising campaign, "Explore emerging horizons with Columbus" will soon be seen in leading American fashion magazines.

We understand that you are a leading importer of men's wear in America. We invite you to visit our website to explore the details of our organization, manufacturing facilities, and product spectrum. Our interactive website will give you an idea about our creative range, attractive packaging, and testimonials from satisfied customers across the world. We shall be pleased to submit our offer to you on receipt of a specific enquiry.

In case you have any queries, please do not hesitate to contact us. We will be happy to reply with the necessary details.

Assuring you of our best attention.

Yours sincerely

PK Singh
Export Manager

(g) Port/airport of despatch and port/airport of destination
(h) Mode of transportation, e.g., by sea/air/road/rail
(i) Payment terms
(j) Name and address of the exporter's bank
(k) Despatch schedule

The exporter should not forget to mention the date up to which the offer is valid for acceptance. This is essential because the costs of inputs such as raw materials, consumables, machinery, and manpower may rise within any time period. In addition, there could be changes in the freight rates, insurance premiums, duties and taxes, etc. The offer validity clause helps the exporter to revise the offer taking into account recent changes.

On receipt of this offer, the overseas buyer may like to initiate negotiations with the seller in terms of price, quantity and quality of goods, packaging, despatch schedule, payment terms, etc. Once both the parties are satisfied with their own end of the bargain, the buyer may release a purchase order or a letter of intent in favor of the seller. At this point, the seller must study the purchase order and confirm agreement with all the conditions laid down by the buyer. If the seller has any reservations, these must be sorted out with the buyer immediately. The seller can then issue a Proforma Invoice in favour of the buyer, which is an advance bill containing various terms and conditions agreed between buyer and seller. If satisfied with the contents of the Proforma Invoice, the buyer approaches a bank to establish a Letter of Credit (L/C) in favour of the seller. If the transaction is on Document against Payment (DP) basis, or Document against Acceptance (DA) basis and no L/C is involved, the buyer can instruct the seller to proceed with the execution of the order.

PROCESSING AN EXPORT ORDER

The processing of an export order can be divided in two different categories.
1. Pre-despatch procedure
2. Post-despatch procedure

This classification will help understand various formalities an exporter has to complete at different stages. It also highlights the role of various agencies involved in the successful execution of an export order. As export transactions involve the government agencies of two countries, it is necessary to ensure compliance with rules and regulations of the countries of both the buyer and the seller. Also, since such transactions involve foreign exchange, government agencies, like, the Reserve Bank of India (RBI) and the Excise and Customs department in India, are very vigilant and expect the exporters to comply with relevant regulations in force. An Indian exporter has to comply with the Foreign Exchange Management Act (FEMA), which binds the exporter to ensure the following:

1. Details regarding value of export, mode of payment, amount of payment received, etc., are provided to the RBI from time to time.
2. The amount of foreign exchange earned against exports from India is repatriated within the time specified by RBI.

Hence, following the correct procedure and ensuring meticulous documentation help the exporter transport cargo to overseas customers without delays. It also helps the exporter to comply with various rules and regulations of both the exporting and the host country.

Pre-despatch Procedure

After the Purchase Order (PO)/L/C is received, the exporter must ensure that it complies with the RBI norms related to permitted currencies and the methods of payment. The expression 'permitted currency' is used in the RBI manual to indicate a foreign currency which is freely convertible, i.e., a currency which is permitted by the rules and regulations of the country concerned to be converted into major reserve currencies like the US Dollar and the Pound Sterling, and for which a fairly active market exists that deals against the major currency. Some of the other currencies permitted are the Euro and the Japanese Yen. The RBI allows exporters to receive directly from buyers payments in the form of bank drafts, cheques, pay orders, foreign currency notes, or foreign currency traveller's cheques, subject to conditions. Normally, the payment must be received through the medium of an authorized dealer. Here, an authorized dealer means a bank, which is authorized by RBI to deal in the foreign currencies listed.

Once satisfied with all the terms and conditions of the transaction, the exporter will initiate the following actions.

1. If a manufacturer-exporter, the exporter will issue a Work Order and circulate it to various intra-organizational departments, such as finance, materials, planning, manufacturing, quality control, etc. The Work Order will contain all the details similar to Proforma Invoice so that the concerned department becomes fully aware of commitments made by marketing/exports department to the customer; in terms of quality and quantity of the material ordered, delivery, payment terms, order value, etc.

2. If a merchant exporter, the exporter will place the order with a vendor/s. The exporter will issue a Purchase Order in favour of the vendor(s) and will communicate all requirements in order to execute the order as committed to the overseas customer. The exporter will ensure that the vendor delivers the goods well in advance of the shipment deadline. The merchant exporter may establish a back-to-back L/C in favour of the vendor for effecting the payment. Alternatively the exporter and the vendor can decide the mode of payment with mutual consent.

After the work order is received by the various departments within the organization, they initiate the manufacturing process. The exporter will simultaneously approach his/her bank to avail of the packing credit, which is the pre-shipment credit given by banks in India on interest rates lower than normal in order to make funds available to Indian exporters at interest rates comparable with the international norm. Packing credit is given both in Indian Rupees as well as foreign currencies, as per the needs of exporter. The exporter can either avail of this credit in person or pass it on to the supporting manufacturer.

Once the finances are available, the exporter can procure the raw materials and consumables for the export cargo. The exporter has to ensure that the goods are manufactured as per international standards, such as the BS (British Standards), DIN (German Standards), JIS (Japanese Standards), etc., as specified by the buyer. A number of overseas buyers insist on in-process quality control right from raw material procurement stage till the goods are packed. Such inspections are either carried out by the representative of the buyer or by a third party inspection agency nominated by the buyer. The exporter has to cooperate with the inspection and should make goods and facilities available for the same. Such facilities may include material handling equipment, quality control equipment/instruments, testing lab facilities, etc. The exporter must keep enough time margin, so that in case of rejection on quality parameters at any stage, he/she can remanufacture and still meet the despatch deadline. In certain cases, due to last minute rejection by the quality control department, the exporter does not have time to remanufacture the goods and has to request the importer to extend the validity of L/C for shipment. Once the goods are accepted, the inspection authorities will issue a pre-shipment inspection certificate.

Excise Clearance of Export Goods

Central Excise duty is an indirect tax levied on goods manufactured in India. This duty is levied in terms of the Central Excise Act, 1944, and the rates of duty, ad valorem or specific, are prescribed under schedule I and II of the Central Excise Tariff Act, 1985.

Exporters of almost all excisable goods except hides, skins, leather, and salt and exports to all countries except to Nepal and Bhutan can claim exemption from Central Excise Duties. As the payment for exports to Nepal and Bhutan are in Indian Rupees, they do not qualify for excise duty exemption.

Excise clearance of export goods can be carried out in three ways:
1. The exporter can pay the excise duty and claim the refund after the goods have been exported. Alternatively, duty drawback can be claimed on inputs used in manufacturing the products exported.

2. The second method involves exporting the goods under bond without payment of excise duty. After the goods are exported and proof of export is submitted, the bond is released. It is a common practice for regular exporters to have a running bond for this purpose.

3. Exporters who are members of EPCs are exempted from submitting a bond to the excise authorities. Instead, they have to only submit an undertaking to the Central Excise department on Form UT-1, against which they can clear the goods for exports. This undertaking is to be executed on a stamp paper of Rs. 250 and is valid for one calendar year. The format of letter of undertaking is as per Annexure 1.

General Procedure for Excise Clearance

Some procedures are common to export under bond or duty pre-paid. The documents required for this are invoice and ARE-1 (ARE stands for application for removal of excisable goods) forms. The invoice is to be prominently marked as 'FOR EXPORT WITHOUT PAYMENT OF DUTY'. ARE-1 has to be filled in five copies.

Assessable value in ARE-1 form is usually the FOB value of the consignment in Indian Rupees at the current rate of exchange. A debit entry has to be made in running bond account equal to duty value as shown in invoice and ARE-1 form. The formats of Excise Invoice and ARE-1 forms are as per Annexures 2 and 3 respectively.

Disposal of ARE-1 Form

Three alternatives exist for the disposal of ARE-1 forms.

1. Export under supervision of excise officer In this case, the excise officer supervises the sealing of export cargo and endorses all the five copies of ARE-1 form. He gives original, duplicate, and quintuplicate copies to the exporter, sends the triplicate copy to the bond authority and retains the quadruplicate. The exporter then sends the original, duplicate, and quintuplicate copies to the customs officer at the port, who returns the original and quintuplicate copies to the exporter after the goods are exported. The customs officer then sends the duplicate copy to the bond authority, which will now have two copies of the ARE-1 form, including the triplicate from the excise officer. This confirms to the bond authority that the goods for which duty exemption was claimed have been exported. Figure 13.1 shows the flow diagram of this procedure.

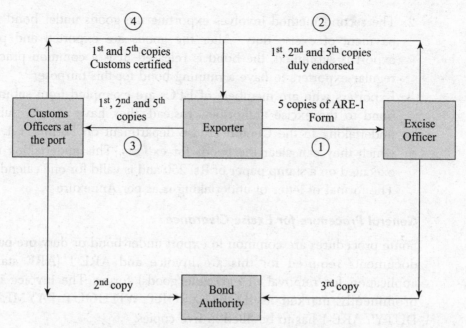

Fig. 13.1 Export under supervision of excise officer

2. Export under self-sealing and self-certification
This facility is only accorded to regular exporters with a good track record. In this case, it is the exporter who seals the goods and certifies ARE-1 forms and sends the original, duplicate, and quintuplicate copies along with goods to the customs officer at the port. The exporter also sends the triplicate and quadruplicate to the superintendent of excise, who in turn sends the third copy to the office where the exporter has executed the bond. After the goods are exported, the customs officer at the port sends the duplicate to the bond

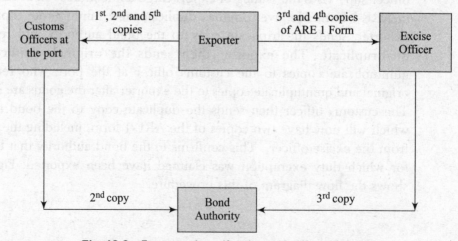

Fig. 13.2 Export under self sealing and self-certification

authority. This enables the bond authority to ascertain the export of goods for which duty exemption was claimed. Figure 13.2 shows the flow diagram of this procedure.

3. Export after payment of duty under claim of rebate   The preceding two cases discussed the procedure when goods are exported under excise bond. In the third option, the exporter pays the excise duty first and then claims the rebate on the duty paid. In this case, the procedure remains the same, except that the duplicate copy of ARE-1 is sent by the customs officer and the triplicate copy is sent by the excise superintendent to the officer to whom the rebate claim is filed. In case the rebate is claimed electronically, these copies will be sent to excise rebate audit section at the place of export. Figure 13.3 shows the flow diagram of this procedure.

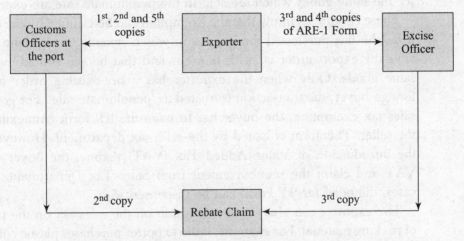

Fig. 13.3   Export after payment of duty under claim of rebate

Sales Tax Clearance for Exports

In India, sales tax is imposed by the state government as well as the central government. According to article 286(1) (b) of the Constitution of India, the imposition of sales tax by state governments is prohibited on exports and imports. Also, because Central Sales Tax (CST) is leviable only on inter-state transactions, there is no CST on sale during export/import. The export sales are from sales tax in order to provide a competitive edge to Indian goods abroad. Section 5 of the CST Act has been formulated to determine when sale is in the course of export/import. According to this Act, a sale or purchase of goods is deemed to be in course of export of the goods out of Indian territory only if

(a) either the sale or purchase occasions such export

Or

(b) The sale or purchase is effected by a transfer of documents of title to goods after the goods have crossed the Indian Customs Department. However, such sales rarely take place in exports, because exports are mostly against firm contracts.

There is also a provision for the exemption of sales tax on the goods, which are purchased for eventual exports by a merchant exporter or an export house. Such a sale is called 'penultimate sale'. The conditions for availing this exemption are that the penultimate sale (i.e., last but one sale) is

(a) for the purpose of complying with an agreement or order in relation to export,

(b) that such a sale is made after the agreement or order in relation to export, and

(c) the same goods which are sold in the penultimate sale are exported.

These conditions imply that the exemption can be claimed by the exporter if he/she has purchased the goods (on which exemption is claimed) only after the export order is with him/her and that he/she should export the same goods. Only when the exporter has a pre-existing order from the foreign buyer, the transaction is treated as 'penultimate sale'. For getting the sales tax exemption, the buyer has to issue the 'H' form (Annexure 4), to the seller. This form is issued by the sales tax department. However, since the introduction of Value Added Tax (VAT) regime, the buyer can pay VAT and claim the reimbursement from Sales Tax Department. In such cases, the need for 'H' Form can be dispensed with.

The exporter can also claim exemption on the sales tax on the purchase of packing material. For example, if the exporter purchases plastic containers, which are used for export production, it is deemed as 'export sale'.

Octroi Clearance of Export Goods

Entry tax, also known as Octroi duty is levied by certain states in India for inter-state transactions. Exporters can however claim exemption from this duty by submitting form EP at the entry point to the Octroi authority. Annexure 5 shows the format of form EP.

Planning the Voyage

The exporter has to plan the voyage in consultation with his Freight Forwarder. This is because the exporter relies on the expertise and the experience of the freight forwarder. In France, it is said that a freight forwarder should care for the cargo in his custody, as a father would care for his family. Hence a forwarder may not recommend the cheapest shipping line to the exporter if he thinks that the safety of the cargo is at stake. The forwarder will explain the pros and cons of using the cheapest shipping line, so that the exporter can take a decision based on the holistic knowledge of the situation. The quality and reliability of service rendered by a freight forwarder becomes the basis of his long-term relations with the exporter. Conventional wisdom continues to hold that freight-forwarders should be consulted by all first-time exporters.

The following factors may help the exporter and the freight forwarder determine the mode of transport, routing, etc.

- Nature of the goods (capital goods, commodities, fragile, perishable, dangerous etc.)
- Voyage (duration, with/without transshipment)
- Time factor (urgent or normal delivery)
- Cost factor (cost Vs speed and/or safety)
- Containerized or break-bulk

The exporter also has to decide whether the goods have to be sea freighted, air freighted, or sent by multi modal transport, i.e., a combination of road, rail, sea, and air transportation. Normally, air transportation is preferred for high value, low volume cargo and sea transportation for low value, high volume cargo. For example, a large consignment weighing 300 tonnes will be ideal for sea freight. But for a consignment weighing 300 kg, air freight as well as sea freight can be considered. The freight forwarder can find out if any cheap commodity rates or consolidation rates are being offered by air carriers. The exporter in such a case can utilize air transportation, which at times can be cheaper and obviously speedier than surface transportation. Hence, a good working relationship between the exporter and freight forwarder is essential for mutual growth.

If the export contract is being executed without a letter of credit, on FOB or on cost and freight (C&F) terms, the exporter must insure the cargo against all risks of loss or damage during the entire course of transit. In such a case, if the goods are damaged before reaching the buyer, the exporter can claim the damages from the insurance company. This is a precautionary measure very often ignored by exporters. Such a cover is very useful in case of transactions on DP or DA basis. Particularly in case of DA transactions, the buyer may refuse to accept the goods and not make a payment if they are found damaged or short supplied.

Post Despatch Procedure

Once the export consignment is ready for despatch and once all the clearances are obtained, the exporter will prepare and send the following documents to his freight forwarding agent well in advance of the shipment.

- Invoice
- Packing List
- Guaranteed Remittance (GR) form in duplicate to conform to exchange control regulations
- ARE1 form for excise clearance in five copies
- Sales Tax exemption form
- Pre-shipment inspection certificate issued by Export Inspection Council and/or any other third party inspection agency nominated by the overseas buyer
- Form N1 for Octroi clearance (as required by certain states within India)
- Copy of Letter of Credit and/or Purchase Order

On receipt of these documents, the freight forwarder will

1. complete the octroi formalities so that export cargo can reach the port of despatch duly exempted from payment of octroi duty.
2. obtain the port permit so that the truck/vehicle carrying export consignment can enter port premises.
3. complete the customs formalities, such as preparing the shipping bill so that the customs examination of the cargo can be conducted.
4. book the space on the ship/flight depending on the L/C conditions and the directions from the exporters. (While doing so, the freight forwarder has to take into consideration various conditions such as last date of shipment, last date of negotiations of the documents against the L/C, trans-shipment allowed or not allowed, etc.)
5. get the customs clearance and ensure that the cargo is placed on board the ship/aircraft.
6. obtain the following documents thereafter and send them to the exporter for negotiations with the bank.
   (a) Customs attested invoice duly signed by the customs authority to certify that the goods have been checked and found in order.
   (b) Copies of packing list
   (c) Duplicate copy of GR-1 form. The original copy of GR-1 form is sent by the customs authority to the regional office of RBI for further foreign exchange regulatory procedures.
   (d) Duplicate copy of ARE-1 form (for claiming excise rebate)
   (e) Certificate of origin (if required) for commercial or political reasons.
   (f) Full set of negotiable and non-negotiable copies of Bill of Lading obtained from the shipping line (Airway bill in case of air cargo)
   (g) Copies of shipping bill
   (h) Copy of letter of credit and/or purchase order

If the transaction is under a L/C, a time gap of about 15 to 21 days is normally allowed between the last date of shipment and last date of negotiation of the documents. This is done in order to help the freight forwarder complete all the port formalities, and get all the relevant documents so that they can be sent back to the exporter for submission to the bank for further negotiations.

On receipt of the above documents, the exporter must check each and every document to ensure that all the terms and conditions of the L/C are complied with. The common discrepancies in the documents could be spelling mistakes, inaccurate description of cargo on B/L, shipment after expiry of L/C, (bill of lading dated later than the last date of shipment given on letter of credit), etc.

The exporter sends shipment details such as B/L/ Airway Bill number and date, name of the ship, voyage number/ flight number expected date of arrival of the ship at the port of destination etc. to the buyer abroad. If the contract is on FOB or C&F basis, the exporter requests the importer to cover the insurance. The exporter also sends the shipment details to the importer's insurance company through e-mail/ fax, so that suitable insurance cover is provided to the cargo. If the contract is on CIF basis, the exporter covers the insurance. Similarly, if the contract is on C&F or CIF basis, the exporter pays the ocean freight and gets the B/L stamped as 'Freight Prepaid'. However, in case of FOB contracts, the ocean freight is paid by the buyer at the destination and the B/L is stamped 'Freight to Pay'.

NEGOTIATION OF DOCUMENTS

The exporter then makes a covering note for the negotiating bank as designated on letter of credit and encloses the following documents for negotiations.

- Commercial Invoice
- Packing list
- Original copy of GR-1 form
- Set of negotiable copies of B/L duly endorsed by the exporter in favor of importer or consignee. The B/L can be endorsed by signing on its reverse side.
- Set of non-negotiable copies of B/L
- Certificate of origin (if demanded by the buyer)
- Certificate of pre-shipment inspection (if demanded by the buyer)
- Copy of insurance policy (in case of CIF contract)
- Copy of L/C / P/O

Scrutiny of Documents

The negotiating bank will scrutinize the documents listed above and if they comply with the conditions of L/C, the bank will pay to the exporter accordingly. The bank would also ensure the following:

1. The serial number mentioned on the duplicate copy of the GR form presented to them tallies with the GR form number recorded on the B/L. Also that the duplicate copy of GR form is duly verified and certified by the Customs.
2. If the transaction is on C&F or CIF basis, and the buyer proposes to pay the freight at the destination, then the freight amount deducted is the actual amount of freight as indicated on the B/L or airway bill, or as declared in GR form, whichever is less.
3. If the contract is on a FOB basis, and the seller proposes to pay the freight, the actual freight amount is added in the invoice. In such a case, a 'freight prepaid' B/L /airway bill is accepted by the bank.
4. If the marine insurance premium is proposed to be paid by the seller on behalf of the buyer, the invoice includes the actual amount paid and the same is received from the overseas buyer.
5. No discrepancies are found in the documents with regard to description of goods exported, value of export, or the country of destination.

If the letter of credit is for payment at sight, the payment is made immediately. In case of 'usance letter of credit' where the exporter has sold the goods to the buyer on credit basis, the bank will pay to the exporter after the credit period is over. According to FEMA, an exporter can extend credit to a foreign buyer up to six months from the date of shipment, which is also the date of B/L. In case the exporter wants to extend a longer credit, he/she has to specifically seek the permission of RBI for the same.

In case the order is on a DP basis, the negotiating bank will send the documents to the buyer's bank abroad on collection basis. In this case, the shipping documents are handed over to the buyer only after the bank has received the payment equal to the invoice amount. The buyer's bank will then remit this amount to the exporter after deducting their commission. When the transaction is on DA basis, the buyer's bank will release the shipping documents to the buyer, who in turn can get the custody of the cargo from the shipping line against the documents. The buyer will release the payment subject to the acceptance of the goods.

It can be observed from the above discussions that L/C provides maximum safety to both buyers and sellers. Transactions against D/P basis have the advantage that no letter of credit charges are involved. However, the seller is at a risk if the buyer does not pay to the seller's bank and does not get the shipping documents released. In such an eventuality, the buyer's bank will have to return the shipping documents to the negotiating bank and the exporter has to get the cargo back to India at his/her own expenses. For this, a clearance from the RBI is required. In case of transactions on DA basis, the exporter is at maximum risk. This is because the overseas buyer may refuse to pay for the goods. The exporter then has no recourse. The only precaution an exporter can take is to obtain a credit worthiness report of the buyer from the ECGC and obtain their commercial risk coverage. Even then, the exporter is liable to RBI for default under FEMA. The exporter has to then represent his/her case to RBI explaining the reasons for not realizing the export proceeds and requesting the RBI for GR waiver. RBI considers GR waiver in case it is convinced that the export proceeds could not be received despite all due precautions from the exporter. In such cases, the exporter must convince RBI about the intended good faith and also that he/she has not defaulted intentionally.

Realization of Export Proceeds in Special Circumstances

Normally, an exporter must realize export proceeds against a transaction on the due date for payment as mentioned in the purchase order/ L/C, or within six months from the date of shipment of the goods which ever is earlier. In case the goods are exported to Indian-owned warehouses established with the permission of RBI, this limit is 15 months from the date of shipment. However, there are some exceptions to this rule.

Exports on Longer Credit Period

Sometimes the exporter may have to give a longer credit period to the overseas buyer to win the contract. This is in case the importer's country is facing Balance of Payment (BoP) problems and does not allow the remittance within six months. Exporters must then submit their application for RBI approval for such transactions on form ECT. This should be routed through the exporter's bank to the concerned regional office of RBI.

Short Supplies and Shut-out Shipments

When an exporter is unable to ship the entire lot of cargo covered by the GR form already filed with Customs, he/she must give notice of short-shipment to the Customs in prescribed form. The exporter must obtain the short shipment notice certified by Customs and submit it to the authorized dealer for onward submission to RBI. Sometimes, the cargo is entirely shut out and there is no ship immediately available to carry the goods to the destination. In such a case, the exporter must notify the Customs department in a prescribed form enclosing therewith the unused duplicate copy of GR form and shipping bill. Customs then would physically verify the goods and if the goods are found actually shut out; they would certify the exporter's notice and forward it to RBI along with the unused duplicate copy of the GR form. The Customs authorities would then cancel the original copy of the GR form. If the cargo is shipped subsequently, a fresh GR form would have to be used.

Export by Air

In this case, the exporter obtains the airway bill from the airline or its authorized agent in exchange of cargo. The airway bill not being a negotiable shipping document, the exporter is at the risk of losing the value of exported goods if they are consigned directly to overseas buyer/consignee and not to the overseas branch or a corresponding bank of an authorized dealer. This is true in cases where the transaction is conducted without a L/C. In such cases, exporters must consign the goods to the overseas branch or the corresponding bank of the authorized dealer with an instruction to deliver the documents only against payment from the buyer. Such a precaution is, however, not necessary in case the exporter has received advance payment from the overseas buyer.

Where air cargo is shipped under consolidation, the airline company's master airway bill will be issued to the consolidating cargo agent who in turn will issue his own house airway bills (HAWBs) to individual shippers. Authorized dealers will negotiate HAWBs only if the relative letter of credit specifically provides for negotiation of these documents in lieu of the airway bill issued by the airline company. Authorized dealers will, however, accept freely HAWBs where the documents are to be sent on collection basis.

Exports by Rail/Road Transport

Exporters sending their goods to neighbouring countries by road transport must submit the GR form at the customs station at the border from where the vehicle would cross into another country. In such a case, the GR form may either be submitted to the customs by the transporter or the exporter's agent at the border. The same procedure is adopted while exporting by barges or country crafts.

In case of transportation by rail to Pakistan or Bangladesh, GR forms can be submitted to the customs officers present at the designated railway station at the time of loading the cargo on the train. This facilitates the passage of cargo to the importing country without any formalities at the border. Exporters can obtain the list of designated stations from Indian Railways. If the exporter is unable to load the goods at the designated railway station, GR forms must be presented to the customs at the borderland station for completing the formalities.

ROLE OF BANKS IN AN EXPORT-IMPORT TRANSACTION

Banks play a crucial role in export-import transactions. This is because the buyer and the seller are located in different countries. They want to conduct business, but do not have any knowledge about each other's credibility, reputation, and business standing in the market. There is always an apprehension in the mind of the exporter about the payment against exports. The exporter is apprehensive about despatching the valuable cargo and then waiting for the payment. The importer, on the other hand, is not sure that the exporter would in fact despatch the right quantity and right quality of goods ordered. Banks play the role of a mediator or a bridge, which links the exporter and importer. The foundation of this bridge is the trust in the banking system throughout the world. The exporter and the importer may not have met each other and they may not have any knowledge about each other's business reputation or credibility in the market. But because of the presence of the bank as a facilitator of the transaction, both feel safe and secure to conduct business. Hence, the bank plays the role of a financer, facilitator, mediator, as well as guarantor in international business.

Bank as a Financer

In India, banks provide pre-shipment credit known as packing credit to exporters. This credit is available at an interest rate, which is lower than the current market rate. Exporters can avail of packing credit in Indian Rupees as well as in foreign exchange. Credit in foreign exchange may be utilized to pay for imported inputs in manufacturing export goods. Packing credit may be liquidated against export proceeds received from abroad. Banks also provide post-shipment finance to make funds available during the credit period. For example, if an exporter extends 60 days credit to an overseas buyer, the exporter can avail of post shipment credit from the date of despatch of the goods till the date of receipt of payment. Like pre-shipment credit, post-shipment credit too is offered as a soft loan by banks. For details, please refer to chapter five on the methods of financing exporters.

Bank as a Facilitator

Facilitation is the most important role banks play in export-import transactions. The bank provides L/C facilities to the importer, so that he can despatch the goods and get payment from the negotiating bank in his/

her own country. Similarly, the importer is also assured that the negotiating bank will pay to the exporter only after ensuring that the exporter has despatched the goods and fulfilled all L/C obligations. In case of a transaction on DP or DA terms, the exporter's bank facilitates the transactions by sending the documents to the importer's bank on collection basis. The importer's bank facilitates the transactions by releasing the shipping documents only after the importer has paid the invoice value in case of DP transactions. For DA transactions, the importer's bank arranges to collect the payment on due date and remit the same to the exporter's bank.

Bank as a Regulator

As an authorized dealer in foreign currency, the bank has to ensure that the exporter complies with the various guidelines issued by RBI from time to time. Hence, the bank has an important role to play as a regulator to ensure that the exporter's transactions are within these guidelines. With the help of exchange regulation forms such as Guaranteed Remittance (GR), SDF, PP, and SOFTEX forms, the bank can ensure that the payments of export invoices are received only through appropriate banking channels. According to RBI, it will be however, in order for authorized dealers to handle documents in cases where the exporter has received the export proceeds directly from the overseas buyer in the form of bank draft, pay order, banker's cheques, personal cheque, foreign currency traveller's cheques etc. without any monetary limit provided the exporter's track record is good, he is a customer of the concerned authorized dealer and prima facie the instrument represents payment for exports. Hence there is a lot of flexibility provided for receipt of export proceeds from abroad if the bank is convinced about the integrity of the exporter and the genuineness of the transaction.

In the pre-economic liberalization era before the 1990s, there were very strict norms laid down by the RBI for compliance under Foreign Exchange Regulation Act (FERA). This was in view of the paucity of foreign exchange in India and also due to the closed-door economic regime, which was in vogue at that time. But after the government opened the doors of economy to foreign goods, FERA, which regulated the foreign exchange market, was changed to the Foreign Exchange Management Act (FEMA) that emphasizes more on the management, rather than regulation, of foreign exchange. Hence, the role of the bank, too, has changed significantly from that of a regulator to a manager of the foreign exchange market in India.

SUMMARY

The execution of an export order follows a sequence of procedures and involves compliance with various rules and regulations of the home country as well as the country of destination, coordination with various government and non-government agencies, correct documentation, and the completion of various formalities to avail prevailing tax and duty concessions. While doing this, it is also of utmost importance for an exporter to constantly communicate with his/her freight forwarder, overseas customer, bank, insurance companies, etc. In many organizations, it is a common practice to follow a checklist of activities to be performed right from the moment an export order is received till the time it is executed and the payment received. Some times, this checklist may also cover after sales service, customer complaints, warranty claims, returned goods, etc. An organization has to expand its body of knowledge and has to inculcate a culture of learning through experience. It is very important to maintain a record of past transactions, important documents and interaction with the customers in order to build a management information system (MIS). This helps organizations run smoothly and ensures that even if a key employee leaves the organization, the commitments to the customer are not affected.

One of the key functions of an export department is to complete the many pre- and post-despatch formalities, such as excise clearance of export goods without payment of duty, claiming sales tax exemption, and octroi duty exemption on export goods. The record registers and relevant documents of the exporter are routinely audited by excise, customs, and sales tax officials to confirm compliance with norms. The exporter has to take due care to maintain correct records in order to satisfy the auditors. Incorrect record keeping, erroneous documentation, and concealment of facts leads to penalties and legal actions. It is, therefore, advisable for an exporter to seek the guidance of procedural experts in case of any doubts or difficulty in understanding the provisions of law.

Lastly, banks have a major role to play in any export transaction. They are a bridge of trust between a seller and his overseas buyer. Exporters are well advised to seek guidance from their bankers regarding availability of pre and post-shipment credits at concessional rates of interest, the creditworthiness of the overseas buyer, the genuineness of letters of credit received from abroad, and the various provisions of FEMA applicable to exporters. In addition to this, the exporter can seek help from other institutions such as the Reserve Bank of India, Export-Import Bank of India, ECGC, etc., in order to avail various benefits offered by the governments to promote exports from India.

CONCEPT REVIEW QUESTIONS

1. How will you execute an export order? Discuss the procedure starting from the receipt of Purchase Order/Letter of Credit up to despatch of material to the port.
2. Explain the post-despatch procedure highlighting various export documents and their importance.
3. As a regular exporter, which of the two methods of excise clearance of export goods would you prefer? Clearance under bond or clearance under duty refund? Give reasons in support of your answer.
4. Write a short note on the following:
   (a) Excise clearance of export goods
   (b) Sales tax clearance of export goods
5. Discuss the various factors you would consider while deciding the mode(s) of transportation for your export consignment.
6. What is the role of a freight forwarder in the execution of an export order? Discuss the various steps taken by a freight forwarder with the help of a flow diagram.
7. List the documents submitted by an exporter while negotiating the documents with the bank. How does the bank scrutinize the documents before clearing the payment to the exporter?
8. Discuss the procedure to be followed for realization of export proceeds under following circumstances:
   (a) Credit period longer than normally allowed by RBI
   (b) Short supplies and shut-out shipments
   (c) Export by air
9. How does a bank help an organization in export-import transactions?
10. Which role of the bank is most important in export trade:
    (a) A financier
    (b) A facilitator
    (c) A regulator
    Support your answer with reasons.

OBJECTIVE QUESTIONS

Choose the correct option.
1. Which of the following act governs foreign exchange rules in India?
   (a) FERA
   (b) FEMA

    (c) FDI

    (d) FII

2. What is the time duration in which an Indian exporter is expected to realize export proceeds?

    (a) 6 months from the date of receipt of purchase order/letter of credit

    (b) 6 months from the date of despatch of goods from the factory

    (c) 6 months from the date of shipment

    (d) 6 months from the date of receipt of goods by the overseas buyer

3. As per RBI manual, which of the following is the permitted currency for export transaction?

    (a) Malaysian Ringitt

    (b) Chinese Yuan

    (c) Srilankan Rupee

    (d) US Dollar

4. Which of the following statements is TRUE?

    (a) Excise duty and sales tax are both exempted for export goods

    (b) Only excise duty is exempted for export goods

    (c) Only sales tax is exempted on export goods

    (d) None of the above.

5. Which of the following factor is NOT considered to determine mode of transport for export cargo?

    (a) Nature of goods

    (b) Freight rate

    (c) Credit worthiness of buyer

    (d) Safety of cargo

6. Which of the following is the correct full form of FEMA?

    (a) Foreign Exchange Mechanism Act

    (b) Foreign Exchange Management Act

7. ARE form stands for

    (a) Application for removal of excisable goods

    (b) Application for receipt of excisable goods

State whether the following questions are True or False.

8. Export under self-sealing and self-certification for excise purposes is not permitted to first time exporters

9. Imposition of sales tax by state governments is permitted on exports and imports

10. Exporter is at no risk if the air cargo is consigned directly to overseas buyer/consignee in absence of a letter of credit

EXERCISES

1. Prepare a checklist of activities to be performed right from the moment an export order is received till the time it is executed and the payment received.
2. Visit the website of Reserve Bank of India and study the various provisions in FEMA applicable to exporters from India.
3. Prepare a covering letter addressed to the Foreign Exchange Department of any bank in India, requesting them to negotiate export documents against your overseas purchase order/letter of credit.
4. Visit the nearest post office and enquire about the documentation to be done for exporting goods by post parcel.
5. Find out which are the Indian states where octroi duty is applicable.

SELECT REFERENCES

Wood, Barnes and Murphy, Wardlow, 2002, *International Logistics,* AMACOM Publication, New York.
www.customs.gov.in last accessed on 25th July 2007
www.rbi.org.in last accessed on 24th July 2007

ANNEXURE I

100 Rs.

Entered in 335-P Register at Sr. No. 11/04 on Pg. 60.

FORM UT-1

Letter of Undertaking

For Removal of export of excisable goods without payment of duty

To,

The President of India (hereinafter called the "President"), acting through the Assistant Commissioner of Central Excise or Deputy Commissioner of Central Excise or the Maritime Commissioner or such Central Excise Officer duly authorised by the Central Board of Excise and Customs, constituted under the Central Board of Revenue Act, 1963 (54 of 1963) (hereinafter called "the Board") DIV-I CGO, Complex, A.B. Road, Indore (Address of the office.).

I/We Dee Tee Industries Ltd, (R.M.R.Division) 59-8, Sector 'C' Sanwer Road Industrial Estate, Indore (Address of the Factory) having Central Excise Registration No. AAACD6052GXM002 Dtd. 05/12/2001, hereinafter called " the Undertaker(s) including my/our respective heirs, executors/ administrators, legal representatives / successors and assigns by these presents, hereby jointly and severally undertake on this 7ᵗʰ day of January 2004 to the President.

(a) To Export the excisable goods removed from my/our factory/warehouse/ approved place of storage without payment of duty under rule 19 of the Central Excise Rules, 2002 within six month from the date of such removal or such extended period as may be permitted by the jurisdictional Assistant Commissioner of Central Excise duly authorised by the Board:

(b) To observes all the provision of the Central Excise Rules, 2002 and all such amendments thereto as may be issued from time to time to be observed, in respect of export of excisable goods to a foreign country:

(c) To export the goods to the satisfaction of the Assistant Commissioner of Central Excise or the deputy Commissioner of Central Excise having jurisdiction over the factory of production or manufacture:

(Contd)

Annexure I (*Contd*)

50 RS.

- 2 -

(d)   Pay the Excise duty payable on such excisable goods in the event of failure to export them, along with an amount equal to twenty four percent interest per annum on the amount of duty not paid, from the date of removal for export till date of payment.

I/we declare that this undertaking is given under the orders of the Board for the performance of enacts in which the public are interested.

For Dee-Tee Industries Ltd.

Signature(s) undertaker(s).

P. G. PUROHIT
General Manager

Date : 7th January 2004

Place : Indore

Witnesses	Name and Address	Occupation
1.	BABU CHACKO 203 Indraprastha Appts., N/30-31 Anoop Nagar, INDORE	Private Service
2.	SURESH RAI 28/33 Pologround Indl. Estate INDORE	Private Service

Executed before me

Date:

Place: Indore

Accepted by me on this .... day of .... (Month) .... (Year)....................... of Central Excise, (Designation) for and on behalf of the President of India.

*The stamp duty rates stand revised at Rs 250.

ANNEXURE 2

INVOICE

ORIGINAL FOR BUYER

Invoice for removal of Excisable goods from Factory on without
payment of duty under Rule 19 of Central Excise Rules 2002

ISO-9001

PRE AUTHENTICATION

Dee Tee Industries Limited

UNIT - II (R.M.R. Division)
59-B, Sector 'C', Sanwer Road, Industrial Estate, INDORE - 452 015 (INDIA)
Tel. No. : (0091-731) 2720433, 2720006, Fax : (0091-731) 2720302
E-mail : deetee @deeteegroup.com Visit us at : www.deeteegroup.com
Range - II, Division - Indore, 2nd Floor, C.G.O. Complex, A.B. Road, Indore

Estd. 1970

ECC No.	: AAACD6052GXM002
Regn. No.	: AAACD6052GXM002
MPST No.	: 0102/XVIII/1342/2/S Dt. 1-4-97
CST No.	: 0102/XVIII/0902/C Dt. 1-4-97
TIN	: 23080201342
P.L.A.	: 34/PLA/RII/CHAP.72.82&84

0000001

Name & Address Of The Consignee : 40000489			
EAST SEA CORPORATION	Party's CST No. :		
625-4, SANGDO-DONG, NAM-KU	Party's LST No. :		
POHANG CITY, GYEONGBUK	Party's ECC No. :		
790-828 SOUTH	P.O. No. : PO/DTA/070227		
KOREA	S.O. No. / Date : SE 60282109 31/03/2007		

INVOICE NO.	INVOICE DATE
RX / 70000001	11/04/2007

Preparation Date :	11/04/2007
Preparation Time :	13:51:52
Removal Date / Time :	11/04/07 / 1500 Hrs.
Packaging Details :	BOX NO. 1 TO 5
No. Of Packages :	5
Freight Details :	PAID
RR/LR No. / Date :	

Vehicle No. :	
Transporter :	XPS
Agent :	EAST SEA CORPORATION
Destination :	INCHEON (KOREA)

TIN No :

Payment Terms : Net 30 Days		Delivery Terms :
Doc Through :		

ITEM NO.	ITEM DESCRIPTION	CHAPTER/TARIFF NO	COMMODITY CLASS	QUANTITY	UOM	RATE	TOTAL AMOUNT
AS PER ANNEXURE							
						Material Value Rs.	442,000.00
						Ass. Value	442,000.00
						Basic Excise Duty @16%	70,720.00
						Education Cess On BED @2%	1,414.40
						Higher Edu Cess On BED @1%	707.20

Total Amount in Words :		Total Amount Rs. :	514,841.60
Rupees FIVE LAC FOURTEEN THOUSAND EIGHT HUNDRED FORTY ONE AND PAISE SIXTY ONLY			

Excise Duty Payable in Figures :	70,720.00		
Excise Duty Payable In Words :	Rupees SEVENTY THOUSAND SEVEN HUNDRED TWENTY AND PAISE ZERO ONLY		
Ed. Cess Payable in Figures :	1,414.40	A.R.E.1 No. / Date :	ARE NO.01/2007-08 Dt.11/04/07
Ed. Cess Payable In Words :	Rupees ONE THOUSAND FOUR HUNDRED FOURTEEN AND PAISE FORTY ONLY	U/T No. / Date :	93 Dt. 18/01/2007
Higher Ed.Cess in Figures :	707.20		
Higher Ed Cess in Words :	Rupees SEVEN HUNDRED SEVEN AND PAISE TWENTY ONLY		

REMARKS :-

Certified that the particulars given above are true & correct and the amount indicated represent
the price actually charged & that there is no flow of additional consideration directly or indirectly
from the buyer.
1. Please check the goods before taking the delivery.
2. Our responsibility of all sorts ceases as soon as the goods leave our factory.
3. Subject to INDORE Jurisdiction.
4. E. & O.E.

For Dee Tee Industries Limited
UNIT - II (R.M.R. Division)

BABU CHACKO
Sr. Manager (Export)
Authorised Signatory

(Contd)

Annexure 2 (*Contd*)

Dee Tee Industries Limited
UNIT - II (R.M.R. Division)
59-B, Sector 'C', Sanwer Road Industrial Estate, INDORE - 452 015 (INDIA)
Tel. No. : (0091-731) 2720433, 2720008, Fax : (0091-731) 2720302
E-mail : deetee@deeteegroup.com Visit us at : www.deeteegroup.com
ANNEXURE

ISO-9001

ANNEXURE   Page: 1 of 1

INVOICE NO.: RX/ 70000001   INVOICE DATE : 11/04/2007

ITEM DESCRIPTION	CHAPTER NO. / COMMODITY CLASS	QUANTITY	UOM	RATE (Rs.)	TOTAL AMOUNT
1 WORK ROLL 73.5MM DIA X 1440MM LENGTH	8455 90 00 METAL ROLLING MILL ROLLS&PARTS	26.00	EA	17,000.00	442,000.00
				TOTAL AMOUNT Rs.:	442,000.00

For Dee Tee Industries Limited
UNIT - II (R.M.R. Division)

BABU CHACKO
Authorised Signatory (Exports)

ANNEXURE 3

FORM A. R. E. 1

Application for removal of excisable goods for export by *(Air/Sea* ////////)

EXPORT UNDER SIP

Range...... **II**

Division...**I**....Address......**C.G.O. Complex, Indore (M.P.)**

Commissionerate......**Indore (M.P.)**

A.R.E.1 No.....**01/07-08**........... Date **11:06:07**

To,

Superintendent of Central Excise (Full Postal Address)....**C.G.O. Complex, Indore (M.P.)**

1) Particulars of (Asst./Deputy Commissioner of Central Excise / //////////////// //////// ///////// with whom b//// / Undertaking is executed* and his complete postal Address

The Deputy Commissioner of Central Excise, Division I, Indore (M.P.)

2) I/We **Dee Tee Industries Ltd. (R.M.G. Division), Indore (M.P.)**

Purpose to export the undermentioned consignment to ......**KOREA**........ (country of destination) By ////////// under c/////////// under ////////// undertaking*

Particulars of manufacturers of goods and central excise registration No.	No. and Description of Packages	Gross Weight / Net Weight	Marks and Nos. on Packages	Quantity of Goods	Description of Goods	VALUE		DUTY			No. & Date of Invoice under which duty was Paid/No. & date of bond / undertaking entered Rule "9"	Amount of rebate claimed	Remarks
						Rs.	P.	Rate %	Amount Rs.	P.			
1	2	3	4	5	6	7		8	9		10	11	12
Dee Tee Industries Ltd. 59-B, Sector C Sanwer Road Industrial Estate Indore (M.P.) C. Ex. Reg. No. AAACD 6052 OXM001	5 Nos. wooden boxes having Sr. No. 1 To 5	Nt. Wt. Kgs. 1195 Gr. Wt. Kgs. 1437	ESC INCHEON KOREA DEE TEE INDORE INDIA	26 Nos.	ROLLS FOR COLD ROLLING MILLS Soft Null 73.5mm Dia x 144mm Case @ 25 cm BED S & H Edu. Cess @ 1% (Conversion rate 42.50)	442000		16%	70720.00 1414.40 707.20		Inv. No. 7000001 dated 11.06.07 Export/ Letter of Under taking No. 93 dated 18.01.07	NIL	Export/ Letter of Under taking

3 I/We hereby certify that the above mentioned goods have been manufactured.
a) availing facility/without availing facility* of CENVAT credit under CENVAT credit Rules, 2002
b) availing facility/without availing facility* under Notification 21/2004 –Central Excise (N.T.) dated the 6th June, 2004 issued under rule 18 of Central Excise Rules, 2002
c) availing facility/without availing facility* under Notification 43/2001 –Central Excise (N.T.) dated the 26th June, 2001 issued under rule 19 of Central Excise (No.2) Rules 2001.
I/We hereby declare that the export in discharge of the export obligation under a quantity based advance license / under claim of duty drawback under customs and Central Excise duties drawback rules, 1995.

A. Amount of Bond ....
B. Amount of duty involved on goods cleared for export duty not yet exported ....
C. Balance as credit as on day ....
Time of Removal ....**1600 Hrs.**... Date ...**11.06.07**..

Rs. ....
Rs. ....
Rs. ....

5) I/We hereby declare that the above particulars are true and correctly stated.

Signature of Owner or his authorised agent with date Name in block letters and designation (SEAL)

*Strike out whichever is not applicable.

(P.T.O.)

Original	-	White
Duplicate	-	Buf
Triplicate	-	Pink
Quadruplicate	-	Green
Quintuplicate (Optional)	-	Blue

ANNEXURE 4

ANNEXURE 5

Octroi

FORM "EP"

(Vide Rule 5 of the Export Promotion Rules 1976)

To,

The Deputy Assessor and Collector (Octroi),
Municipal Corporation of Greater Bombay.

We, M/s. Auditra Engineering Co. Pvt. Ltd.. of C-5, Laxmi Towers, 'C' Wing, 6th Floor, Bandra Kurla Complex, Bandra (East), Bombay – 400 051 do hereby declare that the articles specified below are imported into Greater Bombay for the purpose of Export to Foreign Country, viz. _____ from Bombay per Vessel and are to be consigned to _____ at _____ be exempted from duty of Octroi

We are the registered Exporters as provided for under the Export Promotion Rules 1976 and Our Registration No. is **NEP-10.**/EP/06 08

Particulars of the Consignment Imported

No. & date of Import documents	No. of packages & Description of articles	Import Mark, if any	Weight & Value as per Import documents	Rate of Octroi in %	Amount of Octroi Leviable In Rs.	No. & Date of documents of Export	6 1/4 % amount of Octroi in Rs.
(1)	(2)	(3)	(4)	(5)	(6)	(7)	(8)
Bill No. 0023 Dt. 22/5/c	C1 wordes for		65 kgs			17/6/214 21 6/4/06	
	Exp No. 413		Rs. 33221/				
	Circulas Circ Bride		Rs. Thirty three thousand two hundred twenty one only				

For AUDITRA ENGINEERING CO. PVT. LTD.,

For AUDITRA ENGINEERING CO. PVT. LTD.

AUTHORISED SIGNATORY.

address: C-5 Laxmi Tower, 'C' Wing, 6th Floor, Bandra Kurla Complex, Bandra (E), BOMBAY-400 05

(OUR REF. NO. 592/138881/c   DATED 27/4/06)

(Contd)

Annexure 5 *(Contd)*

PART A
CERTIFICATION BY THE CENTRAL EXCISE OFFICER

1. Certified that duty has been paid by debit entry in the Personal Ledger Account No .... and / or CENVAT Account Entry No. .... or recorded as payable in daily stock Account, on the goods described overleaf.

    OR *U/T 93 dtd. 18/01/07*
    certified that the owner has entered into ~~Bond~~ No. .... Under rule 19 of central excise (No.2) Rules, 2002 with the *Deputy Commissioner* .... (F. No *VIII (AONL2)* 50-31/2005) E-7), duly accepted by the Assistant Commissioner / Deputy Commissioner of central Excise ...... *Indore* .... on .... *18.10.1.07* ... (Date)

2. Certified that I have opened and examined the Packages No. .... and found that the particulars stated and the description of goods, given overleaf and the packing list (if any) are correct and that all the packages have been stuffed in the container No .... with marks ....) and the same has been sealed with Central Excise Seal / One Time Seal (OTS) No ....

3. I have verified with the records, the exporter is only availing the export incentives, as specified in box No. 6 and found it to be true.

4. Certified that I have drawn three representative samples from the consignment (wherever necessary) and have handed over two sets there of duly sealed to exporter/his authorised representative.

Place *Indore*
Date *11.04.07*

<table>
<tr><td>Signature</td><td>Signature</td></tr>
<tr><td>(Name in Block Letters)</td><td>(Name in Block Letter)</td></tr>
<tr><td>Superintendent of Central Excise</td><td>Inspector of Central Excise</td></tr>
</table>

PART B
CERTIFICATION BY THE CUSTOM OFFICER

Certified that the consignment was shipped under my supervision under shipping Bill No. .... Dated ....by S. S./Flight No .... which left on the .... day of ....(Month)................(Year)

OR

Certified that the above mentioned consignment was stuffed in Container No. .... belonging to Shipping Line................. bassed on the "Let Export Order"Given on ....day of..................(month) .... (year) on the Shipping Bill No................. dated.................. and sealed by seal/one time lock No. ....in my supervision and the container was handed over to the Custodian M/s. .... for being shipped via .... (Name of the Port).

OR

Certified that the above mentioned consignment has been duly identified and has passed the land frontier today at .... in its original condition under Bill of Exports No. ....

Place ....

Date ....

<table>
<tr><td>Signature</td></tr>
<tr><td>(Name and Designation of the)</td></tr>
<tr><td>Customs Office in Block Letters (Seal)</td></tr>
</table>

PART C
EXPORTS BY POST

Certified that the consignment describe, overleaf has been despatched by foreign post to .... on .... day of 200.....................,

Place ....
Date ....

Signature of Post Master (Seal)

PART D
REBATE SANCTION ORDER
(On Original, Duplicate and Triplicate)

Refund Order No. .... Dated .... Rebate of Rs. .... (Rupees ....) sanctioned vide cheque No. .... Dated ....

Place ....
Date ....

* Strike out in applicable portion

Notification No. 19/2004-C.E. N.T), dated 6-9-2004

Assistant/ Deputy Commissioner / Maritime
Commissioner Central Excise

14 Information Technology and International Business

Learning Objectives

After studying this chapter, you will be able to understand
- the importance of Information Technology (IT) in international business
- the concepts of e-procurement, e-marketing, and e-logistics

Computerization has changed the way business is conducted the world over. No aspect of business has remained untouched by the information technology (IT) revolution. This is especially true of international business where people located in different parts of the world conduct transactions with each other. The activities of international business include, manufacturing, in-land transportation, customs and excise matters, port operations, shipping, clearing and forwarding, etc. During the course of these transactions, a large number of documents are created and exchanged. Many of these documents or the information contained therein is repeated. While creating and mailing these documents before the advent of IT, hundreds of man-hours would be lost in repetitive operations. Innovations in IT have revolutionized international business; the use of technology in managing and processing information, especially in large organizations helps save time, bring down costs, and reduce manpower. Manual data input and transfer has now become not only obsolete, but also irrational.

In international business today, IT finds maximum utility in the following areas:

1. Electronic Procurement
2. Electronic Marketing
3. Electronic Logistics

A modern competitive enterprise seeks to hold an edge over the market. IT helps provide this competitive advantage through its various application tools. By adopting these tools in various areas of business, the organization can gain many advantages in terms of accessibility to a customer or supplier in any part of the world, speed of operations, reduction in operational cost, reduction in paperwork, reduction in man power, etc. Due to the reach of the internet it is possible to conduct buying and selling transactions irrespective of geographical location. Internet banking helps in the speedy execution of payments and settlement of accounts. A website can be a virtual showroom, where products can be displayed, demonstrated, and sold. Such a website can also provide various after-sales service tips and suggestions, launch discussion forums, ask for customer feedback, and educate the customer. IT application such as Electronic Data Interchange (EDI) has also enabled logistics operations to be paperless.

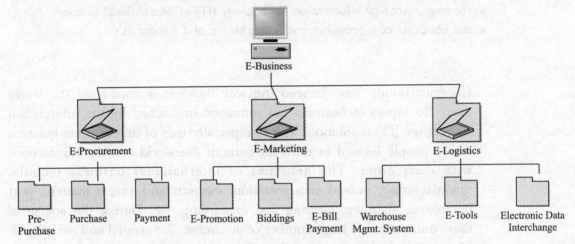

Fig. 14.1 IT: Making international business paperless

For example, for a ship, which is loaded at the New York port for delivery of cargo at Mumbai, the shipping line creates a cargo manifest that lists down the material on board the ship. Such manifests contain hundreds of items, which have to be entered into a computer and sent to the agent of the shipping line in Mumbai through satellite link. The agent takes a printout and files it with the customs department at Mumbai port, where it is entered again into the computer system of the customs department. This is a repetitive and time-wasting operation. With EDI, it is possible to link the shipping agent's computer with the computer of the customs department at the port. The entire data and the documents can thus be transferred into the customs department's computer within minutes. Similarly, on any working day, hundreds of shipping bills and bills of entry are manually presented to the customs department by shippers or their representatives. EDI eliminates this manual operation, where customs departments have to re-enter hundreds of documents into their computers. Instead, EDI ensures these documents are electronically transferred.

ELECTRONIC PROCUREMENT

E-procurement essentially comprises a number of inter-related methods for improving the procurement process through the use of electronic systems and processes. The need for e-procurement stems from the fact that in today's globalized world, a manufacturer can source inputs such as raw materials, components, machinery, and consumables from any part of the world. The manufacturer is constantly looking for suppliers who can offer quality materials at the most competitive rates. The internet has become a favourite hunting ground for the best bargains. Small companies can purchase their inputs through various websites, which sell a variety of items. However, for the larger organizations, electronic procurement is a systematically outlined process. Here, enterprises use automated applications to streamline buying both production and non-production goods and services (Hoque 2000).

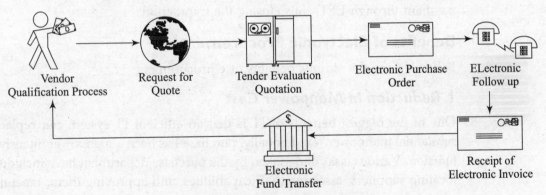

Vendor Qualification Process   Request for Quote   Tender Evaluation Quotation   Electronic Purchase Order   ELectronic Follow up

Electronic Fund Transfer   Receipt of Electronic Invoice

Fig. 14.2   E-procurement process

The entire electronic procurement process can be divided into three major components: pre-purchase, purchase, and payment activities. Pre-purchase activity can begin with a Request For Purchase (RFP) generated by the user department and sent to the purchase department. The electronic platform helps to plan pre-purchase activities starting with the vendor pre-qualification process. Vendors are invited to register their interest in a prescribed application form. They are asked to provide information about their organization, availability of resources, such as manpower, machinery, and monetary resources. Reference letters from their bankers help establish their standing in the market. A list of their present customers is also sought to guage their market base. The short-listed vendors are registered and whenever there is a requirement of their services, a Request for Quote (RFQ) is sent to them. In case of very large purchase orders, vendors are invited to bid in a competitive bidding process. Tender evaluation tools help identify the most suitable bid. A number of companies resort to reverse auctions, whereby they announce the auction process on their website and ask the vendors to make their bids before the deadline. The bids are then opened and evaluated, before the contract is awarded to the selected vendor with the most suitable offer. This process is called a reverse auction because in this case the auction is for procurement instead of a sale.

Once shortlisted to make the supplies, the vendor is issued an Electronic Purchase Order (EPO) and paid an order advance through an Electronic Fund Transfer (EFT). The order is electronically monitored throughout its execution process. In many cases, an electronic vendor management and inventory system automatically generates EPOs in favour of approved vendors. After the vendor has shipped the cargo, he/she can send an electronic invoice to the buyer. Based on this invoice and after the receipt of other shipping documents and quality reports, the buyer can release the payment through EFT, thus closing the transaction.

Benefits of Electronic Procurement

Following are the various benefits of e-procurement.

1. Reduction in Manpower Cost

One of the biggest benefits of IT is that an efficient IT system can replace substantial manpower. Traditionally, purchase has been a manpower intensive function. Various tasks undertaken by the purchase department have included locating suppliers, assessing their capabilities, and approving them; creating a list of approved vendors, sending enquiries to them, evaluating their offers, negotiating with them; placing orders, following up orders and receipt of material; liasoning with the quality control department for approval of quality of goods supplied; coordinating with finance department for effecting the payments against supplies, etc. In an e-procurement most of these functions are performed electronically, and manpower cost, thus, is substantially saved.

2. Reduction in Purchase Cycle Time

Due to a ready database of approved vendors and availability of e-mail, the entire procurement process, right from floating an enquiry to effecting the payment, can be carried out electronically. This reduces repeated visits to vendors who could be located in different parts of the world, cuts down the techno-commercial negotiation process, including the receipt, to shipping documents and effecting of payments.

3. Wider Choice of Vendors

The organization can reach a wider vendor base through its website, online bulletin boards or private bid boards, e-mails, etc. In the pre-electronic era, buyers would confine their search only to domestic markets or to well known international sources. Small companies with limited resources had no opportunity to reach a potential big buyer. All this has now changed; even a small supplier in any part of the world can learn about the requirements of a particular buyer and post offers. In fact, large organizations like America's Wal-Mart and France's Carrefour procure a substantial proportion of their requirements from small manufacturers.

4. Better Prices for the Purchased Goods

E-procurement creates a very competitive environment in which, buyers have a wide choice of suppliers. Buyers can thus get a quality, which they desire at an attractive price. A supplier has to compete on a global basis in order to get an order. Hence, buyers can enjoy the benefit of competition and procure goods at competitive rates.

5. Reduction in Transaction Cost

In a paperless environment, where the procurement process and payments are electronically driven, the delays are minimum, human errors are fewer, the process is transparent, and the result is a reduction in transaction cost.

6. Fewer Human Errors

Repetitive paper work or data entry work can result in human errors in various stages of order processing. But if the entire process is conducted on a common electronic platform, the paper work and repetitive data entry work is eliminated to a very large extent. Reduction in human errors itself is a cost saving component and can cut down the delays and accelerate the order processing cycle.

7. Better Relations with the Vendors

Traditionally a buyer would create a large vendor base, as he/she did not want to be dependent upon a few sources of supply. This used to result in insecurity on both ends, which was not conducive to a good vendor-buyer relationship. E-procurement enables a buyer to rely on smaller number of suppliers because of better connectivity and transparency. This leads to mutual trust, dependence, and a long-term relationship between a buyer and a seller. Also, with e-procurement there is better visibility of orders throughout the enterprise.

8. Better Compliance with Regulations

Any international transaction has to comply with three sets of laws: first, that of the buyer's country; second, that of the seller's country; and third, international regulations. The e-procurement platform can be built taking into account compliance with all the three sets of regulations. Also, it can take into account international cyber laws which govern web-based transactions.

ELECTRONIC MARKETING

Internet has changed the way we exchange goods for money. It has broken geographical barriers between buyers and sellers. The internet enables a manufacturer in India to sell his/her goods to a customer in any part of the world through the World Wide Web. It is necessary, however, that the buyer has access to internet and has the necessary know-how and desire to make online purchases.

The internet has provided a very effective platform for electronic marketing or e-marketing. E-marketing means using digital technologies to help sell your goods or services. This is different from a conventional market place, where sellers display their goods and buyers can touch and feel the goods and bargain with sellers. In case of e-marketing, sellers can display photographs, video films, and specifications of their products. In most cases, the prices are also displayed so that buyers have a clear idea about the product and the price. A number of websites have tied up with logistics service providers to deliver goods at the customer's doorstep. In such a case, the landed prices are also quoted by the seller.

Figure 14.3 shows a seller with a website; the buyer too has access to the internet. The buyer studies the information about the goods listed/displayed on the website. If the specifications or the details of the goods meet the buyers's requirements and if the buyer is satisfied with the price, he/she can purchase the goods through credit card. The seller can get paid through electronic fund transfer and ship the goods to the buyer. This is a typical Business to Customer (B2C) transaction involving a direct interface between the buyer and the seller through the internet. A number of products such as DVDs, music CDs, books, gifts, airline tickets, etc., are widely sold over the internet. Also a number of websites sell used goods of all kinds over the internet. Some of the very successful B2C enterprises are Amazon, eBay, Dell Computers, etc.

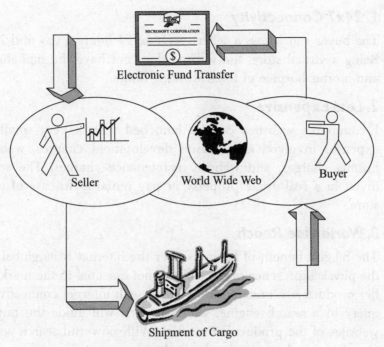

Fig. 14.3 Electronic marketing

Another type of transaction on the internet is between Business to Business (B2B). E-business has so far been more influential in the B2B domain because of greater penetration of computer use among businesses than households, the suitability of B2B products and services to online sales, and the much larger volume (and value) of B2B transactions (Fletcher 2004).

An example of a B2B transaction is the portal of a shipping line, where an exporter can log on to find the voyage schedules, freight rates, and can also book the cargo. Another form of B2B transaction is online bidding. In this case, the buyer; say an automobile manufacturer, invites the suppliers of wind shields to participate in a tender. This tender has an opening and a closing date. The bids are opened to locate the most suitable bidder in terms of price, adherence to technical specifications, delivery schedules, and meeting other terms and conditions of the buyer. As discussed before, this bidding process constitutes a 'reverse auction'. Because business buying practices differ dramatically from consumer buying practices, the B2B virtual market places must offer services that are quite distinct from a simple e-retailer (Hoque 2000).

Benefits of E-Marketing

Following are the various benefits of e-marketing.

1. 24x7 Connectivity

The buyer can access a seller's website 24 hours a day and 7 days a week. Being a virtual store, the website does not have the limitations of a brick and mortar hospice of fixed working hours.

2. Less Expensive

E-commerce websites can be launched with a very small budget. The expenses involved are website development charges, web-space rental, hosting charges, and website maintenance charges. The seller need not invest in a real estate property or pay rental as in case of a conventional store.

3. Worldwide Reach

The biggest benefit of business over the internet is its global reach. Hence the physical presence of the seller is not essential in the markets where his/her products are in demand. A buyer with internet connectivity will feed a query in a search engine, which in turn will guide the buyer to various websites of the products of interest. With powerful search engines such as, Google, a product search takes only a few seconds.

4. Online Payment Facility

The buyer can make online payments via credit card. This facility speeds up the transaction, assuring the seller of payment. Of late, there have been internet security concerns regarding online payments. But due to various innovations such as firewalls, online payments are more secure than ever before.

5. Measurement of Effectiveness

By putting a counter on the website, the seller can count the number of visitors to the website and the number of buyers who actually made on-line purchases. In case the website is not found to be effective it can be modified to obtain the desired results.

6. Ease of Operation

The buyer need not leave the comfort of office or home to purchase goods on the internet. The payment can be made with a click of the mouse and the goods can be delivered at the buyer's door step.

7. User-friendliness

Most e-marketing websites are very easy to use. The buyer is guided through various procedures to purchase the goods on-line. Many sellers have established call centres to be in direct touch with the buyer.

8. Personalized Service

Visitors to the websites are normally advised to register themselves, so that each time they visit the website they are recognized and provided suitable services. This gives a personal touch to the transaction. Many websites recognize regular buyers and frequent visitors and give them special attention.

9. Creation of Consumer Databases

The seller can keep a data base of the name, age, address, sex, contact numbers, and important dates, such as birthdays and marriage anniversaries of online buyers. They can also track the buying behaviour of the frequent buyer, his/her preferences and on-line expenditure, etc. This provides a better insight into the expectations of the buyer. However, this particular aspect of the internet is also seen as a disadvantage by consumers, who may regard it as invasion of privacy.

ELECTRONIC LOGISTICS

Electronic logistics is the use of web-based technologies to support warehousing and transportation management processes. E-logistics enables distribution to couple routing optimization with inventory tracking and tracing information (Norris et al 2000).

In international trade and distribution, computerization is slowly but surely taking hold of every aspect of business. From computerized trade leads available through the department of commerce, to electronic letters of credit, to telecommunicated documents, to computerized freight booking, tracing and documentation system, to electronic freight tariffs, automated freight payment systems, computerized loss and damage reporting, automated freight payment systems, to computerized duty drawback and customs house clearance systems, almost everything is computerized to some extent (Wood and Wardlow, 2002).

Exhibit 14.1 Catching up with the latest technologies in India

Freight Operation Information System

The freight operation information system or FOIS comprises of rake management system (RMS) and terminal management system (TMS). The RMS tracks and manages freight wagons and has been implemented in all major locations in India. The TMS helps find information about the freight at the freight terminal and to know the status of train arrivals, departures, etc.

To achieve higher standards in freight movements, the Indian railways plans to use the Radio Frequency Identification System (RFID) for tracking

(Contd)

Exhibit 14.1 (Contd)

wagons and consignments. The basic reason behind the use of RFID in wagons and consignments is to help customers know where their consignments have actually reached. According to the Centre for Railway Information Systems (CRIS), an RFID chip embedded in all wagons and sheds would read and register the data for both the railways and customers' use. After the implementation of this application, accurate wagon data would be obtained from the Indian Railways' freight operating information system.

Source: CII Logistics & Freight News Dated 10.5.2007

There is a tremendous scope of the application of IT in logistics. In fact, modern supply chains are held together by the strength of IT, through its ability to transmit huge amount of data speedily, or make global data available to expedite the decision-making process.

Due to the advantages offered by IT, many logistics providers are planning to handle majority of their commercial transactions electronically. Also, exporters are already using IT for various activities ranging from e-procurement of goods to availing transportation services on the net.

Important Electronic Tools

Shipping lines are keen to encourage their customers to use the internet and have developed a number of attractive tools. The biggest benefit of these tools is that both shippers as well as shipping lines gain by using them. Following are some of the important tools:

- Electronic receipt of vessel schedule information
- Tracking and tracing of cargo
- Remote bill of lading (B/L) printing
- Single data entry reporting
- Exception reporting
- Online tendering, etc.

Electronic Receipt of Vessel Schedule Information

Shippers can visit a logistics portal to check the schedule of different shipping lines and choose what suits their supply chains the best. This saves shippers time and effort. The shipping lines, too, benefit as they do not have to inform individual shippers about their voyage schedules. At present, the only limitation to this system is that not every portal maintains information about every shipping line, nor does every shipping line provide updated information on their sites or related portals.

Hence, it is necessary for the shipper to Surf various portals.

Tracking and Tracing of Cargo

The biggest benefit shippers enjoy as far as e-logistics is concerned, is tracking and tracing the cargo. With e-connectivity they need to spend less time per enquiry with shipping lines about the status of their cargo and significantly improve their supply chain visibility. However, different portals offer different services. For example, some shipping lines can track a container's movement in and out of various warehouses in transit, while others can track only inland haulage moves. Still others can monitor only the ocean leg of the voyage. No carrier offers complete door-to-door visibility of the cargo.

Remote B/L Printing

The main benefits of this facility are reduced production and distribution costs for the carriers. The shipper's gain is fast and error-free receipt of documents. More and more shippers are using this facility and are demanding simplified transmission of transport documents. One of the reasons for this is error-free transmission of B/L. Shipping lines normally despatch the B/L within 48 hours of vessel sailing. However, if an error owing to the incorrect completion of instructions or other reasons is discovered on arrival, the shipper has to return the documents to the shipping line. With the remotely printed B/L, shippers can check the B/L in advance before final printing.

Single Data Entry Reporting

With the aligned system of documentation, the format of various shipping documents is now standardized. Information once keyed in any document will automatically appear in all aligned documents. This system saves repetitive data entries and also saves substantial time and cost.

Exception Reporting

Shippers across the world, who work tirelessly towards manufacture of quality products, also want reliable delivery schedules. Exception reporting by the shipping line helps the shipper to know if there are any deviations from the instructions, which he/she has given to the shipping line. For example, if there is a delay in arrival of a ship at the port of destination, an exception report will help the shipper know about it in advance. The shipper can then take corrective action to minimize losses.

Online Tendering

To find out the ocean freight rates from various shipping lines, the shipper has to send an enquiry separately to each shipper. Online tendering helps the shipper to send out rate enquiries to as many shipping lines as desired by merely pressing a button. Today, in the era of rationalization, mergers, and acquisitions, the shipper's global requirements are getting increasingly complex. A number of multinationals have operations in up to 200 countries across the world. They have a cargo flow running in thousands of TEUs, and involving hundreds of different ship routes. Online tendering helps them get competitive quotations from shipping lines operating on various routes. These multinationals maintain databases of such quotations in order to choose the most competitive rates on various routes.

According to a Switzerland-based business consultancy firm, Capgemini, the top five IT-supported logistics services listed by customer companies were warehouse management (65%), transport management (63%), consignment tracking and event management (63%), web based communication (57%), and transport planning (38%).

As warehousing is an important component of logistics, which is supported by IT, it would be interesting to discuss the role of IT in managing a warehouse.

Warehouse Management Software (WMS)

Warehousing is defined as "that part of a firm's logistics system that stores products (raw materials, parts, goods-in-process, finished goods) at and between points of origin and point of consumption" (Lambert, Stock, and Ellaram, 1998). Hence, the basic function of a warehouse is the storage of a variety of goods. Figure 14.4 illustrates a typical warehouse operation.

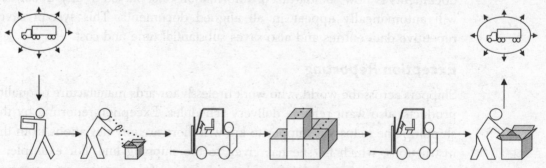

Fig. 14.4   Warehousing functions

The basic functions of a warehouse are
- Receiving goods from the supplier
- Ensuring the quality of received material
- Arranging the proper and safe storage of material
- Retrieval of the goods as required
- Despatching the finished goods to the user

Most warehouses are designed and equipped to undertake these basic functions. However, as the complexity of business grows, warehouses are expected to offer more value added services, such as:

- Cross docking
- Bar coding
- Bonding facilities
- Inventory control
- Accounting activity
- Pick and pack
- Documentation
- Order processing
- Reverse logistics
- Light manufacturing
- Assembly
- Welding
- Order customizing
- Localization

These warehouses are run by sophisticated state-of-the-art warehouse management software, which link the manufacturer with multi-locational warehouses. The software keeps track of material and replenishes stocks whenever necessary. Many of the software are EDI enabled, which can be integrated with the customer and transport carrier EDI systems. They typically perform the following functions:

- *Inventory management* The system records incoming inventory and places the material at the suitable place in the warehouse.
- *Order processing* The system receives the orders, prepares the pick list of the items to be despatched, and prepares invoice, packing list and other despatch documents.
- *Bar coding and labelling* WMS generates bar codes for the products. A bar code is a machine-readable representation of product information. It also helps to trace the product and can reduce the instances of shoplifting.
- *Stock location and productivity management* WMS helps in locating the stocks within the warehouse. It also leads the stock pickers to proper location and identifies the item to be picked. This reduces the picking time for an order, thereby increasing the productivity of warehouse personnel.
- *Management reporting* The system informs if the orders are executed in time, the time required from the receipt of order to delivery of material, the number of orders picked per day, and overtime required for order execution, etc.

Exhibit 14.2 shows the scanned files of individual items received by the warehouse, which are then transferred to WMS, which in turn compares scanned files with the intake register and produces a detailed invoice-wise variance report as shown in Exhibit 14.3. Exhibit 14.4 shows the scanner, which is used to scan the bar-coded tags of imported cargo.

Exhibit 14.2 JEBEL ALI Distribution Centre-DUBAI

Scanned IMPORT.INTAKE Files

Received Date: 20/12/2006 Intake # 0299

S.No	Brand	Location	File Name	QTY	Boxes	Box Nos.	Run Date	Remarks
1	ADAMS	JBEL ALI DC	13225703 VOU	1582	30	01-30	22.12.06	IMPORT
2	ADAMS	JBEL ALI DC	41223814 VOU	1722	30	31-60	22.12.06	IMPORT
3	ADAMS	JBEL ALI DC	02222113 VOU	2015	30	61-90	23.12.06	IMPORT
4	ADAMS	JBEL ALI DC	06241911 VOU	2515	30	91-120	24.12.06	IMPORT
5	ADAMS	JBEL ALI DC	02234211 VOU	2481	30	121-150	24.12.06	IMPORT
6	ADAMS	JBEL ALI DC	06245514 VOU	424	4	151-154	24.12.06	IMPORT
			SCANNED QTY	10739	154			
			INVOICE QTY	10741	154			

Courtesy: Jawad Business Group, Dubai, UAE

Exhibit 14.3 Variance Report

Scanned			Invoice			Variance		
Style	Colour	Qty Recd	Style	Colour	Qty Recd	Style	Colour	Qty Recd
150150	2	2				150150	2	2
150151	2	2				150151	2	2
150154	2	636	150154	2	633	0	0	3
150158	6	1				150158	6	1
150383	2	634	150383	2	639	0	0	−5
151074	7	354	151074	7	653	0	0	1
151127	30	629	151127	30	629	0	0	0
151847	52	812	151847	52	805	0	0	7
152037	67	489	152037	67	488	0	0	1
152038	7	563	152038	7	564	0	0	−1
152583	32	297	152583	32	294	0	0	3
152588	76	949	152588	76	942	0	0	7
152597	7	930	152597	7	942	0	0	12
152598	76	4				152598	76	4
152605	95	719	152605	95	719	0	0	0
153104	46	942	153104	48	942	0	0	0
153105	7	234	153105	7	234	0	0	0
153216	8	1111	153216	8	1126	0	0	−15
153217	26	1131	153217	26	4431	0	0	0
Grand Total		10739			10741			−2

Courtesy: Jawad Business Group, Dubai, UAE

Exhibit 14.4   Barcode Scanner

Courtesy: Jawad Business Group, Dubai, UAE

Benefits of a Warehouse Management Software

Traditionally, the various warehousing functions are carried out manually.

However, by installing a suitable WMS, an organization can enjoy the following benefits:

1. Error-free documentation work
2. Tighter inventory control
3. Better utilization of warehousing space
4. Faster storage and retrieval of goods
5. Higher productivity of the warehouse staff
6. Better coordination with supplier as well as customer

These benefits make WMS an integral part of modern warehousing and logistics operations.

Exhibit 14.5   Dnata's FIFO Boosts Warehouse Efficiency and Customer Service

The global enterprise Dnata Cargo has adopted the First In First Out (FIFO) concept at its Dubai International Airport terminals, with a new storage process enabling shipments to leave warehouses in chronological order to optimize warehouse facilities and speed up cargo movement to aircraft.

The FIFO process was introduced by Dnata to streamline its cargo supply chain for saving space, time, and resources. In this configuration, the operation radically departs from conventional warehouse operations—here shipments are stored in various locations until retrieved for loading—and is particularly valuable for airlines and carriers who need to fill last-minute cargo space availability.

Source: The Supply Chain & Logistics Link, Issue 14/2006

Radio-Frequency-Identification (RFID)

RFID tags are very small in size and they consist of an antenna and a chip that contains an electronic product code (EPC). These tags have a much larger product data storage capacity as compared to a bar code. A RFID tag can store all the information about the description of the product, its specifications, manufacturing location and date, the sources of the components from which it is made, and product expiry date (where it is relevant). The RFID tags emit signals, which can be read by special scanner, thereby confirming the presence of the product. This is the advantage enjoyed by RFID tags over barcodes. To read barcodes, line-of-sight scanners are required, where as RFID tags can be read by strategically placed scanners. Earlier RFID tags were used only for high end applications due to their very high per unit cost. But recent innovations have caused the price of the tags to plummet and their performance to improve: in 2000, RFID tags cost $1 each; they now cost 25 to 40 cents and are widely expected to cost no more than 5 cents apiece in a few years (exhibit) (Niemeyer, Pak and Ramaswamy 2007).

Exhibit 14.6

Wal-Mart recently announced that it wanted its top 100 suppliers, by 2005, to begin fitting their cases and pallets with radio-frequency-identification (RFID) tags—chips that can automatically transmit to a special scanner all of the information about a container's contents or about individual products. A number of these suppliers were tempted to do more than just affix chips to the goods they shipped to Wal-Mart; they also looked to implement RFID technology more broadly in their organizations in the hope of cutting their own supply chain costs. Retailers and consumer products manufacturers, aware of Wal-Mart's interest in RFID, also began eyeing it as the next supply chain technology to invest in.

Source: Smart tags for your supply chain, www.mckinsey.com.

Technology, however, is fast-evolving, and soon 'voice code' technology may replace bar codes and compete with RFID technology. The voice code is unique and can be used by anyone who speaks. The person, who handles a cargo with a Voice Code handset, can document his distribution to a central accounting system through verbal communication.

Electronic Data Interchange (EDI)

EDI is defined as the computer-to-computer transfer of commercial or administrative transactions using a predefined standard to structure data related to the transaction (Kalakota and Winton). In such a case, transaction means carrying out functions like consignment instructions, payment of customs duty, processing of duty draw back applications, DEPB applications, etc. The need for such electronic links between various agencies involved in logistics operations was felt worldwide, because of the increasing number of transactions. The United Nations Trade Data Elements Directory (UNTDED) contains the 'data elements,' which are assembled into 'segments', which are further grouped into a message using 'syntax rules'. These rules are devised by the UN for computerization of trade data and their electronic transmission and are called rules for Electronic Data Interchange for Administration, Commerce, and Transport (EDIFACT). EDI refers to the computer-to-computer transmission of business information from one business computer to another in standard data formats. It is used mostly in large organizations and their satellite suppliers working together over a private network called a Value-Added-Network (VAN) (Nelson and Nelson, 2001).

There is a very close relationship between EDI and international business. EDI was first used in 1948, immediately after World War II when huge amount of humanitarian aid material arrived in Berlin as air cargo from different parts of the world. To sort out different materials described in different languages, a standard format was devised, which was to be filled in by all air carriers before unloading the cargo. This helped in the standardization of information inputs.

Since then, EDI has developed tremendously and enables the free flow of information across continents. It handles large amount of information, which controls and regulates the movement of cargo, containers, ships, and aircraft. Such information is useful only if it arrives before the cargo.

According to the United Nations Conference on Trade and Development (UNCTAD), the cost of voluminous paperwork, formalities, delays, and errors constitutes about 10 per cent of the final value of the goods. It is interesting to note that an international transaction involves 30 different parties, 60 original documents, 360 document copies, all of which must be checked, transmitted and re-entered into computers located at different places. This leads to very high transaction costs, particularly in developing countries. The UN body estimates this cost to be US$ 400 billion per year, which can be cut by a quarter with effective EDI.

Figure 14.5 illustrates the flow of cargo and related documents in a typical international transaction.

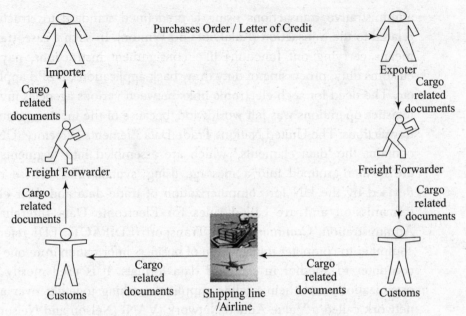

Purchases Order / Letter of Credit

Importer

Expoter

Cargo related documents

Cargo related documents

Freight Forwarder

Freight Forwarder

Cargo related documents

Cargo related documents

Customs

Cargo related documents

Shipping line /Airline

Cargo related documents

Customs

Fig. 14.5 Typical International Trade Transaction

The EDI effectively knits together exporter, importer, freight forwarders, shipping lines, and customs department in different countries. For example, when an importer receives a consignment, he/she is immediately alerted by the computer system about the material, which is short in supply. This helps the importer follow up with the exporter to expedite the delivery of the relevant material. Simultaneously, the freight broker's computer also receives the information about the inbound cargo. This computer scans the information and uses all the relevant data to prepare automated broken interface (ABI) entry data, which is transmitted to customs department. Hence EDI system effectively eliminates manual data inputs, fax messaging, photo-copying, and other related activities.

Customs and EDI

Every consignment entering or leaving a country must clear the customs barrier. The customs officials in most of the countries have to operate under tremendous pressure of the physical examination of cargo, completion of paperwork, collection of customs dues, maintenance of cargo in bonded warehouses, etc. On the one hand, they have to comply with governmental rules and regulations, and on the other hand they have to expedite the clearance of cargo, which is legally entering the country with appropriate documents.

Following are the reasons for which many countries are adopting EDI and advising shippers to transact with customs department electronically instead of paper.

1. The liberalization of economies across the world has given a boost to world trade. This has resulted in an increased volume of cargo to be examined by customs department at ports, airports, and land borders.
2. Technology has enabled increasing the speeds and sizes of ships and aircraft, which bring in larger quantities of cargo for customs clearance.
3. The scope of the customs departments worldwide have widened and now covers areas, such as intellectual property rights, toxic wastes, and endangered species among others.
4. Governments, international agencies, and NGOs demand accurate statistical data related to international trade with greater frequency.
5. EDI helps customs departments cope with increasing demands on their time. It is emerging as a useful tool of transaction for customs departments in many developed and developing countries.

Benefits of EDI

As a result of the various benefits offered by EDI, more and more links of global supply chains are getting connected through EDI. Electronic connectivity for exchange of trade documents speeds up international transaction and delivers the following benefits:

1. EDI saves repetitive data entry work at various points.
2. EDI enables error-free and quick transmission of data from one point to another. Many of the problems arising from data entry errors can, therefore, be minimized.
3. EDI helps exporters and importers to practice the 'just-in-time' inventory concept, thereby reducing inventory-carrying costs.
4. EDI improves the cash flow position of exporters by quick processing of invoices and drawback applications.
5. EDI speeds up the customs clearance by reducing the transit time of the cargo.
6. EDI reduces the 'turn-around time' of the ships at the ports.
7. EDI improves the efficiency of port authorities and helps them earn more revenues.
8. EDI reduces the paperwork, thereby saving a company's efforts and expenses towards maintenance of records, filing cabinets, and storage systems. EDI also saves the time taken for retrieval of a document in a paperless office. Also, there is a substantial reduction in postage costs.

SUMMARY

Technology is changing at a very fast pace. Various aspects of electronic business such as e-procurement, e-marketing, e-logistics use a number of technology products. The life cycle of technology products is very short. What we are using today may become obsolete tomorrow.

We are living in a knowledge-driven era, where everyone has access to information thanks to internet and a variety of other sources of information. However, the market is dominated by those, who translate information into knowledge and use the knowledge to improve productivity and efficiency of their enterprises. India is enjoying an enviable position because of its leadership in the area of information technology. A number of business solutions are developed in India for world wide applications. However, such applications take a long time to be implemented in India itself.

Supply Chain Management is emerging as an area where companies are trying to improve their efficiency in order to have a competitive edge. Some of the technological tools in supply chain domain are bar coding and Radio Frequency Identity (RFID) tags. Developed countries started using bar codes first and now they are implementing RFID. Wal-Mart has taken the lead in implementation of RFID. However, in India, we are still lagging behind in the implementation of these tools. Some of the Indian companies who have an exposure to overseas markets have adopted these tools. Similarly Electronic Data Interchange (EDI) is capable of creating paperless offices and speedy transfer of documents and data. But in this area also India lags behind. Indian ports can improve their operational efficiency by adopting EDI and reduce port congestion.

Retail revolution in domestic market, coupled with improvement in infrastructure and entry of foreign retail giants will see a number of these new technology tools being used in India.

CONCEPT REVIEW QUESTIONS

1. What is the working mechanism of e-procurement? In what ways is it different from conventional procurement?
2. Information technology has revolutionized various aspects of international business. Do you support this argument? Discuss with reasons.
3. Discuss the advantages and disadvantages of
   (a) E-procurement
   (b) E-marketing
   (c) E-logistics

4. How does e-marketing complement conventional marketing? Discuss with examples.

5. How can a company survive and grow purely on the basis of e-marketing? Develop a business model to support your answer.

6. Explain the internet based tools offered by shipping lines to shippers as a part of their e-logistics efforts.

7. What are the various functions of Warehouse Management Software? How do they benefit the user?

8. Define Electronic Data Interchange (EDI) and discuss the value added features of EDI which speed up international transactions.

9. What is the relationship between EDI and international trade? What are the various benefits of EDI to international trade?

10. How is the logistics industry benefited by information technology? What are the various e-commerce tools available to the logistics industry? Explain in detail.

OBJECTIVE QUESTIONS

Choose the correct option.

1. Which of the following is NOT used in international business?
   (a) Electronic Fund Transfer
   (b) Electronic Data Interchange
   (c) Electronic Currency
   (d) Radio Frequency Identification

2. Which of the following is NOT a benefit of e-procurement?
   (a) Reduction in transaction cost
   (b) Reduction in choice of vendors
   (c) Fewer human errors
   (d) Reduction in purchase cycle time

3. Which of the following company uses ONLY the e-marketing platform?
   (a) Microsoft
   (b) Acer Computers
   (c) Dell Computers
   (d) Amazon.com

4. Which of the following products is ideal for e-marketing?
   (a) Perfumes
   (b) Books
   (c) Footwear
   (d) Garments

5. Which of the following is NOT among the top five logistics services supported by IT?
   (a) B2B logistics hubs
   (b) Warehouse Management
   (c) Transport Management
   (d) Transport Planning
6. The major hurdle in the wider application of RFID is?
   (a) Lack of awareness about RFID
   (b) Yet to be proven technology
   (c) Popularity of bar coding
   (d) High per unit cost
7. Which of the following statements is TRUE?
   (a) EDI is a substitute to e-mail.
   (b) EDI can be replaced by voice code technology.
   (c) EDI is operated on value-added-network.
   (d) Only small companies use EDI.

EXERCISES

1. Assume that you are a large manufacturer of garments. List down the important parameters for adding e-procurement facility to your company website to procure fabrics for your production.
2. Design a B2C website for your company to promote high quality leather goods like ladies footwear, handbags, fashion accessories, etc. to your potential customers in Europe and America.
3. Design a B2B website to offer your services as a 3PL operator.
4. Visit the websites of Amazon.com and eBay to compare their features and the services offered by them.
5. Visit the website of Maersk Logistics and study the various e-logistics services offered by them.

SELECT REFERENCES

Australian Government Department of Finance and Administration and Australian Government Information Management Office, *Strategic guide to e-procurement*, May 2006.

Fletcher, Richard, Jim Bell and Rod McNaughton, 2004, *International E-Business Marketing*, Thomson Learning.

Hoque, Faisal, 2000, *e-Enterprise—Business Models, Architecture and Components,* Cambridge University Press.

Kalakota, Ravi and Andrew Whinston, 2004, *Frontiers of Electronic Commerce,* Pearson Education India.

Lambert, Douglas M., James R. Stock, and Lisa M. Ellaram, 1998, *Fundamentals of Logistics Management,* Irwin McGraw Hill, New York.

Nelson, Anne and William Nelson, 2001, *Building Electronic Commerce with Web Data Construction,* Addison Wesley, Boston.

Norris, Grant, James R. Hurley, Kenneth M., John R. Dunleavy, John D Balls, 2000, *E-business and ERP, Transforming the Enterprise,* John Wiley & Sons, Inc., New York.

Supply Chain and Logistics Group, Dubai, "A hybrid world of technology logistics and supply chain", *The Link,* Issue 14/2006.

Supply Chain and Logistics Group, Dubai, *LXE develops Voice Code—A Superior Version of Bar Code,* The Link, Issue 14/2006.

Wood, Barnes and Murphy Wardlow, 2002, International Logistics, second edition, AMACOM Publication.

www.businesslink.uk, last accessed on 29th July 2007.

www.capgemini.com, last accessed on 29th July 2007.

www.mckinsey.com, Niemeyer Alex, Minsok H. Pak, Sanjay E. Ramaswamy, *Smart Tags for Your Supply Chain,* last visited on 29th July 2007.

15 Export Incentive Schemes

Learning Objectives

After studying this chapter, you will be able to understand

- the rationale behind the export incentives
- duty exemption schemes
- duty remission schemes
- the Export Promotion Capital Goods scheme
- the concept of Special Economic Zones

The international market is a very complex and competitive arena, in which, only the fittest survives. Merely producing a good quality product, putting in place an efficient supply chain, and aggressively promoting the product in the overseas market is not enough. The product should also be competitively priced so that the customer finds it a good value for money. This is possible only if the product is not burdened with taxes and duties at various points during its progression from the raw material stage to the final product bound for the overseas markets.

Every country in the world is trying to earn a share in the global trade. This is due to the lowering of trade barriers since the inception of the World Trade Organization (WTO), increased import bills, and increased global competition in the domestic market. Also, most developing countries borrow heavily from financial institutions like the World Bank and the International Monetary Fund (IMF) and other sources to finance their developmental activities and reduce the balance of payment deficits. It is therefore imperative that the import bills as well as foreign loans be paid back in foreign exchange. In order to achieve this, earning foreign exchange through various export activities is the need of the hour.

In order to motivate organizations to export and earn precious foreign exchange, governments offer certain incentives. These incentives help reduce the tax burden of the exporters and also achieve a competitive price-edge for their products in foreign markets. However, being a member of WTO, each country has to ensure that the incentives offered by its government do not give an unfair advantage to the exporters. Thus, no country is to give special trading advantages to another or to discriminate against its all nations stand on an equal basis and share the benefits of any move towards lower trade barriers (Branch). Also, all export incentives have to comply with WTO norms and should be in line with its various principles.

In India, the framework of export incentives in the form of duty exemption and remission schemes has been devised keeping in mind the interests of exporters as well as the commitments India has made to WTO. The duty exemption scheme helps exporters import duty-free inputs required for manufacturing export products. The Advance Authorization Scheme (AAS) and the Duty Free Import Authorization (DFIA) scheme are examples of duty exemption schemes. The duty remission schemes enable post-exports replenishment/remission of duty on inputs. This includes (a) Duty Drawback and (b) Duty Exemption Passbook (DEPB) schemes.

In addition to this, the Export Promotion Capital Goods (EPCG) scheme enables exporters to import capital goods at concessional rate of duty and suitable export obligation.

The incentives detailed above are available to all eligible exporters in India. In addition, the government has launched the very ambitious scheme of Special Economic Zones (SEZs) in order to reduce bureaucratic hurdles in importing inputs for exports and exporting finished products from India. These SEZs are modelled on the highly successful Chinese Economic Zones. It is expected that the SEZs will be the engines of growth in international trade for India.

DUTY EXEMPTION SCHEMES

An exporter has to face cut-throat competition in international markets. To be successful, in addition to good quality and prompt delivery, price competitiveness is an important factor. If products bound for foreign markets are burdened with duties and taxes similar to domestic market, they will not be price competitive and, thus, will find little demand overseas. Following are the two duty exemption schemes offered by the Government of India to reduce the customs duty burden on export products.

Advance Authorization Scheme

An exporter can use this scheme to import the inputs required for the execution of his/her export orders without payment of customs duty. This facility is available to both manufacturer exporters as well as merchant exporters. As duty free raw material can be imported before the final product is exported, this scheme is called the Advance Authorization Scheme. *This scheme was earlier known* as the *Advance Licence Scheme.* Advance authorizations are exempted from payment of basic customs duty, additional customs duty, education cess, antidumping duty, and safeguard duty, if any.

Along with raw materials, other inputs such as fuel and oil can be imported under this licence. Each item, which is allowed to be imported is mentioned on the advance authorization along with its value and the quantity to be imported. While computing the value of advance authorization, the margin for normal wastage is built in so that adequate quantity of raw material can be imported. This authorization however cannot be used for import of prohibited items.

An exporter who avails of this facility of advance authorization has to accept the export obligation of the value indicated on the authorization. The export obligation has to be fulfilled within the prescribed time limit as mentioned on the authorization. The exporter has to execute a Bank Guarantee/Letter of Undertaking confirming that he/she will fulfill the export obligations within the prescribed time limit. The validity of authorization is as per the prevailing foreign trade policy.

Advance authorization can also be availed after the completion of the export process. In this case, export obligation is fulfilled first and the imports are carried out afterwards.

Important Features of Advance Authorization

Following are the important features of advance authorization.
1. Advance authorization is issued only to the actual user. Neither the authorization, nor the material imported against it is transferable even after the export obligation is fulfilled. However, once the export obligation is complete, the authorization holder can dispose off the product manufactured out of duty free inputs.
2. Advance authorization is issued to manufacturer exporters or merchant exporters who are tied to supplementary manufacturers.
3. Advance authorization can be issued for
   (a) Physical exports
   (b) Intermediate supplies
   (c) Deemed exports
   (d) Sale to SEZ units
4. In case the advance authorization is availed on a post exports basis, the need for Bank Guarantee/Letter of Undertaking is waived.
5. In case of project exports, the export obligation has to be fulfilled within the duration of the execution of the project.

6. Advance authorization can also be used for job work. In such a case, inputs are imported free of cost and re-exported after the job work. An allowance for suitable wastage is given as per industry norms.

7. The quantum of imports allowed are decided on the basis of standard input-output norms (SION), as notified by the Directorate General of Foreign Trade (DGFT). For example, for manufacturing a product weighing 1 kg, the raw material required is 1.25 kg. Here, the SION would be 1.25:1, and a wastage of 0.25 kg is allowed after giving due consideration to the method of production. The exporter has to ensure a positive value addition for exports.

$$\text{Value Addition VA} = \frac{A - B}{B} \times 100$$

where A is FOB value of export realized and B is CIF value covered by authorization.

Advance authorizations can also be issued on the basis of adhoc norms or self declared norms as per the foreign trade policy.

8. An exporter can apply for advance authorization by filling the prescribed form given in the foreign trade policy and by submitting the same to the office of the DGFT. Annexure 1 shows the Application for Advance Licence, which is similar to present day application for advance authorization. The exporter can despatch the goods in anticipation of advance authorization after submitting the application form to DGFT.

A special facility of annual advance authorization is provided to status holders such as export houses/trading houses/star trading houses/super star trading houses, etc. This facility helps them to procure their inputs on an annual basis. Entitlement in terms of CIF value of imports shall be up to 300% of the Free on Board (FOB) value of physical export and/or FOR value of deemed export in the preceding licencing year or Rs. 1 crore, whichever value is higher.

Duty Free Import Authorization Scheme

This scheme is similar to the advance authorization scheme with the following differences:

1. **Entitlement** The DFIA scheme is applicable only to products for which SION have been notified. Advance authorization on the other hand can be issued on basis of ad hoc norms or self declared norms.

2. **Value addition** A minimum 20% value addition shall be required for issuance of such authorization, except for items in the gems and jewellery sector, for which value addition would be as per the provisions given in the foreign trade policy.

3. **Transferability** On fulfillment of export obligations, DFIA or inputs imported can be transferred. This facility is not available for advance authorization.

DUTY REMISSION SCHEMES

Duty Drawback Scheme

There are two types of duties levied on a manufacturer in India; (a) excise duty on inputs and finished products, and (b) customs duty on the inputs, which are imported. The duty drawback scheme enables the exporter to claim the refund of these duties from the government. Under section 75 of the Customs Act, duty drawback can be claimed on those inputs, which are used in the manufacture of goods that are eventually exported. Under section 74 of the Customs Act, duty drawback can be claimed when imported goods are re-exported without any value addition or change and the articles are easily identifiable.

Duty drawback is equal to (a) customs duty paid on imported inputs, including special additional duty (SAD) plus (b) excise duty paid on indigenous inputs. Duty paid on packing material is also eligible. However, if the inputs are obtained without payment of customs/excise duty, no drawback will be paid.

There is no duty drawback available on other taxes and duties, such as sales tax and octroi. In case customs duty has been paid on part of the inputs, proportionate drawback will be available. Drawback is, however, available on processing and job work, where there is no manufacturing process taking place and the identity of goods has not changed. Drawback is also available on duty paid on packing material.

Procedure to claim duty drawback

Step 1 The exporter has to ensure that the drawback rate for the product that he/she is exporting is fixed by the Directorate of Drawback, under the Department of Revenue, Ministry of Finance. For fixing these rates, data is collected from the industry and the rates are revised generally on 1st June every year. While revising the rates, the effect of the annual budget on different inputs is taken into consideration. Exporters must keep themselves updated on the relevant rates by referring to the drawback schedule published by the government.

The rates are fixed under rule 3 of Drawback Rules where average quantity and value of each class of inputs imported or manufactured in India are considered. These rates, which are called All Industry Rates (AIR) are fixed for broad category of products, including packing material. The drawback rates are shown under customs and central excise heads. Customs head includes customs duty, surcharge, and SAD. The excise duty includes full basic duty, special excise duty, and counter vailing duty (CVD). It is possible for the exporter to avail drawback only under the customs head; for excise component, the exporter can avail CENVAT credit, which can be utilized for paying the duty on other goods sold in India.

While fixing all industry rates, weighted averages of consumption of various inputs, both imported and indigenous, are considered. Hence, the individual exporter need not prove the actual duties paid while claiming duty drawback. AIR is fixed as a percentage of the FOB value of export goods. In such a case, a ceiling of the maximum amount of drawback payable is defined so that even if the exporter has managed to get a higher FOB price for his/her goods, drawback claim remains within the ceiling limits.

Step 2 If the drawback rate is not fixed, the exporter has to apply for the fixation of rate by submitting the details to the Jurisdictional Commissioner of central excise. The drawback rate thus fixed is called the brand rate. The exporter has to submit an application for the fixation of brand rate within 60 days of export, which can be extended by another 30 days under special circumstances. A maximum extension up to one year can be given for filing the application due to abnormal circumstances as given in the relevant circular.

If an exporter feels that the AIR for his/her category is fixed at a lower rate than the actual duty paid, he/she can apply under rule 7 of Drawback Rules for the fixation of special brand rate, within 30 days of export. The conditions under which an exporter can apply for the special brand rate are as follows:

(a) If the AIR is less than 80 per cent of the duties paid.
(b) If the rate is not less than one per cent of the FOB value of the product, except when the amount of drawback per shipment is more than Rs. 500.
(c) The value of the imported material is not more than the export value. In other words, there should be no negative value addition.

Step 3 For claiming the drawback, an exporter must show the details of the inputs for which he/she is eligible to make a claim. The details, including description and quantities of the goods, are to be given on the drawback copy of the 'shipping bill'. The exporter must also make the declaration on the shipping bill that a claim of drawback is being made on the materials, containers, and packing materials on which customs and excise duties have been paid. The drawback copy of the shipping bill, which is in triplicate, should be marked as 'Drawback Claim Copy' and should be submitted with duty pre-receipt on the reverse side with revenue stamp. This copy should be endorsed by the customs officer at the port of despatch or at the land customs barrier, confirming that the goods have been exported.

Duty Drawback on Re-export

There are instances when the imported goods, which are used or unused have to be re-exported. This can happen in case of goods imported for exhibition, which remain unsold and have to be sent back to their country of origin. Also, in case of goods being rejected or in case of wrong shipments, etc., goods have to be re-exported. Section 74 of the Customs Act provides for such eventualities and allows the claim of duty drawback on the customs duty originally paid. The conditions attached to making such claims are the following:

1. The re-exported goods should be identifiable as having been imported earlier.
2. Such goods are re-exported within two years from the date of payment of duty when they were imported.
3. The original bill of entry under which the goods were imported should be submitted.
4. Such goods are subjected for inspection by customs authorities for verification and 98 per cent of the customs duty paid while importing is refunded as drawback.
5. Goods can be re-exported to any party (who need not be the original supplier) and re-export can take place from any port.

In case imported goods were used or in possession of the importer before re-export, the drawback is allowed at a reduced percentage. The rates of drawback depend on the duration of re-use or possession by the importer. For example, if the material is used up to six months, 85 per cent of the duty is refunded; from six months to one year, 70 per cent of the duty is refunded.

Duty Entitlement Pass Book Scheme

The Duty Entitlement Pass Book Scheme (DEPB) is devised for those exporters who wish to avail the facility of importing various inputs and other approved items under DEPB scheme on *post-export basis*. As such, this scheme operates in a procedure exactly opposite to that of Advance Authorisation Scheme, which allows imports prior to exports.

Under this scheme, the DEPB rates for various items are fixed and announced by the licencing authorities. The criteria for fixation of DEPB rates are the (SION) rates are fixed as a percentage of the FOB. An exporter may apply for credit at specified percentage of FOB value of exports made in freely convertible currency or payment made from foreign currency account of SEZ unit. or SEZ developer in case of supply by DTA. Annexure 2 gives a sample application form for DEPB.

Under this scheme, the exporter is issued a passbook in which the amount of DEPB entitlement is credited at the time of exports on the basis of actual amount of FOB value of exports as per the bank certificate. This credit can be utilized for payment of import duty including SAD, while importing the various items allowed for imports under DEPB scheme. This enables the exporter to neutralize the incidence of customs duty on the import content of export product. If the credit amount in DEPB is less than the import duty payable, the exporter can pay the balance in cash. In this case, two separate entries are made in the Bill of Entry. The exporter has to register DEPB with the customs house.

It is worth noting that capital goods are not allowed for imports under this scheme. Another condition is that export realization should be in hard currencies such as the US Dollar, the Pound Sterling, the Euro, the Yen etc. This facility is not available for exports to Nepal, Bhutan, etc. where exports from India are allowed in Indian Rupees.

To avail this facility, the exporter has to use a blue shipping bill on which a declaration has to be made in the prescribed form. The shipping bill must provide the serial number of the export product and the DEPB entitlement rate as mentioned in the DEPB schedule published by the DGFT.

Exhibit 15.1   DEPB's life-saving

The Duty Entitlement Pass Book (DEPB) scheme for exporters, which has been extended by a year yet again, may soon find a successor. After several unsuccessful attempts at getting an alternative WTO compatible scheme drafted by experts, the commerce department is now banking on the wisdom of its own officials and exporters to come up with an appropriate scheme. Union Commerce minister Kamal Nath has asked exporters to give their recommendations by 31 May. What is interesting though, is the fact that the minister refrained from giving a time-frame within which the new scheme would be drafted. Exporters are very clear about the fact that they would like an overlap between the new scheme and the old to help in smooth transaction. If the Commerce department fails to come up with the replacement scheme in the next six-eight months, it would have no choice other than push for another extension of the existing scheme. Given the popularity of DEPB scheme in its current form, exporters certainly would not complain even if the scheme is extended indefinitely*.

Source: The Economic Times dated 23 April 2007
*The government has yet again extended this scheme till May, 2009.

EXPORT PROMOTION CAPITAL GOODS SCHEME

The EPCG scheme allows the import of capital goods for pre production, production, and post production (including CKD (Complete Knock Down)/ SKD (Semi-knock Down) thereof as well as computer software systems at five per cent customs duty, subject to an export obligation equivalent to eight times the duty saved on capital goods imported under the EPCG scheme to be fulfilled in eight years reckoned from the authorization issue-date.

This scheme enables exporters to import capital goods inclusive of plant, machinery, components, and spare parts of machinery required for goods-production. There is an exemption on additional custom duty and CVD. Other items eligible to be imported under this scheme are:

(a) Computer software
(b) Jigs
(c) Fixtures
(d) Dies
(e) Moulds
(f) Spares for existing plant and machinery
(g) Second hand capital goods up to 10 years old

This scheme can be availed by both manufacturer exporters as well as merchant exporters. In case of merchant exporters, the capital goods imported must be installed in the factory of the supporting manufacturer. Also, the name and address of the supporting manufacturer must appear on the EPCG licence and the merchant exporter and supporting manufacturer must jointly and severely execute and bond with bank guarantee that they will fulfill the export obligation.

The amount of export obligation to be fulfilled is eight times the duty saved on imported capital goods and the time period allowed for this is eight years. In case of sick units under the Board for Industrial and Financial Reconstruction (BIFR) units under Agricultural Export Zones and for EPCG licences of Rs. 100 crore or more, the time period given is 12 years. It is mandatory that the exporter fulfills export obligations by exporting the goods capable of being manufactured by the capital goods imported under the scheme. For example, if an exporter imports a metal cutting machine, the export item should be made out of metal. The exporter cannot fulfill his/her obligation by exporting plastic goods. Certain category of deemed exports are also permissible for fulfilling the export obligation.

In case EPCG authorization fails to fulfill prescribed export obligation, the exporter shall pay duties of customs plus interest as prescribed by the customs authority. Such facilities can be availed by the EPCG authorization holder to exit at his/her option. In case the exporter is unable to fulfill the obligation in the specified period, a customs duty plus 15% interest is applicable. A bond as well as a Letter of Undertaking is to be given by the importer of capital goods. The manufacturer-exporter with an export turnover of Rs one crore is exempted from bank guarantee provided the exporter has a clean track record. Similar facility is also given to status holders (such as export houses, trading houses, etc.). It is possible for the licence holder to procure a machine from India; in this case the machinery manufacturer in India can import components for the machinery at a concessional rate of five per cent. Here, the export obligation has to be borne by the licence holder and not by the Indian machinery manufacturer.

SPECIAL ECONOMIC ZONES

India is presently the fastest growing economy in the world, after China. In the recent past, India has maintained a healthy growth of seven-eight per cent per annum. Export is identified as a thrust area and a major driver of the future economic growth. For the fiscal year April–March 2006–07, export earnings witnessed an impressive rise of 23.9 per cent. This has been the fifth successive year to witness a more than 20 per cent rate of growth. The service sector in India has seen a major expansion in the last few years. However, the full potential of the manufacturing sector has still not been exploited. China has raced past India due to its superior infrastructure. The SEZs in China have contributed substantially to the nation's economic growth. These enclaves are created as pockets of excellence, where world-class infrastructure is attracting huge foreign investments.

After carefully studying the Chinese SEZs, India too has decided to create similar zones that will provide a platform to exporters as well as foreign investors to create their manufacturing base. It is expected that the creation of Indian SEZs will provide the much-needed boost to exports as well as foreign direct investment (FDI) in India. A policy was introduced on 1 April 2000 for setting up of SEZs in India with the view to provide an internationally competitive and hassle-free environment for exports.

An SEZ is a specifically delineated duty free enclave and shall be deemed to be foreign territory for the purposes of trade operations and duties and tariffs. At the moment there are a number of SEZs operating in the country. The locations are Santa Cruz (Maharashtra), Kochi (Kerala), Kandla and Surat (Gujarat), Chennai (Tamilnadu), Visakhapattanam (Andhra Pradesh), Falta (West Bengal), Noida (Uttar Pradesh), and Indore (Madhya Pradesh). There are many more proposals for the establishment of SEZs by large industrial groups across India. Any private/public/joint sector or state government or its agencies can set up an SEZ. Even foreign companies are permitted to establish an SEZ.

Setting up a Special Economic Zone

The Handbook of Procedures (Vol. I) gives detailed guidelines for establishment of SEZs. Some of the terms and conditions for setting up SEZs are:

- Only units approved under the SEZ scheme would be permitted to be located in that SEZ.
- The SEZ units shall abide by local laws, rules, regulations or bye-laws with regard to area planning, sewage disposal, pollution control, and the like. They shall also comply with industrial and labour laws as may be locally applicable.
- Such SEZs shall make security arrangements to fulfill all the requirements of laws, rules, and procedures applicable.
- The SEZ should have a minimum area of 1000 hectares and at least 25 per cent of the area is to be earmarked for developing industrial area for setting up of units.
- Minimum area of 1000 hectares will not be applicable to product-specific and port/airport-based SEZs.
- Wherever the SEZs are landlocked, an Inland Container Depot (ICD) will be an integral part of that SEZ.

The following steps are to be taken for setting up an SEZ.

Step 1 Submit 15 copies of the application in the prescribed form to the Chief Secretary of the state giving details, such as proposed location of the project, existing and proposed infrastructure, distance from the nearest railhead, bus station, airport, and financial details, including promoter's own equity, foreign equity, if any, borrowed funds, etc. The application should also specify whether the proposed zone will be a product-specific zone or a multi-product SEZ.

Step 2 The state government will forward the application to the central government with environmental clearance and commitment to provide facilities such as water, electricity, and other services, full exemption on electricity duty, state sales tax, octroi, mandi tax, turn over tax, and any other duty/cess or levies on the supply of goods from the Domestic Tariff Area (DTA) to SEZ units. Also, the state government has to delegate powers under the Industrial Disputes Act and other related labour acts to the Development Commissioner and commit single point clearances system and minimum inspections requirement under state laws/rules.

Step 3 An inter-ministerial committee in the Department of Commerce will review the proposal and after confirming the viability of the project, and the commitment of the applicant and the state government, an approval for the project will be granted.

Recent Changes in Government Policy on SEZs

The Government of India changed its policy on SEZs in April 2007 in the wake of protests against the acquisition of land in Nandigram by the state government in West Bengal. Accordingly, the government has put a cap of 5000 hectares on the maximum size of SEZs. Also, the state governments are not empowered to acquire the land for SEZs on behalf of private developers.

Exhibit 15.2 States can't acquire land for SEZ projects

Mega Proposals Virtually Ruled Out; Developers Face Stringent Norms

The government has overhauled its policy on Special Economic Zones (SEZs), making large, multi-product SEZs virtually impossible to build. The empowered group of ministers, headed by foreign minister Pranab Mukherjee, which met in the political shadow of the Nandigram violence, has changed several binding parameters:

- The size cannot exceed 5,000 hectares (12,500 acres) — Earlier, there was only a lower limit of 1,000 hectares. State governments can impose lower ceilings, if they so choose.
- At least 50 per cent of the area has to be earmarked for processing for all SEZs — Earlier, the norm was 35 per cent for multi-product SEZs and 50% for sector specific SEZs.
- A state government cannot acquire land for an SEZ on behalf of private developers, nor can state governments form joint ventures with private developers if they do not already have land in possession to offer the project. States can acquire land to develop SEZs on their own, provided they stick to the new relief and rehabilitation package to be announced soon.
- SEZs will have tougher export obligations to meet — instead of being merely net foreign exchange earners; they will also have to gross export earnings at least equivalent to their purchases from the domestic tariff area.

Source: The Economic Times dated 6 April 2007

Setting up a Unit in a Special Economic Zone

Ever since the announcement of the SEZ scheme, several companies have showed interest and have set up their units in SEZs across India. With the entry of private SEZ promoters like Reliance, which is proposing to set up a huge SEZ near Mumbai, a number of Indian and foreign companies are likely to start their operations in SEZs in order to avail various facilities, world class infrastructure, and a business-friendly bureaucratic environment.

Setting up a unit in the SEZ involves the following steps:

Step 1 Submit three copies of the application in the format prescribed in the Handbook of Procedures, Vol.1 to the Development Commissioner of the SEZ for setting up a manufacturing, trading, or service unit in the SEZ.

Step 2 Approval will be given by the Unit Approval Committee headed by the Development Commissioner after getting clearance from the Department of Policy and Promotion/Board of Approvals wherever necessary.

Step 3 As a part of setting up a unit in an SEZ, the applicant has to accept the following obligations:

- To achieve positive net foreign exchange earning as per the formula given in the Handbook of Procedures, Vol.1. The applicant also has to give a legal undertaking to the Development Commissioner.
- To provide periodic reports to the Development Commissioner and zone customs in the prescribed format.
- To execute a bond with the zone customs for their operation in the SEZ.
- A company, which is set up with FDI has to be incorporated under the Indian Companies Act with the Registrar of Companies for undertaking Indian operations.

Step 4 The SEZ unit has to operate within the guidelines that are provided along with the letter of approval. There will be an annual review of performance by the Development Commissioner of each operational unit. The annual review will also cover compliance with the conditions of approval as per the guidelines for monitoring the performance of Export-Oriented Units (EOU)/Special Economic Zones (SEZ)/Software Technology Parks (STP)/Electronic Hardware Technology Parks (EHTP) units.

Incentive/Facilities Available for SEZ Units

The following facilities are given to SEZ units to ensure smooth operations and a competitive edge in the international market.

Customs and Excise

- SEZ units are free to import or procure from the domestic sources, all their requirements of capital goods, raw materials, consumables, spares, packing materials, office equipment, DG sets, etc., on a duty free basis for implementation of their project in the zone without any licence or specific approval.
- SEZ units can utilize goods imported or locally procured over the approval period of five years.
- Domestic sales by SEZ units are exempted from SAD.

- SEZ units are allowed to sell finished products and by-products in the Domestic Tariff Area on payment of applicable customs duty.
- SEZ units are allowed to sell rejects, waste, and scrap in domestic market on payment of applicable customs duty on the transaction value.

Income tax

SEZ units are allowed
- Physical export benefits.
- 100 per cent Income Tax exemption (10A) for the first five years and 50 per cent for two years thereafter.
- Reinvestment allowance to the extent of 50 per cent of ploughed back profits.
- Carrying forward of losses.

Foreign Direct Investment

- Manufacturing units in SEZs are allowed 100 per cent FDI under the automatic route, except for units dealing with arms and ammunition, explosives, atomic substances, narcotics, hazardous chemicals, distillation and brewing of alcoholic drinks and cigarettes, cigars, and manufactured tobacco substitutes.
- There is no cap on foreign investments for SSI reserved items.

Banking/Insurance/External Commercial Borrowings

- Banks can set up off-shore banking units (OBUs) in SEZs. OBUs are allowed 100 per cent Income Tax exemption on profit for three years and 50 per cent for next two years.
- External commercial borrowings (ECBs) by units up to US$ 500 million a year is allowed without any maturity restriction.
- SEZs have the freedom to bring in export proceeds without any time limit.
- SEZ units can maintain 100 per cent of export proceeds in foreign currency account and can make overseas investment from it.
- SEZ units are exempted from interest rate surcharge on import finance.
- SEZ units allowed to 'write-off' unrealized export bills.

Central Sales Tax Act

- SEZ units are exempted to make sales from Domestic Tariff Area to SEZ units.

Service Tax

- SEZ units enjoy exemption from service tax.

Environment

- SEZs are permitted to have non-polluting industries in IT and facilities like golf courses, desalination plants, and hotels, and non-polluting service industries in the Coastal Regulation Zone Area.

Companies Act

- Managers working in SEZs are given an enhanced remuneration limit of Rs. 2.4 crore per annum.
- The office of the Registrar of Companies is to open regional offices in SEZs.

Drugs and Cosmetics

- SEZs are exempted from port restriction under drugs and cosmetics rules.

Sub-Contracting/Contract Farming

- SEZ units may sub-contract part of the production or production process through units in the Domestic Tariff Area or through other EOU/SEZ units.
- SEZ units may also sub-contract part of their production process abroad.
- Agriculture/Horticulture processing SEZ units are allowed to provide inputs and equipment to contract farmers in the Domestic Tariff Area to promote production of goods as per the requirement of importing countries.

It is however worth noting that there is no change in the labour laws with respect to SEZs. Normal labour laws are applicable to SEZs, which are enforced by the respective state governments.

SUMMARY

Competitiveness is the key to success in international market. Success depends upon factors, such as offering a product which is perceived as good value for money, efficient logistics and supply chain management, and creating an awareness in the consumer's mind by a combination of publicity measures including advertisements. Export incentives are given all over the world in different forms to provide the product cost competitiveness. For example, a manufacturer must have access to good quality raw material, which can be procured from any source in the world at an international price. Advance licence and duty drawback schemes enable the manufacturer to be free of the burden of import duty. The manufacturer can then compete in the international market on equal terms with overseas competitors. The EOU scheme aims to provide all export incentives and to remove bureaucratic hurdles so that the delays in production and order execution can be avoided and exporters can meet their delivery commitments with overseas buyers. In light of the immense success China achieved with its SEZ scheme, India too has adopted this scheme. However, there are major differences between Indian and Chinese SEZs. For example, in India an SEZ should have a minimum area of 1000 hectares out of which 25 per cent area is to be earmarked for developing industries. Also, there is a limit of 5000 hectares on the maximum size of SEZs. The Chinese model is different, with only six large, concentrated and government-backed SEZs. India, on the other hand, has 162 scattered SEZs with the help of private partnership. Also, before creating strategically located SEZs with excellent facilities, China developed world-class infrastructure in terms of roads, power generation, telecom network, ports, and airports. This attracted a large amount of FDI in Chinese SEZs. In contrast, India is trying to promote its SEZs without the support of adequate infrastructure. Another major hurdle for Indian SEZs is its labour laws. China has more flexible labour laws, which enable SEZ units to hire and fire labour according to need. Separate labour laws exist for SEZs and DTAs in China. In contrast, Indian SEZs have to comply with labour laws prevailing for DTAs. Further, the Indian government has to face the compulsions of democracy while acquiring land for SEZs, creating infrastructure, etc., which the Chinese government does not face. Finally, Chinese SEZs have now been operational for years, whereas India is still grappling with various issues. As a result, only a few SEZs in India are presently operational and the majority of Indian SEZs are still far from commencing their operations.

CONCEPT REVIEW QUESTIONS

1. What is the rationale behind providing export incentives to exporters? List down the various export incentives available in India.
2. As an exporter of steel tubes, what steps would you take to claim duty drawback on various inputs?
3. In what way are the Advance Licence and Duty Entitlement Passbook schemes each other's opposite? Which scheme would you prefer if you are a regular exporter?
4. Write a short note on the various export incentives available in India.
5. What is a Special Economic Zone (SEZ)? How is the SEZ scheme likely to contribute towards the economic growth of India?

6. Assume that you are a manufacturer of surgical gloves with 75 per cent of your earnings coming from exports. Would you prefer to be located in an SEZ or operate from Domestic Tariff Area (DTA)? Give reasons in support of your answer.

7. Write a short essay on the reasons for the interest shown by the large business houses in India to set up SEZs. What according to you is the downside of the SEZ scheme?

8. What steps must a foreign investor take to set up a unit in a SEZ in India?

OBJECTIVE QUESTIONS

Choose the correct option.

1. On which of the following components is duty drawback available?
   (a) Octroi
   (b) Sales tax
   (c) Special Additional Duty (SAD)
   (d) Duty paid on packing material

2. Brand rate is the drawback rate fixed for
   (a) Those export items for which exporter has to specially apply because drawback rate is not already fixed.
   (b) Rate applicable to a particular brand of product.
   (c) Those export items where exporter feels that the drawback rate is less than the actual duty paid by him/her.

3. Duty drawback on re-export is not applicable under the following conditions:
   (a) Re-exported goods are identifiable as having been imported.
   (b) Goods are re-exported within one year from date of payment of duty when they were imported.

4. Which of the following statement is NOT true?
   (a) Advance licence can be issued for deemed export
   (b) Advance licence is issued only to actual user
   (c) Advance licence can be availed on post-export basis
   (d) Advance licence facility is available only to manufacturer exporters

5. Which one of the following obligations does a unit in an SEZ have to accept?
   (a) To export 100 per cent output of the unit
   (b) To source raw material only from overseas sources
   (c) To achieve a positive net foreign exchange earning
   (d) To employ only Indian nationals

State whether the following statements are True or False.

6. Exporters can avail of DEPB scheme on a post-export basis.
7. Capital goods are allowed for imports under DEPB scheme.
8. In case of the EPCG scheme, the amount of export obligation is 10 times the duty saved on imported capital goods.
9. Computer software can be imported under the EPCG scheme.
10. Foreign companies are permitted to establish SEZs.

SELECT REFERENCES

Branch, Allan, *Export Practice and Management*, Thomson Learning, Australia.

Foreign Trade Policy, 1 September 2004–31 March 2009. w.e.f. 1.4.2007. Ministry of Commerce and Industry, Department of Commerce, Government of India.

Handbook of Procedures, Vol. I, 1 September 2004–31 March 2009, w.e.f. 1.4.2007, Ministry of Commerce and Industry, Department of Commerce, Government of India.

www.cmie.com, last visited on 10th June 2007.

www.dateyvs.com, last visited on 5th June 2007.

www.sezindia.com, last visited on 10th June 2007.

SPECIAL PROBLEMS OF SPECIAL ECONOMIC ZONES

Case Study

Economic reforms in India have always been a two-edged sword. On the one hand, the government has to take initiatives to boost the foreign trade and to attract FDI. This is to boost exports, facilitate imports, and to generate employment opportunities in the country. On the other hand, the government also has had to face resistance from opposition parties, who represent the voices of people directly affected by the government's policies.

The agitating population at Nandigram in West Bengal is an example of opposition to the Indian government's SEZ policy. In the face of fierce opposition to the West Bengal state government's efforts to acquire the land for developing SEZ at Nandigram, the Union Government has now amended its SEZ policy. The new policy has two major implications:

1. State governments cannot acquire land for SEZs on behalf of private developers or form JVs with them if they do not have land for the proposed SEZs.
2. There is now a cap of 5000 hectares on the size of SEZs.

The changes in SEZ policy have forced developers like Reliance, who were planning to develop an SEZ of 10,000 hectares, to redefine their strategies. Another problem is that with every election and with every change of state government, the decisions taken and clearances given by previous governments are put under review by succeeding governments. This further delays the implementation of policies.

India is a parliamentary democracy, where every new initiative has to be approved by the majority, only then can it be translated into reality. To obtain this majority is a time-consuming process, which creates delays in implementing new developmental ideas. China does not face such compulsions and is way ahead of India in economic development.

Questions
1. Trace the history of SEZs in India and find out how the SEZ policy has evolved since its inception.
2. List the reasons for which the government had to change its policies and comment whether such changes could have been avoided.
3. Compare the Indian model of SEZs with the Chinese model.
4. In the light of your findings, prepare a plan of action for successful implementation of projects, which are important for economic development of India.

ANNEXURE I

APPENDIX – 10B
APPLICATION FORM FOR GRANT OF ADVANCE LICENCE UNDER THE DUTY EXEMPTION SCHEME

Notes:
1. Please see Paragraph 4.1.1 of the policy & paragraph 4.4, 4.42, 4.5, 4.7 of this Handbook (Vol.I).
2. Please read the general instruction given at appendix 1 before filling this Application.
3. Please submit 2 copies of this application (10 copies if no Standard input – output norms are fixed).

FOR OFFICIAL USE

File No:..   Date: ....

1.	Name and Address of the applicant :		**Dee Tee Industries Ltd.** 28/33, Pologround Industrial Estate Indore - 452015 INDIA
2.	I.E. Code No. :		1188000489
3. (a)	Name and Address of the manufacturer/ supporting/ co- manufacturer :		**Dee Tee Industries Ltd.** 28/33, Pologround Industrial Estate Indore - 452015 INDIA
(b)	Type of <u>Medium Scale</u> Registration No. (3411/S1A/1mo/95) Date 7/7/95 Unit		
4.	Total FOB Value of exports excluding Commission:	Rs. 5235493	In currency US Dollars of exports In US $ 107505
5.	Total CIF Value of import	Rs. 2312000	In currency US Dollar & Euro In US $ 47474
6.	Value Addition		126.44%
7.	Application fee : (a)	Bank Receipt /D.D No. and date	Rs. 4625. Challan no. 357/10 Dtd. 05/10/02
	(b)	Issued by	Central Bank of India, Siyaganj Br. Jawaher Marg, Indore
8.	Port of Registration		Mumbai
9.	Sr. No. of Standard Input – Output Norms		C-1770
10.	Supply Order No.		L/C No.5519708 dt.27/09/02 of M/s.Ghassan Andraos & Partner Co., Syria & No.DTI/5184 dt.28/08/02 of M/s. Universal Tubes & Plastic, Industries Ltd., U.A.E

(Contd)

Annexure I (Contd)

11.	Name and address of the project Authority/ Ultimate Export	:	M/s Ghassan Andraos & Partner Co., Syria & M/s. Universal Tube & Plastic Industries Ltd., U.A.E
12.	Delivery Period of supply	:	12/24 Weeks.

(Column 11 and 12 are applicable for Advance Licence for intermediate supply and Advance Licence for deemed export)

13.	If the application is for Advance Licence for deemed export; indicate:		
	(i) Credit under which Project is financed	:	N.A.
	(ii) Method by which the order is procured	:	N.A.

14. Details of outstanding export obligation against Advance Licence including Annual Advance Licence/Pre-export DEPB issued under Duty Exemption Scheme.

S.No.	Licence No. and Date	CIF Value (Rs.)	FOB Value (Rs.)	Percentage of Export obligation fulfilled		Date of Expiry of export obligation period
				Quantity Wise	Value Wise	
1	P/L 0243033 10/11/00	US $ 9769 (Rs. 420000)	US $ 31000 (Rs. 1335000)	100%	100%	10/11/02
2	1110001519/ 2/03/00 21/2/01	US $ 16246 (Rs. 739200)	US $ 49000 (Rs. 2229500)	100%	100%	20/8/02
3	1110002593/ 2/03/00 20/9/01	US $ 22337 (Rs. 1027500)	US $ 48730 (Rs. 2241600)	100%	100%	19/3/03
4	1110001064/ 2/03/00 13/11/00	US $ 25078 (Rs. 1116000)	US $ 49667 (Rs. 2210207)	100%	100%	12/5/02
5	1110003769/ 2/03/00 19/06/02	US $ 51862 (Rs. 2437500)	US $ 71000 (Rs. 3337000)	Not yet utilized	Not yet utilized	-
6	1110004498/ 2/03/00 24/09/02	US $17478 (Rs. 847700)	US $49479 (Rs. 2424000)	,,	,,	-

15. Detail of the product to be exported/supplied (Resultant Products).

S. No.	Resultant product (s)		Total Quantity	Unit of Measurement		FOB Value	
	Name, Technical characteristic and quality	ITC (HC) Code		Name	Code	In Rupees	In freely convertible currency (FCC)
1.	Tube Forming Rolls(Roll Set)	84559000	17000 Kgs.	KILOGRAM	12	5235493	US $ 107505

Annexure I (Contd)

16. Detail of Items sought to be Imported Duty free (Arranged Item wise)

S. No.	Import Item			Unit of Measurement		Total CIF value		Total exemption from Customs duty
	Name, Technical characteristic and quality	ITC (HC) Code	Total Quantity	Name	Code	Rs.	In free foreign exchange	
1.	Alloy Tool Steel Round Bar confirming to AISI D3 / D2 or equivalent. <u>Technical Characteristic</u> C - 0 to 2% Si - 0 to 0.4% Mn - 0.15 to 0.45% Cr. - 12% Max. Mo - 0 to 2.8% W - 0 to 0.6% V - 0 to 1.1% P - 0 to 0.05% S - 0 to 0.05%	7228 3011	28900 Kgs.	Kilogram	12	2312000	US $ 47474	30 % Basic duty Rs. 693600 16% CVD – Rs. 480896 4% Addl. Duty Rs. 139460

17. Export Performance during the preceding 3 years : –

SL. No.	Year	FOB Value (Rs.)
1	1999-00	16825222
2	2000-01	19407284
3	2001-02	33677681

18. Details of other materials to be used in resultant product and sought to be imported/procured from sources other than the licence on which drawback benefits is to be availed.

(This column need not be filled if benefit of drawback is not being sought) N.A.

S.No.	Resultant product (s) (Name, Techni--cal characteristics and quality)	Total quantity	Imported Item			Indigenously procured item		
			Name, Technical characteristics and quality	Quantity and unit of measurement	CIF Value	Name, Technical characteristics and quality	Quantity and unit of measurement	Value
	N.A.	-	-	-	-	-	-	-

(Contd)

Annexure I (Contd)

DECLARATION/UNDERTAKING

1. I/We hereby declare that the particulars and the statements made in this application are true and correct to the best of my / our knowledge and belief and nothing has been concealed or held therefrom.

2. I/We fully understand that any information furnished in the application if proved incorrect or false will render me/us liable for any penal action or other consequences as may be prescribed in law or otherwise warranted.

3. I/We undertake to abide by the provisions of the Foreign Trade (Development and Regulation) Act, 1992, the Rules and Orders framed thereunder, the Export and Import Policy and the Handbook of Procedures.

4. I/We further declare that no export proceeds are outstanding beyond the prescribed period as laid down by the RBI, or such extended period for which RBI permission has been obtained.

5. I hereby certify that I am authorized to verify and sign this declaration as per Paragraph 9.9 of the Policy.

For Dee-Tee Industries Ltd.

Place: Indore   Signature of the Applicant: _____
                                                      Director
                 Name: ARADHYA BAHETI

Date: 07/10/02   Designation: DIRECTOR

                 Official Address: DEE TEE INDUSTRIES LTD.
                                      28/33 POLOGROUND
                                      INDUSTRIAL ESTATE
                                      INDORE – 452015 (M.P.)
                                      INDIA

                 Tele. No.:   0731- 422101 TO 06

                 E-Mail Address: deetee@sancharnet.in

Documents to be enclosed with the application form:

---

1. Bank Receipts (in duplicate)/ Demand Draft evidencing payment of application fee in terms of Appendix 29.

2. Project Authority Certificate in cases of application for Advance Licence for deemed export and a copy of invalidation letter in case of application for Advance Licence for intermediate supply.

ANNEXURE 2

<u>APPENDIX – 10C</u>

APPLICATION FORM FOR DUTY ENTITLEMENT PASS BOOK (DEPB) ON POST EXPORT BASIS

Notes: 1. Please see Paragraph 4.43 of this Handbook.
2. Please read the general instruction given at Appendix 1 before filling this Application.
3. Please submit 2 copies of this application form.

FOR OFFICIAL USE

File No...   Date:.............................

IEC No...   Branch Code.....................

1. Name and Address of the Applicant :   **Dee Tee Industries Ltd.**
28/33 Pologround Industrial Estate
Indore 452 015 (M.P.)
INDIA

2. FOB Value of Exports   :   In Figures: Rs. 21,17,559
In Words: Rs. Twenty one Lac
Seventeen Thousand
Five Hundred Fifty Nin

3. Total DEPB entitlement claimed   :   In Figure: Rs. 1,28,700
In Words: Rs. One Lac Twenty E
Thousand Seven Hunc

4. Application Fee   :   Rs. 645

Bank Receipt EFT/DD No.   :   Challan No. 589/7 dated 21/07/04

Issued by   :   Central Bank of India, Siyaganj Br.,
Indore.

5. Port of Registration   :   JNPT

6. Application for Transferable Licence :   Yes

7. Details of Export Made

(Contd)

Annexure 2 (Contd)

Sl. No.	Shipping Bill No. + Date + Port of Export	Date of Let Export Order	BRC No. + Date	Invoice No.	Sl. No. of Invoice	Product Group	DEPB S. No.	Item Description
1.	2.	3.	4.	5.	6.	7.	8.	9.
1	2531778 13/01/04 JNPT	16/01/04	10/020093/04 09/02/04	Exp/080	1	61	409	Slitting Cutters made of Steel
2	2538872 17/01/04 JNPT	20/01/04	11/020044/04 24/01/04	Exp/084	2	61	409	"
3	2658075 17/03/04 JNPT	19/03/04	10/020212/04 25/03/04	Exp/095	3	61	409	"
4	2677774 26/03/04 JNPT	27/03/04	10/020262/04 08/04/04	Exp/099	4	61	301	Spindle made of Steel
5	2677596 26/03/04 JNPT	27/03/04	10/020262/04 08/04/04	Exp/101	5	61	238	Saws made from High Speed Steel Sheet
6	2693681 02/04/04 JNPT	06/04/04	14/020312/04 27/04/04	Exp/104	6	61	409	Slitting Cutters made of Steel
7	2718949 17/04/04 JNPT	20/04/04	12/020327/04 29/04/04	Exp/002	7	61	409	"
8	2735728 28/04/04 JNPT	30/04/04	11/020339/04 07/05/04	Exp/005	8	61	238	Saws made from High Speed Steel Sheet
9	2762777 12/05/04 JNPT	18/05/04	10/020408/04 01/06/04	Exp/008	9	61	238	"

(Contd)

Annexure 2 *(Contd)*

FOB in Free Foreign Exchange		Exchange Rate on the Date of let Export Order	Total FOB (In Rs.)	Computation of Capped Value				
Currency	Value		[(11)*(12)]	Unit of Measure ment in the unit of Value Cap	Export Quantity in U/M	Value Cap	FOB per U [(13) / (15)]	Capped Value [minimum o (16) & (17) : (17) as the case may be*
10.	11.	12.	13.	14.	15.	16.	17.	18.
AUSD	12972	33.550	429520	N. A.	N. A.	N. A.	N. A.	N. A.
US $	6106	45.400	271395	"	"	"	"	"
US $	4171	45.100	186519	"	"	"	"	"
US $	1975	45.100	89696	"	"	"	"	"
US $	1405	45.100	61031	"	"	"	"	"
US $	19723	44.600	853398	"	"	"	"	"
US $	1162	44.600	48189	"	"	"	"	"
US $	1773	44.600	79144	"	"	"	"	"
US $	2282	43.950	98667	"	"	"	"	"

DEPB Rate (In %)	DEPB Entitlement (With out Cut) 15 * 18 * 19 / 100	Cut Application (If Any in %)	Actual DEPB Entitlement 20 * [1 - (21) / 100]
19.	20.	21.	22.
8 %	34361.60	Nil	34362.00
8 %	21711.60	"	21712.00
5 %	9325.95	"	9326.00
7 %	6278.72	"	6279.00
5 %	3051.55	"	3052.00
5 %	42669.90	"	42670.00
5 %	2409.45	"	2409.00
5 %	3957.20	"	3957.00
5 %	4933.35	"	4933.00

In case there is no value cap on the product, the capped value would be equal to the FOB Value per unit of measurement (U/M) as at column (17) of the table above. Else it would be the minimum of columns (16) and (17).

(Contd)

Annexure 2 (Contd)

DECLARATION / UNDERTAKING

1. I / we hereby declare that the particulars and the statements made in this application are true and correct to the best of my / our knowledge and belief and nothing has been concealed or held there from.

2. I / We fully understand that any information furnished in the application if proved incorrect or false will render me/us liable for any penal action or other consequences as may be prescribed in law or otherwise warranted.

3. I / We undertake to abide by the provisions of the Foreign Trade (Development and Regulation) Act, 1992, the Rules and Orders framed thereunder, the Export and Import Policy and the Handbook of Procedures.

4. I / We hereby declare that no DEPB has been claimed earlier pertaining to the particulars of the Shipping Bills given above.

5. I / We further declare that no export proceeds are outstanding beyond the prescribed period as laid down by the RBI, or such extended period for which RBI permission has been obtained.

6. I hereby certify that I am authorized to verify and sign this declaration as per Paragraph 9.9 of the Policy.

7. I / We further declare that in case of non-realization of export proceeds or lesser realization of export proceeds, we shall pay, in cash, an amount equivalent to the DEPB entitlement already obtained on the non-realization or lesser realized value of export proceeds together with 15% interest reckoned from the date of duty free imports effected under DEPB to the date of payment.

For Dee-Tee Industries Ltd.,

Aradhya Baheti

Director.

Signature of the Applicant	:	
Name	:	ARADHYA BAHETI
Designation	:	DIRECTOR
Official Address	:	Dee Tee Industries Ltd. 28/33 Pologround Indl. Estate, Indore 452 015 (M.P.) INDIA
Tel. No.		0731 - 2422101-106
Residential Address		22, Old Palasia A.B. Road, INDORE
E-mail Address	:	deetee@sancharnet.in

Date: 20/07/04

Place: Indore

(Contd)

Annexure 2 (Contd)

Documents to be enclosed with the Application Form

---

1. Bank Receipts (in duplicate) / Demand Draft evidencing payment of application fee in terms of Appendix 29.

2. E.P. Copy of DEPB Shipping Bills. In Case of Exports through notified Land Customs under paragraph 4.40, the Bill of Export may be accepted in lieu of shipping bill.

3. Bank Certificate of exports and realization as given in Appendix – 22.

16 Doing Business with Middle East Countries

Learning Objectives

After studying this chapter, you will be able to understand
- the geo-political and economic systems in the Middle East countries.
- about the industries, companies, and market structure of the countries in the region.

The Middle East is a region with numerous business opportunities, yet, like all markets, it carries its own set of risk factors. Before doing business in the Middle East, therefore, it is imperative to learn and understand the region's business culture, etiquette, and legal framework along with its many potential and available business and investment opportunities.

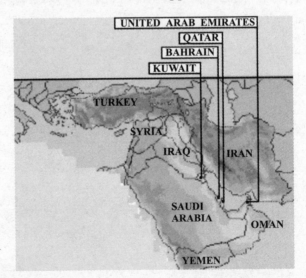

The Middle East (also known as West Asia or the Gulf) region has unique historical and cultural significance. For millennia, Gulf countries have been at the crossroads of trade between Europe, Asia, and Africa, facilitating international trade. The Middle East presents an array of market types, ranging from the poor Yemen and middle-income Iran, to wealthy Saudi Arabia, the United Arab Emirates (UAE), Qatar, and Kuwait.

Business opportunities in the Middle East depend considerably on the movement of the price and production levels of oil. High oil prices are largely beneficial to the region because of the additional revenue created.

OVERVIEW

The Middle East has housed some of the most advanced cultures of time, like the Muslim Caliphate, and the early stages of the Ottoman Empire. Today, the region is characterized by strong political tensions, like the Palestine/Israel conflict, Iraq, the contentious rights to water resources, as well as a number of smaller, yet important issues, such as the Syrian presence in Lebanon, border disagreements between Syria and Turkey, between Saudi Arabia and Yemen, and the civil rights of Shiite minorities in Iraq and Bahrain.

Countries such as Kuwait, Oman, Qatar, Saudi Arabia, and the UAE have registered population growth rates exceeding 3.5 per cent in recent years, while Bahrain has recorded rates below the two per cent average of developing nations.

Although the region is plagued by extreme hot climate, limited groundwater and rainfall, it enjoys abundant natural resources; specifically crude-oil reserves.

Business Environment

Recent changes in policies have transformed the region's economic outlook and the way trading partners and domestic and foreign investors view the Middle East.

The region is closer than ever to resolving the long-standing Arab-Israeli conflict. This conflict had adversely affected economic development in certain Gulf countries; accentuating macroeconomic imbalances and diverting resources from productive investments in infrastructure and in the social sectors. By aggravating perceptions of socio-political risks, it has discouraged investment in certain countries. The conflict situation has also inhibited efficient regional projects for electricity, water management, and tourism.

The Iraq war and subsequent unrest too has created a great deal of uncertainty but most Gulf economies have weathered that storm reasonably well and have continued to register growth.

The establishment of a comprehensive, just, and durable peace in the Middle East is expected to result in a significant economic peace dividend, provided it is accompanied by sound economic policies. The worth of the peace dividend is currently difficult to estimate, but reduced military spending over the time, could lead to higher capital formation and less severe resource 'misallocation'. The impact is expected to be large but will probably materialize with some lag.

Answers about the political, legal, and cultural aspects relating to Gulf countries are a pre-requisite for doing business with people of the region. In many sectors, they insist on a local partner; although imports are, in general, duty free in countries like UAE. They import many items, such as electronics, information technology, garments, and agricultural products.

Expatriates account for about 70 per cent of the population in the UAE Qatar, and Kuwait, and 60 per cent in Bahrain. Expatriates are employed not only in unskilled jobs, but fill many skilled and managerial positions as well.

Key Regional Business Issues

Regional issues important to commercial success include:
- Importance of agents and their changing role
- Choice of a local investment partner
- Degree of market risk
- Taxation matters
- Changing demographics
- Bureaucratic culture
- Key role of chambers of commerce
- Arab-Israeli relations
- Importance of negotiations
- Need for a different emphasis in marketing
- Visa requirements

Business Opportunities in the Middle East

The Middle East enjoys certain enormous advantages. It has great financial and natural resources, well-developed infrastructure in most countries, heavy investment in education, and a strategic location, close and accessible to all world markets, especially Europe, Africa, and Asia. We can also expect the Gulf economies to begin to grow at much higher rates. This expected growth indeed illustrates that this region provides enormous business and investment opportunities.

Country Analysis

In this section, information on countries such as United Arab Emirates, Oman, and Qatar are given, from the point of doing business with the people in those countries. The countries have been selected on the basis of their importance and economic meaningfulness in the Indian context.

United Arab Emirates—UAE

The United Arab Emirates (UAE) is one of the world's major oil producers with the fifth-largest proven oil reserves in the Gulf. The UAE has been a member of the Organization of the Petroleum Exporting Countries (OPEC) since 1967. The Abu Dhabi emirate is the hub of the oil and gas industry, followed by Dubai, Sharjah, and Ras al Khaimah emirates. Natural gas accounts for 64 per cent of UAE's energy consumption.

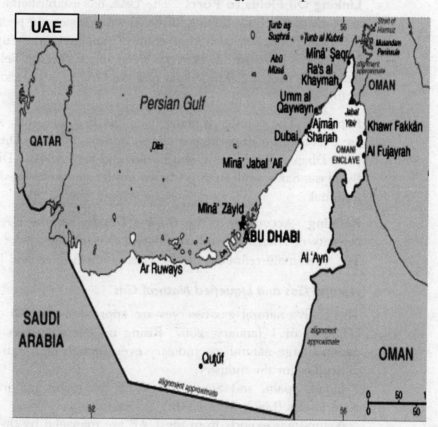

Oil Sector

On an average, the UAE produces three million barrels per day of total oil liquids, of which 2.5 million barrels is crude oil. The UAE also produces an estimated 300,000 barrels of natural gas liquids (NGLs) every day.

According to *Oil & Gas Journal (OGJ)*, the UAE's oil reserves were 97.6 billion barrels as of 1 January, 2007. Among the emirates, the Abu Dhabi emirate leads the others with a capacity of 92.2 billion barrels, followed by Dubai with four billion barrels, and Sharjah with 1.5 billion barrels.

The Abu Dhabi National Oil Company (ADNOC), is the premier government organization which operates 17 subsidiary companies in the oil and natural gas sectors.

The Supreme Petroleum Council, under the government, formulates the energy policy, and oil is the main focus of the UAE's hydrocarbon policy. Foreign investors have a relatively limited role outside of exploration, although they are involved in establishing links with importers from other countries.

Linking Oil Fields to Ports   The UAE has established a wide and strong network of pipelines linking oil fields with processing plants and exit ports for trade. There are also cross-country pipelines primarily for natural gas injection to increase oil recovery levels in existing oil fields. The Dolphin natural gas project linking Qatar and the UAE is a remarkable achievement in this sector.

Exports   The country is situated on the Persian Gulf , and several ports are available for exporting crude oil and natural gas. The main ports are: Jabel Dhana, Zirku Island, Das Island, and Ruwais. Abu Dhabi's Asab, Bab, Bu Hasa, Sahil, and Shah oil fields are located near the Jabel Dhana port terminal.

Refining   According to the *Oil and Gas Journal*, the UAE had a refining capacity of 781,250 barrels per day at five facilities, as of 1 January, 2007. The three main refineries are Ruwais, Umm Al-Nar, and Jebel Ali.

Natural Gas and Liquefied Natural Gas

The UAE's natural gas reserves are approximately 215 trillion cubic feet (TCF) as of 1 January, 2007. Rising oil energy prices have helped the nation's large natural gas industry even though high extraction costs pose difficulties for the industry.

Japan, Spain, and South Korea are the major importers of Liquefied Natural Gas (LNG) from UAE.

Natural gas exports from the UAE are managed by the Abu Dhabi Gas Liquefaction Co. (ADGAS), and are limited to LNG and liquids. The National Gas Shipping Company (NGSCO) handles exports from the LNG plant, and operates eight LNG carriers.

Country Overview

- Location: Middle East, bordering the Gulf of Oman and the Persian Gulf, between Oman and Saudi Arabia

- Independence: 2 December 1971 (from UK)
- Population: (2006E) 4,444,011

Economic Overview

- Currency/Exchange Rate (6/22/2007): 1 U.S. Dollar = 3.67 UAE Dirhams
- Inflation Rate (2006E): 9.5 per cent.
- Gross Domestic Product (2006E): $129.5 billion
- Real GDP Growth Rate (2006E): 8.9 per cent.
- Exports (2006E): $137 billion
- Exports–Commodities: Crude oil 45%, natural gas, re-exports, dried fish, dates
- Exports–Partners (2005E): Japan 24.5%, South Korea 9.8%, Thailand 5.6%, India 4.3%
- Imports (2006E): $88.9 billion
- Imports–Commodities: Machinery and transport equipment, chemicals, food
- Imports–Partners (2005E): UK 10 per cent, China 9.7 per cent, US 9.4 per cent, India 9.2 per cent, Germany 5.9 per cent, Japan 5.4 per cent, France 4.7 per cent, Singapore 4.1 per cent

Energy Overview

- Proven Oil Reserves (1 January, 2007E): 97.6 billion barrels
- Oil Production (2006E): 2.9 million barrels per day, of which 2.5 million was crude oil.
- Oil Consumption (2006E): 423,000 barrels per day
- Crude Oil Distillation Capacity (2007E): 781,000 barrels per day
- Proven Natural Gas Reserves (1 January, 2007E): 214 trillion cubic feet

Oil and Gas Industry

- Organization: Abu Dhabi National Oil Company (ADNOC); operates 17 subsidiary companies in the upstream, midstream, and downstream oil and gas sectors.
- Ports: Abu Dhabi: Das Island, Delma Island, Jebel as Dhanna, Ruwais, Abu al Bukhush, Al Mubarraz, Zirku Island, Port Zayed, Umm al Nar Dubai: Jebel Ali, Fateh, Port Rashid. Sharjah: Mubarak
- Major Oil Fields: Abu Dhabi: 'Asab, Bab, Bu Hasa, Al-Zakum Dubai: Fallah, Fateh, Southwest Fateh, Margham, Rashid. Sharjah: Mubarak (near Abu Musa Island)
- Major Natural Gas Fields (production, Bcf/d): Abu Dhabi: Abu al-Bukhush, Bab, Bu Hasa, Umm Shaif, Zakum

- Major Refineries: Ruwais (350,000 bbl/d), Umm al-Nar (150,000 bbl/d), Jebal Ali - Dubai (120,000),

OMAN

Background

Oman's business is heavily reliant on oil revenues, which account for about 75 per cent of the country's export earnings. The government has devoted considerable resources to oil exploration and production activities. The government has also introduced policies aimed at diversifying the country's business to other sectors in the recent years.

Oil

Oman has invested heavily in oil recovery projects at the country's oil fields. According to the *OGJ*, oil reserves in Oman stood at 5.5 billion barrels, as of January 2007. Oman's oil fields are generally smaller, more widely scattered, and pose higher production costs compared to other Persian Gulf countries. An oil well in Oman on an average produces only around 400 barrels per day, about one-tenth of that in neighbouring countries.

Oman is not a member of OPEC, though it is a significant exporter of oil. Most of Oman's crude oil exports go to Asian countries, with China, India, Japan, South Korea, and Thailand being the largest importers.

Petroleum Development Oman (PDO), which is 60 per cent owned by the Omani government, accounts for more than 90 per cent of the country's oil reserves and 85 per cent of production. The company is controlled by the government through Oman's oil ministry. Several foreign companies are involved in exploration activities, with Occidental Petroleum holding the largest market share. Oman's government manages its investments in the downstream sector through the state-owned Oman Oil Company (OOC).

Ports, Pipeline Network, and Export Terminals   Oman has linked oil fields to the pipelines for delivering crude oil to the country's oil export terminal at Mina al-Fahal, near the capital Muscat.

Downstream Activities   According to the *OGJ*, Oman has 100,000 (billion barrels per day) bbl/d of refining capacity at its major plant, the government-owned Oman Refinery Company's (ORC) facility at Mina al-Fahal.

Natural Gas

Oman exports significant amounts of LNG to many countries. Expanding natural gas production has become the main focus of Oman's strategy to diversify its business away from the oil sector. Over the past several years, authorities have expanded the natural gas-based industries, such as petrochemicals, power generation, and the use of natural gas as a feedstock. However, despite the recent rise in production, additional natural gas reserves have not been explored as speedily as the government had hoped. Nearly two-thirds of Oman's LNG exports go to South Korea and Japan; Taiwan, Spain, France, and the United States are other major importers. Oman has a pipeline for natural gas exports to the UAE.

Government-owned companies dominate Oman's natural gas sector. However, increasingly, the government has begun to enlist foreign companies in new exploration and production projects. Although the public sector remains a major player, foreign companies, such as Indago Petroleum, Occidental Petroleum, and Thailand's PTTEP also have a share of the upstream market. LNG activities are primarily controlled by the Oman Liquefied Natural Gas Company (OLNGC), a consortium led by the central government (51 per cent equity), Shell (30 per cent), and several other foreign companies.

Production and Exports

Natural gas production in Oman has risen significantly during the last 10 years. The government has intensified its efforts to locate additional natural gas sources to help meet the rising domestic natural gas requirements as well as to increase exports.

The government is currently working on several exploration and production (E&P) projects, and hopes to increase natural gas production significantly over the next decade.

Linking Oil Fields

Oman's domestic natural gas pipeline system is controlled by public sector major, the Oman Gas Company. They have contracted the management of the network to a consortium of private companies. Oman's natural gas network spans about 1100 miles, linking production centers to the country's LNG terminals, power plants, and ports for exports.

Country Overview

- Chief of State: Sultan Qaboos bin Said al Said
- Location: Middle East, bordering the Arabian Sea, Gulf of Oman, and Persian Gulf, between Yemen and UAE
- Population (July 2006E): 3,102,299 (note: includes 577,293 non-nationals)

Economic Overview

- Minister of Commerce and Industry: Maqbool bin Ali Sultan
- Currency/Exchange Rate (April 6, 2007): 1 USD = 0.385 Omani Rial (OMR)
- Inflation Rate (2006E): 3.2 per cent
- Gross Domestic Product (2006E): $38.8 billion
- Real GDP Growth Rate (2006E): 4.2 per cent
- Exports (2006E): $23.5 billion
- Exports–Commodities: Petroleum, re-exports, fish, metals, textiles
- Exports–Partners (2005E): China 21.6 per cent, South Korea 19.4 per cent, Japan 14.2 per cent, Thailand 12.6 per cent, UAE 7.1 per cent, Taiwan 4.1 per cent
- Imports (2006E): $13.0 billion
- Imports—Commodities: Machinery and transport equipment, manufactured goods, food, livestock, lubricants
- Import–Partners (2005E): UAE 22.4 per cent, Japan 15.8 per cent, UK 7.7 per cent, US 6.7 per cent, Germany 5.8 per cent, India 4.2 per cent

Energy Overview

- Minister of Oil and Gas: Muhammad bin Hamad bin Sayf al-Ruhmi
- Proven Oil Reserves (1 January, 2007E): 5.5 billion barrels
- Oil Production (2006E): 743,000 barrels per day, of which 91% was crude oil.
- Oil Consumption (2006E): 64,000 barrels per day
- Crude Oil Distillation Capacity (1 January, 2007E): 85,000 barrels per day
- Proven Natural Gas Reserves (1 January, 2007E): 30 trillion cubic feet
- Natural Gas Production (2004E): 607 billion cubic feet
- Natural Gas Consumption (2004E): 239 billion cubic feet

Oil and Gas Industry

- Organization: Petroleum Development Oman (PDO) controls all oil and natural gas resources. PDO is a partnership between the Omani government (60%), Royal Dutch/Shell (34%), Total (4%), and Partex (2%). Oman Oil Company (OOC) is the investment arm of the Ministry of Petroleum.
- Major Oil/Gas Ports: Mina al-Fahal
- Selected Foreign Company Involvement: BG, BP, CNPC, Indago Petroleum, Occidental Petroleum, Partex, PTTEP, Shell, Total
- Major Oil Fields: Yibal, Qarn Alam, Athel-Marmul, Bahja-Rima-Jalmud, Nimr, Karim Cluster, Harweel Cluster, Mukhaizna, Safah
- Major Refineries (capacity): Mina al-Fahal (85,000 bbl/d)

Qatar

Background

Although a small country compared to Oman and Saudi Arabia, Qatar holds the world's third largest natural gas reserves and is the single largest supplier of liquefied natural gas. Qatar is part of the OPEC and exports remarkable amount of oil.

While Qatar is a significant oil producer, the government has devoted more resources to the export of natural gas in recent years, particularly for export. The revenues from the oil and natural gas sectors together contribute 60 per cent of the country's national income.

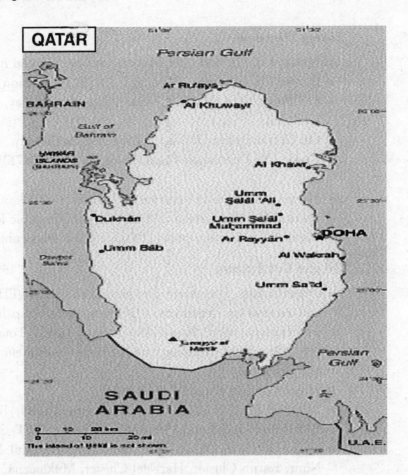

Oil Sector

According to the *OGJ*, Qatar has oil reserves of more than 15 billion barrels as of 2007. The onshore Dukhan field, located along the west coast of the peninsula, is the country's largest producing oil field. Qatar also has six offshore fields: Bul Hanine, Maydan Mahzam, Id al-Shargi North Dome, al-Shaheen, al-Rayyan, and al-Khalij. Oil accounts for 15 per cent of domestic energy consumption, while 80 per cent of Qatar's energy consumption is fuelled by natural gas.

Qatar Petroleum (QP), a public sector undertaking, controls all aspects of Qatar's oil sector, including exploration, production, refining, transport, and storage. QP produces about half of the country's total crude oil output. However, QP often engages foreign companies through production sharing contracts, in which QP typically takes a majority equity share. QP has control on Qatar's downstream oil sector, operating the country's entire oil pipeline network and sole refinery through its subsidiary, the National Oil Distribution Company (NODCO).

Exploration and Production

The government has focused on Enhanced Oil Recovery (EOR) projects particularly at the onshore Dukhan field, Qatar's largest oil field. Most new exploration and production (E&P) work is being carried out by multinational oil companies in offshore areas through production sharing contracts.

Short-Term Energy Outlook

As Qatar has been trying to develop the country's large natural gas reserves, production of condensate and natural gas liquids (NGLs) will increase. This may be an important source of future oil production increases.

Exports

Qatar has three major export terminals: Umm Said, Halul Island, and Ras Laffan. The latter is the newest of the three ports and is mainly used to export liquefied natural gas. Industry sources report that Qatar typically exports around 600,000 bbl of crude oil and about 20,000 bbl of refined petroleum products, per day. Most of Qatar's oil exports are sent to Asian economies, with Japan being the single largest receiver (380,000 bbl of crude per day in 2006, according to IEA statistics).

Country Overview

- Location: Middle East, peninsula bordering the Persian Gulf and Saudi Arabia
- Population (July 2007E): 907,229

Economic Overview

- Currency/Exchange Rate(11 May, 2007): 1 US Dollar=3.64 Qatari Rial
- Inflation Rate (2006E): 10.7%
- Gross Domestic Product (2006E): $27.5 billion
- Real GDP Growth Rate (2006E): 6.9%
- Exports (2006E): $38.9 billion
- Exports–Commodities: Liquefied natural gas (LNG), petroleum products, fertilizers
- Exports–Major Partners: Japan (36.9%), South Korea (19.4%), Singapore (8.2%)
- Imports (2006E): $12.9 billion
- Imports–Commodites: Machniery and transport equipment, food, chemicals
- Imports-Major Partners: France (11.4%), Japan (10.4%), US (10.3%), Germany (8.3%), Saudi Arabia (7.2%), UK (6.9%), Italy (6.5%), South Korea (5.5%), UAE (4.8%)

Energy Overview

- Proven Oil Reserves (1 January, 2007 E): 15.2 billion barrels
- Oil Production (2006E): 1.1 million barrels per day, of which 74 per cent was crude oil.
- Oil Consumption (2006E): 99,000 barrels per day
- Crude Oil Distillation Capactiy(1 January, 2007E): 200,000 barrels per day
- Proven Natural Gas Reserves(1 January, 2007E): 910.5 trillion cubic feet
- Natural Gas Production: 1,383 billion cubic feet
- Natural Gas Consumption: 477 billion cubic feet

Oil and Gas Industry

- Organization: Qatar Petroleum–Exploration, production, refining and distribution; Qatar Liquefied Gas Company and Ras Laffan LNG Company–Production and marketing of liquefied natural gas (LNG)
- Major Ports: Umm Said, Ras Laffan
- Foreign Company Involvement: Anadarko Petroleum, BP Chevron, ExxonMobil, Maesk Oil, Marubeni, Mitsui, Occidental Petroleum, Shell
- Major Oil Fields: Dukhan, Bul Hanine, Maydan Mahzam, al-Shaheen, al-Rayyan
- Major Natural Gas Fields: North Field
- Major Refineries: Umm Said (200,000 bbl/d capacity)
  Source: Adapted from Country Analysis Briefs, www.eia.doe.gov

SUMMARY

The need to improve modest economic growth rates and to diversify, urgent demographic and fiscal pressures, and in some cases, declining oil reserves, are likely to drive considerable structural change in Gulf economies. This would boost international business opportunities.

CONCEPT REVIEW QUESTIONS

1. Discuss the economic structure of Middle East countries?
2. What are the advantages of doing business with Middle East countries?
3. Discuss the salient features of the UAE and Oman economies?

SELECT REFERENCES

Growth and Stability in the Middle East and North Africa – Summary, from website of IMF (www.imf.org accessed on 15 November 2007).

International Financial Statistics, IMF, 2004.

Paul, Justin, and S Subhash, 2005, "International Migration and Its Impact with reference to Gulf migration–Some perspectives, Management and Labour Studies". *Journal of XLRI*, Vol. 30, No.1, February 2005, pp 38-50

Paul, Justin, 2008, Business Environment–Text and Cases, McGraw-Hill, New Delhi.

Rashid, Amjad (ed. 1989), *To the Gulf and Back: Studies on the Economic Impact of Asian Migration*, ILO ARTEP, New Delhi.

Transcript of a Press Briefing on the Economic Outlook in the Middle East and North Africa, Dubai International Convention Centre, Dubai, United Arab Emirates on 18 September, 2003, from the website of IMF www.imf.org accessed on 30 October 2007.

World Bank report overview on Middle East and North Africa Region 2005, Economic Developments, from Website of World Bank (www.worldbank.org accessed on 12 November 2007).

www.countrywatch.com last accessed on 10th November 2007.

Yousef, Tarik M., *Macroeconomic Aspects of the New Demography in the Middle East and North Africa*, Department of Economics, School of Foreign Service, Georgetown University, Washington

17 Doing Business with ASEAN Countries

Learning Objectives

After studying this chapter, you will be able to understand
- the business opportunities in the ASEAN countries
- the characteristic features of countries such as Singapore
- the importance of ASEAN as a regional trade block
- how to conduct business successfully with ASEAN countries

OVERVIEW

The Association of South East Asian Nations or ASEAN was established on 8 August 1967 in Bangkok by five original member countries, namely, Indonesia, Malaysia, Philippines, Singapore, and Thailand. Brunei Darussalam joined the bloc on 8 January 1984, Vietnam on 28 July 1995, Laos and Myanmar on 23 July 1997, and Cambodia on 30 April 1999.

The ASEAN region has a population of about 500 million, a total area of 4.5 million square kilometers, a combined gross domestic product of US$ 737 billion, and a total trade of US$ 720 billion

Brunei Darussalam	Combodia	Indonesia	Laos	Malaysia
Myanmar	Philippines	Singapore	Thailand	Vietnam

Fig. 17.1 Member countries of ASEAN

---

*This chapter has been co-authored by Dr. Justin Paul, Mr. Aditya Singh and Mr. Rajiv Koche.

BUSINESS OPPORTUNITIES AND COUNTRY ANALYSES

It is important to look at the business opportunities in important ASEAN countries. Let us discuss the business environment and new avenues for exports and imports in countries such as Malaysia, Singapore, The Philippines Thailand and Indonesia.

Malaysia

According to the 2005 World Competitiveness Report published by the International Institute for Management Development based in Switzerland, Malaysia is ranked the

- 10th most competitive nation among 30 countries, for nations with a population of more than 20 million;
- 6th on international trade; and
- 8th on economic performance.

To fine-tune its policies and incentives in order to enhance Malaysia's investment environment and competitiveness, the Malaysian government has introduced several measures including

- increased transparency of processes as key initiatives for all government departments;
- provision of specific assistance to investors to enable them to implement their projects without delay;
- liberalization of the policy on the employment of expatriates; and
- provision of customized incentive packages to capital and technology-intensive projects.

Malaysia offers investors with educated, skilled and trainable workforce; well-developed infrastructure; vibrant business environment; and safe and comfortable living conditions.

The various industries, with potential for collaboration in Malaysia, included the following.

Aerospace

The Malaysian aerospace industry is categorized into four sub-sectors:

1. Light craft assembly
2. Parts and components manufacture
3. Maintenance / repair activities
4. Design and development

The aerospace industry offers opportunities for the transfer of advanced technologies in engineering, electrical, electronics and composite materials, as well as manufacturing and systems integration. The Malaysian government is promoting this industry, and for this reason, all products and activities related to the industry are provided with attractive incentives.

Biotechnology

With the establishment of the Malaysian Biotech Corporation (MBC), Malaysia, one of the 12 mega-biodiversity countries in the world, has been actively promoting the development of biotechnology. MBC was set up to oversee, promote, and coordinate the development of biotechnology industry.

Among the areas being promoted are food and agro biotechnology; bio-pharmaceuticals (antibodies and vaccines); nutraceuticals; bio-diagnostics; industrial enzymes; and bio-active compounds for healthcare.

Foreign-based companies with expertise in this area are being invited to take advantage of the incentives provided by the government. Companies can take advantage of the attractive incentive package, in the form of full tax exemption for up to 10 years.

Electronics

The electronics industry is the leading industry in Malaysia's manufacturing sector, as evident by the presence of more than 900 companies valued at more than US$ 65 billion.

The US has been the largest source of foreign investments in the industry, mostly in the electronic components sub-sector. In this sub-sector, US companies are mainly concentrated in the semiconductor industry. Some of the US companies doing business in Malaysia are:

- Motorola
- Western Digital
- Komag
- Intel
- Advanced Micro Devices (AMD)
- On Semiconductor
- Free scale Semiconductor

Many of these companies have undertaken R&D activities in collaboration with Malaysian universities. There are also a number of US electronic manufacturers, such as Agilent, Finisar, and Seagate which have set up operations, including relocating their design and development (D&D) activities to Malaysia.

Malaysia is one of the largest semiconductor producers in the world. The industry has moved up the value-chain into wafer fabrication activities and the design of integrated circuits (ICs).

Further the country welcomes investments not only in the semiconductor industry, but also in the manufacture of other products and activities, such as

- Integrated circuit design

- Production of digital telecommunications equipment
- Production of automated data processing equipment
- Manufacturing of flat panel displays
- Manufacturing of digital audio-visual equipment
- Multimedia products

Services

The services sector (excluding government services) accounts for more than 50 per cent of Malaysia's GDP.

The key manufacturing related services promoted in Malaysia include regional establishments, such as:

- Operational Headquarters (OHQs)
- International Procurement Centres (IPCs)
- Regional Distribution Centres (RDCs)
- Regional Offices (ROs)
- Representative Offices (REs)

In order to attract and accelerate investment inflows into the manufacturing related services sector, the Malaysian government has put in place several fiscal and non-fiscal incentives. These include full income tax exemption for 10 years for Operational Headquarters, International Procurement Centres, and Regional Distribution Centres.

Malaysia is also fast becoming an important hub for call centres, data centres, and back office operations. It has been ranked among the world's top three destinations for offshore services along with India and China.

Multinational companies (MNCs) which have set up such operations in Malaysia, include:

- Dell (call centre)
- BMW and HSBC (data centres)
- Standard Chartered Bank, DHL and Shell (back office operations)
- Citibank (back office operations)

Other service activities, which can be considered for investment by foreign companies include franchising and servicing the oil and gas industry.

Franchising

Over the past few years, the franchising industry in Malaysia, valued at more than US$ 2.8 billion, has grown at 10 per cent annually. Currently, more than 320 franchise systems and approximately 8,300 franchising outlets operate in Malaysia. Around 40 per cent of the franchises are foreign, with US franchises accounting for 70 per cent of those.

Exports

Of India's exports to Malaysia, the live animal product-group comprising fish, meat, dairy products, etc., has a significant share. Other Indian products of importance in the Malaysian total imports are fats, oils, textiles, and footwear.

Edible oils, wood and wood products, and natural rubber constitute the most important exports from Malaysia. For these items India offers an important market for Malaysia.

The Philippines

The Philippines, through its first one hundred years of independence, has proven its resilience in facing the economic and political challenges that marred its history. Although not left untouched by the Asian currency chaos and stock market volatility of 1997, The Philippines has been spared from the banking and real estate crises that rocked its East Asian neighbours.

Robust export growth, prudent fiscal policies, deregulation and liberalization of key sectors of the economy, and close supervision of the liberalized financial sector have supported the country's relatively conservative but steady economic growth in the last decade.

Island of Opportunities

The Philippines offers more than just an investor-friendly environment. Together with the fundamental economic reforms that transformed The Philippine economy into a promising investment location for international business operations, an entire range of opportunities awaits the investor who is on the lookout for lucrative business ventures. A sampling of these opportunities follows.

ASEAN Free Trade Area

With the transformation of ASEAN into a free trade area, the region represents a common market with a growing population currently estimated at about 458 million. As the ASEAN economies increasingly integrate with each other within the framework of the ASEAN Free Trade Area agreement (AFTA), The Philippines is the natural and most strategic location for firms that want access to the large ASEAN market and its trade opportunities in the future.

To promote intra- and inter-regional investments, ASEAN has adopted collective investment schemes, namely:

Sub-Regional growth triangles A sub-regional growth triangle such as the East Asia Growth Area (EAGA), which consists of Brunei, Indonesia,

Malaysia, and The Philippines, aims to exploit the complementary comparative advantages and resource endowments of the less developed areas of the participating countries. Cooperation at the sub-regional growth areas is informal and largely driven by the private sector with the governments concerned playing a supporting and facilitating role.

ASEAN Industrial Cooperation Scheme (AICO) Under AICO, which was implemented in 1996, approved AICO products will enjoy preferential tariff rates of 0–5%. Other attractive incentives include local content accreditation, where applicable, and other non-tariff incentives to be provided by the participating member countries.

ASEAN Investment Area (AIA) The AIA scheme aims to promote greater private sector participation in investment projects and to create a more investor-friendly environment. The implementation of the ASEAN plan of action on cooperation and promotion of foreign direct investment and intra-ASEAN investment will help lay the foundation for the establishment of the AIA.

Banking Industry

Since the banking industry's liberalization in 1994, foreign banks have been allowed to establish branches in The Philippines. Furthermore, an unlimited number of new entrants may now enter into joint ventures/buy existing domestic banks.

In a recent assessment of the overall banking industry in the region, an internationally known investment firm observed the following about The Philippine banking system (Manila Bulletin, 20 September, 1997):

1. The Philippines has adequate rules and regulations governing the banking system. This is manifested in the strong capital adequacy, asset quality, management earnings, liquidity, operating environment, and transparency of The Philippines banks.
2. Domestic banks remain solid and healthy, comparable with their counterparts in Singapore, Hong Kong, and India.

Bank supervision is sound and is further being strengthened by limiting bank exposure to the real estate sector, prescribing a liquidity cover on all foreign exchange liabilities of foreign currency deposit units, and imposing mandatory provision for bad loans, among others.

A lower, more easily rectified degree of vulnerability makes The Philippines banks better able to withstand the prevailing pressures, political or otherwise, than Thai and Malaysian banks.

Information Technology Industry

The Philippines information technology (IT) industry has exhibited steady growth in the last decade. Data extracted by the National Information Technology Council (NITC) coordination group show a bullish outlook for the industry. The NITC 2000 envisions The Philippines as the Knowledge Center in Asia in the 21st century.

The development in the local IT industry is supported by the continuing liberalization of related industries. For example, the entry of new players in the telecommunications sector triggered huge additional investments among companies.

The main strength of The Philippines in the IT sector is the capability of the Filipino IT professional. Quality and expertise distinguish the Filipino IT professional. Filipinos find it easy working on Database Management System (DBMS) as well as fourth generation languages.

The Filipino IT professional is now renowned the world over for his/her creativity, trainability, and professionalism in addition to proficiency in the English language. Industry insiders estimate that more than 100,000 Filipino IT professionals, many of them trained in local companies, are now gainfully employed across the globe. As international demand for IT expertise and quality continues to rise, Filipino professionals have the choice of working in the country or overseas.

Tourism Industry

Recent reforms instituted by the government in The Philippines ensure that tourism will continue to play a pivotal role in the coming millennium. According to the Department of Tourism (DOT), the tourism industry has performed beyond expectations, along the following parameters:

1. Visitor arrivals grew at above 15 per cent annually.
2. Majority of the tourism investments went into development of tourism, estate hotels, resorts, and tourist transport operations.

The natural and geographic resources of The Philippines appeal to various types of visitors. Tourists around the world come not only to visit world-renowned tourist spots but also to hunt for shopping bargains and to participate in year-round cultural and sports festivities. The metropolitan cities of Manila, Cebu, and Davao are favourite destinations of business travellers and conventioners. Those looking for adventure tourism can find their way to still unspoiled sites, which are now being eyed for development by investors.

The government is undertaking a comprehensive approach to tourism development in order to improve access to tourism areas. Various ongoing programmes are aimed to develop and upgrade accommodation and conventioned facilities, transportation network, telecommunication systems, airport and seaport terminals, electrification, and other infrastructure projects. Likewise, investments in the tourism and leisure sector are encouraged through a wide range of fiscal and other types of incentives. These incentives are embodied in the laws described in the section on investment incentives.

The government has identified 11 growth networks/corridors scattered around the country that are currently under various stages of implementation. Four of these areas are in the investment promotion stage.

Calabarzon Calabarzon is a large-scale multi-sectoral project complex planned in a region contiguous to metropolitan Manila. Calabarzon is composed of the Southern Luzon provinces of Cavite, Laguna, Batangas, Rizal, Quezon, and Aurora. The region has been transformed from an agro-base rural economy to a thriving industrial/urban-base economy. Calabarzon is now the site of at least 51 major private industrial estates and ecozones.

Cagayan-Iligan Corridor Lying along the northern coast of the Mindanao Island, the Cagayan-Iligan Corridor unites the two cities of Cagayan de Oro in Misamis Oriental, an agro-industrial centre, and Iligan City in Lanao del Norte, an industrial hub. The corridor abounds in the supply of hydroelectric power and is home to several industrial plants, including an integrated steel mill facility of the National Steel Corporation. It is being promoted as an ideal location for investments in metals (engineering arid metalworking) construction and Infrastructure, oleo chemicals and basic chemicals, and agriculture/aquaculture and agro-forestry.

North Quad The Northwestern Luzon Growth Quadrangle, or North Quad, integrates the coastal provinces of Ilocos Norte, Ilocos Sur, La Union, Pangasinan, and the inland areas of Abra and Southern Benguet at the northeastern tip of Luzon. Due to its location, it is considered an ideal gateway for trade with China, Taiwan, Hong Kong, Korea, Japan, and the ASEAN. The region is envisioned to be an industrial, financial, and tourist haven. Possible investment areas include, the development and expansion of existing infrastructure, agri-industrial estates, and tourism centres.

Socsargen Socsargen is the more popular name for the areas of South Cotabato, Sultan Kudarat, Sarangani, and General Santos City. This economic growth corridor contains abundant agriculture and natural resources, as well as modern physical infrastructure including an international airport. The area also offers access to nearby ASEAN growth markets. The Philippine, US, and Japanese governments have allocated US$ 200 million for the development of projects in this area.

Special Economic and Freeport Zones

Two of the more attractive investment sites in Asia today are the Subic Bay Freeport (SBF) and Special Economic Zone and the Clark Special Economic Zone (CSEZ). These sites are former US military facilities converted for civilian use. The vision for the 67,000-hectare SBF is to create a self-sustaining industrial, commercial, financial, and investment center, in addition to its existing international seaport, which can anchor 600 ships. The CSEZ, which spans some 33,653 hectares, is being converted into a special economic zone and its 1,620-hectare civil aviation complex into a world-class international airport.

Registered enterprises in both SBF and CSEZ enjoy various investment incentives, including access to first-class commercial, residential, and tourist facilities.

Special Economic Zone under The Philippine Economic Zone Authority

With the continuous inflow of foreign direct investments, ecozones have mushroomed across the country. Companies and landed families have diversified into the development of ecozones to consolidate operations, tap the growing export market, and benefit from the fiscal perks from The Philippine Economic Zone Authority (PEZA). At least 76 ecozones have been approved and registered under the PEZA.

Infrastructure and Build-Operate-Transfer Projects

Economic reforms instituted by the Ramos administration have allowed wider participation by the private sector, particularly foreign investors, in almost every aspect of the economy. In addition to the government's revitalized privatization programme, the landmark Build-Operate-Transfer (BOT) legislation redefined the government's role by prescribing the legal and administrative framework for private investment in infrastructure and other development projects–areas previously exclusive to public investments.

Initially and successfully applied to power sector development, BOT contractual arrangements are gaining ground in other infrastructure sectors. Forty-four of these projects are power-related; the remaining involve a variety of sectors including roads, airport, water, rail/mass transit, resort development, agriculture, and solid waste management.

India's exports of gems and jewellery to The Philippines, accounting for nearly 10 per cent of Philippines' global imports, are the only product group where India has a reasonable presence.

The fact that not a single item from The Philippines attracted even one per cent share of India's total imports, points out that Filipino goods have poor visibility in Indian markets.

Thailand

Bilateral trade between India and Thailand reached US $ two billion in 2004 and is expected to double by 2007, according to a Thai Foreign ministry statement. The two countries have signed a Free Trade Agreement that has opened up huge opportunities for bilateral trade.

India's primary imports from Thailand are machinery, electronic appliances, textiles, plastic material, transport equipment, vegetable oils, and latex while its main exports to the country include jewelry, gemstones, steel, pharmaceuticals and ferrous metal ores. Fats, oils, and prepared food stuff also form a sizeable part of Indian exports to the Southeast Asian nation.

Thailand offers the following advantages:

Metal prices are 15 to 30 per cent lower than the price prevailing in many countries. For example, aluminum prices are 30 per cent and steel prices 18 per cent lesser than in India. This opens opportunity to import automotive components from Thailand.

The Thai economy is likely to show a healthy growth rate and many construction activities have been announced by Thailand. India can export construction material, such as cement, to Thailand.

Indian companies can also explore with Thailand the avenues for development of software and electronic industry in that country.

Singapore

As indicated, the structure of trade flows between Singapore and India is quite skewed in favour of the former. While in the case of India, gems and jewellery is the only product-group having a sizable share in Singapore's global imports, several items from Singapore have made inroads in the Indian market. These include organic chemicals, electrical goods, machinery, artificial resins and plastic materials, and non-ferrous metals, among others.

Additional Market Access

Singapore can provide very little tariff preference (or concession) to other countries through bilateral free trade agreement, because it applies tariff rates only on few commodity lines like the beverages industry. The tariff rates of many other commodities or tariff lines (5690 lines) is zero. India does not have export competitiveness in the four products where Singapore can probably give some preferential tariff.

It should be remembered that although Singapore has a very low level of tariff rates, it has not bound a large number of industrial products in the WTO. Singapore has given tariff binding for only 65 per cent of industrial products/lines. Further, a large number of lines (2506) are bound at 10 per cent. A large share of Singapore's trade is subject to non-tariff barriers. The import prohibitions are imposed under various orders and licence measures due to concerns regarding public safety, health, environment, etc. It is very difficult, almost impossible, for Singapore to give preference to the Indian market by removing these barriers. Singapore has signed bilateral FTAs with a large number of countries, including the US and Japan. Singapore is probably interested in FTAs with these countries because it is highly dependent upon the markets, investments, and technology of high-income large economies. Singapore has already concluded an agreement with New Zealand. A large share of Singapore's exports is in the form of re-exports. So it would be difficult to apply any value addition norms.

Gateway to South East Asian Economies

It is generally said that a bilateral agreement with Singapore can provide a gateway to the markets of South East Asian countries. As far as India's exports are concerned, it can even export now to East and South East Asian countries via Singapore without much hindrance. It is debatable how the FTA will help in increasing India's market access to these countries. In this context, we should explore the possibility of India's Free Trade Agreements with other countries of the region, viz. Indonesia, Malaysia, Thailand, or even Vietnam. It should be remembered that a large number of products/ lines for Intra-ASEAN trade have been subjected to negligible tariff (0–5%). Hence, one can say that India can enter the markets of ASEAN countries (other than Singapore) through Singapore. However, it is not a simple process because the clause on the rule of origin is very high. Hence, it is very difficult to expect that the Indo-Singapore bilateral free trade agreement will provide an easy entrance to the ASEAN market via Singapore. In this context, one should remember that Singapore is an important 'trading hub' in the region.

Enhancement of Investment and Financial Flows

These days, FTAs are not restricted to only bilateral trade, but include a number of other provisions, which may enhance cooperation in the field of investment, joint ventures, and other areas. The differential treatment given to domestic and foreign investors (and other related measures) can be an index into the extent of economic cooperation in other fields. Singapore gives a number of incentives in the form of tax holidays, exemption, concessional tax rates, and exemption on taxable income and non-tax incentives. Bilateral FTAs may lead to gains in political stabilities through economic diplomacies. Since the 1990s, India has been following the policy of 'Look east'. Singapore can take the mantle of advancing Indian interests in the world, particularly Asia. It has been advancing China's interest, even as it has maintained close military, intelligence, and economic contacts with the US (a difficult balancing act, so far made possible by the US' desire to engage China and to maintain a presence in Southeast Asia). In the case of Singapore, one is dealing with an authoritarian state. There are very few purely commercial transactions with Singaporean private firms.

Cooperation in Select Sectors

A better strategy, perhaps, would be to deepen cooperation in select sectors like information technology, electronics, etc. The electronic industry is the most important manufacturing sector of Singapore's economy. Singapore produces, imports, and exports different components of the electronic industry. The main products are computer and data processing equipment, telecommunication equipment, electronic valves, etc. A major share of Singapore's merchandise trade is concentrated in this sector, particularly in data processing machines. On the other hand, India has shown a remarkable growth in IT software industry, with a large number of MNCs operating from India. This shows that there are significant prospects for enhancing India–Singapore trade in IT, particularly, software, electronics, tele-communications, and e-commerce.

Indonesia

Looking at the share of Indian products in Indonesia's imports, we see the share of prepared foodstuffs was nearly halved between 1993 and 2004. Nevertheless, this item still accounted for 10 per cent of Indonesia's total imports. No other product from India enjoyed an appreciable share in the Indonesian market. Future opportunities exists in export of motor cycles, pick-up trucks, construction material, steel, aluminum and aluminum products, engineering items, software and hardware, textiles, etc.

While India may not have a large share in the Indonesian import market, Indonesia accounted for nearly 30 per cent of India's total imports of edible oils between 2000 and 2005. Further, its share in textile yarns and pulp and waste paper was also impressive at 8.1 per cent and 9.3 per cent, respectively. In future too, the import of edible oil, especially palm oil, and petroleum products can form a large part of India's imports from Indonesia.

ASEAN COUNTRIES AND TRADE WITH INDIA

Since the economic liberalization of 1991, India and the Indian market have undergone a paradigm shift. There have been fundamental and irreversible changes in the economy, government policies, outlook of business and industry, in general. These can be summed up, as follows:

- From an agro-based economy, India has emerged as a service-oriented entity.
- From a shortage economy of foreign exchange, India has now become a surplus economy.
- The low economic growth of the past has given way to a high-growth economy in the long-term.
- Following the success of the service sector, manufacturing is emerging as a high growth sector and is now a front-runner in the emerging knowledge-based new economy.
- The government is continuing with reforms and liberalization, not out of compulsion but out of conviction.
- India has its own multinationals competing on the global platform based on their quality and efficiency. This is a big change from an era when local companies were afraid of multinational companies.

Trade relations

ASEAN as a region and most of its founding members have displayed great dynamism. While SAARC (The South Asian Association for Regional Cooperation, of which India is the largest constituent) could not really match the impressive achievements of ASEAN or its member-states, both India and ASEAN as a whole have attained growth in exports at rates higher than the global average in last two decades.

The two-way trade between India and ASEAN countries jumped by nearly four times between 1991 and 2004 and surpassed the $12 billion mark.

Among ASEAN members, Singapore and Malaysia have been India's most prominent trading partners while the country's trade with Vietnam has been the least in value terms. During the East Asian crisis, trade turnover declined in absolute terms. The decline was essentially due to the sharp fall in Indian exports. In subsequent years, there has been a recovery and trade flow has once again regained its positive trend. The growth in India's exports to ASEAN in recent years has been much higher in comparison to other important destinations.

In the beginning, just two countries, namely Singapore and Malaysia accounted for more that 90 per cent of India's total imports from ASEAN-5. Although the combined share of the two has come down over the years, they still enjoy a dominant position and accounted for over 65 per cent of Indian imports from the ASEAN-5 in 2004. So far as India's aggregate balance of trade with the ASEAN-5 is concerned, India has posted a deficit in each year since 1994, which has become more pronounced in the last five years. Such a huge gap results from the relatively higher deficits with Singapore and Malaysia and India's simultaneous inability to generate matching surplus elsewhere in the region even when the balance of trade is in its favour.

Overall, the product concentration in India's imports from ASEAN is far higher than that in India's exports to the region. Inter-temporal changes in product composition highlights that while India's exports to ASEAN are becoming increasingly less concentrated; concentration in its imports from the region has been rising. At the bilateral level also, product concentration is found to be relatively higher for India's imports than its exports, excepting the case of Thailand.

Other factors facilitating a smooth trade between the two trading partners are:
- Similarity in culture
- Large percentage of Indian expatriates in almost all ASEAN countries
- None too adverse exchange rate
- Easy travel and transportation facilities
- High internal growth rate achieved by economy of both trade blocks

Trade relations between India and ASEAN are based on following fundamental principles:
- Mutual respect for the independence, sovereignty, equality, territorial integrity, and national identity of all nations
- The right of every state to lead its national existence free from external interference, subversion or coercion
- Non-interference in the internal affairs of one another
- Settlement of differences or disputes in peaceful manner
- Renunciation of the threat or use of force
- Effective cooperation among themselves

Table 17.1 shows India's trade rate with ASEAN-5 countries.

Table 17.1 Growth in India's Trade with ASEAN Region and Select Individual Member Countries

	Average CAGR (%)	Minimum CAGR (%)	Maximum CAGR (%)
ASEAN Total			
Total Trade	11.1	19.8	5.2
India's Exports	6.1	16.5	0.3

(Contd)

(Contd)

India's Imports	15.6	23.6	8.4
Indonesia			
Total Trade	20.1	37.7	6.2
India's Exports	8.7	30.8	-0.9
India's Imports	36.3	57.0	15.8
Malaysia			
Total Trade	14.7	26.4	5.1
India's Exports	10.6	21.0	0.5
India's Imports	17.5	30.5	7.8
Singapore			
Total Trade	10.5	16.7	3.7
India's Exports	10.3	19.2	1.6
India's Imports	10.6	15.6	4.7
Philippines			
Total Trade	11.8	59.8	-0.4
India's Exports	10.7	59.8	-4.6
India's Imports	15.8	60.1	21.5
Thailand			
Total Trade	1.4	−2.5	6.8
India's Exports	−3.3	−7.3	3.2
India's Imports	22.6	30.1	13.2

Source: Enhancing India – ASEAN Trade, study by Confederation of Indian Industry, 2006

The trend in the growth rates in the pre-crisis and post-crisis periods for ASEAN as a whole is reflected more sharply when the corresponding CAGRs for the ASEAN-5 countries are evaluated individually. The slowdown in the growth of the total two-way trade from 1991–96 to 1997–2001 is replicated for Indonesia, Malaysia, Singapore, and The Philippines, with the extent for deceleration being maximum in the case of The Philippines and minimum in the case of Singapore. Among the ASEAN-5, the only exception to this was Thailand, for which the CAGR of total bilateral trade turned from negative 2.5% to a positive 6.8% between the two sub-periods.

By and large, a similar pattern is obtained if we take India's exports and imports separately, with Singapore being the relatively least impacted among the five ASEAN countries.

Table 17.2 Share of India's Exports to and Imports from ASEAN in India's Global
Exports/Imports

	Exports (%)	Imports (%)
1991	11.1	7.7
1992	8.3	7.0
1993	9.8	8.0
1994	9.3	9.4
1995	9.3	10.3
1996	13.1	12.2
1997	10.6	12.0
1998	5.9	13.3
1999	6.1	13.8
2000	7.5	13.8
2001	8.0	13.1
2002	8.2	12.9
2003	8.8	13.1
2004	8.8	12.0

Source: Enhancing India – ASEAN Trade, study by CII, 2006

Thus, post 1991, while India's progressive integration with the global
economy and its 'Look east' policy have helped improve both its exports to
and imports from ASEAN till 1996, post 1997 the situation changed as
India's imports from the region continued to grow (barring 2001), but exports
did not show adequate growth. This can be partly explained by the following
factors:

- Indian exports in the software field increased; but mostly to American
  and European countries.
- India-made products like steel, electronics, rubber etc., became less
  competitive compared to corresponding products manufactured in the
  ASEAN countries.
- Consumption of the listed products increased rapidly in India, thus
  presenting a less attractive market overseas.

Exports only grew after 2002 when Indian electronic goods industry
became competitive.

Nevertheless, ASEAN's position in India's total trade relative to India's
two major trading partners (namely EU and North America) improved
between 1991–92 and 2003–04. The geographical analysis of the trade shows
that just two countries, namely Singapore and Malaysia accounted for more
than 50 per cent of India's total imports from the ASEAN-5.

Table 17.3 Country-wise Distribution of India's Trade with ASEAN-5

% Share in India's Total Exports to ASEAN-5			
	1991	1996	2004
Indonesia	11.6	21.2	15.8
Malaysia	14.6	18.1	23.4
Singapore	21.6	24.8	33.8
Philippines	4.0	20.2	6.6
Thailand	48.0	15.7	20.3
% Share in India's Total Imports from ASEAN-5			
	1991	1996	2004
Indonesia	3.8	12.5	20.2
Malaysia	21.9	28.5	26.0
Singapore	68.8	49.0	44.7
Philippines	1.1	4.2	1.2
Thailand	4.3	5.7	7.8

Source: Enhancing India – ASEAN Trade, CII Study, 2006

Although their combined share came down over the years, the two countries still enjoyed a dominant position and accounted for over 70% of India's imports from ASEAN-5 in 2004.

Country-wise Trading Opportunities

Export-Import business opportunities have been discussed country-wise in the following section.

Product Composition: India's Exports

A comparison of the composition of India's exports to ASEAN for the years 1991–92 and 2003–04 shows that there has not been any significant change in our major exports to the region. India's main exports to ASEAN in both the selected periods were gems and jewellery, oil meals, machinery and instruments, drugs and pharmaceuticals, meat and preparations, cotton yarn, fabrics, and made-ups.

The emergence of electronic goods as one of the leading items in Indian export basket to ASEAN in the last few years has captured the attention of investors and traders.

India's Imports

While the composition of India's exports to ASEAN has not seen much change the same cannot be said about its imports from the region. Electronic goods have emerged as the single-most important constituent, accounting for nearly 30 per cent of total imports from ASEAN to India in the recent past. Edible vegetable oils have also gained prominence and witnessed an upsurge in the share of Indian imports from ASEAN countries over the last 15 years.

Market Penetration

A critical assessment of shares commanded by India and ASEAN in each other's overall trade brings to the fore the asymmetrical nature of trade flow between the two trading partners. We have already seen ASEAN's pre-eminent position in India's global exports and imports (see tables).

Table 17.4 Share in Imports Market during 1991-2004—India vis-à-vis ASEAN-5

	Indonesia's share in India's imports	India' share in Indonesia's imports	Malaysia' share in India's imports	India' share in Malaysia's imports
1991	0.29	0.87	1.64	0.77
1992	0.30	0.79	1.85	0.89
1993	0.47	1.18	1.01	0.87
1994	1.09	0.99	2.07	0.69
1995	1.10	1.18	2.38	0.71
1996	1.47	2.02	3.35	0.94
1997	1.77	1.67	3.04	0.96
1998	1.72	1.07	4.49	0.80
1999	2.05	1.15	4.53	0.81
2000	2.31	1.57	3.87	0.88
2001	2.53	1.41	3.25	1.03
2002	2.53	1.44	3.22	1.11
2003	2.66	1.40	3.42	1.03
2004	2.7	1.72	3.19	1.12

Source: Enhancing India – ASEAN Trade, CII Study, 2006

On the other hand, the share of Thailand has been low and that of The Philippines just marginal. Therefore, it follows that while Singapore, Malaysia, and Indonesia occupy fairly respectable share in India's total imports, the converse is not true. Also, India's presence in the import map of both The Philippines and Thailand is yet to develop on a significant scale, and vice-versa.

MARKET SHARE: A COMPARATIVE ASSESSMENT

In the context of India's sluggish share in ASEAN's global imports, it is worth noting the magnificence in China's robust and impressive share in

ASEAN imports over the years. Further, there has also been a growing trend in the share of intra-regional sources in ASEAN's world imports.

However, as the previous section reveals, there are a few products in which India has managed to improve its share in the ASEAN import-market since 1993. However, India's performance in this regard pales into insignificance when compared to that of China. The products in which India lost market share saw a concomitant and substantial increase in the share of China, e.g., textiles and apparel for Indonesia, and hides and leather for Malaysia as well as Singapore. Even in areas where India registered an increase in import-market share, for instance, stone/cement/ceramics for Indonesia; footwear for Malaysia; vegetable products for The Philippines, China had outperformed India.

Again, there were many instances where potential imports were diverted away from India to greater intra-ASEAN trade (prepared foodstuffs in the case of Indonesia; plastics, gems and jewellery in the case of The Philippines; fish, meat and other animal products in the case of Thailand).

Table 17.5 Indonesia's Imports of Select Products—Share of India, and Intra-ASEAN (%)

	India		Intra-ASEAN	
	1995	2004	1995	2004
Base metal and metal articles	1.5	2.4	5.6	12.9
Stone/cement/ceramics	0.6	2.0	10.5	12.7
Textiles and apparel	2.3	1.5	3.2	6.5
Hides and leather	0.4	1.6	1.1	6.7
Chemicals	1.5	3.1	9.0	23.7
Prepared foodstuffs	19.7	9.9	13.3	26.8
Vegetable products	1.3	2.3	7.8	17.0

Source: Enhancing India – ASEAN Trade, CII Study, 2006

Table 17.6 The Philippines Imports of Select Products—Share of India and Intra-ASEAN (%)

	India		Intra-ASEAN	
	1995	2004	1995	2004
Footwear	1.6	5.1	18.3	17.0
Textiles and apparel	2.8	4.3	15.2	18.5
Hides and leather	5.3	2.0	20.9	25.3
Prepared foodstuffs	5.2	2.4	22.5	22.9
Fats and Oils	0.4	4.0	65.1	61.5
Vegetable products	2.1	3.8	24.3	24.2
Live animal	10.6	11.7	28.4	32.6

Source: Enhancing India – ASEAN Trade, CII Study, 2006

Table 17.7 Thailand's Imports of Select Products—Share of India and Intra-ASEAN (%)

	India		Intra-ASEAN	
	1995	2004	1995	2004
Antiques and works of art	0.0	4.6	15.5	13.6
Gems	0.1	5.7	13.6	5.7
Footwear	4.5	0.9	7.2	10.8
Hides and leather	1.6	3.4	5.0	9.4
Chemicals	0.4	2.0	9.3	15.7
Prepared foodstuffs	10.5	12.6	5.4	11.6
Fats and oils	0.0	19.1	59.7	32.5
Live animal	7.2	5.2	12.7	17.3

Source: Enhancing India – ASEAN Trade, CII Study, 2006

Table 17.8 Singapore's Imports of Select Products—Share of India and Intra-ASEAN (%)

	India		Intra-ASEAN	
	1995	2004	1995	2004
Base metal and metal articles	2.6	3.28	13.1	15.6
Gems	10.3	12.9	5.7	18.4
Textiles and apparel	3.3	3.7	33.6	40.9
Hides and leather	3.9	2.1	12.9	9.8
Plastics	1.4	0.88	26.4	22.8
Chemicals	0.9	2.7	5.4	7.6
Vegetable products	3.4	4.39	38.7	44.3
Live animals	3.1	2.2	47.8	33.9

Source: Enhancing India – ASEAN Trade, CII Study, 2006

Expanding Trade with other ASEAN countries

Trade with other ASEAN countries (namely, Brunei, Cambodia, Laos, Myanmar and Vietnam) as of 2004 is rather low (Table 17.9), with the exception of Myanmar whose share in India's total trade exceeds that of The Philippines. The reasons inhibiting augmented bilateral trade are many including high shipping costs, lack of contact between the business communities, relatively lower volume of demand, etc.

Table 17.9   India's Trade with BCLMV* in 2003–04

Country	Exports to			Imports from		
	Value ($ Million)	Growth (%)	% Share in India's Total	Value ($ Million)	Growth (%)	% Share in India's total
Brunei	2.86	−13.7	0.01	0.36	134.6	0.00
Cambodia	11.29	43.8	0.03	1.12	−15.7	0.00
Laos	3.16	−49.3	0.01	0.04	n.a	0.00
Myanmar	60.89	15.5	0.14	374.43	106.1	0.73
Vietnam	218.17	−3.4	0.50	18.91	52.6	0.04

*BCLMV = Brunei, Cambodia, Laos, Myanmar and Vietnam
Source: Enhancing India – ASEAN Trade, CII Study, 2006

At any rate, alongwith India's focus on ASEAN-5, it is also equally important to expand the two-way trade between India and BCLMV (Brunei, Cambodia, Laos, Myanmar, and Vietnam) in the interest of promoting overall India–ASEAN trade relations. So it is imperative that India engages the BCLMV countries to realize the available opportunities in a mutually beneficial manner.

SUMMARY

It would hardly be an exaggeration to stress the prime importance of accelerating the momentum of India–ASEAN trade and pushing it into a higher growth trajectory. In view of the wide diversity in the resource-base, size and maturity of markets, degree of openness, intensity of trade, stage of development, technological competence, and institutional capacity, significant complementarities exist between the two trading partners.

ASEAN countries are very important from the point of exporting and importing. They have comparative advantage in some sectors in which they specialize for export purpose. At the same time, they also need to import certain goods. It is worth visiting websites like asean.org and countrywatch.com to understand the latest trends and business environment in those countries.

CONCEPT REVIEW QUESTIONS

1. Discuss the international business opportunities in the ASEAN countries.
2. Discuss and debate the strategic importance of Singapore in ASEAN region.

3. Do you think that ASEAN countries are more important, as compared to countries in other regions, such as the Middle East, from the point of view of conducting business? If so, validate your arguments.

4. Compare and analyse business opportunities in Thailand and Singapore based on the information given and with the help of internet-based research.

OBJECTIVE QUESTIONS

State whether the following statements are True or False.

1. Singapore's share in India's imports is more than any other ASEAN country.
2. Most people in The Philippines cannot speak English fluently.
3. Malay and Chinese languages are widely used in Singapore.
4. India and Thailand have signed a bilateral free trade agreement.
5. Vietnam currency is known as Dong.
6. Baht is the currency of Thailand.

SELECT REFERENCES

ASEAN secretariat, ASEAN FREE TRADE and Update, 2006, New Delhi

Enhancing India–ASEAN trade, Study by CII, 2006, New Delhi

Mehta, Rajesh, 2006, "Economic cooperation between India and Singapore", *Economic and Political Weekly*, Mumbai

www.adb.org, last accessed on 2nd May, 2007

www.asean.org, last accessed on 2nd May, 2007

www.countrywatch.org, last accessed on 4th March, 2007

18 Doing Business with Australia and New Zealand

Learning Objectives

After studying this chapter, you will be able to understand
- the characteristic features of Australian and New Zealand economies
- the recent trends and patterns in Australian and New Zealand business

Australia

The Commonwealth of Australia is a federation, which was established on 1 January, 1901. It consists of six states, previously, each a separate British colony—New South Wales, Queensland, Victoria, South Australia, Western Australia, and Tasmania and the sparsely populated Northern Territory, which now has a territorial government elected by its own citizens. The commonwealth also includes the 940 square miles of the Capital Territory in which the national capital, Canberra, is located, and which also has a locally elected government.

Geographic Description

Australia's 7,686,850 sq kms (2,967,909 sq. miles) landmass lies on the Indo-Australian Plate. Surrounded by the Indian, Southern, and Pacific Oceans, Australia is separated from Asia by the Arafura and Timor Seas. Australia has a total of 25,760 kms (16,007 miles) of coastline and claims an extensive Exclusive Economic Zone (EEZ) of 8,148,250 sq kms (3,146,057 sq. miles).

Australia has an enviable Western-style capitalist economy, with a per capita GDP on par with the four dominant West European economies. Rising output in the domestic economy has been offsetting the global slump, and business and consumer confidence remains robust. Australia's emphasis on reforms, low inflation, and growing ties with China are other key factors that drive the businesses there.

Australia has achieved a strong economic growth over the last decade, with a four per cent average annual increase in its real gross domestic product (GDP), making it one of the world's fastest growing industrialized countries. Japan is Australia's largest export market, with the Association of South East Asian Nations (ASEAN) member countries in the second place, followed by China (including Hong Kong). The US is Australia's fourth largest market, followed by South Korea, New Zealand, and the UK.

Aboriginal settlers arrived on the continent from Southeast Asia about 40,000 years before the first Europeans began exploration in the 17th century. No formal territorial claims were made until 1770, when Capt. James Cook took possession in the name of Great Britain. Six colonies were created in the late 18th and 19th centuries; they federated and became the Commonwealth of Australia in 1901. The country took advantage of its natural resources to rapidly develop its agricultural and manufacturing industries.

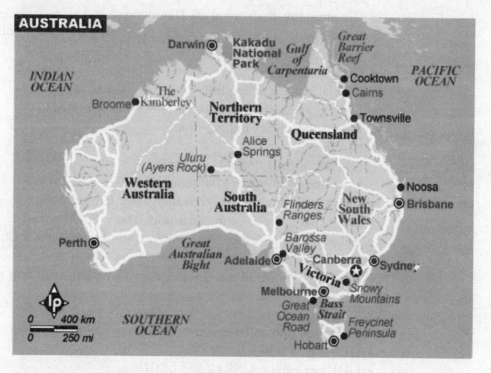

Legal Structure

Australia's judicial system is mostly based on British law. The state has an extremely good record on transparency and was, in fact, ranked 9 (out of 146 countries) in Transparency International's Corruption Perceptions Index in 2004. It scored 8.8, which was far above the Asian average of 3.8 and the

Western Europe average of 7.9, although it scored marginally lower than both New Zealand and Singapore.

Australia, however, compares poorly against its regional peers and other OECD (Organisation for Economic Co-operation and Development) states, as far as timely implementation of trade contracts is concerned. Indeed, while it takes only 11 separate procedures to enforce a contract in Australia, compared to an average of 18 among OECD states and 24 in East Asian and Pacific states, according to World Bank data, the whole process itself takes an average of 320 days in Australia, compared to 213 and 193 days in other nations, respectively.

Country Indicators

- Official name: Commonwealth of Australia
- Head of State: Queen Elizabeth II (since 1952), represented by Governor General
- Government: Parliamentary Democracy
- Ruling party: Liberal Party (LP)– National Party (NP) coalition
- Area: 7,682,850 square km
- Capital: Canberra
- Official language: English
- Currency: Australian dollar (A$) = 100 cents
- Population: 20.23 million (2004)
- Sex ratio:
  - At birth: 1.05 male(s)/female
  - Under 15 years 1.05 male(s)/female
- Infant mortality rate: 4.76 deaths/1,000 live births
- Life expectancy at birth: total population: 80.26 years
- Religions: Anglican 26.1%, Roman Catholic 26%, other Christian 24.3%, non-Christian 11%, others 12.6%
- Literacy: (People of age 15 and above who can read and write) 100%

Economy

- Exchange rate: A$ 1.057 per US$ (May, 2008)
- GDP—US$ 936.4 bn (2007)
- GDP per capita: US$ 42,553 (2007)
- GDP composition:
  - Agriculture: 3.5%
  - Industry: 26.3%
  - Services: 70.2% (2003 est.)

- Labour force: 9.82 million (2003)
- Unemployment: 6.00%
- Agriculture products: wheat, barley, sugarcane, fruits; cattle, sheep, poultry
- Industries: mining, industrial and transportation equipment, food processing, chemicals, steel
- Current account balance : $-30.14 billion (2003)
- Exports: $68.67 billion (2003 est.)
- Export commodities: coal, gold, meat, wool, alumina, iron ore, wheat, machinery and transport equipment
- Exports (major partners): Japan 18.1%, US 8.7%, China 8.4%, South Korea 7.4%, New Zealand 7.4%, UK 6.7% (2003)
- Imports: $82.91 billion (2003 est.)
- Import commodities: machinery and transport equipment, computers and office machines, telecommunication equipment and parts; crude oil and petroleum products
- Imports (major partners): US 16%, Japan 12.5%, China 11%, Germany 6.1%, UK 4.2% (2003)
- Foreign debt: US$ 176.80 billion (2003)
- Oil production: 731,000 bpd (2003)
- Balance of trade: US$ 10.40 billion (2003)

Australian Banking and Financial System

Australian banking history can be divided into the following four eras.

Private Banks

The first bank of Australia, the Bank of New South Wales was formed in 1817. Its purpose was to be a bank of issue, so that its banknotes would provide a sound currency. Soon, competition started to develop in the economy and a private banking system began to emerge. The banking system at that time took deposits and reloaned the money by discounting bills of exchange. There were no central banks and each bank could print its own banknotes on the securities of the assets. As long as the assets of a bank were believed to be sound, its notes were freely accepted.

The Commonwealth Bank Era

In the wake of the crisis in the banking system, the Commonwealth Bank was formed by the federal government in 1911 to issue notes which would be backed by the resources of the nation. This solved the currency problem. Notes issued by the CBA (Commonwealth Bank Authority) were accepted as legal tender. From 1894 to 1979, only three banks failed in Australia. Banking became more controlled during the World War II when the central bank dictated the overdraft rates and, later, the statutory reserve ratios and the liquid asset ratios.

The Reserve Bank Era

The Reserve Bank of Australia was created in 1959 and subsequently, the CBA's banking powers were transferred to it. However, the banking system itself was governed by tight controls.

Deregulation Era

Between 1983 and 1985, the system was deregulated by (a) floating the Australian dollar in December 1983 and (b) granting 16 banking licences to foreign banks in 1985. These steps intensified the competition in the domestic lending market. Banks started reducing the rates and the securities they required.

Present status of the Australian Banking System

In recent years, the Australian banking system has grown phenomenally in terms of total assets. Profitability has been strong. Lately, the housing sector boom dominated the Australian banking system. The economy is low on inflation and interest rates, which fuelled the growth of housing sector loans. Credit growth fuelled the subsequent rise in property prices.

Other factors that contributed to the profitability of the Australian banking system are strong growth in non-interest income and containment of costs. Banks are increasingly entering the fund management business and a major chunk of their revenue is coming from this diversified portfolio.

Monetary and Exchange Rate System

The Australian monetary system requires no minimum reserves of its banks. The policy framework is inflation targeted, under which the Reserve Bank sets policy to achieve an inflation rate of 2–3 per cent on average. The bank and the government determine the target inflation rate.

Monetary policy is set in terms of an operating target for the cash rate, which is the interest rate on overnight loans made between institutions in the money market. When the Reserve Bank Board decides that a change in monetary policy should occur, it specifies a new target for the cash rate. A decision to ease policy will reflect in a new lower target cash rate, while a decision to tighten policy will reflect in a new higher target level for the cash rate.

The Reserve Bank uses its domestic market operations, sometimes called open market operations, to influence the cash rate. On the days when monetary policy is being changed, market operations are aimed at moving the cash rate to a new target level.

The cash rate is determined in the money market as a result of the interaction of demand for and supply of overnight funds. The Reserve Bank's ability to pursue successfully a target for the cash rate stems from its control over the supply of funds, which banks use to settle transactions among themselves.

Exchange Rates

Date	US Dollar	Australian Dollar
5th March 2008	1 USD	1.08119 AUD
1st March 2005	1 USD	1.27437 AUD
1st March 2004	1 USD	1.29451 AUD
1st March 2003	1 USD	1.64609 AUD
1st March 2002	1 USD	1.93162 AUD
1st March 2001	1 USD	1.90041 AUD

According to Moody's credit rating agency, strengths for the country are:
- strong growth performance over the past few years, demonstrating the economy's ability to withstand international cyclical fluctuations;
- open trade policies and a market-oriented regulatory regime, providing a favorable environment for growth and investment;
- the healthy budgetary and public debt situation maintained over the medium term, while a vigilant stance towards monetary policy ensuring price stability; and
- stable political institutions underpinning the pragmatic policy stance of successive governments, and allowing for the relatively peaceful resolution of potentially divisive issues.

Capital Market

The history of the Australian stock market started with the setting up of six independent stock exchanges. Adelaide was established in 1887, Brisbane and Melbourne in 1884, Hobart in 1882, Perth in 1889, and Sydney in 1871.

During the mining booms of the time, provincial exchanges were established in Ballarat, Gympie, Charters Towers, Zeehan, Queenstown, and Kalgurli, to name a few. They catered for the need to raise capital for the large number of mining companies, which were being established. Most of these provincial exchanges closed down when the mining companies ceased their operations.

There was also a stock exchange in Launceston, Tasmania, which later merged with the Hobart Stock Exchange.

From 1903 to 1937, the state stock exchanges met on an informal basis. In 1936, Sydney took the lead in formalizing the association. Initially, this involved the exchanges in Adelaide, Brisbane, Hobart, and Sydney; Melbourne and Perth joined soon after. The Australian Associated Stock Exchanges (AASE) was established in 1937. Through the AASE, the exchanges gradually brought in common listing requirements for companies and uniform brokerage and other rules for stock broking firms. They also set the ground rules for commissions and the flotation of government and semi-government loan raisings.

The Australian Stock Exchange Limited (ASX) was formed on 1 April 1987 through incorporation under legislation of the Australian Parliament. Formation of the national stock exchange involved amalgamation of the six independent stock exchanges that had operated in the state capitals.

History of Trading

During the last century, there have been three different forms of trading on the Australian stock exchanges.

The earliest was the call system, which was an auction system. In this, a stock exchange employee, the Caller, called the name of each listed security in turn while members bid, offered, sold or bought the stock at each call. This system proved inadequate to handle the increased volume of trading during the mining booms.

The call system was replaced by the post system in the early 1960s. This involved stocks being quoted on 'posts' or 'boards'. 'Chalkies' were employed by the Stock Exchange and it was their function to record in chalk the bids and offers of the operators (employees of stockbrokers) and the sales made.

Finally, in 1987 the Stock Exchange Automated Trading System (SEATS) was introduced. This enables computerized screen trading from stockbrokers' offices.

In producing the information available here relating to stockbrokers, stock broking firms and listed companies, reference has been made to the ASX archives, State library collections and the published histories of the individual Stock Exchanges.

In June 1992, the domestic market capitalization was $198 billion. By the end of 2005, market capitalization had increased to $750 billion. While finance and insurance and the other services sectors (which includes communications and media stocks) have grown most dramatically, there also has been an overall strong growth in various industry sectors of the market.

Commerce in Australia

The bigwigs of the Australian business and economy are:

- Qantas Airways Ltd: Australia's national airline
- Commonwealth Bank of Australia (CBA AU), Australia's second biggest lender
- Woodside Petroleum Ltd. (WPL AU), Australia's second biggest oil producer
- Newcrest Mining Ltd. (NCM AU), Australia's biggest gold miner
- Amcor, the world's largest maker of plastic bottles for soda drinks
- Woolworths Ltd., Australia's biggest grocer
- Metcash, Australia's biggest grocery wholesaler
- BHP, the "Big Australian" steelmaker

Australia's top 10 companies are known for overall leadership, quality of products and services, the long-term vision of management, innovation in responding to customers' needs, and financial soundness. The top 10 companies are:

1. Woolworths
2. Harvey Norman
3. Westfield Holdings
4. Qantas Airways
5. Foster's Brewing
6. Commonwealth Bank of Australia
7. BHP-Billiton
8. Mayne Nickless
9. Brambles Industries
10. News Corp.

The top 10 MNCs conducting business in Australia are:

1. Microsoft
2. General Electric
3. Nokia
4. McDonald's
5. IBM
6. Coca-Cola
7. Visa International

8. Intel
9. Walt Disney
10. Nestle

Investment Opportunities in Australia

From its strong mineral, petroleum and agricultural base, Australian industry has diversified in recent years and is now energetically embracing the modern knowledge-driven economy. Innovation and a strong entrepreneurial spirit have driven Australia's economy to world-class achievements. With a welcoming attitude to foreign investment and a proven track record of attracting successful projects, Australia is a great investment location.

There are many investment opportunities available, of which real estate is the primary avenue. Offshore investors are welcome and subject only to Federal Investment Board Review, which normally is not difficult to obtain. Australia has a land mass nearly the size of the United States, but with only a tenth of the population, leaving large areas of undeveloped land. There are also multiple unit development projects in the planning stages, as well as single-family homes, commercial opportunities, or just rural/farm properties. All these present an investment opportunity better than anywhere else in the world.

Investment opportunities are also present in the following areas.

- Biotechnology
- Food and Beverages
- Furniture and Forest Products
- Information and Communication Technology
- International Education and Training
- Marine and Defence
- Mineral and Petroleum
- Mining/Oil and Gas Equipment and Services
- New Technologies, Renewable Energy and Environment
- Wood Processing/Pulp Mills

Exports from Australia

According to the Australian Bureau of Statistics (ABS), in 2003–04 there were 30,788 exporting businesses. This comprised 29,555 goods exporters and 2,139 service exporters–excluding services (like tourism and education) and those businesses with annual exports amounting to less less than $10,000.

New Zealand topped the list of importers, with 13,754 Australian businesses having exported to the country. This indicates that many exporters find exporting to New Zealand relatively easy and that often it is a good 'nursery' to start with when learning the craft of exporting. The Australian New Zealand Closer Economic Relationship (CER)—now over two decades old—has given Australian companies, especially small businesses, a kick-start into exporting.

The United States is the second key market for services and elaborately transformed manufactures (ETMs). Many small and medium businesses get their start in the US, given the size of the market, and the FTA helps provide more opportunities to these companies.

Singapore is in the third place and then come the UK and Hong Kong. Singapore and Hong Kong have many wholesale trading houses and act as a hub port for exporters. For instance, Singapore has played the role of a gateway port for Southeast Asia, while Hong Kong has played a similar role in Northeast Asia—particularly before China opened up to international trade and commerce.

Australia's trade with India is on the upswing. India is a major exporter of brainpower and Australia, along with the USA, Canada, and the UK is a main beneficiary. A significant area of Indo-Australian economic cooperation is information technology (IT), which has been a major contributor to India's recent economic resurgence and has close links with education. Infrastructure is also a focal point of Indo-Australian trade and investment. Many Australian engineers, project managers, and research specialists are making contributions to Indian infrastructure development projects.

Government Assistance for Exporters

The federal government has instituted a lot of bodies that look into growth of trade and assist exporters through investment and provide proper channels to further their trade. Some of the bodies and programmes are as follows.

TradeWatch

This is a new interactive online information service for Australians doing business overseas. The service focuses on market access issues in a progressively expanding range of Australian key markets. It enables business to feed in directly market-specific concerns, which will be factored into the government's market access strategies.

Department of Foreign Affairs and Trade

Working with Austrade, the department uses its worldwide network of missions to facilitate contacts between Australians and commercial business people.

Austrade

Austrade or the Australian Trade Commission is a government agency that provides a wide range of export and investment services to Australian companies through over 90 offices in Australia and around the world.

TradeStart

TradeStart is a branch of Austrade that operates as a partnership between Austrade and local partners, including chambers of commerce, private sector organizations, and state and territory governments to ensure small and medium companies in regional Australia get the support they need to succeed in international markets.

New Exporter Development Programme

The programme is a package of services designed to assist small and medium-sized Australian companies develop their businesses overseas and make their first export sale.

New Zealand

New Zealand's economy is heavily dependent on overseas trade. Traditionally, a large portion of the country's exports, mainly agricultural products, were exported to the United Kingdom. However, in the past 20 years, New Zealand has adapted to a changing world in which Asia is more dominant. The nation's largest merchandise export markets are now Australia, the United States, and Japan. New Zealand has developed its agriculture and manufacturing industries to suit the needs of niche markets, moving away from dependence on dairy, meat, and wool exports. Industries like forestry, horticulture, fishing, and tourism have become more significant.

Over the past 20 years the government has transformed New Zealand from an agrarian economy dependent on concessionary British market access to a more industrialized, free market economy that can compete globally. This dynamic growth has boosted real incomes (but left behind many at the bottom of the ladder), broadened and deepened the technological capabilities of the industrial sector, and contained inflationary pressures. Per capita income has been rising and is now 80 per cent of the level of the four largest EU economies.

Political Structure

New Zealand is a democratic monarchy within the Commonwealth. The executive power is vested in the governor-general, who represents the British Crown. The legislature is a unicameral parliament with 120 representatives, elections for which are held every three years. During these elections, 61 members are directly elected, six are elected for Maori seats, and a further 53 are appointed from party lists.

Country Indicators

- Capital: Wellington
- Population: 3,993,817 (July 2004 est.)

- Ethnic groups: New Zealand European 74.5%, Maori 9.7%, other European 4.6%, Pacific Islander 3.8%, Asian and others 7.4%
- Religions: Anglican 24%, Presbyterian 18%, Roman Catholic 15%, Methodist 5%, Baptist 2%, other Protestant 3%, unspecified or none 33% (1986)
- Literacy: people of age 15 and over who can read and write 99%
- Languages: English (official), Maori (official)

Economy

- Exchange rate: 1.251 NZD per US$ (March 2008)
- GDP (Purchasing Power Parity): $ 117.69 bn (2008)
- GDP per capita (PPP): $27,785 (2008)
- GDP real growth: 3.5% (2003 est.)
- GDP composition:
  - Agriculture: 4.8%
  - Industry: 27.4%
  - Services: 67.8% (2003 est.)
- Investment (gross fixed): 20.9% of GDP (2003)
- Inflation rate (consumer prices) : 1.8% (2003)
- Labour force: 2.008 million (2003 est.)
- Unemployment: 4.7% (2003)
- Agriculture products: wheat, barley, potatoes, pulses, fruits, vegetables; wool, beef, dairy products; fish
- Industries: food processing, wood and paper products, textiles, machinery, transportation equipment, banking and insurance, tourism, mining
- Industrial production growth rate: 1.3% (2003 est.)
- Current account balance: $-3.446 billion (2003)
- Exports: $15.86 billion (2003 est.)
- Export commodities: dairy products, meat, wool, wood and wood products, fish, machinery
- Export (major partners): Australia 21.8%, US 14.6%, Japan 11%, China 4.9%, UK 4.8% (2003)
- Imports: $16.06 billion (2003 est.)
- Import commodities: machinery and equipment, vehicles and aircraft, petroleum, electronics, textiles, plastics
- Import (major partners): Australia 22.2%, US 11.8%, Japan 11.8%, China 9%, Germany 5.3% (2003)

Exchange Rates

Date	US Dollar	New Zealand Dollar
1st March 2008	1 USD	1.25109 NZD
1st March 2005	1 USD	1.37552 NZD
1st March 2004	1 USD	1.45096 NZD
1st March 2003	1 USD	1.79211 NZD
1st March 2002	1 USD	2.36686 NZD
1st March 2001	1 USD	2.30946 NZD

Tax Structure

There are three basic tax rates in New Zealand.
- Taxable income up to $38,000–the tax rate is 19.5 per cent
- Taxable income $38,001 to $60,000 inclusive–the tax rate is 33 per cent
- Taxable income $60,001 and over–the tax rate is 39 per cent.

The non-declaration rate is 45 cents. The non-declaration rate is used when employees do not provide their employers with an IRD (Inland Revenue Department) number.

SUMMARY

Australia and New Zealand are important business destinations. They provide many opportunities for exporting firms and multinational enterprises. Australia is also an ideal place for people to live because of its pleasant climate throughout the year. In recent decades, Australia has transformed itself into an internationally competitive, advanced market economy.

New Zealand, the island located near Australia has also attracted companies from all over the world It is worth noting that New Zealand is heavily dependent on trade–particularly in agricultural products–to drive growth, and it has been affected by the global economic slowdown and the slump in commodity prices.

CONCEPT REVIEW QUESTIONS

1. Compare and discuss the country indicators of Australia and New Zealand.
2. Elucidate the important aspects of doing business in New Zealand.
3. Discuss the business environment in Australia and New Zealand.

OBJECTIVE QUESTIONS

State whether the following questions are True or False
1. Sydney is part of the state known as New South Wales.
2. Tasmania and Western Australia are a part of a single state in Australia.
3. Canberra is the capital of Australia
4. People call the natives of New Zealand as Kiwis.
5. Maori is the ancient and native language used in Australia.

SELECT REFERENCES

Asian Pacific Journal of Economic Literature
Australian Economic Review
The Economist
www.aph.gov.au/library/INTGUIDE/ECON/economy.htm accused on 22nd
    July 2007
www.asx.com.au accessed on 20th July 2007
www.countrywatch.com accessed on 24th July 2007
www.rba.gov.au accessed on 21st July 2007
www.stats.govt.nz accessed on 22nd July 2007

19 Doing Business with China and Japan

Learning Objectives

After studying this chapter, you will be able to understand
- the characteristic features of the economies of China and Japan
- the business environment and opportunities in China and Japan

China

Country Overview

China, the world's most populous country, is one of the driving forces of global exports today. As the world's largest consumer of steel and other raw materials and the leading producer of electronic goods, toys, etc, China's role in the world economy is second only to the USA. So it is imperative that we – students, business analysts, entrepreneurs, researchers, etc. – understand the economic environment of this giant nation, in order to perceive and exploit the possible business opportunities there.

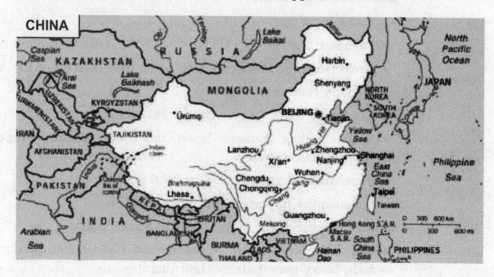

China has emerged as the fastest growing market in the world during the last 20 years. With an annual economic growth averaging eight to nine per cent, the size of the Chinese economy has quadrupled since the 1970s. China has transformed itself from a rural to an urban society, from an agricultural to a manufacturing economy, and from a centrally-controlled and planned economy to a state-managed market economy.

China's accession to WTO in 2001, has led to tremendous business opportunities for companies the worldover. Legal, economic, political, and social changes within China and the adoption of new policies have fostered openings and challenges for companies interested in starting or expanding business in China.

Country Indicators

- Population: 1.3 billion (approximately)
- Location/Size: Eastern Asia/3.7 million square miles (9.6 million square kilometers, slightly smaller than the United States)
- Major Cities: Beijing (capital), Shanghai, Tianjin, Guangzhou, Shenyang, Wuhan, Chengdu, Hong Kong
- Languages: Mandarin (official), many local dialects
- Ethnic Groups: Han Chinese (92%); Zhuang, Uygur, Hui, Yi, Miao, Manchu, Mongol, Buyi, Korean, others (8%)
- Religion: Officially atheist; Daoist (Taoist), Buddhist, Muslim (1-2%), Christian (3-4%)

Business Indicators

- Currency: Yuan
- Exchange Rate (2007): US$1 = 6.5 to 7.5 Yuan/Renminbi
- Gross Domestic Product (2004): $1.65 trillion (2005): $1.89 trillion
- Inflation Rate (2005): 3.9%
- Current Account Surplus (2005): $81.6 billion
- Major Trading Partners: Japan, the United States, European Union, South Korea, Taiwan
- Merchandise Exports (2005): $757.6 billion
- Merchandise Imports (2005): $674.7 billion
- Merchandise Trade Surplus (2005): $83.0 billion
- Major Export Products: Light industrial and textile products, mineral fuels, heavy manufactures, agricultural goods.

- Major Imports: Machinery, steel, chemicals, miscellaneous manufactures, industrial materials, grain.

Statistical note: All data reported here exclude Hong Kong, a former British colony, which reverted to China on 1 July, 1997.

Other Important Indicators

- Service Sector 32%
  Primary Sector 15%
  Industrial Sector 53%
- Oil: World's Largest Consumer Importer of 4.6 million barrels/day
- Natural Gas: Not a major fuel but large reserves
- Coal: 65% of China's energy consumption
  Largest Consumer and Producer of Coal
- Electricity: 30 GW shortage in 2005, characterized by fragmentation

China's exports have grown at above 35 per cent per annum over the last few years and the trade surplus within the corresponding period has been in the range of US$ 55 to 65 billion. China has a mixed economy, with a combination of state-owned and private firms. A number of state-owned firms in China have undergone partial or full privatization in recent years. The government has encouraged foreign investment in certain sectors of the economy; further, China has several "special economic zones" in which foreign investors receive preferable tax, tariff, and investment treatment.

In the late 1970s, China began to move away from orthodox communism. Its success in reforming a socialist economic system, i.e., attempting to manage a market-oriented economy while keeping a communist political system intact is widely appreciated across the world.

China's top trading partners are: EU, USA, Japan, Hong Kong, ASEAN, Taiwan Province, Russia, Australia, and Canada.

The Chinese central bank, in July 2005, delinked its currency from the US Dollar to which it was formerly pegged. The Chinese Yuan now floats within a very narrow band against a basket of currencies from the country's major trading partners. China has also implemented Capital Account Convertibility.

Competitiveness Balance Sheet of China

Strengths

A. Government Efficiency

1. Political parties understand current economic challenges.
2. Protectionism in the economy does not affect the conduct of business.

B. Productivity in Business

1. The labour force is remarkably efficient.
2. Societal values support competitiveness.
3. The competitiveness of the economy is not hindered by brain drain.

Weakness

1. International experience of senior managers is generally low.
2. Credit does not flow easily from banks to business.
3. Finance skills are not readily available.
4. Private property is not adequately protected.

With China's entry into the WTO in 2001, the Chinese government made a number of specific commitments to trade and investment liberalization which, if fully implemented, would substantially open the Chinese economy to foreign firms.

Despite moves toward privatization, much of China's economy remains controlled by large State Owned Enterprises (SOEs). Restructuring the SOE sector, including the privatization of some enterprises, is a major priority of the government, as is the restructuring of the banking sector.

Balance of Payment

In recent years, China's Balance of Payment (BOP) has been characterized by a surplus in its current and capital account.

Sectors Favourable for Foreign Investors

Post liberalization, China has emerged as the most favoured destination for foreign investment. Japan, South Korea, Taiwan, and the United States are China's most important sources of Foreign Direct Investment (FDI). The China State Commission of Economics and Trade declares that China encourages foreign investment in the following areas:

1. Agroeconomic projects like the retooling of low-and medium-yield farmland and the development of high yield varieties.
2. Construction of infrastructural facilities in sectors including energy and communications, and basic industrial projects, such as the production of key raw materials.
3. State designated pillar industries, including machinery, electronics, petrochemicals, and automobile.
4. Projects capable of introducing advanced technologies to improve economic returns and productivity of domestic enterprises.

5. Projects that can increase foreign exchange earning through export.
6. Technologies and equipment helpful for pollution control and environment protection.
7. Emerging industrial technologies and equipment, such as bio-chemical, telecom networking systems, isotope radiation and laser, and the development of oceanic energy.
8. Projects that can make good use of labour-force and natural resources.

Pharmaceutical Industry

The Chinese pharmaceutical industry structure is poised to become one of the largest pharmaceutical-producing countries in the world after its accession to WTO. Traditionally, the industry was small-scale, with a scattered geographical layout, and outdated manufacturing technology and management structure. The domestic Chinese pharmaceutical industry also has weak international trading competitiveness, coupled with a lack of patented pharmaceuticals developed in-house. Having joined the WTO, China has integrated into the global economy. This international competition placed an intense pressure on the Chinese pharmaceutical industry, and further opened the doors to a lucrative market for non-Chinese companies, especially pharmaceutical producers and manufacturers. Following the entry into WTO, the industry environment has changed over the last 10 years. Accession to the WTO has led to transparency and the strengthening of commercial legal procedures, including the tightening of rules on intellectual property, tariff reduction, and market access to non-Chinese suppliers engaging in the distribution of pharmaceuticals. All such moves have created additional business opportunities for non-Chinese pharmaceutical companies for export in China. China, as of 2007, reportedly has nearly 6000 domestic pharmaceutical manufactures and around 14,000 pharmaceutical distributors. By 2010, it is expected to become the fifth largest pharmaceuticals market in the world. The output of the industry crossed US $140 billion in 2004. Around 29 per cent of the pharmaceutical industry is foreign-funded, with nearly all big pharma majors registering their presence in China.

Japan

Country Overview

Japan is the world's fourth largest energy consumer and the second largest energy importer (after the United States). Japan has taken important steps towards economic deregulation and restructuring.

Government-industry cooperation, a strong work ethics, mastery of high technology, and a small defence allocation (1% of GDP) helped Japan advance with extraordinary pace to become the second most technologically-powerful economy in the world after the US. One notable characteristic of the economy is the teamwork of manufacturers, suppliers, and distributors in closely-knit groups called *keiretsu*. A second basic feature has been the guarantee of lifetime employment to a substantial portion of the urban labour force. However, both these features are now being eroded. Industry, the most important sector of Japanese economy, is heavily dependent on imported raw materials and fuels. The tiny agricultural sector is highly subsidized and protected, with crop yields among the highest in the world. Usually self sufficient in rice, Japan imports about 50 per cent of its requirements of other grain and fodder crops. Japan maintains one of the world's largest fishing fleets and accounts for nearly 15 per cent of the global catch.

For three decades, the overall real economic growth had been impressive: a 10% average in the 1960s, a five per cent average in the 1970s, and a four per cent average in the 1980s. Growth slowed down markedly in the 1990s, largely because of the after effects of over investment during the late 1980s.

Robotics constitutes a key long-term economic strength with Japan possessing 410,000 of the world's 720,000 "working robots."

Country Indicators

- Population (2004): 127.3 million
- Location/Size: Eastern Asia - island chain between the North Pacific Ocean and the Sea of Japan/145,882 square miles
- Major Cities: Tokyo (capital), Osaka (Kansai), Nagoya, Fukuoka/ Kitakyushu, Sapporo
- Languages: Japanese
- Ethnic Groups: Japanese (99%)
- Religion: Shinto and Buddhist (84%), others (16%)
- Income Tax: 7.5% among middle income group professionals
- Neighbours: North Korea, South Korea, Russia, China
- Size: 377,835 sq. km. (water: 3,091 sq km)
- Political system: Parliamentary Government
- Judicial system
  Similar to European Civil Law system
  Judicial review of legislative acts
- Administrative system
  Forty-seven prefectures
- Foreign relations
  Temporary member of United Nations Security Council
  Member: G-7, WTO

Business Indicators

- Currency: Yen
- Exchange Rate (May 2008): US$ 1 = 105 Yen (2007 Dec), US$ 1 = 90 Yen (2008 Dec)
- Gross Domestic Product (GDP, at market exchange rate) (2004): $5 trillion (approximately)
- Major Trading Partners: United States, Germany, Asian NIEs, China, OPEC
- Total Merchandise Exports (2004): $522.4 billion
- Total Merchandise Imports (2004): $395.9 billion

- Major Export Products: Machinery and transport equipment; chemical and other manufactured goods
- Major Import Products: Chemical and other manufactured goods; machinery and transport equipment; mineral fuels; foodstuffs; crude oil.
- Transport infrastructure:
  - Airports 174
  - Seaports and Terminals 10
  - Railways network 23,577 km (Bullet train)
  - Roadways network 1,177,278 km
  - Waterways network 1,770 km
- Communication:
  - Landline users 71.149 million
  - Mobile phone users 86.658 million
  - Internet users 12.962 million

At the beginning of the 21st century, the Japanese government has pressed for structural reforms in Japan's economy. In one major change, the government reversed the previous policy of increasing government spending to stimulate the country's economy. The Bank of Japan*, however, has adopted an expansionary monetary policy, which has provided some stimulus to the economy.

Japan remains important to the world energy sector as one of the major exporters of energy-sector capital equipment, engineering, construction, and project management services. All the same, Japan imports oil and natural gas, particularly from Gulf countries.

For a country that boasts of some of the best manufacturers in the world, Japan's service sector remains strikingly poor. Individual consumers struggle with outdated and inefficient services. Hence, the sector presents a huge opportunity for Japan in the future. Foreign companies that can offer their expertise in the service sector can encash the opportunities.

Foreign Investments in Japan

Foreign direct investment (FDI) in Japan has increased steadily, thanks to regulatory reforms in finance, communications, and distribution, as well as the global rise in mergers and acquisitions (M&A).

Between developed countries, 80 per cent of total FDI takes the form of M&A. Thus, Japan will need to undertake institutional reforms to facilitate cross-border M&A.

Japan's Strengths

The Japanese economy has shown signs of improved health in recent years.

---

*The Bank of Japan is the central bank in Japan.

Corporate restructuring and other reforms have resulted in the highest corporate profits in about 15 years. It is now expected that rising corporate profits will increase business investment and subsequently bring about sustained growth led by private demand, as the recovery in the corporate sector will spill over to the household sector.

Japan's strengths include, its huge domestic market that accounts for about 12% of global GDP, skilled human resources, advanced technological capabilities, a predictable business environment supported by strong legal institutions and the rule of law, and a well-developed production/distribution infrastructure, all of which demonstrate the vast potential of Japan as an investment destination. This is supported by the fact that UNCTAD ranks Japan 16 out of 140 countries on its Inward FDI Potential Index. Geographically, Japan is also positioned to function as an international business hub for the fast-growing East Asian region. In addition to this potential, Japan's stable, social and economic conditions make the country one of the top investment choices for foreign companies seeking business opportunities in Asia.

In light of Japan's market size, technological capabilities and social conditions, promising fields for inward FDI include information/communication, environmental technology, medical care businesses, leisure and tourism, and biotechnology. Other industries such as auto parts may present good investment opportunities.

Advantages of conducting business in Japan

1. The world's second-largest market
2. The hub of Asia's growing economies
3. Abundant highly skilled human resources
4. Innovative technologies
5. Efficient infrastructure for dynamic business activities
6. Reformed legal framework for investment
7. Multiple market opportunities
8. Living environment

Areas with Business Opportunities

Business opportunities with Japan mostly lie in the following areas.

(i) Information and Communications Technology (ICT)

From research and development through design and manufacturing, the ICT industry has become one of Japan's strong fields, based on advanced technology. Japan's information and communications market is also enormous, compared to other countries.

(ii) Environment

Japan is the world's most advanced nation in the field of environmental technology, including soil pollution cleanup and fuel-cell batteries. Japan has also achieved the number one position in the world in solar power generation. Japan's environmental business is a promising field, supported by cutting-edge technology and rapid growth.

(iii) Health Care Business

Supported by the national health insurance system, Japan's national healthcare expenses have reached 30 trillion yen. Boasting the longest average lifespan in the world, Japan's demands for health maintenance and improvement services and its healthcare, nursing, and welfare-related markets are expanding rapidly. There are, thus, opportunities for exporting pharmaceutical products.

(iv) Nanotechnology

Japan is a world leader in nanotechnology. In particular, Japan maintains a strong technological advantage in the field of carbon nanotubes, which can be used in products such as thin displays and fuel cells.

(v) Wholesale and Retail

As the world's second-largest market, Japan is an attractive place for wholesale and retail-related businesses from overseas. One after the other, many leading foreign firms are entering the Japanese market. In particular, chains of members-only, cash-and-carry, warehouse-type wholesalers, hypermarkets, and manufacturers' outlets are expanding across Japan.

SUMMARY

It is important to recognize that there are opportunities for importing many manufactured items and capital goods from Japan because the brand 'Made in Japan' has become synonymous with 'quality' in many parts of the world. It makes sense for importers in other countries to compare items made in Japan, if they want to build trust among their customers. The 'Made in Japan' brand has become very popular in the world market, although items from Japan are relatively more expensive. At the same time, 'Made in China' does not command the same credibility in international markets. Many people regard 'Made in China' as 'fake' or inferior'. Nonetheless, Chinese goods have captured more foreign market share, because of their low pricing.

CONCEPT REVIEW QUESTIONS

1. Discuss the business environment and international business opportunities in China.
2. Compare the country and economic indicators of China and Japan.
3. Discuss the important aspects of doing business with Japan.

OBJECTIVE QUESTIONS

State whether the following questions are True or False
1. Nagoya is a major port city in Japan.
2. Exchange rate of the Japanese Yen is always quoted in terms of 100 Yen against US Dollar.
3. The Chinese Currency is called 'Yuan'.

SELECT REFERENCES

Chandran R., 2005, *International Business*, Jaico Publishers, Mumbai

Gavusgil, Tamer, Ghauri, Pervez N., and Agrawal, Milind R., 2002, *Doing Business in Emerging Markets*, Sage Publications, London.

Kuppuswami, Palanivel, and S. Neema, 2006, *Project Report on Japan and China*, under Prof. Justin Paul, Indian Institute of Management Indore.

www.countrywatch.com accessed on 8th March, 2007.

Test Your Knowledge

I. FILL IN THE BLANKS

1. The _____ treaty, signed on February 7, 1992, was aimed at transforming the (European) Economic and Monetary Union into a common Central Bank and a new currency.

2. Out of the 15 countries in the European Union, _____, _____ and _____ decided not to join the EMU, whereas _____, despite its desire to become a member, was unable to join as it did not meet the eligibility criteria relating to inflation, interest rates, exchange rates and fiscal deficit in 1999. This country met eligibility criteria later and joined Euro.

3. SWIFT stands for _____.

4. _____, a company wholly owned by the Government of India, provides export credit insurance support to exporters and banks.

5. _____ is a document through which the buyer's bank guarantees invoice payments to a supplier; it promises to pay the beneficiary if the buyer fails to pay.

6. The exposure of an MNC's consolidated financial statements to exchange rate fluctuations is known as _____ exposure.

7. An exporter prepares the _____ to give an idea to the importer that "if you place the order with me and when I will export, your invoice will look like this".

8. _____ stock offering is the stock issued in the US (due to the liquidity of the new-issues market there) by non-US firms or governments.

9. _____ are sold in countries other than the country represented by the currency denominating them.

10. _____-style currency options are similar to _____-style options except that they can only be exercised on the expiration date.

11. The limit on holdings by individual FIIs in a company has been raised from _____ of the companies shares, while the aggregate limit has been increased from _____.

12. _____ can only be applied if the dumping is hurting the industry in the importing country.

13. The Agriculture agreement distinguishes between support programs that stimulate production _____, and those that are considered to have _____.

14. Upto the end of _____ round, textile and clothing quotas were negotiated bilaterally and governed the rules of MFA.

15. Under GATS, once a government has made a commitment to open a service sector to foreign competition, it must normally not restrict money being transferred out of the country as _____ (current transaction) in that sector.

16. The agreement on Trade Related Aspects of Intellectual Property Rights (TRIPS) of the WTO came into effect on _____. This is also sometimes referred to as _____ agreement.

17. The purpose of patent is to _____ for technological advances.

18. India has already removed the _____ such as restricted list, canalized list, etc. on _____ as per decision made by WTO.

19. Removal of QRs does not mean _____ imports. It only means that an item can be imported without import _____ or _____.

20. A common mistake often made in the international arena is to equate _____ with modernization.

21. It is important to recognize, that knowledge of cultural differences is not a factor to _____ but its absence is a contributing factor to _____.

22. The _____, focuses on the degree of equality or inequality, between people in the country's society.

23. _____ involves doing one thing at a time, whereas _____ entails engaging in several activities all at once.

24. Managing and motivating people with vastly different cultural values and attitudes requires _____ in management styles, systems and practices.

25. The focus of trade policies in India has been on liberalization, openness and globalization with a basic thrust on outward oriented _____ promotion activity, removal of _____ and improving _____ of the industry to meet the global market requirements.

26. The erstwhile EXIM policy has been rechristened by the Government of India as _____.

27. The export obligation under the EPCG scheme, is now linked to the duty saved and is _____ times the duty saved.

28. The new policy in India aims at converting four existing EPZs, creating _____ more SEZs and allow setting up of _____ free from SLR and CRR, within the SEZs.

29. The Foreign trade policy 2004-2009, outlays agricultural sector initiatives by earmarking more funds for the development of Agri Export Zones (AEZs) and permitting duty free capital goods under the EPCG scheme. A new scheme called the _____ for promoting the export of fruits, vegetables, flowers, minor forest produce, and their value added products has been introduced.

30. The strategies for global strategic management are: _____, _____, _____, and _____.

31. The term _____ refers to skills within the firm that competitors cannot easily match or imitate.

32. The production costs decline by some characteristics each time the accumulated output doubles. Two factors explain this: (1) _____; (2) _____.

33. Firms pursuing multi-domestic strategy orient themselves towards maximum _____.

34. The benefits of going global are: _____, _____, _____, and _____ by spreading the portfolio of markets served to bring stability of revenues and operations.

35. Structurally, the planning for global markets may be viewed as _____ or _____ or _____.

36. _____ is establishing a foot-hold in foreign markets without capital outlays.

37. In a typical franchisee agreement the _____, someone with an idea for business sells to another person, the _____, the rights to use the business name, sell a product, or provide a service to someone else.

38. Project works undertaken by foreign companies based on the principle of "Build Operate and Transfer (BOT)" are known as _____.

39. Exporting your products through a middleman, who assumes all risks internationally is called _____ in international business.

40. _____ can be defined as a level of greater commitment in which domestic and host countries join to set up manufacturing facilities in an overseas market.

41. The main advantage for direct exporters is that they can have _____ over export, pricing, sales promotion, after-sales-service, etc.

42. The criteria to obtain a TH (trading house) status, a STH (star TH) status and a SSTH (super star TH) status is annual average NFE (Net Foreign exchange) value of exports during three preceding years is _____, _____, and _____ respectively.

43. _____ means that the price quoted includes all costs, including transport and other charges, incurred up to the time the goods are loaded onto a ship for transporting them abroad.

44. An IEC number allotted to any exporter/importer by the DGFT office in India comprises of _____.

45. An exporter can be registered with the Export Promotion Council (EPC) concerned and will be provided with an RCMC of the concerned EPC provided he is _____.

46. The EPCs are non-profit organizations registered under _____ or the _____, as the case may be.

47. When the drawer, i.e. exporter, expects the drawee, i.e. the importer, to make payment immediately upon the draft being presented, the draft is called _____. However, when the exporter agrees to give credit of say 30 days or 60 days, the draft is called _____.

II. TRUE OR FALSE QUESTIONS

1. Anti dumping stands for refusal to off load ships carrying dangerous wastes i.e. Non bio-degradable wastes.

2. Reduction in agricultural subsidies was agreed the in the Uruguay Round of Agreement.

3. Special Import License and General license are of same nomenclature.

4. Multilateral Ministerial conferences of GATT member countries held at Uruguay (September 1986) opened new chapters, towards world trade and globalization

5. Culture is very important as it explains everything that is different from one place to another.

6. Time does not involve the concept of Monochronic versus Polychronic time.

7. The theories of Smith, Ricardo and Heckscher-Ohlin advocate restricted trade due to balance of payment problem.

8. Green field investment generates cash flows in a shorter time than acquisition.

9. In mining sector particularly in Gold, Silver and precious stones only 49% FDI is permitted in India.

10. Trading houses were introduced in India in 1990 after liberalization.

11. Franchising tends to involve longer term commitments than licensing.
12. A contractual agreement does not involve the transfer of technology, process.
13. Under Joint venture, equity positions are held by each of the partners.
14. The application for issue of IEC number is to be submitted in triplicate (3 copies).
15. The prime objective of export promotion council is to promote and develop the exports of the country.
16. Bank issuing the LC must make payment within seven banking days from the date of receipt of documents.
17. Manufacturer-exporter is required neither to pay excise duty nor file the excise bond.
18. Customs endorsement is made on all copies of shipping bill, but not on the ARE-1 form.
19. The port officer issues a Mate's receipt once the cargo is loaded onto the ship.
20. The minimum turnover for Multimodal Transport services is 5 million Indian rupees.
21. If Mate's receipt contains any adverse comments it is known as a "Clean Mate's Receipt".
22. Bill of Lading is a negotiable and transferable document.
23. The shipping line presents the duplicate copy of shipping bill to the preventive officer.
24. The customs appraiser examines the value of goods:
25. The mate's receipt is handed over by the shipping company to the port.
26. SDF form is used for electronically processed bills where as GR form is used for manually processed bills.
27. An exchange rate between two countries' currencies can get affected by changes in a third country's interest rate.
28. The European Central Bank sets the monetary and fiscal policies for the EMU countries.
29. The contravention of Foreign Exchange Management Act is not considered as a criminal offence and civil imprisonment is provided only as a last resort when the recovery of fines has failed.
30. All types of transactions that cause transaction exposure also cause economic exposure.
31. While using the *currency diversification technique* for reducing transaction exposure, the local currency value of future foreign currency inflows will be more stable if the foreign currencies received are highly positively correlated.

32. When firms reduce their economic exposure, they reduce not only the unfavourable effects of their home currency moving in a given direction but also the favourable effects if the home currency moves in the opposite direction.

33. Translation exposure can be reduced by selling forward the foreign currency used to measure a subsidiary's income.

34. The forward premium (or discount) usually reflects the difference between the home and foreign interest rates.

35. While call option premiums increase with the increase in the variability of the currency, for put option premiums the relationship is just opposite.

36. In direct intervention, governments directly influence the economic factors that affect equilibrium exchange rates.

37. Currency futures are traded on an exchange in a standardized form and a fixed quantity.

38. Currency futures are mostly settled with a difference without delivery of currency.

39. Letter of Credit is issued by a Banker undertaking the guarantee for the quantity of the goods shipped.

40. Letter of credit issued by the banker is considered as a part of working capital limit of the exporter.

41. If the real interest rate in a country is low, then the currency of that country is weak.

42. Strengthening of the foreign currency is good from the point of view of importer while it is bad from the point of view of the exporter.

43. IMF lends money to countries to ease pressure on Balance of Payment.

44. GSP is a certificate indicating the fact that the goods which are being exported have originated/manufactured in a particular country.

EXAMPLES

1. Compute the forward discount or premium for the Mexican Peso whose 90 day forward rate is $.098 and spot rate is $.10. State whether your answer is discount or a premium.

2. Bid/Ask rate is US$ 1 = 0.81/0.83 Canadian $. Calculate the spread.

3. A bank bought 15,000 USD from an exporter at 1 USD = Rs 45.26 and covered itself in the inter bank market on the same day, when the exchange rate was 1 USD = 0.84 Euro. The London interbank rates (LIBOR) were 1 Euro = Rs 65.
   Calculate the profit or loss in the transaction.

MULTIPLE CHOICE QUESTIONS

1. Agreement on Agriculture (AOA)
   (a) Easy market access
   (b) Domestic support – subsidies and other programs guarantee farm gate prices and farmers incomes
   (c) To make exports artificially competitive i.e. export subsidies
   (d) All the above

2. ATC stands for
   (a) Authorized textiles control
   (b) Agreement on textiles and clothing
   (c) All to co-operate
   (d) None of the above

3. Agreement on textiles and clothing (ATC) 1995-2004 is a transitional instrument, covering following elements:
   (a) Encompasses yarns, fabrics, clothing, textiles products
   (b) Establishment of TMB (Textile monitoring body)
   (c) Progressive integration of textiles and clothing products into GATT, 1999 rules.
   (d) All of the above.

4. GATT 1947 The fundamental principles of agreement are as follows:
   (a) Most favoured nation treatment by signatory members
   (b) National treatment except payment of customs duty at import time
   (c) Total restrictions on export/import of rice, tea, tobacco, diamonds, garments, leather etc.
   (d) Only (a) and (b).

5. The member countries of WTO have moved to "Product Patent Regime" under
   (a) TRIMs   (b) TRIPs   (c) SAPTA   (d) BoP

6. Through new industrial policy of 1991, the total number of industrial reserved for public sector enterprises was reduced to:
   (a) Five   (b) Eight   (c) Ten   (d) Twelve

7. Under International strategy, firms try to create value by transferring _____ to foreign markets where indigenous competitors lack these skills and products.
   (a) Valuable skills   (b) Products
   (c) Core architecture   (d) Valuable skills and products

8. Under transnational strategy, firms maintain that _____ should not be all one way from home firm to foreign subsidiary
   (a) Flow of skills   (b) Product of offering
   (c) Cultural difference   (d) Both (a) and (b)

9. Multi domestic firms extensively customize both their product offerings and their marketing strategy to suit _____.
   (a) Creation activities
   (b) Different cultural differences
   (c) Research & Development
   (d) Both (a) and (b)

10. "Culture is the collective programming of the mind which distinguishes the members of one human group from another." This is defined by:
    (a) Maslow
    (b) Mc Clellands
    (c) Hofstede
    (d) None of the above

11. Professional culture refers to the shared code of ethics and other commonalities shared by members of a given group:
    (a) Dancers, Film actors and Artists
    (b) Engineers, physicians and accountants
    (c) Sportsperson, Politician and NGOs
    (d) None of the above

12. Priorities of Cultural Values in US are:
    (a) Family security, Family harmony, Parental guidance and Age
    (b) Freedom, Individualism and self – reliance
    (c) Belonging, Group Harmony, Collectiveness and Age/seniority.
    (d) Both (a) and (b)

13. Porter argues that a lack of resources often actually helps countries to become competitive called:
    (a) Absolute Advantage
    (b) Comparative Advantage
    (c) Comparative Disadvantage
    (d) Selected Factor Disadvantage

14. The factors that determine whether a company has to invest abroad in the form of FDI are:
    (a) Cost of Production and Location,
    (b) Strategic rivalry
    (c) Product Life Cycle
    (d) All of the above

15. Quantitative restriction on fertilizer imports have been removed since:
    (a) April 1, 1990.
    (b) April 1, 1991.
    (c) April 1, 2000.
    (d) April 1, 2001.

16. Build, Operate and Transfer (BOT) concept is envisaged in:
    (a) Power generation
    (b) Highways
    (c) Airlines
    (d) Real Estate

17. Foreign companies undertake _____ projects which are based on the principle of build, operate and transfer.
    (a) Consortia
    (b) Turnkey
    (c) Strategic alliance
    (d) Subsidiary

18. In 1999, Bayer AG Germany & Ranbaxy signed an agreement for _____ where Bayer obtained exclusive development and world wide marketing to formulation of ciprofloxacin.
    - (a) Joint venture
    - (b) Strategic alliance
    - (c) Turnkey
    - (d) International Strategic alliance

19. The export strategy provides focused attention to products that have _____ in the country and potential for export competitiveness
    - (a) High Production capacity
    - (b) High distribution capacity
    - (c) High selective capacity
    - (d) None of the above

20. IEC Number when allotted is valid for a period of:
    - (a) 2 years from the date of issue
    - (b) 5 years from the date of issue
    - (c) 10 years from the date of issue
    - (d) It has no expiry date
    - (e) None of the above

21. IEC Number consists of a:
    - (a) 6 digit number
    - (b) 4 digit number
    - (c) 10 digit number
    - (d) None of the above

22. The major functions of export council are:
    - (a) Provide commercially useful information and assistance to their members.
    - (b) Ensuring participation in trade fairs and exhibitions
    - (c) Promoting interaction between the exporting community and govt.
    - (d) All of the above.

23. The various parties to the letter of credit are:
    - (a) Three
    - (b) Four
    - (c) Six
    - (d) Seven

24. The list of documents required for making an IEC application is as follows:
    - (a) Income tax certificate
    - (b) Bank passbook
    - (c) Company registration
    - (d) None of the above

25. Form SOFTEX in respect of export of computer software is to be submitted in:
    - (a) Two copies
    - (b) Three copies
    - (c) Four copies
    - (d) Five copies

26. In order to secure export payments against political and economics risks and get financial assistance from institutions, the exporter must register with
    - (a) Director General of Foreign Trade (DGFT)
    - (b) Apparel Export Promotion Council (AEPC)
    - (c) Registration-cum-Membership Certificate (RCMC)
    - (d) Export Credit and Guarantee Corporation (ECGC)

27. Which of these is not a component of negative list of items
    (a) Prohibited Items
    (b) Dangerous items
    (c) Restricted items
    (d) Canalized Items
28. Which of these is not a Principal Export Document
    (a) Commercial Invoice
    (b) Packing list
    (c) Proforma Invoice
    (d) Bill of Lading
29. In which type of Bill of Exchange are the relative shipping documents such as Bill of lading, marine insurance policy, invoice and other documents sent along with the bill of exchange
    (a) Sight Bill of exchange
    (b) Clean bill of exchange
    (c) Usance bill of exchange
    (d) Documentary bill of exchange
30. What is the maximum commission that an exporter can pay to his agent as per FEMA guidelines
    (a) 10%
    (b) 12.5%
    (c) 15%
    (d) 20%
31. Under which of these circumstances does product liability not apply
    (a) In case of negligence
    (b) In case of smuggling
    (c) Under the principle of strict liability
    (d) Under express/implied warranties
32. The bank which finally collects the documents and claims reimbursement is called the
    (a) Advising bank
    (b) Confirming bank
    (c) Paying bank
    (d) Negotiating bank
33. Under which of these can the negotiating bank make the exporter liable in case of default in payment by the opening bank or importer
    (a) Confirmed letter of credit
    (b) With Recourse letter of credit
    (c) Without recourse letter of credit
    (d) Red clause letter of credit
34. How long can bank finance be extended beyond the initial 180 days
    (a) 45 days
    (b) 90 days
    (c) 135 days
    (d) 180 days
35. When exporter avails post-shipment credit in foreign currency, what is taken as the benchmark for the interest rate
    (a) Benchmark lending rate
    (b) MIBOR
    (c) LIBOR
    (d) Indian Bank rate
36. Which of these is not an essential service provided by C&F agents
    (a) Warehousing before transportation
    (b) Selection of mode of transport
    (c) Cargo insurance
    (d) Warehousing after transportation

37. The number of copies of ARE-1 forms to be made are
    (a) 3   (b) 4   (c) 5   (d) 6

38. Which IncoTerm includes the price of rail transport to port (Including insurance) and getting goods upto the ship
    (a) Ex works   (b) Free Carrier
    (c) Free alongside ship   (d) Free on board

39. The Board of trade is headed by the
    (a) DGFT   (b) Export Minister
    (c) Shipping Manager   (d) Minister of Commerce

40. Which is the apex body of various exporters and export promotion organizations in India
    (a) Trade fair authority of India
    (b) Export Credit Guarantee Corporation of India
    (c) Federation of Indian exporters organization
    (d) Directorate general of commercial intelligence and statistics

41. EDI system got legal recognition under the act
    (a) Right to data act, 1998
    (b) Electronics act, 1996
    (c) Information Technology Act, 2000
    (d) DGFT act, 1999

42. Which document specifies the name of the country where goods are produced
    (a) Shipping bill   (b) Packing note
    (c) Customs Invoice   (d) Certificate of Origin

43. Which of these is not a form of pre-shipment finance
    (a) Advance against export bills sent on collection
    (b) Advances against incentives receivable from Government
    (c) Packing Credit
    (d) Pre-shipment credit in Foreign currency

44. Which of these accurately describes CIF
    (a) FOB + SHIPPING + FREIGHT + INSURANCE
    (b) A+ unloading charges
    (c) B+ customs charges
    (d) C+ transport to importers surroundings

45. What is the full form of UCPDC
    (a) Uniform civil practices for duty on customs
    (b) Unity for common purposes in duty on customs
    (c) Uniform customs and practice for documentary credits
    (d) Uniform customs and purposes for documentary credits

46. FERA was implemented in order to
    (a) Conserve foreign exchange and put it to judicious utilization
    (b) Enable recognition of foreign exchange
    (c) Have an uniform civil law
    (d) Facilitate external trade and maintain an orderly growth of foreign exchange
47. Which of these is not a quality control mechanism
    (a) Consignment-wise inspection   (b) Document verification
    (c) In-process control   (d) Self Certification
48. The endorsement of "Allowed to export under claim for excise rebate" on the ARE-1 form is made by the
    (a) Deck sergeant   (b) First Mate
    (c) Range superintendent   (d) DGFT
49. Which of these is not a port procedure regarding bill of lading
    (a) Carting permission   (b) Mate's receipt
    (c) Bill of Lading   (d) Shipping bill
50. How many days in advance can a Bill of entry be filed at the maximum
    (a) 15 days   (b) 30 days   (c) 45 days   (d) 60 days
51. The certificate of origin will not have
    (a) Shipping port details   (b) Country of origin details
    (c) Description of goods   (d) Chamber of commerce seal
52. The GR form has to be countersigned by the authorized dealer for the export of which of these goods
    (a) Marine life   (b) Spices and condiments
    (c) Jewellery   (d) Automobiles
53. Which of these refers to refund in respect of central excise and customs paid in respect of raw materials and other inputs used
    (a) Excise duty –Refund/Exemption
    (b) Duty Drawback
    (c) Duty free replenishment
    (d) Duty entitlement
54. Which bank instructs another bank in sellers country to advise or confirm credit
    (a) Advising bank   (b) Paying bank
    (c) Confirming bank   (d) Issuing bank
55. Countries   Currencies
    A - China   1 - Lira
    B - Korea   2 - Peso
    C - Mexico   3 - Won
    D - Turkey   4 - Yuan

The correct country-currency pairing is
(a) A-1, B-3, C-4, D-2
(b) A-4, B-2, C-1, D-3
(c) A-2, B-4, C-3, D-1
(d) None of the above

56. Keeping other things constant, logic demands that US dollar should definitely become costlier when
(a) both US interest rate and US inflation rate decreases
(b) the US interest rate increases whereas the US inflation rate decreases
(c) the US interest rate decreases whereas the US inflation rate increases
(d) both US interest rate and US inflation rate increases

57. INCOTERMS are devised and published by
(a) International Chamber of Commerce
(b) World Bank
(c) World Trade Organization
(d) United Nations

58. In relation to INCOTERMS, which of the following is incorrect:
(a) Under the "E"-term (EXW), the seller only makes the goods available to the buyer at the seller's own premises.
(b) Under the "F"-terms (FCA, FAS and FOB), the seller is called upon to deliver the goods to a carrier appointed by the buyer.
(c) Under the "C"-terms (CFR, CIF, CPT and CIP), the seller has to contract for carriage, but without assuming the risk of loss or damage to the goods or additional costs due to events occurring after shipment or dispatch.
(d) Under the "D"-terms (DAF, DES, DEQ, DDU and DDP), the seller has to bear all costs and risks needed to bring the goods to the place of destination.
(e) All are correct

59. A price agreed on CIF basis
(a) does not include the freight charges
(b) includes freight charges up to the port of loading
(c) includes freight charges up to the port of unloading
(d) includes freight charges up to the importer's works

60. Which of the following is not a party to a letter of credit:
(a) Advising Bank   (b) Confirming Bank
(c) Governing Bank   (d) Issuing Bank
(e) Reimbursing Bank

61. The _____ of exchange rate forecasting assumes that an increase in the price level results in the depreciation of a country's currency and vice versa.

(a) Demand-Supply approach
(b) Monetary approach
(c) Asset approach
(d) None of the above

62. Which of the following transactions reflect economic exposure but not transaction exposure:
    (a) a firm's imports/exports denominated in local currency
    (b) a firm's imports/exports denominated in foreign currency
    (c) interest received from foreign investments
    (d) interest owed on foreign funds borrowed

63. An MNC's degree of translation exposure is dependent on the following:
    (a) The proportion of its business conducted by foreign subsidiaries
    (b) The locations of its foreign subsidiaries
    (c) The accounting methods that it uses
    (d) Only (a) and (b)
    (e) All the three

64. Under which of the following hedging techniques, that an MNC uses to eliminate its transaction exposure, the associated cash flows cannot be determined with certainty?
    (a) Forward hedge   (b) Futures hedge
    (c) Money market hedge   (d) Currency option hedge

65. Which of the following is *not* a payment method for international trade?
    (a) prepayment   (b) a bill of exchange
    (c) consignment   (d) factoring
    (e) open account

66. Assume that goods are available to an importer before payment, that payment is made by the importer after the buyer sells the goods, and that the risk to the importer is negligible. Which type of payment method for international trade is likely being used in this example?
    (a) sight draft   (b) time draft
    (c) consignment   (d) letter of credit
    (e) none of the above

67. Which of the following is the purpose for doing business in the international markets ?
    (a) To expand the operations beyond the local geographical limits
    (b) To take the advantage of the tax benefits of the foreign country
    (c) To develop and sell the products for a particular geographical location
    (d) Existence of imperfect markets
    (e) All of the above

68. Which of the following is not a motive for providing funds in the international markets ?
    (a) To take benefit of the high interest rates
    (b) To reduce the default risk by diversification
    (c) To take benefit of the strengthening of the currency
    (d) To take advantage of high inflation rates
    (e) None of the above

69. If a particular bank is short of a foreign currency, the same is generally bought *first* from
    (a) Other Banks
    (b) International corporate lenders
    (c) Open market operations
    (d) International Monetary Fund
    (e) Central Bank of the Country

70. Eurodollars are
    (a) Currency   (b) Deposits   (c) Bonds   (d) Equity
    (e) None of the above

71. Which of the following alternatives is not applicable to American Depository Receipts
    (a) Dollar deposits in Banks
    (b) Certificates representing the ownership of foreign stocks
    (c) These are not actively traded
    (d) Act as substitute for direct investment in foreign stock
    (e) Involves high transaction costs

72. Equilibrium exchange rates between the currencies depend on:
    (a) Quantity of foreign currency demand
    (b) Quantity of foreign currency supply
    (c) Rate remains dynamic over a period of time
    (d) Is affected by the inflation rate
    (e) All the above are correct

73. For which of the following reasons MNCs do not use the forward contracts ?
    (a) To hedge their imports
    (b) To hedge their exports
    (c) To speculate on the currency movements
    (d) To earn arbitrage
    (e) All of the above

74. Which of the following factors does not affect the currency call option premium ?
    (a) Level of the existing spot price relative to strike price

   (b) Length of time before expiration date

   (c) Potential variability of the currency

   (d) All of the above

   (e) None of the above

75. Disadvantage of fixed exchange rate system is

   (a) Risk that the government will alter the exchange rate

   (b) MNCs can engage international trade without worry

   (c) Xchange rates are held constant

   (d) Rates are maintained within boundaries

   (e) None of the above

76. Which is the characteristic/s of the Freely floating exchange rate system?

   (a) Exchange rate values are determined by the market forces

   (b) Country having this system is more insulated from unemployment problems of other countries

   (c) Country having this system is more insulated from inflation of other countries

   (d) Only a and b

   (e) All of the above

77. A call option on Canadian Dollars has a strike price of $ 0.759. The spot rate is $ 0.735. This call option is

   (a) In the money

   (b) Out of the money

   (c) at the money

   (d) at a premium

   (e) at a discount

78. The ADR of an Indian Company is convertible into 2 shares of stock. The share price of the firm was Rs 1250 when BSE closed. When US markets opened, the exchange rate was 1$ = Rs 43. The price of this ADR should be $ _____

   (a) $ 29.07

   (b) $ 60.16

   (c) $ 14.53

   (d) $ 34.16

   (e) None of the above

79. The firm has entered into a forward short contract for $ 154,000 at a rate of Rs 44.56 = 1$ for 90 days. The spot price on maturity was Rs 45.12. The firm has made approximate profit/loss of _____ on the forward contract.

   (a) Profit of Rs 86000

   (b) Loss of Rs 86000

   (c) Profit of $ 1911

    (d) Loss of $ 1754

    (e) No profit or loss on this contract as forward is to hedge the risk

80. While measuring the "Transaction Exposure" one should consider
    (a) net cash flows
    (b) currency variability
    (c) currency correlations
    (d) a and b above
    (e) a, b and c above

81. The degree of Translation Exposure of an MNC is not dependent upon
    (a) accounting methods followed
    (b) proportion of business conducted by subsidiary
    (c) remission of profits to parent company
    (d) products sold by the subsidiary
    (e) (a) and (c)

82. Variability of the following portfolio of currencies is
US $: % of funds to be received = 40%, Standard Deviation = 0.26
Euro: % of funds to be received = 60%, Standard Deviation = 0.38
Correlation Coefficient between US $ and Euro = 1.12
    (a) 0.116   (b) 0.34   (c) 0.258   (d) 0.512
    (e) None of the above

83. "Parallel Loan" does not involve
    (a) back to back loan
    (b) exchange of currencies with a promise to re exchange at a time and rate
    (c) involves swaps of currency
    (d) not recorded in the books of accounts
    (e) All of the above

84. Forward transactions involves exchange of currency at _____ rate.
    (a) Swap rate   (b) Reverse transaction rate
    (c) Forward rate   (d) Spot rate
    (e) None of the above

85. Which of the following is the rate at which a banker is willing to buy foreign currency ?
    (a) spread rate   (b) cross rate   (c) offer rate   (d) bid rate
    (e) ask rate

86. Which of the following theory best defines the relationship between currencies on the basis of rate of inflation
    (a) Interest rate parity theory
    (b) Purchasing power parity theory
    (c) Relative inflation theory
    (d) Foreign exchange parity theory

List of Abbreviations

3PL	:	Third Party Logistics
4PL	:	Fourth Party Logistics
AAS	:	Advance Authorization Scheme
ABI	:	Automated Broken Interface
AIR	:	All Industry Rates
AMS	:	Automatic Manifest System
ARE	:	Application for Removal of Excisable Goods
ASEAN	:	Association of South East Asian Nations
ATA	:	Admission Temporaire
B/E	:	Bill of Entry
B/L	:	Bill of Lading
B2B	:	Business to Business
B2C	:	Business to Customer
BAF	:	Bunkerage Adjustment Factor
BIFR	:	Board for Industrial and Financial Reconstruction
BIN	:	Business Identification Number
BoP	:	Balance of Payment
BOT	:	Build-Operate-Transfer
CAC	:	Capital Account Convertibility
CAF	:	Currency Adjustment Factor
CAGR	:	Compound Annual Growth Rate
CBP	:	Customs and Border Protection
CFR	:	Cost and Freight
CFR	:	Customs Federal Register
CFS	:	Container Freight Stations
CHA	:	Customs House Agent
CIF	:	Cost, Insurance and Freight
CIS	:	Commonwealth of Independent States
CKD	:	Complete Knock Down
CONCOR	:	Container Corporation of India Ltd.

CRIS	:	Centre for Railway Information Systems
CSD	:	Carbonated Soft Drinks
CSEZ	:	Cochin Special Export Zone
CVD	:	Counter Vailing Duty
D&D	:	Design and Development
D/A	:	Documents against Acceptance i.e. Delivery of Transport Document against Acceptance
D/P	:	Documents against Payment i.e. Delivery of Transport Document against Payment
DD	:	Demand Draft
DDP	:	Delivered Duty Paid
DEEC	:	Duty Exemption Entitlement Certificate
DEPB	:	Duty Entitlement Pass Book
DEQ	:	Delivered Ex Quay
DFIA	:	Duty Free Import Authorization
DGCI&S	:	Directorate General of Commercial Intelligence and Statistics
DGFT	:	Director General of Foreign Trade
DPP	:	Damage Protection Plan
DTA	:	Domestic Tariff Area
DWT	:	Dead weight Tonnage
EAGA	:	East Asia Growth Area
ECBs	:	External commercial borrowings
ECGC	:	Export Credit Guarantee Corporation of India Ltd
EDIFACT	:	Electronic Data Interchange for Administration, Commerce, and Transport
EEC	:	European Economic Community
EEFC	:	Exchange Earners Foreign Currency
EEPC	:	Engineering Export Promotion Council
EEZ	:	Exclusive Economic Zone
EFT	:	Electronic Fund Transfer
EGM	:	Export General Manifest
EIA	:	Export Inspection Agency
EIC	:	Export Inspection Council
EIR	:	Equipment Interchange Receipt
EOR	:	Enhanced Oil Recovery
EPC	:	Export Promotion Council
EPCG	:	Export Promotion Capital Goods
EPFG	:	Export Production Finance Guarantee
EPO	:	Electronic Purchase Order
EPZ	:	Export Processing Zone

ERIC	:	Export Risks Insurance Corporation
ETMs	:	Elaborately Transformed Manufactures
EU	:	European Union
EXIM	:	Export–Import
EXW	:	Ex Works
FAK	:	Freight All Kinds
FAS	:	Free Alongside Ship
FCA	:	Free Carrier
FCL	:	Full-container load
FCNR	:	Foreign Currency Non-Resident
FDI	:	Foreign Direct Investment
FEMA	:	Foreign Exchange Management Act
FERA	:	Foreign Exchange Regulation Act
FIB	:	Freight Investigation Bureau
FIEO	:	Federation of Indian Exporters' Organization
FIFO	:	First In First Out
FMCG	:	Fast Moving Consumer Goods
FOB	:	Free On Board
FOC	:	Flag of Convenience
FOIS	:	Freight Operation Information System
FTA	:	Free trade Area
FTZ	:	Free Trade Zone
GATS	:	General Agreement on Trade of Services
GATT	:	General Agreement on Trade and Tariffs
GR	:	Guaranteed Remittance
GRI	:	General Rate Increase
GRT	:	Gross Registered Tonnage
GSP	:	Generalized System of Preference
HAWB	:	House Airway Bills
HS	:	Harmonized system
ICC	:	International Chamber of Commerce
ICD	:	Inland Container Depots
ICs	:	Integrated Circuits
IEC	:	Importer-exporter code
IGM	:	Import General Manifest
IICL	:	International Institute of Container Leasers
IIFT	:	Indian Institute of Foreign Trade
IIP	:	Indian Institute of Packaging
IMF	:	International Monetary Fund

Incoterms	:	International Commercial Terms
IP	:	Intellectual Property
IPR	:	Intellectual Property Rights
IQF	:	Individually Quick Frozen
ITF	:	International Transport Worker's Federation
ITPO	:	India Trade Promotion Organisation
JIT	:	Just-in-time
JNPT	:	Jawaharlal Nehru Port Trust
LC	:	Letter of Credit
LCL	:	Less than container load
LIBOR	:	London Interbank Offered Rate
LNG	:	Liquefied Natural Gas
LO/LO	:	Lift On/Lift Off
LSP	:	Logistics Service Provider
M&A	:	Mergers and Acquisitions
MERCOSUR	:	Southern Cone Common Market
MIS	:	Management Information System
MPEDA	:	Marine Products Export Development Authority
MTO	:	Multi-modal Transport Operator
NAFTA	:	North American Free Trade Area
NGL	:	Natural Gas Liquids
NOE	:	Not Otherwise Enumerated
NOS	:	Not Otherwise Specified
NTB	:	Non Tariff Barriers
OBUs	:	Off-shore Banking Units
OECD	:	Organisation for Economic Co-operation and Development
OPEC	:	Organization of the Petroleum Exporting Countries
OTI	:	Ocean Transportation Intermediaries
PAN	:	Permanent Account Number
PBSEZ	:	Port-Based Special Economic Zone
PCFC	:	Pre-shipment credit for foreign currency
PP	:	Post Parcel
PPP	:	Purchasing Power Parity
QC	:	Quality control
QR	:	Quantitative restrictions
RBI	:	Reserve Bank of India
RCGs	:	Regional Cooperation Groups

RCMC	:	Registration-cum-Membership Certificate
RFC	:	Resident Foreign Currency
RFID	:	Radio Frequency Identification System
RFP	:	Request For Purchase
RFQ	:	Request for Quote
RMS	:	Rake Management System
SAARC	:	South Asian Association for Regional Cooperation
SCI	:	Shipping Corporation of India
SCM	:	Supply Chain Management
SCOPE	:	Standing Committee on Promotion of Exports by Sea
SDF	:	Statutory Declaration Form
SEATS	:	Stock Exchange Automated Trading System
SEZs	:	Special Economic Zones
SION	:	Standard Input-output Norms
SKD	:	Semi-knock Down
SOEs	:	State Owned Enterprises
SPS	:	Sanitary and Phyto-sanitary
STC	:	State Trading Corporation of India
STPIs	:	Software Technology Parks of India
TBT	:	Technical Barriers of Trade
TCF	:	Trillion Cubic Feet
TEU	:	Twenty-feet Equivalent Units
TMS	:	Terminal Management System
TRIPS	:	Trade Related Intellectual Property Rights
UCPDC	:	Uniform Customs and Practice for Documentary Credits
UNCITRAL	:	United Nations Commission on International Trade Law
UNCLOS	:	UN Convention on the Law of the Sea
UNCTAD	:	United Nations Convention of Trade and Development
UNTDED	:	United Nations Trade Data Elements Directory
VAN	:	Value-Added-Network
VAT	:	Value Added Tax
W/M	:	Weight/Measurement
WCO	:	World Customs Organisation
WMS	:	Warehouse Management Software
WTO	:	World Trade Organization
WTPCG	:	Whole Turnover Packing Credit Guarantee
WTPSG	:	Whole Turnover Post-shipment Guarantee

Answers

CHAPTER-END OBJECTIVE QUESTIONS

Chapter 1

1. (d)   2. (d)   3. (d)   4. (d)

Chapter 2

1. False
2. True
3. False
4. True
5. False
6. (d) Bills of Lading
7. (c) Name of the Air carrier

Chapter 3

1. False   2. True   3. True   4. False   5. True   6. (c)
7. (a)

Chapter 6

1. True   2. True   3. True   4. (c)

Chapter 7

1. (c)   2. (a)   3. (b)   4. (c)   5. (d)

Chapter 8

1. (c)   2. (d)   3. (b)   4. (a)   5. (a)
6. False   7. False   8. True   9. True   10. True

Chapter 9

1. (d)   2. (b)   3. (c)   4. (c)   5. (d)
6. True   7. False   8. False   9. True   10. True

Chapter 10

1. (d)   2. (b)   3. (b)   4. (d)   5. (c)   6. False
7. True   8. False   9. True   10. False

Chapter 11

1. (d)	2. (b)	3. (b)	4. (d)	5. (c)	6. False
7. True	8. False	9. True	10. False		

Chapter 12

1. (b)	2. (c)	3. (d)	4. (d)	5. (a)	6. False
7. True	8. False	9. True	10. False		

Chapter 13

1. (b)	2. (c)	3. (d)	4. (a)	5. (c)	6. (b)
7. (a)	8. True	9. True	10. False		

Chapter 14

1. (c)	2. (b)	3. (d)	4. (b)	5. (a)	6. (d)
7. (c)					

Chapter 15

1. (c & d)	2. (a)	3. (b)	4. (d)	5. (c)	6. True
7. False	8. False	9. True	10. True		

Chapter 17

1. True	2. False	3. True	4. True	5. True	6. True
7. (a)					

Chapter 18

1. True	2. False	3. True	4. True	5. False

Chapter 19

1. True	2. False	3. True

TEST YOUR KNOWLEDGE

I. Fill in the Blanks

1. Maastricht
2. Britain, Sweden, Denmark, Greece
3. Society for Worldwide Interbank Financial Telecommunication
4. Export Credit Guarantee Corporation
5. standby letter of credit
6. translation
7. proforma invoice

8. Yankee
9. Eurobonds
10. European, American
11. 5-10%, 24-30%
12. Anti dumping measures
13. directly, no direct effect
14. Uruguay
15. payment for services supplied
16. 01 January 1995, Paris- plus
17. provide a form of protection
18. quantitative restrictions, 01 April 2001
19. duty-free, licences or quotas.
20. westernization
21. success, failure
22. Power Distance Index
23. Mono-chronic time, poly-chronic time
24. variations
25. export, QRs, competitiveness
26. Foreign trade policy
27. eight
28. thirteen, overseas banking units
29. vishesh krishi upaj yojna
30. international, multi-domestic, global, trans-national
31. core competencies
32. learning effects, economies of scales
33. local responsiveness
34. achieving economies of scale, unifying product development, transfer of know-how, diversity of markets.
35. corporate, strategic, tactical
36. licensing
37. franchiser, franchisee
38. turn-key projects
39. indirect marketing
40. joint venturing
41. direct control
42. Rs 50 crore, Rs 250 crore, Rs 750 crore
43. Free-on –board
44. 10 digits
45. a member
46. Companies Act, Society Registration Act
47. Sight draft, Usance draft

II. True or False

1 False	2 True	3 False	4 True	5 False	6 False
7 False	8 False	9 False	10 False	11 True	12 False
13 True	14 False	15 True	16. True	17. True	18. False
19. False	20. True	21. False	22. False	23. False	24. True
25. True	26. True	27. True	28. False	29. True	30. True
31. False	32. True	33. True	34. True	35. False	36. False
37. True	38. True	39. False	40. False (Note: considered for importer)		
41. False	42. False	43. True	44. True		

III. Examples

1. Rate = $[(F/S) - 1] \times 360/90 =$ discount of 8%
2. Spread = [Ask rate – Bid Rate]/Ask rate
   = [0.83-0.81]/0.83 = 2.41 %
3. Bank paid Rs 678900 to exporter (15000 USD x Rs 45.26)
   Bank converted 15000 USD into 12600 Euros (15000 USD × 0.84)
   Rupee equivalent of 12600 Euro = 12600 × Rs 65 = Rs 819000
   Bank's profit = 8,19,000 – 6,78,900 = Rs 1,40,100

Multiple Choice Questions

1 (d)	2 (b)	3 (d)	4 (d)	5 (b)	6 (b)	7 (d)	8 (d)	9 (b)	10 (c)
11 (b)	12 (b)	13 (d)	14 (d)	15 (d)	16 (b)	17 (b)	18 (d)	19 (a)	20 (d)
21 (c)	22 (d)	23 (d)	24 (d)	25 (b)	26. (d)	27. (b)	28. (c)	29. (d)	30. (b)
31. (b)	32. (d)	33. (b)	34. (b)	35. (c)	36. (d)	37. (d)	38. (c)	39. (d)	40. (c)
41. (c)	42. (d)	43. (a)	44. (a)	45. (c)	46. (a)	47. (b)	48. (c)	49. (d)	50 (b)
51. (a)	52. (c)	53. (b)	54. (d)	55. (d)	56. (b)	57. (a)	58. (e)	59. (c)	60. (c)
61. (b)	62. (a)	63. (e)	64. (d)	65. (c)	66. (b)	67. (e)	68. (d)	69. (a)	70. (b)
71. (a)	72 (e)	73. (e)	74. (e)	75. (a)	76. (e)	77. (b)	78. (e)	79. (b)	80. (e)
81. (d)	82. (b)	83. (d)	84. (c)	85. (d)	86. (b)				

Index